IN THE DAYS
OF MY YOUTH
I WAS TOLD
WHAT IT MEANS
TO BE A MAN

IN THE DAYS OF MY YOUTH I WAS TOLD WHAT IT MEANS TO BE A MAN

A Memoir

TOM JUNOD

Doubleday New York

FIRST DOUBLEDAY HARDCOVER EDITION 2026

Published by Doubleday, a division of Penguin Random House LLC, 1745 Broadway, New York, NY 10019.

DOUBLEDAY and the portrayal of an anchor with a dolphin are registered trademarks of Penguin Random House LLC.

Book Two photograph: Marion Ettlinger
Epilogue photograph: Janet Folk Junod

LCCN 2025020113

ISBN 978-0-375-40039-1 (hardcover)
ISBN 978-0-385-54322-4 (ebook)

penguinrandomhouse.com | doubleday.com

Printed in the United States of America
1st Printing

The authorized representative in the EU for product safety and compliance is Penguin Random House Ireland, Morrison Chambers, 32 Nassau Street, Dublin D02 YH68, Ireland, https://eu-contact.penguin.ie.

For Janet, without whom . . .

What about the boy? He saw it all.

—The Who, "Tommy"

Yet why not say what happened?

—Robert Lowell, "Epilogue"

CONTENTS

IN THE DAYS
OF MY YOUTH
I WAS TOLD
WHAT IT MEANS
TO BE A MAN

PROLOGUE

Everybody knew.

Uncle Johnny knew. Mike Labella knew. My aunt Ceil knew, and so did my uncle Harry, my mother's brother. My father's surviving sisters—Liz, Ellie, Millie—all knew, and had known pretty much all their lives. Mr. Rudolph, our next-door neighbor, might not have known, but his wife, Ina, sure did. My older cousins Billy and Betty Ann knew, because of what their parents told them, and my younger cousins Mitchell and Michael knew because my father told them himself, when he was regaling them with his stories, which is to say when he was telling them his secrets.

And what about me? Well, I knew better than anyone else at the service, indeed anyone else alive—my father, after all, had *told* me, and so, in her way, had my mother. But at the same time I knew as little as my brother did, which was nothing at all. I knew, but I couldn't tell, and because I couldn't tell, I couldn't see. And I'm not speaking metaphorically, either. I mean that when the one person who not only knew about my father's double and triple life but had *tasted* it walked into the funeral parlor, she remained invisible to me. *How could I not have seen her?*

I was raised to see her. He brought me up to see her, trained me from an early age to spot beautiful women from across the room so that they, in turn, would spot *me.* And she was indeed beautiful, even though "beautiful" wasn't a word he often used—it was too *blah,* too commonplace. An old pool shark, he liked to put a little English on his English. He preferred "gorgeous" when he was describing the weather and, especially, people's teeth; and "built," "statuesque," "stunning" or "magnificent" when he was describing women, even in front of my mom. And in this case my father was right—even in her late sixties, the woman who showed up at his memorial service was all those things, with gorgeous teeth to boot. She was also the only Black person in the funeral home, and, as such, conspicuous. She wore a short black leather jacket and jeans cut to clamdigger length, and golden high-heeled sandals that elevated her above all the mourners. And yet somehow I didn't see Muntu Law until she sauntered up to the lectern to say a few final words about him, her waist-length braids swaying with her movements, the finial beads making a rattling music.

But I guess there's an obvious explanation for my obliviousness. When my father came home from his nights in New York, he often told the story of some celebrity—maybe Liz Taylor, maybe Ava Gardner—who took one look at him at the Harwyn Club or El Morocco or the Copacabana and "couldn't keep her eyes off . . . *your father.*" Well, that was me, at his memorial service. I couldn't keep my eyes off him, and neither could anyone else. He hadn't given me any instructions, regarding the arrangements—hell, he refused to give me instructions, on the grounds that he was never going to die. All I had to go on was the preference he'd announced when I was a little kid, which was that he didn't want an open casket. "All those people, standing around saying how *good* I look?" he said with a stagey shiver. "For*get* it. Just give me a closed casket draped with an American flag and a picture of me in my *prime.*"

He came close to getting what he wanted, or at least not getting what he didn't want. On a table at the front of the "viewing room" at the Charles J. O'Shea Funeral Home, on Wantagh Avenue, there was, in a glass case, an American flag folded into a tight triangle in honor of his military service, and a framed photograph of him standing in a Muscle Beach bathing suit on the steps of our house in Wantagh, Long Island, built like Charles Atlas, with skin as brown as mahogany. And his corpse didn't have to endure the scrutiny of gawkers lining up at an open casket because, well, there was no corpse and there was no casket. I had him cremated, and the body he bid us to worship as he jogged in place in front of his bedroom mirror dressed in nothing but black bikini underwear—"Look . . . at this body—have you ever seen a body . . . like *this*?"—now occupied a ceramic urn of such aggressive anonymity it made the funeral home spotlight look ironic.

It was his second service. The first was in Atlanta, where he had moved and lived with my mom for the last two years of his life, and it was pretty much *for* Mom, because she was ninety, she didn't fly, she refused to fly, she had never flown, and there was no way she could make the drive to Long Island. The second . . . well, the second was the real one, because Mom wasn't there. He had been married to her for fifty-nine years when he died, but he had *lived*—italics his—largely apart from her, according to his whim. Now, a month after his death on the early morning of September 17, 2006, there was a service for family, friends, and people who saw in his life something to admire and even to emulate. They saw the grandeur of his outsized expectations even if many of those expectations went unmet, which is why, when they went out on a rainy Sunday evening for a final tribute to Lou Junod and came upon his modest ceramic urn, they stopped and did double takes.

Some of them couldn't help making remarks. In Atlanta, my brother Michael's ex-wife crept up to his urn and whispered, "Big Lou, huh? Well, you're not so *big* anymore, are you, Big Lou?" In Long Island, two of his sisters, Ellie and Millie, stood in front of his ashes until Ellie issued Millie a warning—"You do this to me and I swear I'll come back and haunt you from the *grave*." Michael and I, however, stared at what was left of our father with our arms around each other's shoulders, stunned into silence by the spectacle of the genie squeezed back into the bottle. The biggest thing that had ever happened to either of us—the fact that Lou Junod was our father—was over, and when we finally spoke all we could do was simultaneously utter the one word that, against all odds, articulated who he was to us:

"Dad."

And then, of course, we did what we always did, what we still do, even with Dad long gone: we spoke in his voice. We cribbed from his language and his intonations. He had a store of phrases and we borrowed one to say what he surely would have said, faced with such conclusive evidence that he'd been cut down to size: "So . . . it's come . . . to *this*."

And then we hugged each other harder, and began to laugh.

—

It was his funeral. It was also mine. I was ten years younger than Michael and my sister, Cathy—"number two son," Dad called me, doing his best Charlie Chan. I was also, of all his kids, the sickliest, skinniest and weakest, a crybaby who grew up to be a nervous wreck and considered that an achievement. And yet I ended up making all his funeral arrangements, handling everything from start to finish. I ordered his cremation and picked the ill-fitting urn. I planned the service as an entirely secular rite, with no priest, no readings from scripture and no prayers. I picked the music, I hired a chanteuse from New York City to sing "I'll Be Seeing You," I chose "Summer Wind" as the hymn and led the dearly beloved in singing it, and then I delivered the eulogy, taking the title from one of his sayings, one of his *maxims,* "If You're Going to Be a Bear, Be a Grizzly."

"My father—Dad, Pop-Pop—was not like other fathers," I began. "He was not like other people, period." And then I set about trying to enumerate everything that made him so distinctive, as well as to account for the absence of clergy. "A lot of people have told me that he's with Jesus now. Well, with all due respect, I have my doubts, unless, of course, Jesus has shaved his beard, ditched the sandals, and is drinking a martini at the El Morocco, circa 1955, with Frank and Ava.

"This is not to say my father was not a believer. He had a whole belief system. He believed in a lot of things, and what he believed in, he believed in absolutely.

"He believed that there was not a person in the world whose appearance would not be helped by exposure to the sun, or what he called a 'fresh burn.'

"He believed that there was not an ailment in the world that could not be cured by salt water.

"He believed that the way Rhett Butler treated Scarlett was the way all women should be treated, and that Clark Gable was robbed when he didn't win the Oscar for Best Actor in 1939.

"He believed that the lottery was a game of skill, rather than chance, and that he had won it—twice!—but, for some reason, had neglected to turn in the ticket.

"And he believed, to the very end, that he was going to win again—and then, as he said, '*then* I'll teach you how to live.' "

It went without saying that he didn't win again, and that the same sense of outsized expectation that had ennobled him most of his life left him subject to endless indignities before he died. But it also went without saying that he never stopped trying to teach people how to live and that most of those seated in front of me had, at one time or another, paid him heed. He didn't just want so much; he *presumed* so much, and the central presumption of his life was that he knew the secret of being a man. That he believed his life worthy of emulation is what made Michael and me try to emulate it, and also what made me so determined to commandeer his memorial service. I wasn't trying to belittle my dad. I was only trying to get what I wanted since I became his audience at the kitchen table as a little boy—the elusive thing at the tip of my tongue that made me want to be a writer:

The last word.

Michael followed me to the lectern and spoke without notes, offering a symbolic toast with a glass of water standing in for a martini. My nephew Scott followed him, calling his grandfather "Pops" and trying to shake off the nervousness that Dad elicited in him even posthumously. Next up was my godfather Uncle Johnny, telling one of his funny stories about their days together in the service, this one about the time Dad tried to thicken his hair before a dance by sticking his head in a hot oven. Finally, there came Mike Labella, Johnny's brother-in-law, a proud man who admitted, "My whole life, I tried to copy Lou Junod." And then . . . well, silence. Though all the speeches had left the impression that my father was important to the speakers because proximity to him made them *feel* important—indeed, like stars in their own right—there had been no surprises and there had been no tears. The service was a dry-eyed affair, the audacity of his life producing something like appreciation but nothing like grief, and after Mr. Labella found his way back to his seat a powerful force settled over the room: finality. "That's *it*?" I could hear Dad asking. *"How the mighty . . . have fallen."* There was nothing left for me to do but play the song I had chosen for the processional—"My Way," of course—but before I could stand up I became aware of a break in the stillness, like wind on water. I must have anticipated it before it actually registered with me, for I glanced back over my shoulder and from my seat in the front row I saw Muntu Law advancing to the lectern, her long braids swinging heavily, like a beaded curtain.

She was no stranger to me. She was, like most everybody else at the Charles J. O'Shea Funeral Home that rainy evening, Dad's friend, and therefore a friend of the family. He told me—well, he told us: me and Mom—about her when I was just entering my adolescence, in the early 1970s. He represented a handbag line called Valeri, and she had come to work as a "showroom girl." Her name was Erlene back then, Erlene Frazier. She was from Newport News, Virginia. Dad called her "country," but he also saw in her a beauty and vanity commensurate to his own. Not only was she *built, stunning, statuesque* and *magnificent,* with a fashion model's bearing and an album-cover Afro; she was what he considered very few people on this planet, an "equal," as fanatical in dietary matters as he was in sartorial and hygienic ones. She ate no meat. She ate only foods she considered alive, mostly raw vegetables, and not long after she started at Valeri he returned home with a juicer he'd bought at a health-food store in the city and a weekly allotment of carrots he dutifully turned into heaps of pulp that Mom had to clean, cursing under her breath. He didn't even object when she became a Black nationalist and changed her name to Muntu, because he regarded the uncompromising ferocity of her politics as a mark of his own distinction. Sure, she was "adamant—*adamant*!" in her condemnation of "the white man," but at the same time he claimed to be "the only white man she respects." It was an outrageous thing to say to an audience that included his wife, but I never understood it as such because whenever he went on about Muntu he also made sure to mention her boyfriend, Bob Law, who was six foot eight and hosted a radio talk show in New York. He was her *"dude,"* Dad said—he was her *"man,"* and how Dad talked about him somehow defused the threat of how he talked about her.

I had not seen Muntu since the summer of 1977, when I apprenticed in the handbag business not so much as a "showroom boy" but as Lou Junod's son. But Dad had never stopped talking about her, and she maintained a stubborn presence at our kitchen table for as long as he and Mom lived in Wantagh. And now, here she was again, a part of my father's past about to speak at his service, and I felt, in my own helpless heartbeat, the electricity of her return. So did everyone else—people snuck looks at one another, for she exuded not just confidence but *defiance,* and we all just watched and waited until her long and purposeful stride carried her to the lectern. For a moment, she kept her back to us, as if her black leather jacket bore an insignia she wanted us to see; then she turned around, with her hands raised, her palms turned outward, and her long fingers extended. She was sixty-seven years old, and age had only made her more imperious, sharpening her cheekbones, burnishing the bronze of her skin, turning her golden eyes lupine. She was exactly what Dad said—she was *adamant,* and now she brought her palms down on the flat surface of the lectern as decisively as a judge swinging a gavel. For all the queenliness of her stature and bearing, she'd always had a small voice, breathy and almost girlish, but as the crack of her hands resounded around the room she leaned forward and spoke with *authority,* as if from the pulpit. She was "country," all right, and with a voice insolent with enthusiasm and a chin that drove home the beat of each word with a downward stroke, she spoke for him in a way that no one else did or could, with the urgency of ultimatum:

"Can we *all* . . . just *agree* . . . that *this* . . . was a *man* . . ."

I had made myself an authority on my father's life—no, *the* authority. I had compiled a dossier I deemed dispositive, and taken control of a narrative I thought I understood as well as my own. I told his *story,* and I selected the urn as its exclamation point. Now the last word went not to me but rather to a woman who knew him as I never did, and my mind went blank as paper. It wasn't just what she said, or the hallelujah swing of how she said it; it was that she had heard me out, and still felt compelled to come up with a rejoinder. She had *answered* me, and left me to wonder if I had missed the point. Can we all just agree? she asked. Well . . . didn't we? Hadn't we? Wasn't his manhood precisely what I had eulogized, extolled and emulated? But no, there was another story, and it was being told by someone whose presence I hadn't registered until it became unavoidable. Muntu had been there all along, and somehow I hadn't seen her.

And so, Dad, I hadn't seen you.

PLEASE!
DO NOT
DISTURB

Book One

IN THE DAYS OF MY YOUTH I WAS TOLD WHAT IT MEANS TO BE A MAN

1

They had just moved into one of the new split-levels on Britton Street. There were five of them all in a row on the east side of the cul-de-sac, five houses, each built with the master bedroom above the two-car garage, and a bay window to the right of the front door. The houses weren't particularly large, just three bedrooms, and they were kind of stout and squat, like the teakettles that smiled and sang in cartoons. But they were in Wantagh, a step up from neighboring Levittown, and by and large the people who moved into them, like Charlie and Helen Kline, had already started their families in even smaller houses somewhere else. All over Long Island, developers were building split-levels like the ones on Britton Street, and soon enough they became symbolic of suburban conformity. But they never felt anything less than luxurious to many of their inhabitants—anything less than a little *fancy*—and while the Klines' new home was painted an unassuming autumnal gold, the house next door, at 1463, was as turquoise as the Mediterranean Sea.

Helen thought it was a bit much, maybe even a bit too . . . flamboyant, and one afternoon she found out why. Her doorbell rang, and when she answered she saw a man standing at her door who was nearly naked. He was wearing a mesh pullover cut off to exhibit his abdomen, short shorts, and espadrilles, and the skin that he displayed was as brown as her polished dining room table. He introduced himself as her neighbor, and although he was very friendly and welcoming, he struck her as *different* somehow, almost foreign, so much so that she couldn't wait for her husband to come home from work and drink the cocktail she'd mix for him. She wanted to tell him the big news about their new neighborhood:

"Charlie, a homosexual lives next door!"

But Lou Junod turned out to be married to a beautiful woman, and Helen and Charlie Kline found out soon enough what made him so distinctive. It wasn't that he was homosexual, at least in any technical sense. It was that he was *sexual,* in a way uncommon in 1956. He was a tough guy, a rough customer, a man's man who eventually helped Charlie manage his Little League baseball team. But he flaunted himself. He left no doubt about his intentions, and so had a talent for connecting with people across any room he entered, male and female alike—men, because they saw him as an ideal or a rival; women, because they saw him seeing *them.* He frequented clubs in Manhattan, and when Helen and Charlie went out with Fran and Lou, they felt like they were dining on Fifty-Second Street between Fifth and Madison instead of somewhere off Sunrise Highway. The India House in Bellmore was the swankiest restaurant on the South Shore, but Lou didn't even have to call in advance to get the best table. The "captain"—that's what he called the maître d'—led them instinctively to the center of the dining room because they were the best-looking people in the place and they fulfilled the same function as a Cadillac parked by the front door. They were looked at; they were meant to be looked at, and although Helen and Charlie were a handsome couple, they had never had the electric experience of eating dinner with all eyes upon them until they went out with Fran and Lou Junod.

And yet the Klines had something the Junods didn't. They had a baby boy, Raymond, who liked to play on the front lawn at 1463, with the sun in his curly blond hair. He was a beautiful boy, and my parents stared at him with such a stricken longing that they decided to have a beautiful boy of their own. They already had Cathy and Michael, beautiful in their own right—indeed, they were chosen "Levittown's Cutest Twins" when they were two, and given a year's free diaper service as a prize. But "the twins," as most people called Michael and Cathy, were eight years old when my parents moved from Levittown to Wantagh. They were no longer babies. My parents, thanks to Raymond Kline, wanted a baby.

—

In the summer of 1957, when my father was thirty-eight and my mother on the cusp of forty-one, they left my brother and sister in the care of my grandmother and went to Atlantic City. They had honeymooned there; on the wall of my father's bar in the basement hung a framed photograph of them on their wedding night. They are sitting at the threshold of their hotel room; my mother is sitting as if on a tuffet, the crinoline of her wedding dress spreading to fill the door frame, her white teeth on display in a smile that is for the photographer rather than her husband; my father is leaning over and looping a sign on the doorknob that says "Please! Do . . . Not Disturb," black lettering on a white background, the exclamation point the verbal equivalent of a wink. It is a performance on both their parts, one trying to look like the hopeful novice, the other the experienced rogue, but they succeed only in appearing mismatched. It is not a romantic photograph. It is, however, a nostalgic one, an evocation of an innocence that presumably ended when my father shut the door behind them. Ten years later, they returned not only to that place but to that moment when the future beckoned and everything was possible. They brought along a movie camera, and they shot film of each other feeding flocks of pigeons on the boardwalk, my father dressed like a gangster and my mother like an ingénue, pigeons perched on their sleeves as if they were inviting scarecrows. Then, just as ten years before they had conceived my brother and sister, they went back to a hotel room and conceived me.

I was born on April 9, 1958, weighing nine pounds, with my mother under general anesthesia. In the story I would hear again and again, I caught a cold right after I was born, and the cold developed into a case of bronchitis so serious that the priest came to our home to deliver simultaneous baptism and unction, a vaporizer exhaling sacramental breaths. Before the war, I might have died, but in 1958 I was the beneficiary of postwar medicine, and so delivered by tetracycline back into my infancy and childhood, stained but whole. My mother wanted to name me Christian, but my father intervened to spare me an undue burden, and I was christened Thomas Christopher. But there was something else I was called, something I began to hear as soon as my ears began opening to the thorned magic of words:

I was "an accident."

It wasn't people of ill will who told me this discordant news. It was my parents' friends, my aunts and uncles. I was very young when I asked my father, "What does 'accident' mean?" I was in the habit of asking my parents the meanings of words, and so he thought nothing of the question. "It means something that isn't supposed to happen," he answered, and not until I asked "Am I an accident?" did he flash his anger, with his lips contracting like a muscle and the flares erupting in his eyes. "Who told you that?" he asked, and when I said, "Everybody," his anger gave way, and he hoisted me up to his shoulders, as if carrying me into the water. He patted me on the back and with tremendous suppressed force he whispered comfortingly and confidingly in my ear: "*Accident?* You're the furthest thing from an accident! You're our . . . *love baby*!"

I started reading comic books when I was very young. My brother's and sister's friends left them in our house, and I preferred them to the baby books my mother read me. I loved comic books because they were about transformation—especially the transformation from weak to strong. Spider-Man, the Hulk, Thor, Daredevil: they all had origin stories and they all had two births. They were born as babies and then they were born as superheroes. Most of the time, they were born as superheroes because something happened to their parents. Their parents were blown up when the planet they came from was blown up. Their parents were killed by cheap hoods. They didn't have parents in the first place and were taken care of by kindly aunts and uncles who were killed by cheap hoods. They could never save the people they loved the most, so they had to save strangers. I was very weak and sickly but I wanted to be a superhero so I could save my family. But from whom? From what?

I had an origin story of my own and a secret identity. People thought I was an accident but I was really a love baby and that gave me special powers. I was put on earth to keep my family together and in the eyes of those who judged our family by our beauty and our prosperity and the red convertible Thunderbird my father hosed down in the driveway so that it would stay wet and sparkling in the sun, I succeeded. I loved my mommy and my mommy loved me. I loved my daddy and my daddy loved me. I loved my brother and my brother loved me and I loved my sister and my sister loved me. There was no shortage of love in our house. But in the end I was no different from Superman and Batman and Spider-Man: I had my powers because my powers had failed those they were supposed to save. As the love baby, I was supposed to keep my parents together. But there was something I knew about them from the start that I was not meant to know, a secret I could not share with anyone:

My mommy and daddy didn't love each other.

The morning starts with a sound—a snap, crackle and pop, not from the kitchen but rather from the room down the hall where my parents live. It is a sharp sound, like the snap of elastic, and also a multiplicity of sounds, like something popping in fire. I hear it because my ears are tuned to it, because I can't help but hear it, because it's my sound to hear. It doesn't wake me up; I register its report with the sense that I am already awake. But it opens my eyes. Whether I am a baby, a child, a boy or a man, it is and always will be my morning alarm, in that it alarms me and puts me in a state of alert. My heart beats with the sudden knowledge that I am not alone; I am alone with *him,* and my day is no longer my own. He is awake, therefore so am I; he is up, and, as he puts his feet on the floor and takes his first steps, his ankles crack—"an old war wound," he'll explain, as though the words are set to music. Outside my window there is birdsong, but the sound of his ankles is what requires vigilance, like a twig snapping in the forest.

He pauses at the door to my room, and I close my eyes. Sometimes he'll stop and ask, "Are you up?" and I'll be forced to admit my charade, and he'll say, with tender derision, "Phony." But mostly he just slows before continuing down the stairs, and I try to cling to the ease of a world in which he is absent, either asleep or away. But resistance, as he might say, is futile, because I don't just hear him, milling around the kitchen; I smell him. He makes coffee, and I smell it. He burns the bread in the toaster, and I smell it. Sometimes on Sunday mornings, he makes lamb or veal kidneys, and I smell them. Finally, I can't help myself; I follow my nose down his path into the kitchen. It is early, with the yellow sunlight competing for the kitchen table with the leafy, breathing shadows of the trees, and everyone else in the house still in bed, and this man waiting for me in his blue terry-cloth bathrobe, which is short as a miniskirt and exposes his bare legs—"I have great *legs,*" he will say. He is both entirely familiar and utterly foreign to me, brown as a wooden Indian, shiny as shellac, fragrant as a seraglio, and bejeweled as a satrap, with a gold bracelet, an oval ring of gold and black onyx on his pinky, and his army dog tag, cast in gold, nestled in his swirling pelt of black chest hair. It is a color scheme that sets him apart from anyone in my family—my mother's hair is white, though she calls herself a platinum blonde, like a movie star. But his hair is black as shoe polish, despite all the time he spends in the sun. So are the eyebrows that concentrate the green fury of his eyes. So is the hair on his body, and on the backs of his hands and fingers, which have huge whorled knuckles, like walnuts. He is not just different from the rest of us; he seems of a different race, both of us and apart from us, even as he bends over the stove, ribboned in smoke, making me breakfast.

"Hey, buddy-boy," he says, with a spatula in one hand and a saltshaker in the other. "How about some . . . kidneys?"

He is not a cook. My mother is the person who cooks, though she hates cooking. But he is the master of one thing—hunger—and hunger is what draws me to him and his black smoking pan. He has cut the kidneys into crescents, and now, as he salts them, they sizzle and spit, wobbling on the pan's cast iron surface as if trying to escape the heat, as animated as the ends of tiny fingers. Then they stop, and give up their smell, which is what keeps him to myself—they smell like pee, and no one else wants to be in the kitchen when they're cooking. He salts them again, as they turn brown and crisp, and move with a rubbery bounce when he tosses them with the spatula, like dice. "Get me . . . the butter," he says at last. Like everyone else I know, I say "buttah," in the same way I say "wawdah" for "water." But he says "butter" with an internal flutter, with both T's audible in the middle and the R audible at the end, and he says "water" like no one in the world, *wahter,* like it's in a glass, and it's cool, and you want to drink it. "Now watch me," he says. "You add the butter and a little water, and that's how you make . . . the gravy."

He scoops some of the kidneys onto my plate and then dirties them with gravy he spills from the pan, and I sit down to eat, famished but careful, spearing each crescent with my fork. "Hey, mootay-vam," he says, in the pidgin Italian he uses to applaud big eaters, "don't eat 'em all. I still have to make . . . the eggs."

Eggs-uh. A dramatic reading, in two syllables.

"I don't like eggs with kidneys," I say.

"What? No . . . eggs? You don't know what you're missing, my son."

"I don't like how they look with the gravy."

"Very well then," he says, and then doesn't say anything else. He might light a cigarette; he might hum, or whistle, or sing, maybe Sinatra or, more likely, "My Buddy." But he doesn't speak, and I find myself warily and helplessly watching him. I watch him fry his eggs, and pluck toast from the toaster, blackened because burnt toast puts hair on your chest, because burnt toast is good for the . . . teeth. I watch him flatten his toast with his fork and then cut a piece off the end, along with a sliver of egg and a curl of kidney, which he eats with closed eyes, in secret rapture. With each bite, he goes through the same process, taking his time, as fluent with knife and fork as an artist with brushes, until his patience and precision and above all the privacy of his pleasure become unbearable to witness. "Dad . . . can you make me some eggs?"

He lifts an eyebrow. "I knew it was just a matter of time," he says. "Like Joe Louis and Billy Conn: you can run . . . but you can't hide."

"Don't break them, Dad."

"I know, I know . . ."

He gets up, fries two eggs in butter and slides them onto my plate, unbroken and entire. "There," he says. "Don't ever doubt . . . the master."

I pick up my fork with one hand and my knife with the other, and then set upon the eggs with a fury that leaves them a mound of bite-sized pieces, all covered in yellow. He cringes as he watches, his teeth set on edge. "I'll never understand you," he says. " 'Don't break the eggs, don't break the eggs'—and then you *destroy* them."

And so we eat. He opens the paper, the *Daily News,* and begins annotating the margins of the sports pages with a stubby yellow pencil, a combination of letters and numbers in his blocky left-handed printing, each letter in slanting uppercase, a tabloid typeface all his own now assembled like a ransom note to his bookmakers. In a few minutes, I know, the phone will start ringing. But right now, I am his audience, and he, to an extent I can't even begin to imagine, is mine. We circle each other, sitting still in our chairs, and when I look up from my plate he is staring at me, studying me. "For a guy who didn't want any eggs, you eat pretty good," he says.

"I was hungry," I admit.

He bites his lip, the color of which is lighter than the rest of his face and serves, like his eyes, as a reliable indicator of his emotions. Sometimes I see colors in his lips and his eyes that make me terribly nervous, that make my heart beat wildly and my feet start to dance. But sometimes I see something else, I behold something else, an effort to plead his case that is no less volatile, no less transient in the tint it brings to his eyes, than his anger. With his teeth still nipping at the pale flesh of his lower lip, he nods his head, as if suddenly remembering something, and offers an assurance that I interpret as an order I can't possibly disobey:

"Stick with me, buddy-boy," he says. "Stick with . . . your *father.*"

He owns the mornings. This is what I know of him from the start, from the days of my own dawning. My mother owns the nights, because she is always home, in their room, in their bed, while he is out, sleeping in the hotels whose names adorn the coat hangers in his closet and the towels in his bathroom—the Carriage House and the Essex House in New York, the Doral and the Racquet Club and the Diplomat in Florida. And I own the afternoon, because that's when I'm home, free to watch TV, read comic books, or snoop around his closet and his bathroom and the bar he's built for himself in our basement, all of which are as replete with his presence as the pyramids in Egypt are with the ghosts of the Pharaohs. But the mornings belong to him; he even speaks that way, in a language of possession—"I walked in there like I owned it," he will say when he regales us with stories of his adventures in New York City nightclubs, just as he will not hesitate to say, of an up-and-comer in his business, "I made him." I don't doubt him, for when he is home the house is divided, the very day is divided, like an occupied city in the war movies I watch on TV. "Nights are long, since you went away," is what he sings when he sings "My Buddy." But in fact nights are simple when he is away and I am alone with my mother. I eat what I want, I watch what I want, I read what I want, and then she kisses me on the forehead and tells me to turn out the light, "like a good boy." It is enough, to be a good boy for my mother. But then the morning comes, and the crackle of lightning in my father's ankles alerts me not only to his presence but to the encompassing fact of his ownership. Morning is when he comes to my dark room, to say hello when he returns or to say goodbye when he leaves; morning is when he squats by my bed and puts his hand in my hair and talks to me in a fatherly way; morning is when he tries to impart his wisdom; morning is when he is sober, and has something to say; morning is when I listen to my mother and father talking rather than hear them arguing; morning is when he does his exercises and makes his bets; and morning is when he takes me to . . . the beach.

He owns the beach, too—literally. We have two houses, one in Wantagh, at 1463 Britton Street, and one in Westhampton Beach at 879 Dune Road. There is a sign in Wantagh, on Wantagh Avenue, proclaiming it the "Gateway to Jones Beach," which means that my town is the last outpost of civilization before the world opens up and flattens out and turns into sky and sand and sea, planes flying overhead. "Put on a pair of trunks, and let's go to the beach," he'll say—and it is always "a pair of trunks," what he wants me to wear; it is never anything so simple as "a bathing suit," though in truth he wears neither, and goes to the beach nearly naked, in a black bikini indistinguishable in my eyes from the underwear he washes in the sink of the bathroom he claims as his own. Who is my father? He is the man who wears his underwear to the beach, he is the man who drives his red 1960 convertible Thunderbird to the beach with the top down, he is the man who lugs to the beach an enormous black radio with an aerial as tall as I am, and glowing orange tubes inside. Jones Beach is carpeted with people wearing bathing suits and littered with tiny transistor radios playing rock and roll on WABC, a tinny, segmented chorus you hear blanket by imbricated blanket, all the way down to the water. My father plays 45s on a record player installed under the dash of the T-bird and then on his portable black "hi-fi" he plays a radio station whose playlist still includes Sinatra and Brasil '66 and "Music to Watch Girls By," unless he meets Uncle Lenny, who demands opera.

Like most of my uncles, Uncle Lenny is not my uncle and his wife, Aunt Betty, is not my aunt. They are friends, and Lenny Casten, like my father, is a salesman—indeed, another salesman whom my father "made." He used to be . . . *a soda jerk,* my father says. But Uncle Lenny is different from the rest of my father's friends, in that he is nearly an equal and therefore nearly a rival. He is a strapping man, with long skinny legs and long arms and shoulders he keeps thrown back, like a soldier. He is almost as dark as my father, with a mat of curly gray hair on his chest and a high bald crown fringed with gray hair and a gap between his teeth and a nose of shapeless enormity mounted so high on his face that his eyes appear affronted by its intrusion. He is also very loud, with the habit of declaiming his preferences and loyalties—"The best! The best!"—in a gruff booming voice that makes me think he's Russian. But I am not afraid of him, in the way that I am afraid of my father, because there is nothing hidden in his grandiosity, no hint of calculation or menace. Also, when we meet Uncle Lenny, we meet Henry and Tessie, who sit in beach chairs under an umbrella, eating something called yogurt and reading a slablike newspaper with no comics. "That's their *bible,*" my father will explain on the way home, and by "their" he's not referring to Henry and Tessie, but rather to what Henry and Tessie, along with Uncle Lenny and Aunt Betty, are—Jews. A lot of people assume my father is Jewish, because of his honker, his schnozz, which is nearly as monumental as Uncle Lenny's, and because he calls the rest of the people at the beach, with their sunburns and their sand castles, *schnorrers.* But he is not Jewish and so neither is my family, although some kids at Catholic school call me Jew-Nod. We don't listen to opera and eat yogurt and read *The New York Times,* or for that matter *Newsday,* which my father calls "a Jewish paper" because it is so liberal. We are also not like Henry and Tessie, who are exotic to me because they are kindly without being quiet, because they make a fuss over my being able to read their "bible," and because, above all, they seem amused by my father rather than starstruck or terrified. But if we are not Jewish, then what are we? If people don't think my father is Jewish, they tend to think he's Italian, on account of his swarthiness, but we're not that, either. We're nothing. We don't celebrate St. Patty's Day like the McGartys; we don't eat the Italian delicacies of our ancestors like the Labellas. We have no ancestors, except Grandma, my father's mother, who is still alive and lives with Aunt Ellie in Levittown; we have no history, no family tree, no store of knowledge about who came to America, and when; we have no stories except the stories my father tells, about himself. It is not simply that we're ahistorical; it's that our history, and indeed American history itself, begins with Lou Junod, an intensely ethnic man of no ethnicity at all, whose very skin—which he never calls brown, but "black"—is a varnish of self-creation.

My father and I do not sit by the water when we go to Jones Beach to meet Uncle Lenny. We sit far away, in a desert of hot sand, away from the crowds, and away from what my father, above all, can't stand—"other people's kids." And even when we go to the water, it's never for anything as prosaic as taking a swim, or cooling off, like other people do. It's to "run the beach," a prospect my father makes as alluring as eating kidneys. "All right, let's go . . . run the beach," he says, rubbing his hands together in anticipation, and so off I go with Lenny and Lou, two Olympians who ignore the blankets and the sprawled bodies and turn the shoreline into their own arena. They're not just going to run; they're going to run and then every hundred yards they're going to drop down and do twenty push-ups, the way the Jones Beach lifeguards do, "for the lifeguard test." The lifeguards, my father says, are in "some shape," but then so are he and Uncle Lenny—both of them "brutes," in my father's estimation. I am not a brute. I'm just a little boy, emaciated, with what the doctor calls a "protruding rib," which I try to hide with my right elbow, especially in photographs. I get sunburns. I can't do a single push-up, much less twenty. So I tell my father that I'm staying behind and building a sand castle. I promise to stay by the lifeguard's stand, and watch him and Uncle Lenny amble off into the odd perspective afforded by the beach, the shimmering haze that arises from the endless line of waves striking the sand. Lenny is wearing an old-fashioned navy blue swimsuit, squarish across his midsection—trunks—and my father only the filament of his black bikini, and yet sure enough, just as the distance begins to claim them, these two men either indulge or ignore the fact of their nakedness and assume prone positions on the beach for their ceremonial push-ups. Then they get up, and resume running until they disappear and I begin digging, covering myself, like the schnorrers, in an extra skin of sand. I am just about to hit water when an enveloping force seizes me, not a wave, but rather my father, saying, "All right, buddy-boy, you've avoided me long enough. Up and at 'em, here you go, into . . . the drink." Already in a lather from the run, he scoops me up, and totes me under his arm as he makes his way to the waves. But I am scared of the waves, which open and close and flash foaming teeth, and I am scared of the waves because my mother is scared of the waves, and of the water in general—the drink. My mother can't swim. I know this not only because of the way she approaches the ocean, bending at the knees and splashing her neck and arms as if the sea contains handfuls of eau de cologne, but also because when she first met my father back in Brooklyn she told him she was a member of the Dragon Club, the prestigious swim team at the St. George Hotel. "And then when I take your mother to Coney Island I pick her up and try carrying her into the surf, and she screams bloody murder. She panics—panics!—and I say, 'I thought you belonged to the Dragon Club.' And she says, 'I can't swim!' "

He has told this story so many times that it, like many of the stories he tells and tells again, has acquired the authority of scripture. Not only can't my mother swim; she is, as she admits at the end of each telling, biting her lip and shaking her head at the memory of her own youthful self, "a terrible fibber." She looks so beautiful when she says that, radiant both in mischief and in the force of impromptu confession, and I love her so . . . but now, here I am, swept forward in my father's arms with the surf churning before me, and I'm panicking, *panicking*, and when he tells me, "You're just like your mother," it's not a compliment. He puts me down on the sand, saying, "All right, all right . . . ," but as I watch the curve of his brown back slide under the waves, I am picked up, in turn, by Uncle Lenny. "Come with me, Tommy," he says, but in his rough growl my name sounds like Tummy, and I smile instead of cry. And then he tells me something I never knew, a secret: "It's calm on the other side of the breakers. Once you get through, you got it made. You'll see—there's nothing like it in the world!"

I go with him, aloft in his arms until we hit the waves and he says, "Duck." Duck? But I duck, and then . . . we're through, as if we just passed through a secret door in the wall of water. My father stands before us, and behind him the ocean is calm and stretches all the way to France. My presence startles him, and my presence in Lenny Casten's embrace takes him aback. "Tommy! I thought you didn't like the water!" But then he collects himself, and sinking lower beneath the surface, he begins moving slowly backward, away from me, while extending his arms and beckoning with submerged fingers, saying, "Swim! Swim to me! Swim to . . . your father." And I do, in a furious, hopeful, gasping dog paddle, suspended between escape and capture, swimming toward him even as he moves away, somehow understanding that manhood is a matter of admission, and that in order to gain admission I have to brave the deep water.

In Wantagh, he owns Jones Beach. In Westhampton, where the beach belongs to him and he patrols his property to keep out unattractive intruders, he owns the elements themselves. He bought the house in the mid-sixties for $20,000—"cash," he always says, opening his right palm and flicking at a pile of invisible bills with his left thumb, a pantomime of swashbuckling plenty. It is a gray two-bedroom cottage with white shutters and a bunch of Danish modern furniture inside, a separate bunkhouse where my brother and I sleep, an outdoor shower enclosed in cinder blocks painted white, and a wooden deck, also white, upon which members of my family fry like sausage links on a griddle. There is a dune, the other side of which is the ocean, invisible but audible day and night; there is a single strip of blacktopped road, Dune Road, the other side of which is the bay, fragrant with the tang of salt and decomposition; and then there is the sun in the sky, which rules our days. My mother calls my father "the ruler," just as he calls himself "the master" and even "the king," but he bows to the sun as it crosses the sky, charting the course of his day by its movement, waiting until it's "over the yardarm"—around 11 a.m.—to start drinking his rum-and-Cokes and his gin-and-tonics, which my mother fretfully counts until her palms begin to sweat.

"Your father is a sun worshipper," she explains, and though she tries to say these words lightly, she never really succeeds, punctuating her sentence with the same mirthless chuckle—"heh-heh-heh-heh-heh"—she employs when she talks about his gambling and his drinking. As a matter of fact, she cannot speak lightly about anything my father does, because he makes her as nervous as he makes me, and because she scrupulously calls him "your father" instead of "Dad," although sometimes, for a joke, she also calls him El Exigente, "the Demanding One," from the commercials for Savarin coffee. But that's the biggest difference between them. When my father says outlandish things, I know that I'm supposed to think he's funny. But when my mother is trying to be funny, I know she means what she's saying. It's never just a manner of speaking, when my mother is talking about my father. He really is the demanding one. And he really does worship the sun.

He does not go to church on Sundays with my mother and me—he does not go to church at all, except on Christmas and Easter. But then, when I ask him about it, he assures me that he wakes up early and goes to "fisherman's mass," and I know he's lying, especially when my brother, Michael, tells me that the fishermen at fisherman's mass put fishhooks on the collection plate, and my father gives him a look. But that doesn't mean he doesn't pray. He does, to the sun. "Oh, sun, cast your rays upon this humble body," he intones when he steps out onto the deck, resplendently greased in Bain de Soleil or in the volatile "concoction" he makes for himself out of baby oil, iodine, and peroxide. He's joking, but that doesn't make him any less serious about what is, after all, the family religion. We are sun worshippers not simply because we worship the sun but because we have to—it's compulsory. I'd rather stick my face in a comic book but whenever I step out onto the deck my father says, "Stick your face in the sun, son. It's like *fire*."

And it is, tingling like the aftermath of a slap, and therefore occupying all of one's attention—it's possible to lie under the spell of the sun for hours without getting bored. But even the sun, in its beneficence, is not enough for my father, and so not enough for us. He gives us each a reflector, a folding cardboard contraption shaped like a coal chute and covered in foil, constructed for the purpose of redoubling the sun's rays and focusing them on . . . the face. Michael and Cathy, my mom and I: our faces turn silver in the reflected light, as if frozen in the blinding glare of a flashcube that somehow never stops bursting, a snapshot that never ends. But my mother doesn't last, because she, as a Brandshagen, sins against the Junod family religion—she burns. And I can't help opening my eyes, and watching silver blobs of reflected light dance like fish in an aquarium on the walls of the house, until I finally behold my father in his raiment of fire. We have reflectors for our faces; my father has one for his entire *body*. He is encased in it, entombed in it, for its dimensions follow precisely the outline of a coffin. He burns, but his burn is different from my mother's. My mother's burn hurts, and makes her skin peel. My father wants to burn, he implores the sun to burn him, turning darker even as the shine of the reflector makes him lighter, never peeling and never turning pink or red. "There is nothing like a fresh burn," he counsels, and there is no doubt in my mind that he means exactly what he says; there is nothing like it, not even us. He lives close to the sun, so close that I wonder if he's like that tragic Greek hero I read about in one of my Classic Comics, that waxwork angel struck down because the sun melted his wings. Because he's not just worshipping the sun, with his reflector; he's cheating it, stealing its fire, and so even as it exalts him, it punishes him, chaining him to his glowing casket-shaped mirror. It's what makes him different, it's what makes us different, from anybody else, even Uncle Lenny. My mother is a Catholic, and says, "Oh, Jesus," every time I sneeze. Uncle Lenny is a Jew. But my father is a pagan, and paganism is the faith to which he converts us, every day a brand-new baptism.

And so as there is fire, there has to be water, and he owns them both. The sun rises and falls over the sea, and the sea is on the other side of the dune behind the house, and each morning in Westhampton begins with his call—"All right, gid up. It's time to hit . . . the beach." He's kidding around, trying to sound like a drill instructor from the war, but he never says he's kidding, and sometimes, if we don't get up quickly enough, he sprays us with a hose. Michael and I share the bunkhouse in Westhampton, the way we share a room at home in Wantagh, and sometimes friends stay with us, along with our German shepherd, Nikki. But no matter who is with us, they have to "get with the program," my father says. In order to eat breakfast, they have to get up, and "work up an appetite." They have to run the beach.

So do I. I passed some kind of test, when I went into the deep water with Uncle Lenny, and dog-paddled to my retreating father's beseeching arms. Now I've earned the right to continue to be tested, like my brother, although, unlike Michael, I'm not "well-built," but scrawny, a charcoal sketch of a boy in a family of comic-book superheroes. But here I am, somehow, on the beach, following my father's footsteps in the sand, trying to do push-ups when he does, every hundred yards. We do not run fast; he does not run fast, he "jogs," turning around as he goes, snapping his hands open and closed, exhorting us, no matter how many of us—his boys, his underlings—there are. He is performing, as he is in everything he does, and now his performance includes me. "We'll run to the public beach . . . and back," he declares. How far is the public beach? I have no idea, it throbs in the distance as a mottled density of color (other people) in a world otherwise completely composed of blue (ocean, sky) and white (sand, light). But my father is always setting a goal, and so we jog there and back, and when we return to our own private beach our reward stretches infinitely before us: the ocean. We have not gone swimming yet; we have not been allowed to, we've had to "work up a sweat" before swimming as we've had to "work up an appetite" before eating. Am I sweating? Little boys don't sweat. Michael always tells me about the speech our father gave him when he turned thirteen, the one about his glands—"Son, your glands . . . are changing." I'm not sweating, and my glands only change when they swell up in my throat when I get sick, as I so often do. But when my father and my brother and all the men and boys who are with them dive into the sea, I follow. The sun has risen over the water in the east, and when I emerge from under the water to breathe, I see my father do the same, and the joy he experiences he shares, and somehow transmits to me for the rest of my life. "Nectar . . . of the gods!" he exclaims, and yes, there are swimmers in the Olympics, but this is different, this is our own Olympus beyond the waves. We are bathing in water, but also in light, in pure incandescence, the ocean so clean the sun shines through the waves, and my father grabs at it, in handfuls. First, he washes his face, but then he raises the whole sea to his lips, as if in a goblet, and says, "It's so clean you can drink it!" And he does! He scoops a handful of water into his mouth and then spits it out in a stream, as if he were the stone figure in a fountain! He doesn't swallow—no, he's always told me not to swallow salt water, even as he tells me that salt water can cure all my "ailments." But Uncle Lenny, when he is with my father, will sometimes raise his fists to the sky and ask, like a petitioner, "What does he want? WHAT . . . DOES . . . THIS . . . MAN . . . WANT?" And now I know. My favorite book in school is the book about the five Chinese brothers, including the brother who swallows the sea in one gulp and leaves the fish flapping in the sand. My father is like that. He is the man who wants to drink the ocean.

One day, he doesn't tell me to put on my trunks, and we don't go to the beach. Instead, he comes into the bunkhouse whisking his palms together, and asks, "Hey, buddy-boy, how would you like . . . a hot fudge sundae?" He's a salesman like Pavlov is a salesman, and in an instant I'm salivating. *How would I like a hot fudge sundae? What kind of question is that? I love hot fudge sundaes!* "Do you know who makes the best hot fudge sundae . . . in the world?" *I don't! Who?* "A place called Act IV, in Southampton. How about you and me go to Act IV . . . for a hot fudge sundae?" *Really, Dad? Sure!* "Well, then . . . get dressed."

Of course, he is dressed already, the way he dresses when he goes out in Westhampton, especially when he goes, around sunset, "in the shank of the evening," to a hotel down the road called the Dune Deck, where he drinks at the bar and listens to Teddy Wilson from the Benny Goodman orchestra play the piano and sometimes sings "a couple of numbers." It's a uniform, of sorts—an orange sweater with a plunging neckline worn directly against his skin, and a pair of white jeans he calls, after the drumroll caesura, "white ducks." I wear a sweater, too, but with buttons, and then the dressy shorts my mother buys me, and then a pair of bright-white PF Flyers, and off we go, my father and I, "a couple of dudes," as he says, off to consort with "the swells" at Act IV. But we don't go to Act IV, at least not directly. We don't go to Southampton, either. He stops the red T-bird at a house in Shinnecock Hills, small and far away from the ocean, with bristly suburban grass struggling to grow from the sandy soil. We're visiting one of his buyers, he says, but when she meets us at the door she's a *lady*, svelte and stylish, with arms bared by her crewneck top and ankles exposed by her clamdigger pants. She has coppery hair she wears up, off her shoulders, and she walks with a contained contraband strut that makes it seem she's walking on a wire. But what's most striking about her is that she's all alone, with no husband, no kids, no company except a dachshund the same color as her hair. "Oh, he *likes* you," she tells me as she pours my father a drink, not one of his summer drinks but rather a winter one, brown liquor over ice he stirs with his index finger, his tic, his tell, making music as if he's ringing a bell. Then she opens the sliding doors to the backyard, and I follow the dog to the swing set planted on a little scrub-grassed hill. Nobody has to tell me to play; I just do, me and the dog partners in wonderland. But after a while there's a problem: I don't know how to swing on my own. I'm one of those kids who needs a push. I try to get started by moving my feet like Fred Flintstone, but then I stall out and just sit there, missing the comic book I left on the bar where the buyer who lives all alone poured my father a drink. I decide to go find it, but when I try to go back inside the house, I can't. The sliding doors are locked, and when I look inside for my father and the buyer there's nobody home. I go back out to the swings, and stare at the ground while using my feet to give me the illusion of movement and altitude, until my father and the buyer finally walk outside, her face a little brightened, as if, in her absence, she went out to get some color.

"All right," my father says, with his palms going. "Are you ready? Are you ready for . . . a hot fudge sundae?" He turns to the buyer and says, "Can you believe it? The poor kid's never been to Act IV?"

"*Never* been to Act IV?" she says, stooping in front of me with her hands folded and her knees pressed together. "Oh, Tommy—you're gonna *love* it!"

"Can I go inside and get my comic book?" I ask, and for some reason this question causes her to look at my father instead of me.

"Of *course* you can go back inside and get your comic book," she says, and when she releases me by mussing my hair I run as fast as I can and pluck the comic book off the bar as if someone might steal it.

At Act IV, my father's meeting a bunch of his friends from New York City—his "cronies," my mother calls them—and they all greet him like a conquering hero. I can't tell them about the buyer because they're all salesmen and I'm not supposed to talk business with my father's competitors. "Why so quiet?" one of them asks, but once

I open the menu I don't really care that I don't have an answer. I don't even have to open my comic book. Everything on the menu at Act IV is named after a Broadway show and as I look around I see that the restaurant itself is decorated just like my father's basement bar in Wantagh, with black-and-white photographs of celebrities all over the walls. I have to study the menu to see which of the sundaes with funny names is plain hot fudge and spend the rest of the time staring at the singers and movie stars and wondering why my father is not with them, why I can't find a photograph of him up on the wall, way up there and lost among the stars.

2

I have a friend. He is my first. He was born two months before I was. His name is Michael, just like my brother's. Our parents take pictures of us in the crib together and then of us wearing white baby boots and white caps woven from yarn and tied under the chin. We are babies together and then little boys, chronological twins. And our parents are friends.

My father is friendly with Chip and Valerie Schocket, anyway. He works for Chip, or, more precisely, he represents his handbag line, which is called Mr. Chips. But he also goes out with Chip at night to clubs in New York City, and stays with Chip and Valerie in their apartment on Sutton Place. Chip is five years older than my father, and he is sophisticated. He teaches my father things, what my father calls "savoir faire." In my father's bar, there is a framed photo of them together, at a club in Manhattan—the Harwyn Club. I know the name of the club because it's printed on the square black ashtray that sits between them, a lit cigarette aslant in one of the little slots molded into the sides. In the photo, Chip is the teacher, my father the student—Chip is pointing at something and talking, and my father is following his gesture and listening, his lips compressed into a barely discernible smile. They are sitting very close together at a table, and there is an intimacy between them, my father leaning toward his friend as if literally under his wing. They are both wearing black jackets, white shirts, and skinny black ties, and they are both drinking brown liquor from clear glasses set before them. I can tell the color of their drinks even though the photo is in black and white, and everything is the color of either the ash of the cigarette or Chip's hair, which is thinning and going gray and swept off his forehead with oil. The photo predates me, and I study it in order to breathe its strange alluvial air, even though if my mother could she would take it down from the wall and throw it in the garbage can.

My mother hates Chip. She loathes him. It's not something that she has to tell me, or that I have to ask about—I am in such sympathy with her feelings that I feel them too. My father calls him a "kibitzer." But many years later, his son, Michael, will say what he is—"a needler." He needles my mom, and his needling doesn't make her laugh. It makes her flinch. When he visits our house in Wantagh, he sometimes brings thick steaks from his butcher in New York City, and my father cooks them on the grill on the slate patio. But Chip makes a point of asking for ingredients he knows we don't have—ingredients he knows my mother doesn't have. "Where is . . . the kosher salt? *What*—no kosher salt? How can you serve steaks without kosher salt?" He's just teasing, and letting everybody know he's just teasing—well, letting his *audience* know, with a certain wry change of expression, like a winking comedian. The audience includes my father, Valerie, my brother, my sister and even me and Michael, the two little boys. But it doesn't include my mother, who either is not in on the joke or refuses to be, and finds herself alone onstage with him, like the assistant cut in half by the magician. She must be aware of what's happening, because he's looking at *us* as he teases *her*—she must be aware that he is, in my father's words, "playacting." And yet she has no comeback for Chip's remarks, and can't stop herself from becoming flustered, can't stop the stinging moisture from shining in her outraged blue eyes. She shrinks from Chip's voice the way she sometimes shrinks from my father's touch: viscerally. And that's what I feel, prickling my own skin. She's repulsed by him, and the liberties he takes. Sometimes Chip talks to her and to her alone, whispering in her ear, making her knees weak, with intimations not of romance but something even more confidential—secrets he tells only to her. Though not nearly as handsome as my father, he is far from an ugly man, but with his hunched shoulders and pockmarked skin and dark watchful eyes there is something ugly *about* him, and for some reason he has made her his target. I am normally her defender, or at least her witness. And yet like nearly everyone else in my family I fall under his sway. I laugh at his jokes. I call him Uncle Chip.

I don't call Valerie Schocket "Aunt Valerie." I'm not allowed to. My mother won't let me. I called her Aunt Valerie once, and my mother said, "She's not your aunt," as if consanguinity ever mattered with the men and women who came to the house in Wantagh. It's not that she hates Valerie the way she hates Chip. It's that Valerie is so different from her—so much younger. My mother is in her forties, and even her hair strikes me as old-fashioned. She wears bathing suits with skirts attached to them, and has tiny blue veins in her legs like the cursive of a lost language. Valerie is in her twenties, and wears bikinis. She was a model in New York City, and is very dark—almost as dark as my father. In fact, Valerie and my dad are as similar as Valerie and my mom are different. They could be brother and sister, if my father didn't happen to be so much older than she is. She's almost an expression of him, a glimpse of what he'd be like as a woman, with their surface similarity confirming what anyone can see—their deep affinity. She's not even afraid of him. She calls him "Louis," with an extra S, a brassy sibilance that shows she's playing with him. "Louis" somehow sounds less formal than "Lou," and her use of it gives her standing, as if he let her get away with scolding him or beckoning him by snapping her fingers. It's exciting to hear, and also confusing. Why, of all women, is Valerie Schocket the woman he treats as an equal?

Maybe he respects her because she can swim. My mother can't. She can't swim and she refuses to fly, abjuring the foreign elements my father inhabits naturally, air and water. But Valerie is a jet-setter, and not only can she swim; she can water-ski. She was a featured water-skier at Cypress Gardens in Florida, the beauty at the apex of the human pyramid in the wake of the motorboat. There are pictures of her waving from her pinnacle and in the summer of 1961, when the Schockets and the Junods each rent houses on Dune Road in Westhampton Beach, Uncle Chip brings a motorboat of his own, a hulking thing with wooden sides moored in the bay like a dreadnought. The houses are on the bay, rather than the ocean, and very close to one another. We live, that certain summer, three houses away from the Schockets. I don't, however, visit the Schockets, at least not by my own initiative. I like to wander, I like to explore. But the Schockets live on the other side of a border I dare not cross. In truth, I am afraid to, even though my friend Michael lives there. I am afraid to because of the shadows that lurk behind the thicket of pine trees, and because the Schockets have a big black German shepherd named Flag. But mostly I am afraid to because of Valerie, who is not always pleased to see me and not shy about saying so. She is not like my mother, or any other mother I know, in that she is not like Donna Reed in *The Donna Reed Show* or Mrs. Cleaver in *Leave It to Beaver.* She is not always nice, and she's not afraid to send me home, especially when my mother dispatches me to the Schockets' to find my father.

He spends a lot of time with Chip and Valerie and Michael, so much so that I am a little jealous of my friend. My brother also spends a lot of time there, because Valerie is teaching him how to water-ski. My brother is thirteen, and he looks so beautiful behind a boat that Valerie makes him her protégé, while my sister, Cathy, babysits my friend Michael. My mother and I spend a lot of time alone together in the little gray house we rent, and when we cross the two-lane blacktop of Dune Road to go to the ocean, my father is often already there with the Schockets, propped up on an elbow on a towel next to Valerie. When he sees us, he greets us with a wave, as if hailing us from the peak of a mountaintop he is urging us to climb. I run to him and he picks me up and sometimes pits me against Michael, the both of us cradled in our fathers' arms so that we can jab at each other with our feet. He walks down to the water with my mother and watches her stoop at the edge of the surf and refresh herself by splashing water the length of her arms, a dainty, timid gesture that makes her look simultaneously like an old lady and a young girl. Then he strides over to Chip and Valerie and takes Valerie into his arms as he takes me, manhandling her, so that they appear to be a couple showing off at Muscle Beach, or a team of acrobats at the circus, with Valerie's husband the ringmaster who sees all. My father cradles her and carries her to the water, but she doesn't panic as my mother would—Valerie is featherlight and unafraid in his arms, with not only her legs extended but also her toes, and she raises her hand in a practiced wave of farewell as they disappear into the endless surf.

It is a milestone summer, the first that lodges itself in my memory. My father's sister Liz will visit with her husband, Harry, and in the company of Uncle Harry I not only go clamming but also eat clams for the first time—eat with such abandon that I make myself sick, and spend an entire night throwing up clams and Coca-Cola. I also step on a nail on the beach, and my mother drives me into the town of Westhampton Beach, where a doctor gives me a tetanus shot. And years later, when the subject of the summer of 1961 comes up in my family, that's all anyone will remember—the nail I stepped on and the clams I ate. "You were so *sick,*" my mother will say in a manner almost admiring, the way my father tells my brother how beautiful he looked on skis. What no one will mention is what really happened; what remains unsaid is the romance my father conducted with the mother of my first friend in front of anyone who cared to see.

He sings everywhere—in the shower; in the bathroom; in the kitchen, with a smoking pan; in the backyard, with a muddy spade. But he *practices* in the basement, when he's all alone. It's something he disdains, as a matter of principle—"you either have it or you don't." But every once in a while, he descends to the depths of 1463 Britton Street and makes a ritual of recording his own voice. He pours a drink, puts an instrumental recording from Paul Weston and His Orchestra on the big black Fisher hi-fi in the den, and then sings into the microphone of the big reel-to-reel tape recorder he stores in the boiler room. He sings "Autumn Leaves" and "I'll Be Seeing You" and "Long Ago and Far Away" and the songs that he's invited to sing at clubs in Manhattan and Miami and New Orleans and Dallas—the songs I not only hear but hear *about,* from him and his friends. For a man who sings so often in public, he very rarely invites others to sing with him, especially his kids. But when he records himself in the basement, he's not just private. He's solitary, and his singing sounds lonely, a word I wouldn't apply to anything else he does.

Is he a good singer? My mother calls him a "good *crooner,*" as if to make a distinction. And she's right, because he doesn't belt out songs with the vehemence of a Sinatra or the operatic flourishes of Robert Goulet. He sings softly, a little stiffly, with something old-fashioned in his voice, something meant to be heard on a Victrola. But he was good enough to sing in the army, after he was wounded, and he's good enough to bring tears to my mother's eyes when he sings "Silent Night" in church on Christmas Eve. And he's good enough for me. I hear his voice when I'm upstairs in my room and pretty soon I'm heading downstairs, five steps to the living room, six steps to the den, and four steps to the basement where he practices for the dream that never came true.

We have, like most of the other split-level families in Wantagh, a "finished basement." But it's not like the other finished basements because we're not like the other families—it is not a basement divvied up between a family room for Mom and the kids and a workshop where Dad can wear an undershirt and take silent refuge at his tool bench. My dad can't hammer a nail. My dad doesn't even own tools—he has friends do mechanical work for him. And he hasn't worn an undershirt since Clark Gable took off his dress shirt in *It Happened One Night* and dared to stand in front of the camera bare-chested. He doesn't need a place of refuge because the entire world is his refuge, and I can't go down to the basement without being reminded that his life is elsewhere. He has painted the ceiling red, his color, and has built a bar that makes the subterranean portion of our house feel like an after-hours club in Manhattan, or what he calls "a speakeasy." It is not a "home away from home," whatever and wherever that might be. It's the exact opposite, a place inescapably away from home *at* home, right here at 1463 Britton Street.

He stops singing when I come to visit him—when he looks up and says, "*Tommy,*" as if either he's just been discovered or he's just discovered *me.* "Would you care for . . . a drink?" he asks with mock solemnity, and then moves behind the bar, while I sit with my legs dangling off one of the black vinyl stools on the other side of the curved wooden rail. He is dressed for the occasion, wearing either his red satin pajamas with black piping or the uniform he wears around the house or when he's visiting friends around the holidays—gray slacks and a V-neck red sweater worn over a white dress shirt and a narrow black tie. I watch his every move, so he puts on a show, rinsing two dusty glasses in the aluminum sink and then wiping them out very carefully with a soft cloth specially designed not to leave any . . . *lint*. He takes his sweet time, humming to himself the songs that he was just singing, so that when he finally pours his drink into a shaker and rattles it over his shoulder like a conga dancer, I fear it's going to explode. He pours it into one of the clean glasses waiting on the black Formica, a brew as antiseptic as ammonia and effervescent as a wave. Then, and only then, he speaks. "What'll you have?" he asks, and though I know what I'm going to get, I answer, as he has taught me, "A double," before he fills the second glass from a foreshortened bottle of ginger ale. He is lit from behind by the same panel of lights that illuminates the cityscape of liquor bottles from below, and in the inset mirror where the bottles glow green and gold and amber, I can magically see his back at the same time as I watch him raise his glass to his suddenly parched lips. We do not clink glasses; that's not what he does. He says what he also says when I sneeze—"*Salute,*" in the Italian way—and together we drink.

Then one day I follow the music downstairs and behind the bar stands an impostor. A man who is not my father is dressed like my father, in the gray slacks, the red sweater, the white shirt and the narrow black tie—the uniform. He is taller than my father, paler and thinner and much more gray, "distinguished" my mother would call him, and yet he's going through the same motions my father does, carefully cleaning each glass and setting them out on the black counter of the bar to dry. Music is playing on the hi-fi, but he doesn't sing or whistle—he doesn't even hum, and he reminds me of the priests at St. Francis de Chantal, wiping clean the chalice in protracted silence. When I climb up to the black vinyl bar stool, it takes him a while to look at me and say, "Hello, young fella—how can I help you?"

"Who are you?" I ask.

"I'm the bartender," he answers promptly.

"No, you're not. My father is the bartender."

He smiles while staring into a glass he's cleaning, as if what I said made him wistful.

"Not tonight," he says. "And do you know why?"

"Because my parents are having a party?"

"That's right, because it's New Year's Eve."

I go upstairs so that I can change into my pajamas before the guests arrive and then watch through the bars of the balcony as they walk through the front door and pile their coats on the plastic-covered furniture no one uses. They come from what is, to me, the known world: the Roses and the Klines from Britton Street; the McGartys from around the block; Uncle Johnny and Aunt Liz from the part of Wantagh that still has farms; my grandma from Levittown, along with my aunts and their husbands, and my mother's two brothers all the way from Jersey. They are all dressed up, the women wearing pearls as reliably as men wear ties, the husbands in suits of such uniform sobriety that the shiny silk and crinoline of their wives look like plumage in comparison. But no guests are in the same league as my parents because no other woman shines the way my mother does—as though she is sunburned in the middle of winter—and no other man would dare to dress like my dad. When he was traveling in Texas, he bought a jacket in Houston he calls a "smoking jacket" and that I call "Sakowitz," from the name of the store stitched into the black satin lining. Sakowitz is red and black the way Superman's costume is red and blue—the colors don't matter as much as the power required to put it on. The red is red *velvet,* and has a pulse; the black is black silk brocade as complex as the language humans are going to find when we land on Mars. And my dad not only wears Sakowitz; he wears it with a black bow tie that makes him look—a word that ladies say in movies when they slap men across the face—"fresh."

Then the Schockets arrive from Manhattan, as if by flying carpet. Chip is wearing the same color as my mother—black. But Valerie wears a dress as green as the illuminated bottle of crème de menthe in my father's bar is green, as green as my father's jacket is red, as green, indeed, as my father's . . . eyes. It's made of silk, with a wide pleated skirt that's the shape of a bell but still revealing of Valerie's bare legs and green high heels. It's attached to Valerie's tawny shoulders only by two spaghetti straps, and so there's something informal about it, unsettled and tenuous, as if by dressing in it she's undressing. Her lips are bright red, and since the summer she's changed how she wears her hair—it's now in a swirling pixie cut that makes her look like she's trying to act casual for a photographer. Valerie's different from every woman at the party because she's *modern* and wears the Green Dress. My father's different from every man at the party because he's "ahead of his time" and wears the red smoking jacket. They are only like each other and that's what makes *them* a couple.

I watch from the top of the short stairway of the basement for as long as I can. It's what other little kids do at parties all over the world but unlike other little kids I know what I'm looking at. Yes, there is the nonstop surprise of seeing how "grown-ups" behave at a grown-up party, unchaperoned by their children—the antic, mugging, grabby desperation; the performances they put on when they're dancing with people who are not their spouses, hamming it up like "Latin lovers" when they're doing the cha-cha, rhumba and mambo with flowers between their teeth. But while I *see* the Klines and the Roses, the McGartys and the Labellas, I watch *them,* the Junods and the Schockets, Fran and Lou and Chip and Valerie. I watch Chip lean into the necks of the women he's dancing with and whisper into their ears some scandalous remark that causes them to jump and exclaim, "Oh, the things he says!" I watch Valerie dance with one man after another who will, as my mother will say later, "make asses of themselves" over her. I watch my mom, sitting with tightly wound legs and smoking fugitive menthol cigarettes that, instead of making her look older, as cigarettes always do to her friends, make her look younger, like a girl getting away with something—"I'm a *social* smoker," she'll claim. And then I watch my father . . . well, what do I watch my father do? I watch him light cigarettes and have his own cigarettes lit. I watch him drinking brown liquor from a highball glass with music in the ice even when the hi-fi is blaring Pérez Prado. But mostly I watch him being watched—because they all can't help themselves, Chip and Valerie and my mother; he inhabits his red jacket just as he inhabits the speakeasies of New York, and it's just as he says—they can't keep their eyes off . . . your *father.*

I'm found out, eventually—my mom sees me, and leads me by the hand into the basement, where my father says, as if after a long absence: "Tommy! What are you doing up! You're supposed to be in bed!" Then he picks me up, and offers my face to everyone at the party, so that I'm darting in and out, person to person, until I feel like a dizzy dancer, crazy with kisses, a feeling that sticks with me as he climbs the four steps, the six steps and then the five steps to my room. My brother is not in his bed; he is in my parents' room, watching TV as a treat for the festive occasion, and so I'm alone with the sound of the party and the bright lights burning just outside the closed door of my dark room. I must fall asleep, because when I hear all the guests downstairs start counting backward, "Ten, nine, eight, seven, six," it feels like a dream, and later on, when my parents start arguing, I keep telling myself that it must *be* a dream—that I am not really awake, even though every light beyond the crack in my door is blazing. The guests have all gone home, and the argument starts in the kitchen right after my father says good night to the bartender who dressed just like him. My parents don't yell at one another, as they sometimes do; no, their argument is worse than that, a conversation that they don't want their children to hear, its mortal energy expressed in voices so clenched and quiet they are guttural, until they hiss. They are arguing over someone: Valerie. They are arguing over something: divorce. My mother is doing most of the talking, saying, "If you think I'm going to give you a divorce so you can run off with Valerie, you can just forget it." My father keeps telling her, "Don't be ridiculous," but she doesn't sound ridiculous. She sounds, for the first time, as dangerous as he does, even though I keep telling myself I'm dreaming.

I begin to cry, despite not knowing exactly what they're arguing about. I haven't heard the word "divorce" before, at least not in our home, in the intimacy of our kitchen. I don't even know exactly what it means, because it is not just a new word but rather a new concept, like "death" or "cancer." Many years later, Michael will tell me what he heard that night, which he calls the Night of the Green Dress—he will tell me that as he feigned sleep in my parents' room, he heard our mother say, "I'd leave you, if not for the children." But I have to figure out so much on my own, and all I know is that "divorce" and "Valerie" are not just spoken in the same breath—they are bound together forever, as if by rhyme.

—

My parents gave us the tapes as presents. They lived in Florida, or maybe by this time they had moved to the home of my father's favorite sister, Elizabeth, back in Levittown. They were living in straitened circumstances, and so the tapes were exercises in nostalgia—the special nostalgia of those who had lost nearly all they had.

The tapes came from a time in their marriage when they had filmed everything—Little League baseball games, trips to the Catskill Game Farm, parades at Eastern Military Academy, Christmas mornings, Easter afternoons, and New Year's Eve parties. Then they had stopped, and had put the projector away, stacking the blue metal cans of film in the boiler room, next to tubs of curling photographs my mom couldn't organize herself to put into albums. I assumed they had left their home movies behind when they had moved away from their home in Wantagh. I was surprised that they had not only taken their stock of memories with them to Florida but had found someone to transfer them to VHS. The cassette was labeled "1463 Britton Street" and one evening I watched it with my wife, Janet, and my niece Stacey.

I had not seen my parents' home movies in decades, not since they rolled up the screen and boxed the camera. Indeed, I wasn't sure if I had *ever* seen them, for they had ended their practice of filming their lives and ours by the time I was four. And so watching the tape was like watching a curtain rise and fall in the same moment, like watching an era preserved even as it comes to a sudden and final end. I never made it past childhood in my parents' home movies. I was not only an adult as I watched them now on a television screen but an adult who grew up to be a sneak, a snoop, and a spy—an adult whose interest in his family's past is overwhelmingly forensic.

When I press "play," then, I am watching a tape entirely different from the one Janet and Stacey are watching. Sure, the pageantry is the same, the waving, mugging crowds whom time has turned into the lost tribes of Wantagh. They're all there—Uncle Johnny, Uncle Lenny, my two Aunt Lizzes and my two Uncle Harrys, all my aunts and uncles "fake" and "real," the Klines, the Roses, the McGartys, all of them drunk to the gills and dressed to the nines. What Janet sees are the pearls and the dresses of silk and satin—"I can't get over the outfits," she says. What Stacey sees are people she's heard of but never really got to know—for her the past is the past, and only the names are familiar. What I see, however, is what I've *already* seen, what I saw from my perch on top of the steps when I was a little boy. I'm watching something for the first time that I'm seeing for the second, and so while Janet and Stacey fixate on what happened, I can't shake my apprehension about what happens next. I live, in regard to those bygone days and nights, in the perpetual present. It is what I still have in common with the little boy watching from the top of the stairs:

I know what I'm looking for, as if I'm watching my personal Zapruder.

And then there they are. My mother is wearing a black dress with pearls that match her cropped platinum hair, occasionally raising to her lips a social cigarette. Uncle Chip is wearing a black suit and carrying himself with an air of scandal-sheet sophistication, his face marked by a jeweler's eye and a leer. My father is wearing the red velvet smoking jacket with the black brocade and the Sakowitz label printed on black satin lining. And Valerie, of course, is wearing the Green Dress with matching high heels, her lips the color of my father's jacket. It is New Year's Eve, the last day of 1962 staring into the mirror at the first day of 1963; it is, more precisely, the Night of the Green Dress, and it is transpiring once again before my very eyes, Valerie looking like she's dancing the Charleston every time she steps close to my father, even though she's standing still.

Are they happy or they are miserable? Do they still have a chance to be happy instead of miserable? That's what I want to know, now that time has answered so many of the other questions. Then, as the clock swings closer to midnight, they pair off, Chip and my mother stranded in the basement with the other revelers and my father and Valerie alone in the den, at the foot of six steps ascending to the kitchen. She primps him, pulling at the ends of his black bow tie and then swaying back on her heels as she smiles for the camera. I can only guess who's behind the lens—either Mr. Labella or my uncle Harry Nolan—but whoever it is doesn't allow the mechanical eye to blink. He doesn't have to, because Lou and Valerie aren't sharing a secret. They're unashamed, and as she leans back he catches her and scoops her into his arms, one hand around his neck and the other flung like a dancer's, her green high heel hanging from an extended toe. His favorite movie is *Gone with the Wind,* because Rhett Butler "knows how to treat a woman," and now he carries Valerie up the red stairs the way Rhett carries Scarlett before he ravishes her. The camera keeps rolling for their entire ascent, and at the top of the stairs the white door to the kitchen is closed. My father stops, frees one of his hands to turn the knob, and steps through the open door with his prize, Valerie holding tighter now, her hands in his hair. The door shuts, and the camera lingers on it for one, two, three, four, five seconds.

But the door does not reopen.

3

They did not go look at the house as a couple. He went alone, on a lark. He and his wife were new parents, but they were still renting in Brooklyn, a basement apartment that was so damp the twins never stopped coughing. The doctor had told them to get out, suggesting that the fresh air of Long Island might do the kids some good. So one day he told his wife he was taking a ride. He drove straight to Levittown, the development rising out of fields that no one before the war had thought to name. He looked around, and liked what he saw, clean streets curved like smiles, houses being sold like new cars. He went to the sales office, and introduced himself to the salesman at the desk. "Lou Junod," he said. "Bill Levitt," came the answer.

It was the man himself—the Henry Ford of the American suburbs, the builder of tract houses who was also a primary progenitor of the postwar dream. He didn't just buy up the potato fields and name the town he created after himself; he offered home ownership as a reward for service and a promise kept. For $100 down, veterans—white veterans—could buy one of Bill Levitt's houses and move in before the lawn was even seeded. More important, they could move *out* of the places where they'd grown up, out of the Bronx, out of Queens, out of the Lower East Side, out of the damp basement apartment in Brooklyn where babies developed the croup.

Was Lou Junod a veteran? He was, and had a Purple Heart to prove it. He had gone to war, just like everyone else, and had demonstrated, as he said later, that he wasn't yellow, that he didn't have "shit in the blood." But he'd had *two* wars—the war that was like everyone else's and the war that was all his own; the war he fought as an infantryman and the war he enjoyed as a singer. He'd almost lost his life, in the hedgerows of Normandy a month and a half after D-Day. But he'd had the *time* of his life in liberated Paris, where he'd sung with an army big band before audiences of adoring GIs as well as with Django Reinhardt in a hotel room before an audience of three adoring women. The name of the barnstorming revue was *For Men Only.*

He did not tell Bill Levitt about *that* war, because Bill Levitt was in the business of everyone's war, and so, in a way, was Lou Junod. He liked Levitt as Levitt liked him—as a man's man. "We hit it off . . . *immediately,*" he would say, with the house itself evidence of the great visionary's regard. Yes, Levitt was offering "Levitt houses" to veterans for $100 down, and yes, Lou Junod was a veteran of Omar Bradley's First Army. But he had gone to Long Island for a drive, not to buy a house, and he had only $75 in his pocket. He might have been just starting out as a salesman, and yet he understood in his bones that in order to make a sale he had to sell himself. So that's what he did. He entered into a contract for the house on Anvil Lane in Levittown, New York, for "seventy-five dollars and a handshake, because Bill Levitt liked . . . my face."

He was not a young man by the standards of the day. He was thirty, and his wife, Frances, was thirty-three. He had already gotten lucky in the army, when he was wounded but not killed and then when an officer who heard him sing called him off a troop truck heading back to the front. He had already invented and reinvented himself. But he was about to embark on the performance of a lifetime. He was going to be a family man.

He had not made it as a singer. He tried, but New York after the war was different from Paris after the Nazis. He wasn't allowed to sing the songs that had saved his life; instead, he was at the mercy of commercial song pluggers and had to "sing shit." Dick Ballou, one of the bandleaders from *For Men Only,* sent him to get lessons at Carnegie Hall Studios, but the instructor touched his face in an effort to pry open his mouth, and he walked out—"I should have slugged him." Anyway, the problem wasn't his voice but rather his teeth, which were too small for his mouth and made him look like he ate too much licorice. They sapped him of the confidence he had in such abundance in Europe, and whenever he had the chance to make an impression he "got the apple"—the lump in the throat "that's so big you can't even *breathe*." His wife, my mother, finished him off. Before the war, he'd driven rivets in the Brooklyn shipyards, the job that had given him his . . . body. But if she didn't want to be the wife of a riveter, neither did she want to be the wife of a crooner—a showbiz wife. The one time he had the chance to sing on the radio, he came home to an imperturbable silence. Neither his sisters nor Fran Brandshagen gave any indication that they had even heard him. The only person who admitted listening to him was his mother, who gave him a kiss and a glass of whiskey.

He was lucky he had another war, a war that gave him what everyone else had—stories to tell and army buddies to tell them to. He had met Johnny Orto in basic training, an Italian mama's boy from Queens. Johnny was quick-witted, with a talent for ribbing Lou Junod in a way that made him feel special rather than scorned. But Johnny was soft, Johnny was weak, and once, on a long hike, he fainted on the side of the road. To wake him up, the drill sergeant unscrewed his canteen and dumped its contents on "Johnny's . . . privates." My father could be a terrible bully to functionaries who did not give him his due—clerks, taxi drivers, waiters, parking lot attendants. But he made a habit of standing up for men weaker than himself, especially those who, like Johnny, called him by his preferred nickname: *Ace*. "Why don't you try that with *me*, you son of a bitch," he told the sergeant. He could have been sent to the brig, but instead the son of a bitch ordered him to complete the hike with Johnny on his back. The Ace was a "brute" back in those days, and so he bore "Johnny O" back to base as his personal burden, while Johnny promised one day to do the same.

He called the Ace after the war—after the Ace got the apple auditioning for Arthur Godfrey. Johnny had a job selling belts and asked the Ace to join him on a road trip and learn the business. They traveled by train, sample cases in the baggage car, and set up to show Johnny's wares in rooms they rented in the big hotel of whatever city they found themselves in—the William Byrd in Richmond, the Vance in Charlotte, the Winecoff in Atlanta, the New Yorker in Miami. They quickly learned that they were better off as a team than they were individually. Alone, they were just two guys from New York on the make. As a duo, they had chemistry, they had a routine. The Ace would tell stories about his own singularity, Johnny stories about the Ace's vanity, and these buyers, wide-eyed young women "fresh off the farm" or "old maids who were around for the Civil War," had never seen anything like them. They became the Martin and Lewis of the leather goods business, to the extent that later on they would each chafe at the roles they had to play, Johnny O "the second banana," Lou Junod the butt of Johnny's jokes. "Your uncle Johnny has made a *living* off your father," he would complain. "But he tells stories about me because he has no stories of his own." He would never admit that he had made his living off of Johnny. He would never admit—and Johnny would never say, knowing it would end their friendship—that the man he literally carried during the war had for all these years carried him.

He had no education to speak of; back in Brooklyn he had not advanced past the eighth grade. Although his wife had dreamed as a girl of "marrying an officer," he had left the service as a private first class. But he had found his calling; no, better than that, he had found what he called "a license . . . to *steal*." He was the star as a salesman that he could never be as a singer; indeed, he'd finally found a way to cash in on his looks, his charm, what even other men called his *virility,* gaining back the confidence he had lost because of his teeth as a swain to women both married and single, both haggard and in bloom. He might have moved to Levittown, with all the rest of the dog-faced GIs, but he lived like none of them did, with a big red Oldsmobile in the driveway and his bride in furs. Frances didn't want to be a showbiz wife? Well, she was a showbiz wife now, and he didn't hear her complaining.

There is no Bill Levitt in Westhampton. There is no mass migration of GIs buying beach houses for whatever they had in their wallets. There is just another salesman, Mel Arden, who has a divorce to pay for and a house to sell. This time my father has twenty grand in his wallet, or at least that's the way he makes it sound, even though for all I know he buys Mel Arden's house by signing a check. The point is that he pays cash, and when he tells the story he licks the tip of his thumb and whisks imaginary bills from the green stack in his hand. He will speak when he grows old of the days when he was in his . . . prime, and whenever he does I will think of this moment in early 1965, when, at the age of forty-four, he buys a house on the ocean at 879 Dune Road and parks a red Thunderbird convertible in the driveway.

The house is about a mile west of the square gray box he rented a few summers before, and he doesn't have to do a thing to it before moving in—it comes furnished, in a way I absorb forever rather than memorize. There's a brick fireplace, painted white, flanked by bookshelves stocked with mildly salacious and literary hardcovers my parents never crack. There's a dartboard hanging on a white door perforated and turned nearly black by a decade's worth of misses. Instead of a carpet there's a straw mat covering a wooden floor painted black, on which sits a green couch with down-filled cushions that exhale when you sit on them and a black rocking chair with "JFK" printed on the seat-back in gold. There's a fisherman's net draped on the wall over the green couch, entangled with dried starfish, and conch shells on most of the shelves, even one or two on the glass cart that serves as my father's bar. The heat comes through a grate on the floor that hurts when I step on it, sometimes imprinting itself on the soles of my bare feet. My parents keep a black-and-white TV in their room, which has outlandish summer hats and a large straw monkey hanging from nails on the ceiling beams, and at night my entire family crowds on their bed, watching whatever show is broadcast on the one channel we get—the ABC affiliate from New Haven, across the Long Island Sound.

I absorb the details of what we call "the Westhampton house" because I love it so much, as do my brother and sister and, of course, my father. My mother doesn't, first because of my father's drinking, second because she has to clean up after his friends, and third because one of those friends is often Chip Schocket. He does not bring Valerie anymore. He sometimes brings my friend Michael, but Michael's quiet presence is disquieting to my mother. "He's all

Valerie," she says. My mom is also not a beach person, and after she puts in her hours burning up in the sun and avoiding the ocean she likes to drive to town and go shopping. I often accompany her—we hold hands as we walk down Main Street in Westhampton Beach, before she leaves me off at the drugstore so that I can read comic books. Sometimes, though, I don't want to get dressed, I don't want to change out of my wet bathing suit and put on shorts and white socks and PF Flyers, so I stay with my dad while he drinks cocktails and plays Sinatra and Judy Garland—*Judy at Carnegie Hall*—on an old phonograph with an arm as thick as a spare rib. And one afternoon, when my mother is gone, he makes a long-distance phone call—a business call, he says, to a buyer in Florida. There is ceremony to such occasions, because long-distance calls are so expensive, and my father generally conducts his business in private. But on this afternoon he sits on the couch in his bikini and alpaca sweater, with his legs casually crossed like a guest on a TV talk show, and hands me the phone.

"Sing," he says.

"Sing what?"

He doesn't have to tell me. All he has to do is look at me, his right eye slightly asquint. "You know," he says.

And I do. It is the summer of "Fly Me to the Moon," a song I think is about spaceships and astronauts. I sing it all the time, and sometimes my father hears me and says, *"Heeeeey,"* as if he's taken notice, as if I've surprised him. I look at the telephone, the twisty spiraling black cord connecting me to a woman in Florida. My father hasn't told me her name; he hasn't done what he usually does, and made an introduction. But I know I'm singing for . . . a *lady,* and not just because he's told me she's a buyer. No, I feel her, in the sudden intimacy of our connection—her expectation, her receptivity, her kindness, her breathing. I open my mouth and sing into the black depths of the telephone, my words circling down the helixed black cord like water in a drain: "Fly me to the moon, let me play among the stars, let me see what spring is like on . . . Jupiter and Mars. In other words, hold my hand. In other words . . ."

I know what comes next. All along, I've thought "Fly Me to the Moon" is about . . . well, the moon. Now, as I come to the end of my long-distance serenade, I understand it's about kissing—about kissing *ladies.* I understand I have to proposition the lady I'm serenading long-distance, and with that understanding I hear myself for the first time, as if my mouth is singing to a skeptical ear. I hear myself sing, "Baby, kiss me," but then I hear something else, something that's involuntary and sounds like a hiccup, a cough or maybe even a bashful burp. But it's none of those things. It's a giggle, high as a girl's, and as soon as I hear it I know that, like everyone else in my family but *him,* I'm not a singer—that I'm too shy, too abashed and, above all, not enough like my dad. "Oh, you have a *nice* voice, Tawmmy," the lady on the phone says, and though it's the first time I've heard her speak, I'm immediately taken by how generous and kind she sounds, like a mommy instead of like a lady. "I hope I can meet you one day."

I hope I can meet her one day too, and will forget neither how she sounded or how I sounded . . . she, so inviting, like someone speaking with a mouth full of candy, and me, so embarrassed by my giggle that I won't sing again for another forty years.

I have a place on the floor where I watch and listen. It's a place I make for myself, my head resting on a wedge-shaped bolster pillow I take from one of the Danish modern sofas covered in black-and-white plaid. I lie down on the red carpet with a small dish of Junket or a glass of Wink, sometimes with my brother next to me but mostly alone. I watch the twenty-five-inch TV in the wall and I listen to my parents talking about what's on. It's a color TV at a time when many of the shows are still in black and white, but it's my mom and dad's conversation that adds another dimension to what I'm seeing.

I'm too young to know what the word "gossip" means. But what I come to understand watching television with my parents is that nothing is as it seems, and that when my father goes to nightclubs he also gains access to a hidden world of information—or, as they say on *The Man from U.N.C.L.E.* and in James Bond movies, "intelligence." The man knows everything. If my mother says that Tony Bennett has "some head of hair," he will counter that "it's a toupee . . . a piece . . . a *full wig.*" If she admires the stately form of Randolph Scott, my father will inform her that he's "the Queen *Bee*—during the war he used to pick up sailors with Monty Woolley." Often, I'll have no idea what he's talking about, especially when he's talking about women and says that Agnes Moorehead on *Bewitched* is a "big dyke," and that Vivien Leigh, Ava Gardner and Grace Kelly are all "big nymphos." I still listen closely because I'm an eager student of the lesson that even famous people are no more than the sum of their secrets.

But if I learn who and what my father doesn't like—reds like Charlie Chaplin, Jewish intellectuals like David Susskind, hopheads like Robert Mitchum, slobs like Buddy Hackett, degenerates like Fatty Arbuckle and Chuck Berry and sickies like Sal Mineo and Anthony Perkins—I also learn who and what he does. He has, it seems, "a type," so that when he expresses appreciation for a certain woman on television, my mother will suggest he is expressing appreciation for a certain *kind* of woman. He is discriminating in this regard; Liz Taylor is not his type because she's a "dumpy broad with a little bit of a facial hair problem." But Lena Horne? She's my father's type. So is Diahann Carroll. Raquel Welch is my father's type above all, so much so that he cuts out a photo of her from "Walter Scott's Personality Parade" and tapes it to the mirror on the inside of his closet; so much so that everyone in my family refers to her on a first-name basis and alerts my father to her presence on the television simply by shouting "Dad! *Raquel!*"

"Don't be a sneak," my mother says, when she catches me downstairs in my father's bar. Is that what I am? I don't think of myself as a sneak but rather as a spy or, better yet, as a scientist, studying the natural and unnatural phenomena of 1463 Britton Street. I can't help looking because whenever I look, I also find; there is evidence everywhere, especially in the basement, where the walls are striped with photographs the way the Grand Canyon is striped with sediment. My family has stories but no history, and yet there, frame by frame, an unspoken history exists to be pieced together. In one photo, my father is in swaddling clothes, the sepia tone of the print predicting his eventual complexion. In another, he is a little boy in a pageboy haircut, standing on the Coney Island boardwalk with his sister Marie, holding hands with his grandmother and wincing in a self-dramatizing way that is still recognizable to me. In another, he is facing the camera in shorts and cap, his hands in his pockets and a cocky grin on his face, his pose suggesting the child star he wanted to be—"That's the picture that won me the Jackie Coogan contest!" he says. In another, he is angled against a black roadster in a suit and tie, lighting a cigarette and already looking like a gangster. In another, he is posing with my mother at the beach, my mom with platinum pigtails, and he, in a bathing suit, looking away, so that the photographer captures him in profile on his "good side." In another, he is smiling inside a pup tent, in the army now, and then, in the last black-and-white photograph, he is standing before a microphone in boots and his army dress uniform, reborn as a singer, with the members of a big band smiling behind him, the bandleader gesturing with a baton. And in the last photo, in color and closest to the stairs, all of us except my brother are sitting on the beach in the summer of 1961, my mother wearing her skirted and striped one-piece bathing suit and a pink scarf that frames her sunburned face, my father in his blue trunks with his black hair spit-curled by the ocean on his brown forehead, my sister in the back with her arms around both our parents and me in the front with my blond crew cut, scowling as if Uncle Chip is taking the picture or Valerie is asking me to smile.

But that's just the history my father wants us to see. The real mother lode is the deposit of photographs on the walls behind his bar, flanking the mirror and the glowing bottles of liquor. They're not secret, exactly, because they're hanging in plain sight, and among them is the picture of my father and mother on their wedding night in Atlantic City and the newspaper clipping of Levittown's Cutest Twins. But they're also somehow . . . private. They occupy the shadows of my father's dimly lit saloon, and so when I'm not snooping around behind the bar with my mother upstairs in the kitchen I'm sitting in front of the bar on one of the black stools and asking my father to explain them, especially one of the news clippings he keeps in a small black frame. "All Quiet on Anvil Lane," reads the headline, underneath which is a photo of Lou Junod, wearing a suit and tie, pointing at an open Levittown window where he and a neighbor apprehended a "prowler."

"Dad, what's a prowler?"

He looks at me with an expression of nonchalant surprise as he cleans a glass.

"A prowler? Why do you want to know about *prowlers*?" he asks.

"That picture from the newspaper."

"Oh," he says, relaxing as he pours my ginger ale. "He was a Peeping Tom."

I brighten. "Like 'Tom, Tom, the piper's son'?"

"No," my father says. "That's you—you're the piper's son. The Peeping Tom was a sickie. When they arrested him, they found magazines in his car with pictures of women . . . tied up."

I take a breath and don't exhale. Maybe that's who I am, Peeping Tom, because of all my sneaking around and because there's another photograph that transfixes me, that I can't help peeping at, a black-and-white photograph of a woman posing on a diving board in a glistening bikini . . . well, not just posing, but rather caught by the camera in the act of writhing, with her fingers laced behind her head, her elbows extended like vestigial wings, her knees and indeed every other portion of her body bent, articulated from her tossed-back head to her extended feet, so that she seems almost segmented, like some preening, gorgeous insect. I'm not sure who she might be, but she has long platinum hair and wears a lot of lipstick and so I hope that she doesn't just live in my father's world but also mine.

"Dad," I say, "is that Mommy?"

"Who?"

"The lady on the diving board."

He glances at her, smiling to himself and trying not to laugh.

"No, son. That's Jayne Mansfield, at the Fontainebleau Hotel in Miami."

"Who is she?"

"She's an . . . actress."

"Wow. Did you meet her?"

"Yes I did. I sometimes stay at the Fontainebleau."

"She looks like Mommy."

He squints at me with curiosity but not anger.

"Son, Jayne Mansfield is . . . a sexpot."

"Mommy's not a sexpot?"

"No, son. She's a beautiful woman. But she's your mother. And she's my wife."

And that's the difference. The other photos on the wall of the basement are the historical record of the life that led him to us, while the photos behind the bar are the record of the life that led him away. They're from the road, from his nights in Manhattan, from the world of savoir faire he inhabits with Chip and ladies who can't keep their eyes off him, and for that reason I can't get enough of them or the stories that accompany them. There's a photo of Sammy Davis Jr. wearing an ascot in the company of my father's friend Frankie; there's a photo of Doris Day in a showroom in stockinged feet; and, best of all, because it comes with a story, there's a photo of Cary Grant shopping for handbags during the filming in New York of *That Touch of Mink*. He was a little bit of a cheapskate, Cary Grant. His movies might have taught my father about how to behave like . . . a gentleman, not to mention how to dress. But he was a little *tight*, and he came up to the Koret showroom for some handbags he might be able to give as gifts. My father returned from lunch one day and there, sitting on a stack of newspapers with his legs crossed, was Cary Grant, eating an egg-salad sandwich. "Hello, Cary," my father said, without deference or ceremony. "Hello, *Lou*," Cary Grant answered, in that unmistakable voice and unmistakable style, perfectly casual, as though "we'd known each other all our lives," in my father's telling. It's a story he often tells because it's a story I often ask him to tell—because I never get tired either of hearing his Cary Grant impression or being reminded, again and again, that Cary Grant recognized Lou Junod as an equal.

And yet the photograph of Cary Grant is not the celebrity photograph I study the most on my expeditions deep behind the bar. That honor belongs to the photograph of Lloyd Bridges, the star of *Sea Hunt*, one of my favorite shows before it went off the air. I stare at it as though hypnotized, though not for any of the usual reasons . . . not because it's in a place of prominence, like the photo of Jayne Mansfield, or because my father talks about it, like the photo of Cary Grant, or because it demands explanation, like "All Quiet on Anvil Lane." I stare at it because it meets none of those qualifications. It's stashed away in the shadows, low and next to the corner where two walls meet. My father has never told a story about it or, for that matter, about Lloyd Bridges. Most important, I know better than to ask.

It's not even much of a photo, just a record of strangers thrown together at some place that means nothing to them, probably at a hotel. The *Sea Hunt* star is sitting at the table with his hands folded and a cocksure expression on his face, as if he's confiding to the camera that he's above all this and really doesn't give a damn. Four men stand behind him, strenuously smiling, all of them tan enough to suggest a South Florida locale. Two women flank him, one of whom appears to be his middle-aged wife and one of whom appears to be Valerie Schocket.

Could it really be Valerie Schocket? It can't be Valerie Schocket, because Valerie Schocket hasn't been to our house since she divorced Chip and even I know she's no longer welcome. My father wouldn't *dare* hang a photo of Valerie on the wall of his bar, even in an out-of-the-way spot. But if she's not Valerie, who is she? She's my father's type, that's for sure; she's dark, she's tan, with white teeth and a crown of glossy black hair parted in the middle. I would think that maybe she's a model or a local starlet summoned to sit next to the television star, if not for the way she's dressed—in a uniform of some kind; in a white dress shirt, a skinny black tie, and a V-neck sweater that looks red even in a black-and-white photograph; like a man . . .

Exactly like my father.

4

Of all the mysterious photographs on display on the walls and tables of 1463 Britton Street, the one I study most often and intently is not of a woman. It is a photograph my father had made for the same reason he'd once recorded a tape of Cathy and Michael singing "I Love Paris" when they were just five years old—to send to his buyers. He'd hired a professional photographer to come to the house and shoot it and then he'd had it mass-produced in a variety of sizes, so that it could be put in a frame or carried in a wallet. In our house, it can still be found all over the place, so prized that it exists now as a kind of flotsam, turning up in the bottom of my father's drawers, on the shelves of his closet, and loose in the boxes where my parents store their photo albums, like inflationary currency. But the print that I stare at every day is the framed eight-by-ten that sits on an end table in the den made of Italian marble and at eye level when I sprawl on the floor and watch television. I stare at it because it intrudes into my line of sight and gives me no other choice but also because it is a picture of me, as an infant, in my father's embrace.

The photographer shot it in black and white, and did a beautiful job capturing a moment between us—a moment of bliss. My father, wearing a dress shirt open at the neck, is holding me with both hands, tossing his head back and bringing me closer to his exposed skin and his hidden heart, while I, wearing "white to the face" in the form of swaddling clothes, open my toothless mouth in Gerber-esque abandon. The photo looks like an advertisement, and yet the world it advertises I can't recognize. Of course, I recognize *him*, in his enormity, in his swarthiness, and yes, in his love. But I can't recognize myself, and not simply because the photo captures me in larval form, with the hair I now wear in a stern crew cut raised into a comical cowlick. No, what I can't recognize is my happiness, and my absence of fear. The photo is strange to me because I am in my father's grasp, and *I'm not crying*—so now I can't study it without wondering what happened to me and the ecstatic world I once inhabited.

The chewing never stops. The swallowing never starts. There is something in my mouth that used to be steak but, no matter how vigorously I chew, won't go down—something that won't go past the rising gorge in my throat. So I keep chewing, until the masticated meat has the texture and taste of exhausted Juicy Fruit, and I get an idea. I'm sitting at the dinner table, along with the rest of my family, the table round, with a glass top, overhung by a swaying blue lamp on a chain. Given the kind of family we are—the kind of family I imagine us to be—we should be sitting at an endless oblong table, with our father at the head and our mother at the other end, speaking to one another by ear trumpet. Our actual table is too close, too intimate and nonhierarchical, with the hanging lamp touching our huddled faces with an interrogatory light. How can I possibly get away with my plan? How can I take the dead meat out of my mouth and stick it under my seat like a wad of chewing gum?

I am sitting in the chair against the wall, under the window, Cathy and Michael across from me, Mom and Dad to my left and right, facing each other. I keep chewing, and then, staring straight ahead, take the gray bolus of beef out of my mouth while continuing to move my jaws as loudly as possible, as though the extraction never occurred and I'm still struggling to swallow. I am a genius, I think—a master criminal, although, as my hand searches the underside of my chair, I am already facing a problem. No matter how much I've chewed it, steak is not chewing gum, and it doesn't stick. Though I press it as hard as I can into a corner of the chair's metal frame, it falls to the floor in a hideous heap, and our German shepherd Nikki comes over to eat it. I'm caught doing something *disgusting*, as well as breaking the rule against feeding Nikki scraps from the table. I hear my mother say, under her breath, "Oh, Tommy," and then my father repeat my name in an altogether different kind of voice, a stern and commanding one that changes the very vowels:

"Tummay."

I don't look. I can't look, not simply because I'm afraid of him but because I'm afraid of what's going to happen. Dinner has always been difficult for me, and my mother has told me that when I was a baby I was nicknamed "Suppertime Tom" because "all day long you were good as gold, but at suppertime, *watch out*!" But now I'm no longer a baby and still I can't swallow my food or control my emotions and worst of all I can't understand why, which is to say I can't understand why I'm so afraid of my father. No, I'm not the only one, and yes he is a fearsome and formidable man. The other day, he came home late from a road trip and raised such a clamor that he woke up sickly Mrs. Kornhoff next door. When old Mr. Kornhoff came to our house to complain, my father told him, "If you don't get off my steps I'll *throw* you down," and now we don't see Mr. Kornhoff anymore—he hides in his house every time my father pulls his car in the driveway. Everybody is scared to death of Lou Junod. But it's different with me because I'm not just scared of him the way my mother is, I'm scared of him *when* my mother is, so that although I feel all alone I'm scared enough for two.

"Lou," my mother says, with a note of caution, the same voice she uses when he's driving too fast and she's pressing the imaginary brake.

"Frances," my father answers.

"Lou, let him just suck the juices from the meat," my mother says, and extends a hand moist with sweat. "Tommy, you don't have to swallow. Just the suck out the juices, like a good boy . . ."

"Frances, let me handle this. Look at the poor kid. How's he going to put on any muscle sucking out . . . the *juices*?"

And that's when it starts, the thing I want to stop and can't. My face tightens, and my lower lip starts trembling like a worm, no matter how much I bite it, no matter how ruthlessly I try to subdue it with my teeth. I'm squeezing my eyes shut so hard that I'm straining the tendons in my neck, but even through those clenched apertures I can see the faces of Michael and Cathy on the other side of the table, as if from far away. They're indulgent and kind, but there's something else about them—as hard as I'm trying to hold back tears, they're trying to hold back laughter. They're not laughing at me, precisely; they're not mocking me, they're not being cruel. They just think . . . I'm cute. I'm around five or six years old, but to them I'm still Suppertime Tom, and the whole spectacle, the whole routine and ritual, is part of their love for me. I am quaking in terror, but they see me differently from how I see myself, and that realization somehow emboldens me. I sneak a peek at my father the way I would the sun during an eclipse, aware that I am running the risk of being struck blind.

Is he mad at me? He seems to be, with his chin cocked and his teeth nipping the edge of his lower lip. And yet, at the same time, he's not. He's just teasing. He's playing with me, mugging, *acting*, pretending he's mad at me for the benefit of Michael and Cathy and maybe even my mom, his audience. And the thing is, I know this, because my father reaches out and puts his hand on mine, his palm not clammy like my mom's but warm and dry like a fireplace, his pinky ring of black onyx extending from my tiny mitt to tap the glass top of the table. I'm not in trouble—he's *telling* me I'm not in trouble—so I shouldn't cry, I shouldn't have to. But it's too late.

There are forces inside me against which I'm helpless; I'm the little Dutch boy with his finger in the dike, and the pain of holding back what demands release contorts my face into a mask of agony. I must look like I'm about to sneeze, and when at last I surrender to the call of my stinging eyes and quaking jaws I don't just start crying; I start *blubbering*, with a spasmodic recoil that renders my voice insensate and causes the tears to come from my eyes in a spurt, as if instead of sneezing I've wet my pants, and am now stained with the hot proof of my shame.

My father might not have been genuinely angry at me for feeding Nikki scraps from the table but he is angry at me for crying. Or maybe he's just disgusted. Or maybe he's something altogether different, something harder—and more painful—to discern. He raises both hands in a gesture of either disavowal or surrender, and begins staring at my mother as though she's to blame. "What did I do?" he asks. "What did I *do*? I was just teasing. You'd think I was beating him to a pulp, when I've never even laid a hand on him." He stands up, and on his way down to the bar he throws the ice from his highball glass into the sink. I sit miserably, with the hot tears cooling on my face and Nikki waiting for more gray cud from my mouth and what I want to do is follow him, because I realize what I've done. I've hurt him. I've pierced him as he pierced me, and I'm left to figure out why. Did I think he might hit me? Did I think he might humiliate me as he sometimes humiliates my mom? I didn't. He's right—he didn't *do* anything, and what he did do, he did for fun. So why was I so afraid of him? Why did I cry? Why can't I stop crying even when he *pretends* to raise his voice? I have no answer except for the most terrible of all:

I cry because I'm a crybaby.

I cry because I'm weak.

My father has four categories of friends. There are the enablers, like Chip, who get him into trouble, and there are the sidekicks who get him out. There are the rivals, foolhardy enough to presume themselves his equal, and then there are the worshippers, foolhardy enough to presume him their ideal. The worshippers are by far the most numerous, and I can always identify them by the way my father talks about them—by the language that he uses. It's not just that he will sometimes tell me outright that the handbag salesman he happens to be meeting for dinner at "21" "worships . . . your father. It's a little embarrassing, if you want to know the truth. He's up my ass something terrible. Like I'm his idol!" It's that he speaks of men I know to be his closest friends with pity that sometimes crosses over into contempt. Whenever he sees some henpecked stranger at the beck and call of his squirming brood, he is in the habit of shaking his head and muttering to himself, "poor . . . *beggar.*" But that's also how he speaks of Uncle Jimmy Duffy, his boyhood friend; of Uncle Joe McGarty, the father of my best boyhood pal, Robert; and, most of all, of Uncle Johnny. They are, respectively, "poor Jimmy," "poor Joe McGarty," and "poor Johnny," unless he is arguing with my mother, whereupon he will declaim, "Who do you think you're talking to, Joe McGarty?" Or, "What do you think I am, a *mameluke* like Johnny Orto?"

I hate that word, *"mameluke,"* Italian slang that is roughly equivalent to the Yiddish "schmuck," but which in my father's scornful interpretation means a grown-up "mama's boy," a weak man who takes orders from his wife. I also hate how he talks about his supposed friends behind their backs, ranking them against the punishing standard of his own exalted masculinity. And yet the men he considers weakest are also often the men he loves the most, perhaps for the privilege of feeling sorry for them. He feels so sorry for one of our neighbors, Bill Rose, that years later he will avow his love for Bill Rose as soon as his name comes up in conversation, a response so automatic it seems Pavlovian. Mr. Rose, as I call him, lives three split-levels down Britton Street. He is prematurely bald, with a laconic face pinioned between fringes of dark hair encircling the sides of his head and white skin tinged purple under his dejected eyes. It is a comedian's face, and Mr. Rose enjoys a comedian's privileges, my father letting him get away with acts of impertinence that would be fatal to his other friendships. He is allowed to tease my father about the most disastrous dalliance of his life. Back in the late 1950s, my father got a tip about a Japanese company that was coming to the United States to compete with Kodak. He decided to buy ten thousand shares of Fujifilm, only to have his stockbroker, who happened to be my mother's uncle, refuse to make the purchase out of hatred for Japan. "I would be worth . . . *millions,*" he tells anyone who will listen, and so when he visits Bill Rose's backyard, he's greeted by his host pulling back the corners of his eyes and shouting "Fuji photo, Fuji photo!" in a phony Japanese accent.

My father's saving grace is his ability to laugh at himself, even occasionally about his ruinous romance with the stock market. But his response to being kidded depends entirely on the identity of the kidder, and the latitude he gives Bill Rose as a comedian depends entirely on his sympathy for Bill Rose as a tragic figure—as a man who wants to be somewhere else. Mr. Rose was a pilot in World War II, and indeed keeps his flight suit in a valise in his basement. But he was grounded because of a bad heart, and now makes his living as a salesman for Ballantine beer, cringing theatrically when my father drinks Miller ("It's like *water*") and taking my father into his confidence while gazing at jet airliners leaving trails across the sky: "That's where I should be, Lou—up there. That's where I belong." Instead, he is *down here,* not just earthbound but the lowliest of *mamelukes,* subject to the fastidious tyranny of his wife, Alice.

My father, as a rule, flatters women who know how to "keep a house," and lords the prowess of the *balabustas* over my mom as remorselessly as he did the sexual allure of Valerie Schocket. And no one knows how to keep a house like Alice Rose. She is a woman whose skin is almost as tan as my father's, whose "frosted" hair looks like a wig, whose patterned housedresses roll off the assembly line of her sewing machine, and whose kitchen floor has turned yellow with the tireless application of wax. She has a hunger for housekeeping matched only by her hunger for L&M cigarettes, the lipsticked butts of which pile up in the scoured copper ashtray that accompanies her wherever she goes, like a mechanical valet. She is, in my father's estimation, "neat as a pin," but although he wields the phrase to shame my mother, neither does he use it to compliment Alice. He dislikes her because of how she treats her husband, and because of how her son treats me.

Perry Rose is my third friend, after Michael Schocket and Robert McGarty. He is a year older than me and he is "all Alice" in the way Michael Schocket is "all Valerie" and I fear I might be "all Frances" instead of "all Lou." He is pale as a grubworm, and, yes, neat as a pin at a time when the mischievous boys of TV commercials and sitcoms use their ingenuity to come home spattered in mud. He wears his Bermuda shorts with a belt, and his blue canvas boating sneakers with white socks that manage to stand out even against the camouflage of his skin. He touts his ownership of GM stock, reads Classic Comics instead of Marvel, and is the Thurston Howell of our neighborhood, although he also appreciates the witticisms of Paul Lynde on *Hollywood Squares.* He can't go outside without Mrs. Rose inspecting him first, often spitting on her fingertips and refreshing the raised precipice of his crew cut, even as her lips shrivel around her cigarette. He is the only kid I know who openly wants to be a millionaire, as well as the only kid I know whom my father openly distrusts, contriving to keep us apart by summoning me to work with him in the backyard when Perry knocks on our door.

One day, I find out why. Perry doesn't like to run; he likes to skip, and as he comes down the sidewalk I take his hand and join him, the both of us swinging our arms and singing songs as we skip up and down Britton Street. When I return home, my father is waiting for me. With a curled finger he summons me downstairs to the bar, where he sits me down on a stool and explains that boys don't do what I just did with Perry—boys don't skip, and they certainly don't hold hands with other boys. "Do you know what boys who hold hands with other boys are called?" he asks.

"No," I say.

"They're called sissies," he says. "They're called fairies. You don't want to be a . . . *fairy,* do you?"

"No," I say, but I can already feel it, the shame of his accusation finding expression in the shame of my stinging eyes and trembling lips.

"Then stay away from Perry," he says. But of course that's impossible—Perry lives three houses away. Perry is my friend. There's nothing I can do but turn on the waterworks; nothing I can do but look at my father, with his face poised between love and stern dismay, and burst into tears.

I have the best big brother. Michael is a teenager, so he once had a room—and a life—to himself. I, on the other hand, know of no other life but the one I've had with *him,* our beds pressed in parallel against opposing walls, a space the width of a surfboard between them. We share a closet, two chests of drawers with a desk between them, and a radio. Although Michael and Cathy are "the twins," I often tell myself that I'm my brother's *real* twin, and stare at the mirror in search of evidence that we look alike. I try to follow him everywhere he goes and for the most part he lets me tag along, even when he's with his friends. He is remarkably indulgent of my attentions, remarkably patient and remarkably kind.

I have the best-*looking* big brother. I have a big brother who lets me watch whatever I want on television, without complaint, and then watches with me. I have a big brother who protects me from bullies and buys me Rocky Marciano boxing gloves so I can learn to defend myself. I have a big brother who lets me wear his Wantagh Warriors sweatshirt and wrestle with the guys on his wrestling team. I have a big brother who was mentioned in the newspaper when he used his surfboard to save people from drowning in the ocean after a storm in Westhampton. I have a big brother who dreams of being a veterinarian because he not only loves animals but animals love him. I have a big brother who, when my parents give me a transistor radio for my birthday already tuned to the station that plays Frank Sinatra and Dean Martin, turns it to a station that's playing Roy Orbison's "Oh, Pretty Woman," and changes my life. I have a father who is nothing like any of the all-knowing, forbearing, pipe-smoking fathers of the television shows I watch—indeed, my father claims that there is a correlation between pipe smoking and miserliness, and uses "pipe smoker" and "cheapskate" interchangeably—but I have a big brother who is just like Wally on *Leave It to Beaver,* so I can still watch TV without thinking it represents a big con.

My father might make me cry with just a glance. But how can he be a bad father, if Michael has turned out so good? I aspire to be like my brother because my brother aspires to be like my father and has somehow turned out better than my father could ever be—and maybe even bigger, eating a carton of ice cream each night and working out incessantly with the barbells in the basement. In the Charles Atlas advertisement of our lives at 1463 Britton Street, I am and might forever be the ninety-eight-pound weakling who gets sand kicked in his face. But every day Michael shows me that the Dynamic Tension of living with our dad *works,* and can make a Man out of Mac.

My father loves Michael—he calls him "Big Mike," the ultimate accolade. But he disapproves of his weight lifting, for a few reasons. First, Michael doesn't need to lift weights, because as a *Junod,* his body belongs to him as a dispensation of the blood; when my father stands in front of the mirror in adoration of his own physique, he'll often remark, "Never touched . . . a weight." Second, he's afraid that Big Mike is getting *too* big, and is in fact "disfiguring" himself. And finally, he doesn't like that my brother reads "muscle magazines" the way I read comic books—that he's devoted not just to weight lifting, which is manly, but also to "bodybuilding," which is not. My father and brother don't argue very often, but they argue so bitterly over muscle magazines that they become contraband in our room, and I have to sneak looks at them.

They all look like the Incredible Hulk, the bodybuilders whom Michael admires, their musculature so exaggerated that I can see not just their biceps and deltoids but also their stippled veins, their entire circulatory systems on pulsing display. My father's right; they have disfigured themselves, and there's something grotesque about them. But it's not just that their muscles have grown too big. They're all tan, they're all gleaming with oil, they're all either smiling or grimacing with overly white teeth, their bodies erupting from tiny bikinis. They are straining toward some kind of ideal, but in doing so they look artificial, as if what's being exaggerated is not just their anatomies but the very notion of masculinity. In truth, they all look like parodies of . . . my father *himself,* but that's not what he says. My father says they all look like *fags,* and worries that Michael likes to read about them because he's a fag too. I don't know what a fag is, exactly; all I can guess is that fags are like fairies and sissies, but even worse. But what I worry about most is the impossibility of the ideal that my father demands we live by. My brother is an example and exemplar; he is the pure product of the program that my father has instituted in our household in terms of both "physical culture" and manners, his character as perfected as his build. Even as a teenager, he's exactly what my father demands we become, a "gentleman," and if that makes him a "fag" . . . well, what does that make me?

Cathy lives at the end of the hall. Her room is right next to ours, but I don't see her nearly as much as I see Michael. In fact, Cathy is the biggest mystery in my life, even more so than the question of how my father entertains his buyers. She is, however, in no way *mysterious* in her actions or her aspect. If anything, she is the simplest and most straightforward member of my family, the one who aspires to simplicity and straightforwardness though not, in the end, to honesty. Unlike Michael, who is still scarred by his Catholic school experience, she survived the nuns at St. Francis by shrugging them off; unlike Michael, she is popular in high school. She has girlfriends who come over for sleepovers, putting their hair up in curlers and dancing in the basement to a stack of 45s that Cathy plays on a portable phonograph. She has a flattopped boyfriend whom she started dating when she was fourteen, Ronnie Gustafson, the New York State cross-country champion three years in a row, Olympian in his talent and his attitude. She is dirty blond, with skin that tans easily and eyes almost as green as my father's, and has a joshing manner, a talent for mimicry and an unwillingness to take anything too seriously. She likes soul music and girl groups more than she likes the Beatles, and tries to teach me how to dance; she likes to laugh with rough mockery, but she never says an unkind word to me. She's the one who teaches me how to tie my shoes, and puts streamers on the handlebars of my tricycle, and yet there is some essential part of her I never know, and never will.

My parents don't let me. It isn't simply that Cathy's bedroom is the only place in the house where I'm not allowed without permission, and so exists as a closed door at the end of a dark hallway like a room preserved as a memorial for someone already gone. It's that they insist on telling her story and the story they tell I can't recognize. The Cathy who lives at the end of the hall drives fast, smokes cigarettes, bowls in a league on Wednesday nights and relies on my mother to write her papers for school. The Cathy who lives in my parents' narratives is a sort of unsinkable South Shore debutante who might have fulfilled all my parents' wishes for themselves had she not . . . well, *what*? Torn up her knee on a ski trip? Gotten sick? Met Ronnie? It is impossible to reconcile the sister who *is* with the sister who *might have been*, and so my parents seem to mourn her even as they extol her. Cathy put her hand through a pane of glass as a little girl and the doctor who stitched her up said she was lucky she didn't cut a tendon and end up with a *claw*—and yet, in my mother's frequent telling of the story, Cathy might as well have a claw, so bravely does she fight to overcome the handicap that never actually befell her. Though she participates only in intramural sports at Wantagh High, I hear over and over what an athlete she is—that, indeed, she was so good at baseball that when Michael tried out for Little League the coaches wanted Cathy instead. They even tried to change the *rules* so that Cathy could play, although in the end the rules stayed the same and Cathy never joined a team. But intentions matter much more than actual outcomes when my parents speak about Cathy; indeed, they are all that matter, and the legend of my sister grows up alongside my sister herself, the choking vine indistinguishable from the trellised roses. My parents won't hear of anything but what they concocted, and even agree with friends who—as heedlessly as they call me "an accident"—opine that Cathy "should have been the boy."

She should have been the boy. But she is not the boy. She is the center of tumult and division. My father often dismisses "women drivers" with one of his sayings—"They don't get into accidents; they just *cause* them"—and that turns out to be Cathy at home. She doesn't argue so much as she causes arguments, because alone among us she has the courage to disobey. She goes out to the clubs that line the route to Jones Beach, leaving my father either to wait up for her so that he can smell her breath or to get in his car and search for her in the places he thunderingly calls "toilets." She also doesn't wear the country-club clothes my mother buys her on shopping sprees and by the simple act of refusal brings out a side of my mother I have never seen. Cathy likes to tell me stories of how, when she was young, my mother hit her so hard with a hairbrush that my father had to pull the bristles from her arm "with pliers." But I never believe her, first because I am temperamentally skeptical of anything Cathy says and then because Mom treats me "with kid gloves" rather than a hairbrush—because, as she tells my brother and sister, "Tommy poops gold." But I watch the fights that Cathy has with my mother in the basement for the simple reason that they are *fights*, and so require spectators. They are also strangely funny, from my perch on the short staircase that becomes my seat in the bleachers. My mother is so prim and proper that my sister calls her what she detests most—"a snob" and "a phony." But she is *wild* when she fights Cathy. She throws things at Cathy. And not just anything: plates, glasses, items that she picks up from my father's bar and lets fly so hard that they make a whizzing sound before they shatter against the doors of her closet, my mother crying out, "You little bitch!" and my sister poking out her tongue as she dances away from the rain of broken crystal and china. I always root for my mother in her battles with my father. But now I want to stand up and cheer for Cathy, hoping that she can still somehow get away.

For my eighth birthday, I receive a reel-to-reel tape recorder. It's not as big as the wooden one my father used to serenade before he parked it once and for all in the boiler room. It's about the size of a box of cereal, light blue, the thin brown tape suspended between two reels of clear plastic. I guess I could call it a tape player, but I rarely play anything on it. I use it to record, and I'm always amazed that the tape looks the same even after I use it to snoop on my family. I think it should look different somehow. I think it should be scribbled with their words, or maybe turn bright red.

I am known—notorious—in our house for my curiosity. When I was five, I shocked my father and my brother when I accompanied them to the curb where they were putting out our garbage and asked the workers in the garbage truck, "What do you think of the Negro situation in Alabama?" But I'm not nearly as straightforward with my family as I was with our garbagemen. I don't tell them I'm taping them, but rather set up the recorder on the first step to the stairs to the den and turn it on right before we sit down for dinner. It's not a secret, exactly; anyone who goes downstairs to the bathroom has to avoid stepping on the reels as they turn. But the rest of my family thinks the recorder's a toy, and it's not. It's an instrument of power for me, because when I turn it on after dinner—when I find a place where I can listen to it in private—I hear the exact same conversation that I heard at the table and yet it sounds completely different. The tension is gone, and what baffled and unsettled me as it happened now sounds like a play, with everybody practicing their familiar parts. At the same time it becomes a sort of Babel, a record of misunderstanding and miscommunication that makes me wonder what other people would think of us if they only could hear . . . that makes me think, perhaps for the first time, that my family is *crazy.* My father actually sounds silly, like a gangster auditioning to be an actor, his pronouncements spoken as much to himself as to us, his cagey laughter much more essential to his charm than his thoughts on his three political heroes, Barry Goldwater, Douglas MacArthur, and J. Edgar Hoover. I chuckle at my father when I listen to the recorder but that's not why it's so important to me.

It's important to me because when I'm recording my family over dinner I never want to cry.

And then they're gone.

They leave, Michael for Ball State University in Muncie, Indiana, and Cathy for Averett College, a two-year Baptist school in Danville, Virginia, where she is the only Yankee. Why they go where they go, I have no idea; all I know is that I'm alone with my parents at 1463 Britton Street, and embarking on my second life as an only child.

Everything changes, particularly me. I am no longer cute, with my adult teeth growing in as brown as toffee and fissured from all my childhood fevers. And our empty house is a foreign house, an exotic and enchanted house, a house under a spell. Every room is open to me, and so I start exploring, as if we—my scant new family, the five of us now the three of us—have just moved in. Cathy's dark bedroom I visit by myself for the first time. The same with my parents' bedroom, where I not only begin the task of cataloging what I find in my father's closet but lie down on the comforter that covers the broad expanse of bed they share, hearing the air go out of it as I sink into the folds of satin.

I also fall asleep in the upstairs hallway outside the bathroom my mother uses, when she's behind the closed door. We have always spent a lot of time together but now very often it's just us, my father very often away. I accompany her on her shopping sprees, sit next to her at the counters of the luncheonettes she frequents, eat dinner with her in the evening and watch TV with her at night. She is all alone and yet because of me she has no privacy and seeks refuge in a bathroom that is becoming the complement to my father's at the other end of the hall. She doesn't boast the extensive and exotic selection of toiletries he does, although the can of Aqua Net hair spray she keeps on her counter is the exact same size as the can of

Consort he keeps on his. But she is building her own cabinet of curiosities, in the phalanx of bottles and vials she stores behind the mirror. They all look the same because they are all from the same pharmacy, a place on Wantagh Avenue where the proprietors greet her by name and like her so much that they are sometimes willing to "fudge" her prescriptions when she really needs them. They are all amber-colored plastic with white caps, and they are filled with pills whose different shapes and sizes represent a hidden variety behind a uniform front. When I ask what they are she calls them "medicines," though sometimes, when she's talking to my father, I'll hear her saying, "I need a pill," or advising him, "Why don't you take a pill?" But if she's taking medicines, does that mean she's sick? She must be, given the sheer number of medicines in the medicine cabinet, and their relentless accumulation, which reminds me of the rolls of unused cookie dough that crowd a shelf of our refrigerator. And so I worry about her when she disappears behind the bathroom door, and call out to her when I hear her run the faucet because that often means she's crying. "Mom, what are you doing in there?" I'll ask, and when she inevitably answers, "Tommy, I'm going to the john!" I'll lie down parallel with the strip of light under the door and wait her out as patiently as a hunger striker, eventually closing my eyes and sinking into the oblivion of sleep.

I do not run the tape recorder when I eat dinner with my mom. I do when my dad comes home, because he upends our routine and suddenly my mom and I are both nervous wrecks. Suddenly I can't watch the Monkees because he's heard that one of them is homosexual. Suddenly I can't watch *The Flying Nun* because although he doesn't go to church he thinks it's sacrilegious. Suddenly my mother can't serve the "salads" she makes when he's not here—the scoops of tuna fish and cottage cheese plated between crescents of peeled cantaloupe and honeydew—and has to return to the stove like a shell-shocked soldier sent back to the front. She burps when he comes home. Her hands sweat and are at the same time as chilly as the steaks defrosted on the counter. And I place the tape recorder on the step closest to the kitchen, and close the door so that he doesn't see.

The recorder—the fact that the recorder is recording—has

become a secret, now that Michael and Cathy are gone. They used to think it was funny, but I played it for my father once, and he didn't like it, didn't like how he sounded discoursing authoritatively about hairpieces. Since then, he has even asked, "You don't have that *thing* on, do you?" But it's on now, because my parents have been arguing more in the empty house and I want to hear what that sounds like on tape. I want to be able to play it back to them and say, "Here, this is what I hear, *this* is what it sounds like," and make everything better.

My father drinks, and my mother is worried about his drinking. Of course, he does not *get* drunk, because he is not *a* drunk—the very suggestion is an affront to his pride and the cause of their fights. "You look at me like I'm some kind of . . . *rumdum,*" he says to her, swirling the Scotch, the occasional Rob Roy, with the tip of his finger. In truth, she hasn't said a word; she's just fretted. But he can *see* it—he can see her counting each drink, he can see her flinching, he can see her being . . . a martyr. That's what he calls her, and it's strange to me, because at St. Francis de Chantal we pray to "all the martyrs and saints," but he doesn't mean it as a compliment. He says, "You make me out to be the *heavy,* so you can be the . . . martyr," and as her face stiffens, as her eyes narrow and her flickering glance turns cold, I can see he has a point. I attend St. Francis, but my mother *is* St. Frances, with the belligerent dignity of a visionary being consumed by flame.

He makes the ice tinkle in his glass. "Maybe you should have a drink. Maybe it would . . . loosen you up. Maybe if you had a drink instead of a cookie, you wouldn't have to wear . . . a girdle. Maybe you wouldn't have to go . . . to Weight Watchers."

"Your sisters drink *plenty* but I don't notice *them* losing any weight," my mother says.

"Don't talk about my sisters."

My mother doesn't. But she lets a few beats go by, and says, as if starting a new conversation, "I went to see your mother this week. It was good to see her. But she's getting *awfully* heavy—"

"Shuddup," my father says.

And my mother, as she always does when my father tells her to shut up, does what she is told. She shuts up. So do I.

Shuddup is the thunderclap of my childhood, no, the sonic boom of my childhood, the sound that consumes all other sounds, after which I can't hear anything but the buzzing in my ears. It marks the moment when my father reveals himself, when he drops all pretenses, when he no longer worries about having class, when his actorly diction slips, when he stops trying to sound like Cary Grant and sounds instead thick and thuggish, a minor player with a gat stuffed under his coat, my father the cheap hood. "I'm always the heavy" goes his complaint, but now his language itself is heavy, leaden, with a molecular density impossible to bear. We don't cry, my mother and I, because "shuddup" means there can be no response at all. She picks at her food with the tines of her fork and keeps her pale and disconsolate face averted. I squeeze my stinging eyes closed and pray that I can hold back the tears, the prayers turning into a mute vow:

You will *never* shut me up.

When I'm eight, I join Little League. I have to; it's a mass induction. Every boy in my class joins, and many of their fathers coach. Mine doesn't. My father is on the road too much, and I've never had a catch with him, never swung a bat. Although I sleep with my glove under my pillow like my friend Robert does, I go to my first practice with it utterly alien to me and stiff as cardboard.

My father takes me, wearing a pair of gray slacks and a navy blue sweater styled like a double-breasted jacket, with rows of brass buttons. I'm embarrassed by him, for him, because most of the rest of the other dads on hand wear sweatshirts and baseball caps—they look like they should chew tobacco. But he's unself-conscious about how he dresses, what he wears, his margin of difference, and he shocks me by borrowing a left-handed glove from one of the coaches and squatting on his haunches to warm up the pitcher. The pitcher's name is Vinnie. He's a big kid, happy-go-lucky, with fat cheeks, dark skin, black hair and a smile that is shy, perpetual and white, like that of a happy cartoon beaver. His pitches pop in my father's glove while my father calls balls and strikes, his occasional hamminess gentle and encouraging. He evinces obvious pleasure in speaking his battery mate's name, as if "Vinnie" is a nickname he has coined himself. "All right, Vinnie, a little more upstairs, there you go, kid, there you go, Vinnie, *stee-rike* . . ." I'd be jealous—or merely jealous—if the man warming up Vinnie didn't seem like a stranger to me. Instead, I wonder if I'm a stranger to him, wonder if he'd be more like *this* if only I were more like *that* . . . if only I were more like Vinnie.

I am not like Vinnie. It is late March when I report to my first practice with the Sparks, with a cold, wet wind blowing off the bay in Wantagh that gets in my bones. I can't stop shivering, by which I mean the shivers that start in the chill of late winter continue in the warmth of spring. I'm not just a terrible ballplayer; I'm a terrified ballplayer, whose stomach ties itself into a knot when I dress for games and whose teeth chatter when I step to the plate. I take it personally when players for the other team begin heckling me, and want to throw myself at their feet and confess, "You're right, you're right—I *am* no batter!" I never think myself worthy of talking to Vinnie, though before the games he always asks if my father is coming, and if my father shows he always warms Vinnie up. It's a strange interaction, another that lets me know that Dad belongs to *them* more than he belongs to *us*. Do I wish he'd warm me up instead of Vinnie? Well, not exactly; in fact, the prospect fills me with fear. I just wish that when my next-door neighbor Richie Rudolph knocks on the door and asks if I want to have a catch, I didn't have to see my father slipping him a five-dollar bill.

I don't quit, at least not outright. I simply plead an "upset stomach" before games and eventually just stop going to them, even when the Sparks play for the championship, and I don't put on a baseball glove again until well after college. I want to like sports, in the same way Pinocchio wants to be a real boy, but I keep my face buried in comic books until I watch something on TV that sounds like one of my toys—the Super Bowl. It's the first one, before the NFL starts using Roman numerals, and also the first sporting event I watch with my father outside of the occasional boxing match on Friday nights and Saturday afternoons. I have no understanding of football whatsoever. But I'm transfixed by the armor the players wear, and the colors of their uniforms as translated by the big color TV built in our paneled wall—the Green Bay Packers and the Kansas City Chiefs look like superheroes come to life. My parents have also told me that the Packers' coach, Vince Lombardi, is somehow related to us . . . that he's the brother of my aunt Claire, my mom's sister-in-law. Dad claims to have known him back in Brooklyn, along with his father, Enrico, the "old man" he admired for . . . his teeth, as well as his manly preference for bread so stale it was "like a rock." Dad also claims to have drank with Paul Hornung and Max McGee at the Racquet Club in Miami, the two "playboys" of the Packers, Hornung Uncle Vince's favorite before the NFL suspended him for gambling and McGee the star of the game we're watching now. But there's something else that keeps me in the den with my father, something that makes me want to stay until the game ends. He's betting it. In the hours before kickoff, the phones started ringing, and he received a call from his pal Frankie Klein in Miami. Frankie introduced my father to someone called a "bookie," who gave my father something called "points," which means he can bet the losing team and still win. It sounds like a license . . . to *steal.* But my father took the points and bet the Kansas City Chiefs, and he's losing. And it's this—the prospect of my father defeated—that puts the game into a realm beyond sports, because what's happening on the field is irrelevant except as it relates to him. I'm not rooting for him to lose. But I'm not rooting for him to win either. I'm just watching him, watching him pace, watching him curse, watching him mix one drink after another and stir them with the tip of his finger, watching him slam the arm of his chair as the misfortune that grabs the Chiefs on television also grabs *us.* It's not a football game. It's a shared exercise in fate that neither of us can control, and I'm privy to his unfolding agony in a way I'm privy to nothing else in his life. And although the final whistle delivers a terrible decree—my dad has lost a thousand dollars—I find myself immune to his show of temper. My lip doesn't quiver, and I never even think of crying.

The next season, he bets football each weekend, telling us he needs . . . a little *action,* and I watch the games with him. By the time I turn ten, I'm his tout. I exchange my comic books for the football magazines for sale at the candy store whose owner is my father's local bookie, and football becomes my field of study. I'm consumed by its statistical nuances, because they offer the promise of understanding the game in a rational and almost scientific manner, and therefore the world. But my father does not bet rationally. He bets hungrily, greedily, desperately, in response to phone calls that start on Saturday mornings and last through the weekend, a concert of calls before each game like church bells after a war. He bets everything, at first just the games on TV and then games involving teams from colleges we've never heard of. He bets with everyone, bookies who "lay off" action to other bookies, bookies who tempt him with exotic combination bets called "parlays" and "teasers" that allow Dad to adjust "the spread" by as much as ten points in either direction, with one caveat—in order to win one bet, he has to win them all. He does not win them all, which means that I don't win them all, which means that we don't win them all, the Junod family. My father is not a good loser—"Show me a good loser, and I'll show you a loser," is one of his maxims. But he's also a terrible gambler . . . no, an *unlucky* gambler, even with my statistical analysis. We live and mostly die by the caprices of pass-interference penalties, two-point conversions and coaches who inexplicably decide to run out the clock instead of running up the score or vice versa. There are holes in the door to the kitchen and the door to my father's bathroom where he put his fist through them, holes my mother refuses to get fixed because she doesn't want him to forget his transgressions.

And yet . . . I love football. We all do, and look forward to football weekends, which are like parties in front of the firing squad of the television . . . no, wait, two or three televisions, if there are multiple games. There's the big color TV in the wall, the portable color TV my parents watch in their room, and the black-and-white portable I watch when I'm sick. On New Year's Day, when all of the network stations show bowl games, my father puts one of those portables on the obsidian surface of the hi-fi and another on the marble table and amidst the din my mother, in the center of the room, both burps with anxiety and does something like a davening dance as she tries to jinx the kickers from teams my father is betting against. She folds her fingers into what later will become the hand signal for heavy metal music, and puts what she calls "the horns"—or, in her Long Island accent, the "hawns"—on them, so that if the extra point or field goal goes wide, she can say, "See, Lou? That's because I put the *hawns* on them!" But Dad, by this point, usually can't celebrate with her because in the polynomial math of the "teaser" he has to win every game in order not to lose them all.

My mom de-horns her hands and lets them fall despondently to her sides. "Oh, I hate those teasers," she says.

There is a phone in my parents' room. It's on my mother's side of the bed, on her nightstand. It *looks* like my mother—fancy, glitzy, a low-slung "Princess" model, yellow, the first phone I've ever seen with push buttons instead of a dial. But it's my father's phone, because it has a secret, a clear plastic toggle switch that looks like a lost cuff link. Turn the switch one way, the phone rings, and its number is ours. Turn it the other, and the phone sort of *dings,* and the number belongs only to him. Neither my mother nor I know it, nor are we allowed to pick up the dinging phone under any circumstance. It's his "business phone," he says—we can't answer it because the calls he receives on it are from his buyers. But that's not exactly true, because once he starts betting football, he also gets calls from his bookies. It's not hard to figure out which is which: When buyers call, he closes the door and speaks in murmurs. When bookies call, he leaves the door open and we can listen to him bet "ten dollars" or "fifty dollars" or "a hundred dollars" on games. It doesn't sound like much. It doesn't sound that bad until I begin to understand that he's speaking to the bookies in a special language and betting in multiples of ten—that one hundred dollars is really a thousand. I never tell this to my mother; I don't have to. I can tell she's reached the same conclusion because as she stands in the hallway outside the door to her room listening to my father make his bets she's belching and wringing her sweaty hands. And yet even as she frets and worries she never asks him to stop. She keeps putting the horns on place kickers and inviting all their friends to the house at the end of each January for a big "Super Bowl party" even though my father bets and usually loses large sums and sweats through the games like Christ in Gethsemane. Football is not exactly like horse racing, which costs my father a lot of money but which my mother loves—which brings out the girlish gleam in her eyes and makes her look young. She endures football. But she loves football *weekends* because they're better than the alternative . . . because at least he's home. My father is always up to something behind closed doors but when he's betting football he's up to something and the doors are open. It is the family vice.

—

I wish he was a winner. But maybe I'm not a good tout. I must be a bad tout, because if I were better my father wouldn't be a loser. But my father generally doesn't blame me, and even when he does blame me that doesn't stop me from studying football statistics, nor does it stop him from asking my opinion. Indeed, we have a ritual: On Monday mornings, when I'm sitting at the kitchen table eating cereal, he drops the *Daily News* in front of me open to the page with a listing for "THE LATEST LINE." It's in a little box across the gutter from the racing form, upon which he's already scrawled his picks with a ballpoint pen. The line is in tiny type, with three columns—favorite and underdog, and between them "the spread," measured in half-point increments. Sometimes instead of a number there's a word in the middle, "EVEN," but I like figuring out the games where the line is so large that trying to pick a winner feels like doing the Iowa Tests at school: "Ohio State 23 ½ NORTHWESTERN" (home team in CAPS). I do better in the Iowa Tests than I do as a tout. But picking games for my father is the best of two worlds, in that it makes me feel smart and it also makes me feel like a real boy, like Vinnie. He usually gives me about five minutes of library-like silence before, standing behind me, he presses his hand on my shoulder and asks me what seems the most important question of my life:

"Who . . . do you *like*?"

5

My father is a traveling salesman. It's not a phrase spoken in our house, because it's so déclassé—a step above "door-to-door," a setup for jokes about the farmer's daughter. But it fits him, because even when he's brushing his teeth or sitting on . . . the commode, he's making a sale, and also because he travels. That's the word my mother uses, when she's on the phone with her friends or has to explain to the priest at St. Francis de Chantal why she and my father can't be counted on to attend the charity ball—"Well, you know, Lou travels" or "My husband travels." It's an explanation and an excuse, but more than that it's the verb that describes not just him but us, the systole and diastole of our existence. My father leaves and comes back. He departs and he returns. He *travels*—and we wait for him.

Everything depends on how long he's gone. On some days, he's almost like a normal man, a commuter whom my mother drops off at the Long Island Rail Road station in Wantagh just after rush hour and picks up when he arrives with the elevated rumble of the 5:19 from Penn Station, which spills exhausted men down the stairs and escalators like a troop train. On others, he goes to New York City and *stays* there, two nights, three nights, even all week, when it's "Market Week," and he has to "entertain," a word my parents use as intransitively as they use "travel," as if it describes not an action but an essence. Just as I have to ask where he goes, I have to ask who he entertains—and then have to wonder about the answers. "He entertains his *buyers,*" my mom says, her undertone of fretful grievance suggesting that they form an exalted class to whom we all must bow. And yet why are they *his* buyers then? And how, other than singing, does he entertain them? And why, when he comes home, entertaining us—yes, us!—with his stories, with his dispatches he's gathered from the front of his own personal magnetism, does he never mention his buyers but rather the movie stars and starlets whom he saw and who, in turn, saw *him*?

But then, after Market Week, he goes out *on the road,* where he really is gone, his travel best measured in terms of time. He's on the road even when he flies, even when he "gets on a plane"—Eastern, Northeastern, Pan Am, TWA—at JFK and heads "for a couple of weeks" to wherever he can "get some sun," mostly Miami but sometimes Vegas and sometimes more exotic places he keeps secret, at least from me. And if he's a glamorous figure, flying, he's downright heroic when he has to load his car with huge black belted sample cases and drive the immensity of his territory so he can write some orders—or, as he sometimes puts it, "get the paper." I try to help him before he leaves, bringing some of the bags up from the laundry room, stuffing some of them with tissue paper before he layers them carefully in the cases, the new "goods" smelling of animal hides and of paint, not just fresh but *raw,* as though once alive. They're made by Mr. Chips and Lumured, by Letisse and Handi-Bag, by Lou Taylor and Valeri and Koret, and when they're finally packed away in one of his station wagons or his Cadillac or, later, his expansive white Lincoln Continental, he ruffles my hair, kisses my mother on the cheek, and backs down the driveway, Mom waving with one hand and holding my hand with the other, Dad henceforth on the road for five or six weeks, leaving around Valentine's Day and not coming home until just before Easter.

Whenever he leaves I never truly believe that he will come back and when he does come back I never truly believe he will stay. His return is a revelation, first because he *has* returned and is with us, and second because . . . well, he looks, as he tells us, "almost too good." My mother, when he is gone, never fails to tell me how hard he works, how far he has to travel, but now he looks *better* with all those miles on him, better walking in than he did walking out. He has been restored by the road; the road has touched him with fire, and instead of effacing him has made him unbearably vivid, especially when I go with my mom to pick him up at the airport. Strangers at JFK stare at him as if he's . . . *someone,* which would not be so discomfiting if we did not stare at him in the same way, as if the glory of his return didn't also announce the conditions of his return:

That we belong to him.

That he doesn't belong to us.

As I grow older I begin searching for personal artifacts that tell me where he's been. I help him unload and unpack, with an eye for the clothes, the towels, the colognes, the jewelry, the matchbooks and even the chewing gum he picked up while he was gone, his Chiclets, his Dentyne, his Beemans and Black Jack, which he chews not for taste but for sound, a little rat-tat-tat that crackles in the corner of his jaw like his ankles in the morning. I am not particularly observant; I'm just observant about *him,* alert to evidence that reveals inconsistencies in his stories, and when after one long trip he stashes one of his bags in an unaccustomed place, I make it my business to investigate.

The bag is manufactured by a line he once represented, the Koret handbag company, out of New York, and even to my unschooled eyes it's a beauty. It's a tote, deep as a bucket and made of soft butter-colored leather with black handles and trim—a ladies' handbag he has turned into his own. He uses it to transport his "toiletries" and takes it with him wherever he travels; wherever he travels, he brings along his clanking allotment of lotions, fragrances, unguents, ointments, astringents, aerosols, shampoos, dyes, gels, creams, and pastes, some of them combined by whim into concoctions as volatile as unstable elements. He uses the toiletries on himself, to make himself resplendent and gleaming, his skin lubricated and his smell sharp and his thinning hair combed to the side and subject to the fixative of Consort Hair Spray for Men, which he applies until he coughs; but he also uses them to colonize the places he inhabits, even when he's a guest at somebody's home. On the road he stays with Milton Friedman, in Dallas; with Gilbert Brown, in Birmingham; with Irma Carey, in Atlanta; and, for weeks on end, with Frankie Klein, his sidekick in Miami . . . but wherever he goes, he requires his own bathroom for his portable apothecary. Of course, he has the same arrangement at home; the bathroom in the bedroom he shares with Mom belongs entirely to him, a territory marked by the Koret bag squatting on top of the toilet tank and the assorted tubes, bottles, jars, cans, and vials scattered everywhere else. I like to carry the bulging leather bag upstairs, because there is something almost alive about what's inside, alive and trying to get out; but on this day I can't find it in the trunk of his car. I can't find it in his bathroom or on the floor of his walk-in closet, where he sometimes leaves it after he empties it out. I can't find it until I go downstairs and search in our elaborately finished basement, where it sits on the floor of Mom's closet like a mushroom in the dark.

I have no idea what it might be doing there. Mom's closet belongs to her as much as Dad's belongs to him, with the difference that it serves a purely archival purpose. It takes up an entire wall of the basement, four sliding doors behind which are hats stacked in hatboxes, dry-cleaned evening dresses sealed in rustling cellophane, furs I confuse with taxidermy, and the eye-watering smell of mothballs. Mom only opens those doors on Christmas and Easter, the two days a year my father accompanies her to church and she wears chinchilla. And yet there, in the dormant shadows, is the leather tote bag I am looking for. I think of taking it upstairs because I've done Dad the favor of finding it, but at the same time I understand it isn't lost—it's *hidden,* and so I wait for him to take Mom to the track, as he often does when he comes off the road, so that I can open it up and see what's inside.

I am not little anymore, though it is as a boy, rather than as a man, that I contemplate my father's mysteries. I am sixteen years old, a junior in high school, old enough to take care of myself, even to cook for myself. When my parents leave, I usually fry a steak and eat a salad with French dressing, but this time I hurry down to the basement and find the bag crouching in the dark like another petulant child. I turn the lights on, relieved that the bag hasn't gone anywhere. It has a brass zipper with huge leering teeth, and when I pull the slider it makes a striptease sound, slightly embarrassing even though I am all alone. I have no idea what I might find other than the customary exotica of my father's toiletries, but my heart is beating and my mouth is dry. I open the bag and peer inside, surprised that it is nearly empty, an abyss as dark as a wishing well, with water gleaming at the bottom.

The bag contains no toiletries at all, not even the can of Consort or the bottle of Jean Naté, with the big black knob for a cap. Instead, there is a copy of *The Joy of Sex,* and two vibrators, one of them the color of bone, the other of a Hershey bar. I turn on the "white" one first and it jolts me like a joy buzzer hidden in the handshake of a high school smart aleck. I don't know whether to laugh or cry, unprepared as I am for the little-engine-that-could persistence of its clenched movement and also by how loud it is. As a teenager, I am so jittery, especially around my dad, that he has to stop me from drumming my fingers or tapping my toes by calling me "Nerves," and for some reason I think of that appellation as this fierce little machine tap-dances against my palm. It doesn't just make me nervous; it *is* nervous, not to mention ludicrous, a prop in a comedy I'm not old enough to see without the accompaniment of a parent or guardian. I turn it off, try the "Black" one—it is even more teeth-chatteringly frenetic, whirring at a higher pitch—and after I drop both of them back in the bag, I open *The Joy of Sex,* the title of which refers to something I've never experienced. I have never even kissed a girl, and am as terrified of the prospect of having sex as I am embarrassed by the reality of not having it. Now I see it for the first time, see with my own eyes sexual acts depicted in line drawings that are graphic yet . . . classy. Indeed, the first emotion I experience upon opening *The Joy of Sex* is relief—relief that my father is not *in* it, and that maybe he has returned home with a bag of tricks to rekindle the fire of his marriage. My mother and father are normal, and so am I.

And yet I can't sleep that night, somehow afraid that I have left the vibrators switched on and that they are still generating frantic Morse code from the bottom of Dad's man-bag, but I am so taken by the easygoing expertise of *The Joy of Sex* that the next day I search for it again amidst Mom's furs. The bag is gone. My father has moved it from its hiding place and restored it to the floor of his closet, but when I find it and reach my hand inside, all I grasp is the greasy jostle of his toiletries. *The Joy of Sex* has disappeared, along with the two vibrators, as if they were figments of my imagination. I search for them under his bed, in the drawer of the nightstand where he keeps paperback copies of *The Happy Hooker* and *Portnoy's Complaint,* and on the shelf of his closet where I sometimes find his *Playboy*s and, better yet, his *Penthouse*s, as well as *Everything You Always Wanted to Know About Sex but Were Afraid to Ask,* a quack treatise with an alluringly easygoing title. Do I have questions about sex that I am afraid to ask? Sure; but they are often questions about my *father,* and now the most pressing of them has to do with the fate of the book and the "marital aids" in his bag. Where did they go? Where could they have gone? I start listening at night, my ears tuned to the possibility of a battery-powered buzz emerging from his boudoir, but no, there is no such French lullaby, only the sounds of *The Honeymooners* reruns Mom and Dad like to watch together on nights when he is not in New York.

A few days later, Mom and I meet him at the train station in Wantagh for the arrival of the 5:19 and he shocks me by carrying what everyone else is carrying: a briefcase. God knows he needs one; he's in the habit of keeping his papers in manila envelopes, and the briefcase makes him appear more organized and professional. It's made by Samsonite, the company that advertises its products as unbreakable. It's brown and rectangular, its surface elaborately crosshatched in simulation of leather but made out of some kind of plastic, some kind of metal, maybe some kind of alloy only recently invented, hard to the touch, with a steel frame and a lock.

It is as nondescript an accessory as a man as flamboyant as Lou Junod could carry, the equivalent of a gray flannel suit. But right away, I can't keep my eyes off it, because by instinct I know there is something *in* it. His briefcase: of course. That's where he's stashed the vibrators and *The Joy of Sex*. And so I begin looking at it as a safecracker would. I begin watching him both with his briefcase and without it, and realizing, before long, that I am right—he never leaves the Samsonite briefcase open. Ever. He keeps it at the very bottom of his closet or at the bottom of the cavernous trunk of the enormous white Lincoln Continental. He keeps it away from us.

I begin trying to figure out the combination. The lock is the kind with three tumblers, each with ten digits, from 0 to 9—the kind people turn with their thumbs—and it doesn't seem like such a challenge at first, especially with the information I have about my dad. He's a man who bets lucky numbers. He bets his birthday. He bets Mom's birthday, his mom's birthday, the birthdays of his children. He has a private system of numerology, and of all his numbers his luckiest is 343, the draft-lottery number that kept Michael out of Vietnam. It's the first number I try when I try opening the lock. Dad has gone again with Mom to the track, and I have the house to myself, and therefore his closet to myself, and therefore his briefcase to myself, if only I could figure out the combination. But 343 doesn't work, and neither does 323, 325, 926, or 316. I even try my birthday, 409, although it never comes up when Dad is picking the Triple at Roosevelt Raceway. It doesn't work, nothing works, and so I start rolling the tumblers randomly, until my thumb hardens with the beginning of a callus. Finally, in frustration, I take the briefcase in my hands and shake it, just to see what will happen. It replies with a sound like sneakers in the laundry-room dryer, just to let me know it's not empty.

Then one day I get lucky. My father comes home and leaves the briefcase on his bed. The lid's not open, but the latches are sprung, sticking out from the frame at a forty-five-degree angle like the stunted wings of a chicken. And he is in the bathroom, singing, so I creep onto the bed, quiet as the sigh of the puffy satin comforter, and read the three-digit jackpot lining up across the face of the lock. Then I commit it to memory, where even now, so many years later, it remains.

A spell, a charm, the key to Pandora's box and the magic word for the genie in the bottle, the answer that will forever exist as a question:

616.

I receive an opportunity to try it out a few days later. Dad takes Mom to the Cloud Casino at Roosevelt Raceway, where she typically bets favorites and wins $20 for the night and he bets long shots and loses $1,000. I creep into his closet and find the briefcase in its accustomed place, on the shag-carpeted floor, in the slot beneath the lowest shelf. I slide it out, taking care to note its position, its precise angle in degrees and minutes, so that I can return it with my intrusion undetected. In a trembly trance, I roll the tumblers to the three digits that I spied upon my father's bed. I take a breath, and in that moment, the latches spring open, the sound like shots from a small-caliber pistol.

There were always songs—songs he whistled, songs he sang, songs he turned up when they were on the radio and he wanted me to listen too. He didn't just want me to like them; he wanted me to learn from them, as though they were short sermons, sung not by men but by the voice of manhood itself. There was, of course, "My Way," which I played at his memorial service. There was "Smile," which he called "the only good thing Charlie Chaplin ever did" because he loathed Chaplin as "a communist" as much as he loved the lyrics of hopeful resignation he had written for singers like Nat King Cole. There was Matt Monro's "Walk Away," the stiff-upper-lip lament of a lover who finds his true love when he's already spoken for. And then, at last, there was Sammy Davis Jr.'s version of "Once in a Lifetime," with its hard-swinging masculine ethos: "Just once in a lifetime / A man knows a moment / One wonderful moment / When faith takes his hand . . ."

My father believed this, espoused this, lived by this. Though the word was not in his vocabulary, he was at heart an existentialist, and wanted me to be one too—he wanted me to be open to the transformative potential of the moment mastered, the moment during which everything is up for grabs and after which everything is changed forever. I used to ask him how I might recognize what he called "the moment of truth," and he said that it didn't matter whether I was on the field, in the ring, onstage, at the casino or in bed with a woman—"when it's there, you can *taste* it."

He was right, as it turns out, and like a lot of other men I have sought out transformative experiences in the belief that I need to be transformed. Unlike a lot of other men, I have found them while trying to find out the truth about my father.

There is an automatic light overhead, the light in his closet. Although Mom and Dad have gone out and I am alone in the house, I don't want the doors to be wide open, because I don't want to be . . . well, exposed, if they come home and somehow sneak up on me in the middle of my investigation. Unfortunately, a floor-to-ceiling mirror covers the back of each door, and I can see myself, cross-legged in front of the briefcase, revealed as I seek revelation. I do not walk away. I open the lid. And I look.

For a second, I think that my father has stowed in his briefcase something that was once alive—that I am gazing at a package of chicken parts he bought at the supermarket and then forgot about. I told myself that I was opening the briefcase to find *The Joy of Sex* and two vibrators of generic provenance. But while *The Joy of Sex* has not returned, the vibrators have mutated—metastasized—into two dildos so large they seem prosthetic. They are sheathed in sleeves of venous rubber, each remarkably realistic in detail but outlandish in scale, the size of fungo bats. They share space in the briefcase with a stack of invoices and order forms from various handbag lines, as well as several boxes of pornography, all of it on film, in Super 8 format. Dad occasionally brings *Playboy*s and *Penthouse*s home and I do not read them for the articles. But I have never seen real pornography before. Is this real pornography? It is, in that the photos on the boxes depict human beings engaged in undeniable acts of copulation. It's not, in that the acts in the photos are as different from what I imagine to be "normal pornography" as Dad is from normal people. They are extreme even by porno standards. There are about five films, and the only one I can bring myself to look at is the one called *Her Master's Piss*. The rest are captioned in German and scare me. Everything in the briefcase scares me. When I came across the vibrators stashed away in the Koret leather bag with *The Joy of Sex,* I hopefully remembered that they were called marital aids. But these look like *martial* aids—like truncheons, the kind used in riot control. I have no idea what Dad does with them nor with whom.

I have caught him red-handed, after all. At long last, I have produced concrete evidence—incontrovertible proof!—of what I have always suspected, which is that he has a sexual life outside of his marriage. But what kind of sexual life? Instead of providing answers, the contents of the briefcase offer what no sixteen-year-old is prepared to contemplate: possibilities. My father has an entire vocabulary for men and women who are not, to his mind, sexually healthy, and when he comes home from his nights in the city he is keen to report not only which women made eyes at him but also which men were "sickies" and "degenerates," with a subtle difference between them. Do the movies make my dad a sickie? Do the dildos make him a degenerate? And if he is a sickie and a degenerate, what am I?

I push the briefcase back into place, taking care that it lines up with the imprint it left in the shag carpet before . . . well, before curiosity killed the cat. But I hold on to the combination just as tenaciously as it holds on to me, and the next time Mom and Dad go to the track I invite my friend Jack over. Dad likes Jack, because Jack, of all my friends, is the most sexually experienced, and Dad thinks he has something to teach me. Jack succeeds sexually because he is not afraid to tell girls what he wants sexually and walks the halls of Holy Trinity High School with an undisguised leer and an aversion to averting his eyes. He possesses not only the genetic ability to flicker his tongue like a brightly colored lizard in a *National Geographic* special but also the shamelessness necessary to demonstrate his talent in the cafeteria. It continually shocks me that his strategy works—that Jack, with his impertinence, always has pretty girlfriends with whom he has a lot of sex, and I, with the deferential manners my father taught me, am consigned to rifling his drawers and searching his closet for masturbatory fodder. But I cannot watch *Her Master's Piss* by myself, and Jack is the only human with whom I can watch it without shame. I do not show him the dildos, which are so luridly lifelike they might as well have come from a surgical suite. But when he comes over, the projector is already set up in the basement, threaded with obscene celluloid.

The projector belongs to my dad, an artifact from the bygone days when he made a hobby of home movies. I couldn't find a portable screen, but then I don't need to: the sliding doors of Mom's closets are broad and blank, four of them taking up an entire wall. I point the projector at the place where Mom's finery is stored, and after smoking a bowl with Jack in the backyard, I turn it on. A white square of light trembles on the bleached wooden door, alive with a fleeting paisley of imperfections from the dust on the lens. In a few seconds, a woman appears in living color—an artist of some kind, working on a painting, with the canvas on the floor. She is very pale, with black hair and no tan lines. She wears only a smock, until interrupted in her labors by the arrival of four Black men, all of them tall and lanky, wearing leather hoods. They are skinny and potbellied, unimpressively built but for the size of their penises, which, flaccid, are about the size of the rubber appliances in the briefcase. When the sex starts, it looks, well, like sex, or a crowded version of what I imagine sex to be; then, when they tie her up, it doesn't. My mouth falls open, and stays that way. "Holy shit," says Jack, my experienced friend, my spirit guide through worlds I am afraid to navigate. "This is fucked up . . ."

The next time I watch *Her Master's Piss,* I watch it alone, in every sense of the word. I get high again, but I also pour myself a drink from Dad's bar, brown liquor in a highball glass, the tip of my finger toggling the ice, in an effort to look suave and debonair like him, instead of desperate and soiled, like me. Nobody dies in the movie, and yet it feels like a snuff film in the spiritual sense, with levels of coercion and humiliation for which I am still not prepared, and my worldly façade is no match for what I see—for what I witness. I swallow the brown liquor against the gag reflex it elicits, and watch in excitement, fascination and horror until suddenly everything stops, because the film jams. The projector stalls, with its beam of light undimmed, and for a hectic few seconds, the moving image turns into a still photograph of the performers caught in flagrante delicto. Then it begins to burn. A sepia stain spreads across the color print, making it look quaintly antique; then it blackens and as I smell smoke, it snaps, the fevered fulfillment of all I fear. I caught my father, when I opened the briefcase; now I am in turn caught. *I've broken Dad's porno movie,* and all I can think is that the next time he watches he'll know that I tampered with it. If I were another type of kid, another kind of son, I might just toss the film in the garbage and dare him to say something about it—"Hey, Tommy, have you seen my copy of *Her Master's Piss*?" Instead, I feed the film back onto the main spool as if I'm defusing a bomb. It takes an hour, and yet when I finish I still imagine the film flying apart as Dad watches it with some intimate friend in a dark hotel room, the loose end slapping against the projector from the spinning reel, and him wondering about me and the broken thread of our connection.

I always suspected that he was something of a rogue, but the glamour he cultivated made me think he was a rogue like David Niven was a rogue, like Richard Burton was a rogue, like Cary Grant was a rogue, a charming thief who stole only from other dishonest men. Then I opened the simulated-leather Samsonite briefcase and it was like discovering he wasn't a harmless scoundrel after all. He was a killer. But he didn't get away with it, because I had found the murder weapons and now I was possessed of tremendous power.

It was the ultimate power, really—the power to blow up the world. All I had to do was tell my mother, and my parents' marriage would not only have ended; I would have ended it. Should I have told my mother? I think now that I should have, and all these years later still castigate myself for being derelict in my duty to her. But of course I neglected my duty to her in the name of doing it—in the name of protecting her from the terrible truth. And so the power to destroy their marriage became the power to preserve it. I had more power than I'd ever dreamed of, power *over my father,* and yet, because I chose not to exercise it, he had power over me. Yes, he had a secret. But now so did I. He would never know what I knew.

And that became our bond.

There's something in my own closet that we share. It's a bank in the shape of a bottle; a bottle that serves as bank—an amber-colored plastic replica of a quart of Scotch, a couple of feet tall, with a slot at the top. It's so big I have to jam it between my jackets and sweaters, twisting them on their hangers, or else I couldn't close the closet door. But really, the Ballantine's bottle is bigger than that, a lot bigger, because it represents a dream my father and I are supposed to hold in common, its name written on the label in his kerned, jagged hand—"PARIS TRIP." He's been talking about taking me to Paris since I was a little boy, just the two of us, so I can see where he had his greatest triumphs during World War II. Of course, he can't help but sell an adventure I bought long ago, and most mornings when he's home he enters my room without knocking, jingling coins—which he calls "silver"—in the shaker of his hand, crooning, "Hey, buddy-boy, listen . . . to *this,*" before dropping them into the slot. I listen—I have no choice but to listen, for when I drop my occasional quarters into the bank, they make a paltry, tinkling music, but he throws them in by the fistful, with such vehemence that they land with a thunking noise, as if they are gold doubloons—a pirate's booty, pieces of eight. "Heeey," he says, reaching out with his hand to pick up the bottle by the neck. "Look at this, look at this, I can barely *pick it up . . .*"

It's a ritual I've gotten used to. On this morning, however, he doesn't announce himself, or talk about the trip we're saving up for, or even make one of his contributions to the cause. On this morning, his entrance is so stealthy I don't even hear the crackle of his ankles. But then, I don't have to, because I *smell* him. He's showered, shaved, lotioned, lubricated, lacquered, and fragrant not with men's cologne but with an aromatic alloy of soap, hair spray, oil, iodine, witch hazel, deodorant and Jean Naté "after bath splash for women," which is his secret weapon for avoiding "offensive odors." His intent is not olfactory but rather hygienic; he wishes to smell, above all, *clean,* and as a result his "look" may be Mediterranean, even tropical, but his aroma is Arctic.

He's also, and above all, *dressed,* and part of his silence on this morning is the slither of his spit-shined Florsheim shoes across the red shag carpet that covers the floor of my bedroom. He whisks his way to the edge of my bed, where he sits down and studies me before grabbing my shoulder. *"Heeey,"* he says, and immediately I register, from the tone of his voice, that he's not making a sale, he's not enticing me with something only he can provide. I don't open my eyes, not yet anyway, keeping them closed as a matter of hardened habit until at last he gives me a shake, and says, with an authority tender and ominous, "Wake up." I become instantly alert, and there he is in profile, his big honker a shadow in the shadows, his eyes burning like gas mantles, his brown skin finding a way to shine even in the dark.

"How are you feeling?" he asks.

"Good," I say noncommittally.

"You were pretty sick yesterday."

"Yeah . . . it must have been a twenty-four-hour virus."

He bites his lip. He takes his paternal hand off my shoulder and leans forward, angled like a predatory bird. "I've never seen anybody with a *virus* eat the way you ate at the Labellas."

The day before, I went with my pal Ray Labella to buy some weed, and spent so many hours sampling the excellent product that by the time I returned to Ray's house I felt not just stoned but drunk, and passed out in the breakfast nook. The Labellas, family friends of long standing, summoned my father to take me home, but by the time he arrived I might have been too stoned to talk but not to *eat*, especially Mrs. Labella's food. She spent all day cooking her "gravy" for Sunday dinner, but more important, she made platters of food that woke up my mouth, cooking with raisins and parsley and nuts and anchovies. I passed out in the subterranean embrace of the banquette just as Mrs. Labella was putting food on the table, so when my father arrived he was treated to the following spectacle: his son just out of sight, presumably unconscious, and yet every few seconds a *hand* rises from the Naugahyde depths, and snatches a niblet of cantaloupe wrapped in prosciutto or a mushroom dressed in vinegar. I'm well aware that I'm putting myself, or at least the narrative of my illness, at risk; I'm well aware that he is watching me, or, more precisely, my fingers, blindly navigating the groaning board, as Mr. Labella keeps exclaiming that for a kid he thought was dying I'm a real *mootay-vam*—his pidgined pronunciation of "*morte di fame,*" Italian slang for someone dying of hunger. But I've got the munchies, and in this I'm not so different from the old man—a slave to appetite.

Of course, I confess none of this in response to his interrogation from the edge of my bed—he's not going to break me *that* easily. "Well, I never said I had a *stomach* virus," I answer, and as soon as I do I wish I could take it back. He sits up straight, his attention electric, and though I don't own an alarm clock, one seems to be ringing now. There is a caged flutter in my chest, a feeling of my dark room growing large and small, and I prop myself up on an elbow so that he can't accuse me of disrespecting him.

"Tell me something," he says.

"Sure, Dad."

"Were you smoking pot?"

It's still dark outside, but at that moment the birds start singing . . . or maybe that's when they stop.

"No," I say.

"Look at me," he says.

He does not mean, as he often does, that he wants me to look him . . . in the *eye;* no, he wants me to look him *over,* from head to toe; he wants me to *behold* him, there, on the edge of my bed. I obey his command because I have no choice, and see, as I didn't see before, that he is dressed . . . *to the nines,* in a midnight-blue suit; a light blue shirt with a white collar; a patterned red-and-blue tie with a knot as big as my fist; gold cuff links he wears like spurs.

"I'm going to Florida for a few weeks on business," he informs me quietly, his voice almost disconsolate. "I'm leaving today—flying today. Now, let me ask you again: were you smoking pot yesterday?"

"No, Dad."

"Swear . . . on my life."

"What?"

"In an hour, I'm getting on a plane," my father says. "Swear . . . on my *life.*"

He has never hit me. He brags to his friends that he's not the kind of man who hits his kids—that he never *needed* to hit us in order to secure our obedience.

"I swear," I say.

"What do you swear?"

"I swear I didn't smoke pot yesterday."

"On my life?"

"I swear . . . on your life . . . that I didn't smoke pot yesterday."

We both exhale, though not in unison, not in concert, not with any sense of relief. He stands up and wipes his hands on the front of his perfectly tailored trousers, as if there is something on them . . . as if he has just gone to the john and couldn't find a towel. Then he bends over, lurches over, and kisses me hard on my head, so that I feel it in my bones—one of his skull-kisses—and he walks out of my room, into the house, and then into whatever car takes him to the airport, where now he has to await his doom, and knows it. I stay in bed, telling Mom that I'm still sick and can't go to school—telling, that is, a second lie, while waiting for the daylight outside my window to rise and fall, along with his flight to Miami.

Why did he do it? Why did *I* do it? Why did he make me swear on his life and why did I, duly sworn, then violate my pledge? I don't know. I have never known. It wasn't that he was such a stickler for discipline—it wasn't that he cared so much about me smoking pot—and it wasn't that I was so afraid of what would happen if I told the truth. God knows, I feared him, but not like *that,* not that *way*—in general, I wasn't afraid of what he would do to me so much as what he would make me do. And now he has made me do something I can never take back.

I am seventeen years old, and still in high school, at either the end of my junior year or the beginning of my last. Ever since finding what I found in his briefcase—ever since finding the evidence—I have needed to forgive him. Now he needs to forgive me. Now we are even. He corrupted me with a secret stash of pornography and prosthetic extensions of himself. But I have cursed him. I have *killed* him, and even if his flight lands safely and he is somehow spared, I will never get away with it.

6

He worked very hard at being a father, almost as hard as he worked at being . . . Big Lou. He might have been Big Lou to everyone else—or, better yet, the Ace—but to us Dad was always, well, *Dad,* and in that single syllable was the essence of his hold on us. That he was our father was the overwhelming fact of growing up at 1463 Britton

Street. There were other kids we knew, other kids we heard of, who didn't have fathers, due to divorce, untimely death, drunkenness, negligence—"Oh, their father *ran off*." But that's what made us different. We had a father, even when our father was running off or at the very least running around, and we had a father because *he* didn't.

He told us a lot of stories about how he grew up, when we were growing up. I loved hearing them, because hearing them was like turning on the TV on a Saturday afternoon and watching a Jimmy Cagney movie or an episode of the East Side Kids—they were colorful to the precise degree that they were in black and white. He was a tough kid, a scrapper, who lived one step ahead of the landlord on Coney Island Avenue, on Gates Avenue in Bed-Stuy, and in Gerritsen Beach, where his best friends were named Duffy, Smitty and, best of all, Johnny Rail. They'd get into fights or fight each other, and when they came home with a black eye, they'd put a steak over it, then fry the steak up in a pan.

But as much as I enjoyed his stories, I also needed them. They were all I had of him—all I had of his youth, all I had of his "formative years," all I had to *go on* when I was trying to figure out why he was the way he was, even though they never exactly answered the question. They weren't quite lies; they weren't even tall tales. But I never had the sense that my father was telling the whole and hard truth about how he grew up until we asked him about his own father. Then he gave us an answer he repeated without variation over the years, an answer that came as close as he ever could to explaining himself:

"I never had a father."

He calls from the city to tell Michael that he has a surprise for him, something special. He starts early with the calls, dropping hints, building up anticipation, making the sale. "Wait till you see . . . ," Dad says. Ginger, my parents' dog, has died, and Michael, a teenaged innocent, loves animals. "Maybe it's a dog," Michael thinks. "Maybe it's a puppy!"

He runs down to the car when Dad pulls into the driveway and then follows him back into the house. "Hey, buddy-boy, look what I have, look what I have," Dad says, and then puts a package leaking blood from paper wrapping on the table. "A couple of big . . . *steaks,* from Chip's butcher!"

Steak is a staple in our house and at the same time a big deal. That is, it's a staple when Mom buys the meat at the supermarket and a big deal when Dad buys . . . prime beef, from the butcher in New York, which he will cook himself in the oven instead of on the stove.

"Is this a steak or is this a *steak*?" he asks at the table. He chews and swallows the steak from his fork with the gusto of an actor in a television commercial, and drinks beer from a pewter tankard with a glass bottom. He puts the beer down with a thunk and says, "Listen to your *father.* There's only one way to cook a good steak, and that's to broil it."

"How did Grandma cook steaks?" I ask.

"We didn't have steaks. We barely had a pot to piss in. If I wanted a steak, I'd have to go over to Duffy's."

"Were you poor because your father was poor?" It is an innocent question in that I really want to know the answer. It is not an innocent question in that I know what the answer is going to be, and also not to use the word "Grandpa."

And then he says it: "I never *had* a father." And though he has told us this many times before, it never fails to move, surprise, and mystify. On the one hand, the information is entirely consistent with how we think of him—a mythological being who sprang fully formed from Grandma the way Athena sprang from the skull of Zeus. On the other, the information is . . . unreliable. He's not really saying he never had a father, since he tells us stories about his father. He's saying, instead, that he had a father but he wasn't a good father. He's saying he had a father but he didn't like his father. And he's saying, in a way that shows us not just anger but pain, that we should be grateful for the father we have.

"My father," he says, "didn't let me go to Hollywood after I won the Jackie Coogan contest!"

"You were going to go . . . to *Hollywood*?" I ask.

"I was supposed to go with my mother," he says. "We had . . . the train ticket. They were going to give me . . . a screen test. That was what I won. But my father said, 'Forget it.' He told me I was no Jackie Coogan. Nice, huh? A real sweetheart, my father."

"What did your father look like?"

"What did he *look* like?"

"Yes." It is, after all, the question my father asks about every human on earth.

"Well, he was a nice-looking man. Tall, thin—he could wear clothes. He could look . . . elegant, like a gentleman. But he had very . . . thin lips. I don't trust men with thin lips. Usually, they're *cheap.*"

"Was your father . . . cheap?"

"He used all his money for drink," my father says. "You know, he was a very smart man, my father—supposedly an electrical *genius.* That's how he met my mother. He was an electrician and he was doing work at the movie theater where my mother played the piano. He became a *mortician* and invented the embalming machine that's still in use today. He even had a patent for it but he gave it away to his partner . . . for a drink. It was worth . . . *thousands.*"

Nobody says "thousands" the way my father does—he makes money sound like steak.

"He wanted to get me into the *embalming* business," he says. "But I wanted nothing to do with it. Once I went to see him at the funeral parlor and he asked me to come down to the basement. 'I want to *show* you something,' he said. I followed him downstairs and there was a body lying on the slab, covered with a sheet. He pulled the sheet away and said, 'We call them *floaters,* because they pulled him out of the bay. He *shot* himself. Here—you can stick your finger in the hole . . .' I ran out of there and never went back. Oh, he was a real peach, my old man . . ."

My father never mentions his name, or, more precisely, he never *discloses* his name—I don't know the name of my own grandfather. But I can imagine him, gaunt, severe, in a gray suit, with the aspect of a vampire, not only his lips but all his features effaced by his acquaintance with death. Does he scare my father as much as he scares me? Did he scare my father as much as my *father* scares me? He must have, because the only men from his childhood my father talks about fondly are the men he saw on movie screens. He went to the movies every Saturday—"Two features, a newsreel and a cartoon for a *nickel*"—and accepted the tutelage of the men who knew something about manhood. From Fred Astaire, he learned how to dress; from Cary Grant, how to talk; and from Clark Gable, how to treat women. He has a fixation on teaching me and my brother what these men taught him, but none of what we are supposed to learn came from his father.

His father is not supposed to exist. And yet, every so often and always at night, the phone rings, and either my brother or my sister picks it up. A man is on the other end, and Cathy sometimes imitates what he sounds like, in a rough voice she has to sneer to make:

"Is your *fatha* home?"

It's the only thing he says, the only question he asks. He never identifies or introduces himself, and my father generally takes the call in a private place, the same way he takes his calls from his buyers. But we know who he is and once Michael even has the temerity to ask about him. "Dad, why does Grandpa call?"

Dad doesn't even flinch. "He calls to ask for money."

"Why do you give it to him?"

And this time my father does flinch, this time he holds Michael's gaze as if imploring him to understand:

"Because he's my father," he says.

My mother had a father. His name was Herman Brandshagen. He worked for the phone company and took in boarders in their two-story house off Flatbush Avenue. He wore gray suits with a vest crossed officiously by a watch chain. He was scowling and severe in aspect, with dark bushy brows and thick hair patterned white and black like marble and rising straight up off his scalp—hair like my mother would have had if she didn't set and color it so mercilessly. But he was a kindhearted if reticent man, approachable enough that Michael and Cathy named their pet parakeet after him. He built them go-karts and customized their bicycles and when they talked about him—and they talked about "Grandpa Herman" frequently—I felt again as though I had been exiled from the life they led before I was born. I never knew him. He died on the operating table on April 9, 1959, my first birthday, and the coincidence always rattled me; I feared, even as a little boy, that I had something to do with his death, and should apologize to my mother.

She had a mother, too, but she "dropped dead in the street" in 1942, while she was taking my uncle Harry shopping in downtown

Brooklyn. That's all I know about her. My mother never mentioned her name, only how and where she died. My mother was twenty-six when her mother died, but she spoke of the death as though she were much, much younger—as though she were a little girl lost, with tears spangling the outline of her blue eyes. My mother had two terrible wounds that caused her pain she couldn't get over—pain she expressed through glares and flinches that sometimes vied for control of her face and made her anger and her hurt indistinguishable, squaring her jaw and making her look, in my father's term, "belligerent," even when she was fighting tears. The first wound was the story of her mother, Lillian Dineen Brandshagen, dropping dead in the street. The other came later, when she married Louis Junod.

My father has a mother. Her name is Grandma Bess but since she is my only surviving grandparent—other than the one who calls out of the dark and asks for money—she is Grandma to me and Grandma only. I think her last name is Junod, but I'm not sure because nobody ever refers to her that way except my father when he is elaborating on the genetic superiority of the Junods relative to the Brandshagens. The Brandshagens are skinny and weak and when my father beholds me and the ribs that show shamefully under my skin he sometimes says, "You're built like a Brandshagen," or "You're a real Brandshagen," and I'm well aware it's not praise. My father is built the way he's built—a cross between Jack LaLanne and Victor Mature—because he's . . . a Junod. He doesn't get sick because he's . . . a Junod, nor cold in the winter nor sunburned in the summer. Being a Junod is the source of all his strength and immunity and vigor and he must have gotten it from Grandma because he can't have gotten it from the father he never had.

And yet . . . is Grandma really a Junod? She is definitely my father's mother, in that she has the same green eyes as my father and the same elaborate edifice of a nose and the same affronted expression, and if my father put on a white wig no one could tell them apart. But Grandma is not *built* like a Junod and neither is anyone else in his family. Grandma is fat. When my father is out of earshot my mother calls her "heavy" but I can tell she's just trying to be nice and can't say what she really wants to say, which is that Grandma is so fat she's as wide as she is tall and waddles side to side when she walks and has folds in her stockings between her ankles and her feet that look like skin. My father can tell when my mother has put on a pound from eating sweets and is forever trying to convince her to use his slant board "just fifteen minutes a day" so she can pull in her stomach. But it's as if he's blind to how heavy his mother and some of his sisters are, blind to the fact that he does not share his . . . *physique* with any of his siblings, blind to what's clear every time we drive to Levittown to visit his family:

He has a mother and four sisters. But he is the only . . . *Junod*.

My grandma lives with my aunts, and my aunts live one house away from each other on Old Farm Road in Levittown. It's only five and a half miles from Britton Street. But the distance is psychic and emotional more than it is geographical, because Levittown is the place my parents left behind in order to have me. We take the *highway* to Old Farm Road, and the lefts and rights of local travel in Wantagh giving way to the compass points of the trip to Levittown—west on the Southern State, and north on Wantagh Parkway—give me my first lesson in the mysteries of class. My family on Britton Street is different from my father's family on Old Farm Road. We live in a split-level with white marble steps that reflect the sun and they live in Levitt houses. We have fancy cars in the garage and they have Fords and Chevys in the driveway. And we dress for our visit—or, rather, I *am* dressed, by my father and mother. They used to dress Michael like Sinatra, in slacks and a blazer and a fedora, but me they dress in cardigan sweaters and Buster Browns so that when I go to Levittown I feel like Little Lord Fauntleroy holding hands with my mother, who, in my aunts' unanimous opinion, "thinks she's the Queen of Sheba."

We generally visit Levittown on Easter and Christmas and Mother's Day, as well as on Sundays after mass, which my father dodges and my mother attends in big hats and furs I rub my cheek against when I'm bored, like one of her cubs. My father parks the car in front of 106 Old Farm, where without fail we see, through the window, Aunt Elizabeth sitting at the kitchen table. Her husband, Uncle Harry Nolan, greets us at the door, and extends his thick right hand for me to shake. I have no choice; I have to grab his hand in order to get past him, which means in reality that he grabs mine, and begins to squeeze. He also begins to grimace for effect, and since he has the face of a television comedian—big and round, flushed and aggrieved, sweaty with exertion—I do the same, first because I'm hamming it up and then because he keeps tightening his grip and explaining that in the navy his nickname was "Hamhocks" on account of the size and power of his forearms. He was a cook in the navy, and I can smell the pot of stew he keeps bubbling on the stove even as I'm trying to survive his handshake. He draws me closer and closer, so that we're almost face to agonized face before, at long last, he grins and releases my pink and constricted hand and I hear Aunt Liz singing her greeting to my father: "Well, well, look who the cat dragged in."

As Uncle Harry is my father's favorite brother-in-law, Aunt Liz is my father's favorite sister—the only one who sees him as he sees himself. She's no glamour-puss. She is an almost stationary woman, with thin lips and dark hair set in big limp curls, and a habit of wearing housedresses as she witnesses the world just outside her kitchen window. But even in her Long Island citadel she's Brooklyn through and through, and she gives me an idea of what he must have been like . . . of what he must have sounded like . . . before he taught himself to sing and talk. Aunt Liz *berls* the water. She asks me if I need to use the *terlet,* and when she's telling a story and comes to a part where she has to quote herself, she says, "So I says to him, I says . . ." And with invincible pride she calls my father her "brudda," especially when she's talking about all the times no boys would ask her to dance back in Brooklyn once they found out who she was—or once they found out who her *brudda* was. He was feared in Brooklyn, feared both inside and outside the home, because with his father either inebriated or absent altogether, he tried to be the man of the house, even as a teenager, not just *brudda* but *fatha*. His other sisters told him to go to hell. But Aunt Liz accepted his primacy, and liked to see the stricken faces of her would-be suitors when she told them they were dancing with Lou Junod's sister.

We're at 106 Old Farm for about a half hour when the phone starts ringing from 112, Grandma wanting to know where her "Louie" can be. She's famous for this, her worry—her talent for letting her worry do all the work of love—and so we all head down the sidewalk for the house Grandma shares with Aunt Ellie and Uncle Frank. They have an arrangement; Uncle Frank's supposed to own the house, and Grandma's just supposed to live in it, by his leave. But that's not how it works, and as soon as Aunt Ellie opens the door for us I see balding, owlishly bespectacled Frank Peragine, dressed in his work clothes—his white T-shirt and chino pants—asleep on the couch, his rack of bowling trophies sealing his slumber with a sarcophagal flourish. My mother has told me that Uncle Frank needs a lot of rest because "he's nervous," because "he has spells." That makes him sound sick. But even I can see that he's nervous because Grandma makes him nervous—and that he sleeps in a state of fraught surrender in a house divided between two women, only one of whom is his wife.

"You want a Yoo-hoo, Tommy? I bought some Yoo-hoos for you," Aunt Ellie asks, in her squawky, honking voice, which, though loud, seems always to be straining against some unseen impediment, like a broken trumpet. Of course, I accept, because Aunt Ellie's offer of my own personal can of Yoo-hoo is a Levittown ritual as firmly entrenched as my handshake with Uncle Harry. I love Yoo-hoo, a watery chocolate drink advertised by Yogi Berra and packaged in long slim yellow cans, but I don't drink it anywhere else but 112 Old Farm Road, because there I have an audience, there Aunt Ellie always waits for me to take my first sip and then says, "Aw," in a muted tone, wistful and private.

Ellie is the most formidable of my father's sisters, the one who doesn't defer to him, calling him not her "brudda," but "some pain in the ass," right to his face. She's the sister who looks most like him, with a mug dominated by her cavernous nose and the kind of latent outrage memorialized in the funeral masks of emperors and saints, but when he starts what she calls his "bullshit," she waves a hand and says, "Save that for your buyers, Louie. Don't try it on me." She is a sawed-off shotgun of a woman, a self-described "shrimp" who tells every little boy she meets that he is catching up to her, as if the whole world were changing, and she, by her own stubbornness, stays fixed in one place. She's literally got parts missing, holding the cigarettes she chain-smokes between one yellowed finger and the pink stump of the digit she lost in an accident at the factory where she works with Uncle Frank—where she *protects* Uncle Frank from anyone who thinks they can push him around. She is not just the only person in the world who is not afraid of my father. She is the only person in the world my father might be afraid of, and that's why I love her so much.

And yet Ellie Peragine does not occupy the throne at 112. That seat belongs to her mother, wherever the grand dame happens to sit down. And Grandma is *always* sitting down, not just because her bulk discourages her from standing up, but because she's in the habit of accepting homage, even from my mother, who calls her "Mom," and especially from her "Louie," who never comes empty-handed. He makes sure to give her what she loves to get, sometimes a bottle of Shalimar perfume or a bottle of Johnnie Walker Black, but most often a fistful of cash, which he slips into her hand with a whispered word, as if he's tipping a headwaiter. It's the perpetual shock of visiting Levittown: my dad and my grandma don't just look alike; they are alike, in that she is as different from other grandmas as he is different from other fathers. But what is the difference? She certainly *looks* grandmotherly enough, with her inviting corpulence, with her black dress and white bib collar, with her brooch and her fake-pearl earrings the size of jawbreakers and sometimes even a little hat that looks like a doily. Indeed, Aunt Ellie has decorated her living room in "oriental" style, populating it with porcelain figurines, fans, prints, a burbling bamboo fountain, and a slovenly Buddha, and whether Grandma takes a seat on the couch or in the upholstered chair right by the front door, she fits right in—she's the Buddha from Brooklyn, except with a glass of Scotch at the ready, and with . . . well, the same look of wincing distaste that I see on my father's face when she deigns to look at Uncle Frank, unconscious just a few feet away. Grandma lives in Uncle Frank's house, but she doesn't like Uncle Frank, even though he's as gentle and kind and patient as Ellie is volatile and unyielding. Grandma makes faces at Uncle Frank, and little hissing noises—tsk, tsk, tsk—when he has the temerity to get up and walk by. And that's the difference between Grandma and other grandmas, other little old ladies, at least as I imagine and idealize them: she doesn't love unconditionally. She loves in the knowledge that the balance of power on Old Farm Road is the balance of her favor, which—with a couple of exceptions—is capricious, even to children.

"Let me have a look at you," she says to me, after my father dispenses with his tribute and his kiss. I don't know exactly how to respond, because it's not like she's going to ask me any questions I can answer—she's not going to ask me about school or G.I. Joes or comic books. She's going to ask if I have any girlfriends, or if I can sing her a song, both questions that make me shy and nervous. I'm not scared of Grandma. I never have been, because first of all I'm a boy—and according to my mother, Grandma likes boys—and then I'm Louie's son, which gives me special dispensation. But I am scared of disappointing her. She's an inspector, just like my dad, blurting out bad words or telling some off-color story, then seeing how you react. She's an old lady as spoiled and mischievous as a child, and she wants not only to live to one hundred but to have a parade in her honor when she does. She likes candy, but the candy she keeps in front of her in a cut-glass bowl is old-lady candy, little square pillows with sharp edges and pointed corners, their satiny finish pastel colored and striped like the accessories in Grandma's frilly bedroom—the bedroom that reminds my mother of "a bordello," whatever that is. "Grandma, can I have a piece of candy?" I ask. Of course, she says yes—she is, as my father says, "a soft touch, just like your old man." But just as I'm about to reach for the bowl, she plants a greenback in my palm, and says, "You can have a dollar instead." I know she's making me choose; I can have one or the other. But I'm reaching for the candy and closing my hand around the bill at the very same time, and so I say, "I want *both*, Grandma." I have no idea what's going to happen next, and for one giddy moment I'm afraid I'm going to get the same "tsk tsk" she gives Uncle Frank. Instead, she ruffles my hair in the same way my father does, with the same pressure, and says, "Oh, you have a little of the devil in you, Tommy! I *like* that."

I like that too, with nearly a sense of relief, because it means that I'm just like him—that I'm just like *them*.

They're all loud, especially when they're drinking, and they're always drinking. But Aunt Millie's arrival—her reliably late arrival, with her husband, Jack—amplifies the clamor into a din, like a stack of dishes breaking in the uproar of a restaurant kitchen. The front door swings open; she sings her entrance with an eight-to-the-bar *Hay-luh-uh-oh-oh,* and suddenly everyone who was simply shouting is now forced to shout over one another, the change not just quantitative but qualitative. Millie's tall, in heels almost as tall as my dad is "in shoes," and is what my mother calls "brassy," with a Medusa swirl of hair the color of a Mercurochrome stain. She has the face of a rapacious empress, and the blinking "Who, me?" faux-naïveté of a starlet at the Academy Awards. She has nails long enough to saw through the bars of a jail cell, each one decorated with a decal of a butterfly and sometimes festooned with tiny chains. She also lives in Levittown, where she dresses Jack and styles his hair like he's a kept man, but there's something exotic about her, an interloper's force she expresses with cheerful vulgarity and absolute confidence. My father might be Grandma's favorite, but Millie is Grandma's favorite *and* Ellie's favorite, so she's untouchable, invulnerable, at 112—or, as my father grudgingly says, in what is usually one of his highest compliments, "She gets away with murder."

My father doesn't like Millie. Liz, he loves, and calls "honey"; Ellie he defers to, and calls "the Ruler." But he's sixteen years older than Millie, and it took me a while to figure out they were brother and sister. He calls her "Mildred," or else what Ellie calls him: "a pain in the ass." Everybody laughs when pictures are taken and instead of "Say cheese," Millie says, "Say *shit*"—everybody, that is, but my father, who gets the same look on his face that he wears when someone tells a dirty joke. At best, my father *puts up* with dirty jokes, and at best he puts up with his sister Mildred . . . and because he is resistant to her charms, so am I. She doesn't like kids, anyway; she *says* she doesn't like kids, right to my face—"Oh, I hate kids." But then she relents, because I'm "the accident," and that makes us the same. "I'm the *baaaaaby,*" she announces brayingly, like a baby. "I'm the *braaaaaaaat.*"

My father and Millie occupy separate zones of Grandma's affection—Dad is his mother's favorite because he's the boy, Millie because she's the baby. But they're still rivals, because both of them don't know what to do with themselves when they're not the center of attention, and both of them sing. When my father the crooner sings one of his studied ballads, Millie will yell, "Loosen up, Louie," and when Millie sings her big bluesy showstopper, "My Man," my father will ask, "Don't you know another song?" And yet every so often, when everybody's had enough to drink—when Grandma's drank enough to sit down at the upright piano that Ellie keeps in the dining room off the kitchen—they'll sing together, and turn me into a starstruck spectator.

Grandma still remembers not just the songs she used to play when she earned her living playing piano at the silent movies; she remembers the background music, the tried-and-true themes that even I recognize—the music of danger and escape. She remembers how to play the music for when the heroine is tied to the train tracks, and for when the hero on horseback is galloping to save her. And she remembers the music of domestic distress, the music of orphans abandoned and foundlings discovered, the music of heartless evictions. Her children don't sing when she plays these rickety old melodies, with heavy emphasis on the bass clef; they dress up and act them out. Aunt Ellie, Aunt Liz and Mildred—they all wrap their heads in old scarves and enact scenes of piteous woe at the hands of the bill collector, played by my father. He revels in his villainy, twirling an imaginary mustache, while his sisters weep and moan and throw themselves at his feet with clasped hands, begging for his mercy. Since I was old enough to hear my father's stories, I've been hearing how hard he and his family had it—that they were just one step ahead of the landlords and the bill collectors, and had to rely on Grandma's guile just to get by. Now I *see* it, unfolding right in front of me, and though the drama is consistent with my father's romantic interpretation of his past—it's a movie, after all—I gain a sense, as never before, of the facts of their lives:

They were desperate, and they would do anything to survive.

My father's oldest sister lives nearby, in West Hempstead, and comes on most Sunday afternoons to take Grandma "out for a drive"—that is, to dinner. She stops by Aunt Liz's as well, sometimes when we're there for a visit. But she does not often go to Ellie's, and she does not join the music, though she is supposed to have a beautiful singing voice. Indeed, once upon a time Aunt Marie was supposed to have been a rare beauty, with a "gorgeous figure" that drew a line of suitors to the door. But Marie "let herself go," in my father's reliable refrain, and now look at her: "She's a wreck." She looks in fact like Grandma, with the same tottering mass; the same formal taste in clothes; the same two-handed way of carrying a small prim pocketbook, as if waiting for someone to try stealing it; the same white doily pinned to the top of her head, floating on her salt-and-pepper hair. Unlike Ellie, she never says a cross word to my father; unlike Millie, she never says a cross word to me. And yet I'm afraid of her and the crooked teeth that give her a barbed-wire smile. I run away from her and she stomps after me, thinking it's a game, thinking that I'm having fun. But it's no game, because I can't help but remember what my father says in disgust about his older sister Marie—"What she's *done* to herself." When I avoid her embrace she stares at me with her eyes as suddenly big as eyeglasses, and then tries again, softer this time, squatting massively in front of me and touching me on the tip of my nose. She looks like she's about to cry and so I want to cry too, because I can't tell if she's just put a spell on me or lifted one. "Oh, Tommy," she says in a voice of plea and apology. "Don't be like your *fatha*. Don't be ashamed of your . . . aunt *Marie*."

The doorbell rings. I'm nine or ten years old, and the only one home now besides my parents. It's my responsibility to answer, though it's a winter evening and dark. An old man is standing on the marble steps, backing away from the door like a stranger. I've heard the phrase "hat in hand" but never understood its meaning until just now. He is not just old; he is antiquated, in the cut of his clothing and the formality of his manners, and yes, his hat is in his hand. He is thin, with his gray hair combed straight back off his scalp, and though he is deferential he is not at all friendly. "Is your *fatha* home?" he asks, and in that instant I don't have to wait for him to introduce himself. I know him already, through my sister's gravelly impression of the way he sounds on the phone. The man asking for my father is his father, and he looks exactly how I've imagined he would look, as I've feared he would look, without a hint of recognition in his eyes. I call for my father with a bark in my voice, an edge of panic and alarm, just one word—"Dad!"

When he comes downstairs, my father moves quickly through

the open door, nudging me aside and closing the door behind him. I wait for a while in the living room, hoping for his quick return, then sit at the kitchen table under the light of the hanging lamp. I hear my father step back inside and shut the front door. I hear him climbing the stairs and closing the bedroom door. For the rest of the night, I do not hear anything else from him, and when I close my eyes I squeeze them tightly, afraid that my grandfather's severe and stricken face will turn up in my dreams.

It is as if I've seen a ghost. I never meet him again, but he begins to occupy a place in my imagination defined equally by curiosity and fear. I have no idea where he lives or when he dies, only that even when I visit Levittown I have to be careful when I ask about him. Dad avoids the subject, and if he hears me asking Aunt Liz about her father he'll say, "What do you want to talk about *him* for?" because he knows that his sister doesn't detest the man's memory as much as he does. "Oh, he wasn't so bad," she'll explain, after my father leaves the room. "He just drank. He'd go on these terrible binges, two weeks at a time, until he'd ask me to go to the store and buy him chopped meat and tomato juice. He'd cook the chopped meat in the tomato juice, and that's how I knew he was coming out of it."

And yet my aunt's stories are not the only place where my grandfather survives his son's determined disregard. In Grandma's scented room, a small framed photograph stands on the dresser next to the bed. The man in the portrait wears a suit with a vest. His dark hair is combed straight back, and though his sealed lips are thin and unsmiling, they evince a bare hint of self-regard that makes it hard to associate him with the specter who came to our door. He is neither familiar nor familial to me—he does not look like a relative, much less my grandfather, and he is indeed such a persistent stranger that I'm in the habit of asking Grandma who he is. She never responds by informing me, "He's your Grandpa," or even "He's your father's father." Instead, she simply says, "That's Louis Junod," and when I ask her why she keeps his photo by her bed, she answers, like an old madam, "He's the only man who ever turned me on."

7

It's the first day of fifth grade and somebody must have made a mistake. I'm in the wrong class. All my friends—all the smart kids—are in a different class. My head spins, and I begin trying to convince my classmates that they're as miserable as I am, as though we've all wound up in a prison for the falsely accused. "This has to be a dream," I say. "Or maybe a nightmare."

My classmates shrug—who cares? But I do. I care so much I feel something familiar coming on, the way epileptics are supposed to feel the onset of a fit. I can hear it in the distance. My face grows warm, and there's a ringing in my ears. It's not enough that I've wound up in the slow class—I have to *cry* now too? I can't, I won't. I turn around and start talking to the kid behind me. He's new and he's shy, with a head that looks too big for his body and at the same time not fully formed under his crew cut, like a baby's. For some reason, I start talking to him about music, maybe just to show off. I don't just like music; I like that I like music and think it makes me cool. I already argue over "the best songs" and "the best bands" and my favorite songs of the summer that just ended were "Sunshine of Your Love" and "Hello, I Love You" and "Jumpin' Jack Flash" and "Reach Out of the Darkness" by Friend & Lover—they practically made me a hippie. But when I ask the new kid his favorite song, he answers, " 'Snoopy vs. the Red Baron,' " with pursed lips and a little giggle. "Snoopy vs. the Red Baron"? He really *is* a baby. I don't say anything, but I remember what he said and how he said it, and start building a case against him. His name is Timmy Titimski, but in my head I repeat it to myself with my own laugh track, and when I do I don't have to cry anymore.

Then our aged teacher dies and the class becomes ungovernable. We have subs and old nuns who were once fearsome but are now senile. "No more pencils, no more books, no more teacher's dirty looks," we used to sing. But it turned out to be an incantation and now whole days pass with one teacher giving us a writing assignment in the morning and another teacher trying to quell the uproar in the afternoon. There are puddles of pee under desks and in the coat closets. The girls have discovered nail polish and slam books and the boys spitballs, so the school day ends with glistening black threads of spittle running down the chalky surface of the blackboards, like Halloween decorations. There are boys who shoot spitballs at the subs but mostly we shoot at each other on the sly unless a free-for-all breaks out. One day, a sub walks out, and during lunch we are completely unsupervised and left to our straws and our saliva and I see Timmy Titimski standing alone by the blackboard. His lips are pursed and his shoulders are hunched and shaking with timid glee and I stand in front of him to block his exit. He is a noncombatant; he has no straw. I raise mine and point it at his broad forehead. Then I blow. It shouldn't hurt him; it's only a spitball. But it does, grievously, and suddenly even amidst the fracas we are standing alone. Patiently, methodically, one after another, I paint his forehead with spitballs as his pursed lips tremble and his trapped eyes fill with tears. Finally I roll up a piece of tinfoil into a little barb, a tiny spur, and fire it at him. It bounces off but leaves a little mark on his smooth, almost larval skin. I watch it fall and when I look back at him his face crumples and his mouth releases a yielding gasp and tears spurt from his eyes.

Lunch is ending and as kids go back to their desks we are still standing there, a breed apart, victim and scourge. He is sobbing and shaking and as transfixed as I am by what I have done, what I have wrought, I am afraid of getting caught so I take him by the arm and lead him back to his seat, whispering, "Don't tell anyone, don't tell anyone." I am not proud of myself but that hardly matters. I am in the grip of something as surely as he is in the grip of me. A few days later, I look up his name in the phone book and find his address. I have a new bicycle, an orange Raleigh Chopper, with a small wheel in the front and a sissy bar in the back. It's a spoiled boy's bike, but when I descend on the backyard where Timmy Titimski is playing in a sandbox with his younger brothers I feel like a one-man motorcycle gang, despoiling an unsuspecting town of upright citizens somewhere on the edge of the desert. They are building sand castles—what a baby he is!—and I ride my Chopper through them until there's nothing left and Timmy Titimski's agonized face is shining with tears and grief.

The first is not the last. It's just the beginning of what becomes part of my life, and his. I call them my "raids"—as in, when I ask my friends to go along with me, "Do you want to go on a raid?" They don't, after a while; Robert McGarty, my closest friend, even tells me he doesn't know what I have against Timmy Titimski—he *likes* Timmy Titimski, and starts going over to his house to play. But that just makes me feel worse about what I'm doing, and therefore more dangerous to my prey. I ride out alone, with the transistor radio I hang from the handlebars of my Chopper playing the 5th Dimension's "Aquarius," a song that stirs the deepest and most exalted feelings in me, until I find who I'm looking for and lay him to waste. He is not safe anywhere in Wantagh, especially once I figure out the parameters of his paper route, and it is only a matter of time before there's a knock on the door at 1463 Britton Street.

I'm in my room when I hear it. The knock is sharp and curt—more a rap than a knock—but I go downstairs in the usual leaps and bounds, opening the door with my usual sense of expectation. It's dinnertime, my mother in the kitchen, my father on the phone in his room, the light from the setting sun making the sprays of water from the underground sprinkler system look like a garden of spiderwebs. When I open the door, I see Timmy Titimski and his father. Although he is standing a few feet behind his father the way an altar boy stands behind a priest, I see him first—our eyes meet in a moment of mutual shame, but when he bows his head and averts his gaze, I have no choice but to look at the man I'm trying to look past. Mr. Titimski resembles his son, with a head like the bulb of a thermometer. He's wearing a white shirt and a narrow tie. But his hair is dark and curly instead of light brown and downy, and it's pasted damply to his scalp. At first I think he must have gotten wet, walking through the sprinklers. But no, he's sweating. As my father would say, he's in a *lather*—he's "all worked up." He doesn't say hello. "Is your father home?" he says. I run upstairs and tell my father that there's someone at the door.

"Who is it?" he asks.

I don't say anything. I go back downstairs and stay inside, peering through the glass. My father walks past me and opens the door. He extends his hand to Mr. Titimski, who doesn't take it. I keep hoping he's going to threaten to throw Mr. Titimski down the stairs like he threatened Mr. Kornhoff. But he minds his manners, and I stay behind him, occasionally peeking at the boy also hiding behind his dad. I hear Mr. Titimski say, "This has to stop," and after a while my father calls me forth and I step outside onto the white marble stoop. "What do you say?" my father asks.

"I'm sorry," I answer.

"Now shake hands and let bygones be bygones," he says. "And look each other in the eye, like *men*."

I offer my hand to Timmy Titimski and he flinches, his lips pursed with an apprehension of horror. Then he *makes* himself take it, and my father and I stand together and watch them leave, the water from the sprinklers somehow just missing them. I want to watch them get in their car and drive away, but my father turns toward the house, and I open the door for him. "Next time pick on somebody your *own* size," he says, and heads back to his room and his phone.

Two days later, I find him on his paper route with his two brothers. "Timmy Titimski!" I roar, and then spill his newspapers all over some Wantagh lawn, while he cries and one of his brothers tries kicking me in the shins. I laugh like a barbarian sacking a city and the futile efforts of his little brother only deepen my sense of power. When I push him to the ground, he clings to my shins as I wade forward like a giant and the pages of newspapers begin to peel off in the breeze. I know that what I'm doing is wrong. I know that what I'm doing has embarrassed the man I live to impress. I know that I'm a villain, but I can't stop myself, and I've never been so unhappy in my entire life.

He is not running away from me, like prey. He is running right at me, part of a stampede of boys who are indistinguishable from one another. But he has the ball cradled in his arms, so he's the one I have to tackle. We are all wearing white helmets and white pants and white practice jerseys and slumping white socks; the only distinction is the red singlet that half of my teammates pull down over their shoulder pads to show that they are playing offense. I am playing defense. I'm playing the last line of defense, as something called a safety, a word my mother insists on speaking in three syllables, much to my annoyance. Playing "safe-uh-ty" in Little League football is a little like playing outfield in Little League baseball; it means that I'm not very good. But what I love about playing football is that I don't have to be good, only willing. I don't have to prove myself by swinging at a ball and getting a hit. I have to prove myself by hitting.

I am twelve years old, in sixth grade, and I am so desperate to prove myself that I don't know how desperate I am. The running back is bigger than me—taller, anyway, his gigantic shoulder pads comically out of scale with his long, skinny legs—and as he breaks into the open field he heads right at me, as if he has a score to settle or maybe as if I'm completely invisible. But he runs standing straight up, with short skittering steps, like a sandpiper. I dive at his legs when he is at full speed and his knee comes up as my helmet goes down. My vision goes vibrantly black; my ears ring with a thousand echoes of the initial clout and when I stand up I'm staggering and stumbling like . . . a real rumdum. The coach approaches and tries to steady me by my shoulder pads; I can look at his mouth or I can look at his eyes but I can't look at both. He opens his hand in front of my face like he's shooting craps.

"How many fingers?" His mouth moves but no words come out; the words come out of the ringing in my ears, which comes out of the sky.

"Uh . . ."

"Go take a knee."

I take a knee, the position like penance, big black spots tingling before my eyes even when my eyes are closed. I don't go back in but I also don't take my helmet off and I'm smiling like a big palooka too dumb to know he's been knocked out. I'm still smiling when my father picks me up and the coach says, "He got his bell rung a little bit." We walk to the car together and when my father puts his arm around my shoulder pads and says, "Heeeeeey, you got your *bell* rung a little bit," I hear a new sound in his voice, something almost conspiratorial.

I keep my helmet on even in the Cadillac because my head is starting to hurt and also because as my father sings "My Woman,

My Woman, My Wife" along with his eight-track of Robert Goulet I can ring the bell any time I want by snapping my fingernail against the helmet's hard shell, the sound like a ricochet in a TV Western. I imagine never taking it off for the rest of my natural-born days, and when we get back home I march right upstairs and fall into bed in my full uniform. "Oh, he's just a little . . . punchy," my father says to my mother in the kitchen, and she comes to visit me with a cold wet rag as if I have a fever. "Here, take your helmet off like a good boy," she says, and presses the rag against my forehead, asking if I feel woozy. "No, I'm *punchy,*" I say, and the word doesn't just sound good; it feels good, like a cure, and I keep repeating it to myself as I drift off to a black sleep, my helmet and my cleats on the floor next to the bed but my shoulder pads clanking whenever I toss and turn, like armor.

As gambling is the family vice, football becomes the family sport. My parents don't just go to every game; they dress for every game, my mother in furs and my father in a long camel hair coat with a flask in his pocket. He prowls the sideline, taking picturesque nips, while my mother engages in the same full-throated rituals she's developed watching the games my father bets. It's my father I see, when I'm out on the field, but it's my mother I *hear,* as her practiced civility falls away and her Brooklyn bray comes to the fore. "Get 'em, Tommy! Get 'em!" she shouts whenever a play is coming my way, and by God I do—I'm a little hellion out there, piling on and taking cheap shots but also making tackles and, in one sacred moment during a night game, an interception. I boot-black my eyes and wear a white rubber neck roll and when I'm selected for an all-star team I feel that I'm on my way to making myself into a brand-new boy.

I'm a bully but not a tough kid and a lot of the tough kids are not bullies. Billy Knott is both. He lives at the other end of Britton Street, where the split-levels stop and there are cars parked on the lawns of the small houses. He hangs around with other tough kids—or, as we call them in Wantagh, "hoods." What makes him a bully is that he, like me, has picked one kid, weaker than himself, to torture and torment. That kid is my new best friend, Brendan Clancy.

Brendan is my new best friend because my old best friend, Robert McGarty, is disgusted by how I treat Timmy Titimski, among other things. My father doesn't like Brendan because once, on the way to Westhampton, he puked in the back seat of the Cadillac without a word of warning and my father can't get the smell out. But my mother loves him because she feels sorry for him. He is fatherless and he is poor, one of nine children who moved to Wantagh after his father died in his late thirties. He wears pants that ride above his ankles, darned socks, cracked shoes with metal taps on the heels. When he turns twelve, my mother helps out with the cost of a Raleigh Chopper that complements my own, mine orange and black, his black and orange. It's a gift beyond his own family's means and so when it's stolen he lashes out and accuses Billy Knott of stealing it. His accusation isn't baseless—the rumor is that Knott has a black Chopper for sale—but it provides the presumed thief an occasion for necessary outrage. He's a low-ranking tough kid, and now he has the rationale, the necessary moral justification, to be a bully.

Knott begins waiting for Brendan after school, and their meetings quickly become ritual. Knott begins by making an accusation of his own—"Hey, this kid says I stole his bike." Then he says, "Why don't you say I stole your bike *now,*" and yanks on Brendan's uniform tie until the knot shrinks to the size of a SweeTart and Brendan is red in the face. He neither fights nor flees, even when Knott slaps him or doubles him over with a punch to the solar plexus. I don't know what sickens me more—Knott's cruelty, Brendan's submission, or my inaction. But what's most unsettling is not just that I'm standing around and watching my friend's pain and humiliation but rather that I'm standing around and watching in the company of some of the toughest kids in town. I'm part of an audience that includes Richie Loudermilk, a member of Wantagh's one hillbilly family; Jackie Costello, the son of a mobster who lives opulently on one of the canals; and, most fearsome of all, Paul McCracken, whose savage fights attract large crowds and end in shocking acts of violence that go well beyond fisticuffs. I don't feel threatened by them because even though I'm standing among them they barely see me, and because they don't like the spectacle of Billy Knott's sadism any more than I do. They get bored, they light cigarettes, they hock loogies and leave them glistening on the street. They might form a gauntlet around their friend, but they make fun of him all the same, and after a while they tell him to "hurry the fuck up" or to "let the fucking kid go, so we can get the fuck out of here."

But I know Billy Knott's not going to let Brendan go—as a fellow bully, I know he *can't* let Brendan go any more than I can Timmy Titimski. He responds to the impatience of his pals by thinking he has to find new ways to impress them and he responds to Brendan's surrender by thinking he has to find new ways to hurt him, until one afternoon, just down the block from St. Francis, I look up and he has Brendan by the balls. He's slapped him, punched him, kicked him and pulled him by the tie like a dog and now he has grabbed Brendan between the legs and begun squeezing. He has him against the bumper of a stranger's car parked in a stranger's driveway, and Brendan twists and groans and whimpers while Knott keeps yelling at him about the bike. It's a kind of martyrdom, the kind of scene featured in illustrated versions of *The Lives of the Saints,* the haloed victim rolling his eyes toward heaven as he is disemboweled. It's also terribly private and shameful. I avert my eyes and so do the toughs who surround me. An unhappy silence descends; then someone says, "Cough!" like a doctor checking for a hernia. Some of the hoods laugh, and as Knott turns toward them in confusion—are they laughing at Brendan or at him?—a woman in a housedress opens the door and begins yelling at boys on her driveway. "Stop that! Stop that! Let that boy go or I'm going to call the police!" Startled, Knott loosens his grip; Brendan uses the distraction to hop on his old bike and ride away, back through the grounds of the school. He is standing on his pedals, riding so hard and so fast the front wheel wobbles. Knott runs after him, and they disappear beyond the gate. Suddenly, I'm all alone with the hoods and decide that, as my father sometimes says, "discretion is the better part of valor." I kick the kickstand on my own bike and slink toward the St. Francis gate, careful not to ride too fast or too slow.

Brendan is long gone when I reach the road that encircles the school. Knott is not. He is waiting for me, in a little alcove formed by one of the side entrances, a strip of grass and shrubbery formed by a projecting brick wall. He must have been hiding, or maybe taking a whiz, because he steps out of the shadow and says, "Hey, kid—get off your bike, I want to talk to you." I get off my bike and step toward him. We face each other, a foot or two away. He smiles; no, *leers.* He thinks I'm like Brendan, but he's got me all wrong. I swing a haymaker into his face and then another and another and I don't stop when he goes down or even when he begins to bleed. I can't see, I can't hear, I keep windmilling punches with both hands until something gives way in his face and the blood spouting from his nose and staining his teeth seems to darken. Bits of matter cover his cheeks, snot probably, but snot released from some reserve deep inside him, and now he's the one wearing the look of the saint, the sacrifice. The only thing that stops me is his obliteration. I get up, staring at my bloodstained fists in ecstasy and horror, and when I stagger to my bicycle Paul McCracken is standing next to it in his navy blue peacoat. He claps a hand on my shoulder and says, "Good fight, kid." Then he calls to his friend, prostrate in the grass: "Hey, Knott, now you know what it's like to get the *shit* knocked out of you." I don't say anything to him. I hop on my bicycle and ride away, Jackie Costello giving chase. He reaches for the sissy bar of my Raleigh Chopper and comes inches short, so that as I glance back I see him staring at his empty hand with a sardonic smile. Thirty seconds before, I would have fought him and Paul McCracken at the same time, but now I've lost my courage, or maybe my bloodlust. I pedal, hearing the sounds I'm making, the involuntary squeaks that have replaced my breath. I go to Brendan's house, then ride home in the dark. I tell my mother I got into a fight. I tell my father I got into a fight and won. I don't tell either of them that it felt like murder.

A few days later, I'm riding my bicycle home from a pickup tackle football game played on the expansive front lawn of the local public elementary school. My house is in sight; I'm on a street that runs perpendicularly into Britton Street, right into the jeweled vision of 1463. But I also hear a high-pitched sound, a whine that becomes a rasp because there's teeth in it, and for some reason it makes my heart quicken. I look behind me, and in the haze of distance I see a Sting-Ray bicycle advancing at impossible speed and coming relentlessly into focus. And then I hear something even more distinct than the greedy motorized roar—an exultant human sound, a whoop, a war cry. I begin to pedal harder and faster, and keep sneaking glances at what's approaching because I can't believe my eyes. It's a motorbike, a Sting-Ray outfitted with a lawn mower engine, two boys sharing the banana seat. The one steering with his arms extended to the grips of the raised handlebars is wearing a black leather jacket, his black hair short and his cheeks apple red with acne. The one along for the ride is flipping his long hair like a girl but he is the one making the exultant howl and swinging a chain over his head. That they look like members of a motorcycle gang makes me believe for a few hopeful instants that they have nothing to do with me, that they can't possibly have anything to do with me and will pass me by. But they slow down next to me and the hood in the black leather jacket begins reaching for my handlebars, and suddenly I hear myself making those involuntary cries and see myself leaping off my bicycle with my bicycle still moving and running straight to my house. The Raleigh Chopper crashes in a heap behind me and as I run up the marble steps and through the front door I hear their triumphant laughter and then the roar of the motorbike receding back into the neighborhood, turning again into a distant whine. My father is home; he is standing in the living room talking to his friend Barney Allen, "Uncle Barney." But I run right past him, right past both of them, and into my room, slamming the door behind me. I am so afraid that for once I forget to be afraid of my father.

He opens the door and sits on the bed with his hands folded. "*What* . . . just happened?"

"Two boys on a motorbike they were going to kill me they were like Hells Angels they came after me with a chain."

He was smiling as the story spilled from me but when I reach the end he bites his lip and his eyes begin to burn. "They came after you . . . with a *chain*?"

"Yes, a long chain one of them was swinging over his head! He was trying to hit me with it!" By this time, Uncle Barney is standing in the doorway and I feel tears coming on. He's one of my father's Brooklyn cronies, a tough Irishman who sounds exactly like Archie Bunker, speaking his words as if they were caught in his teeth. He's a New York City cop who works in a security detail protecting celebrities. On the wall of my father's bar hangs a black-and-white photo of Uncle Barney and Jackie Onassis, and when he visits the house the two men still descend into the basement to drink and listen to records. He is not a friend my father deems "weak" behind his back but rather "a man's man," which means that he makes my mother nervous. He is not unkind to her, like Chip. But she counts my father's drinks when he is with Barney, and pities his wife, Florence, the way some people pity her.

"Did you know them?" my father asks.

"No."

"How old were they?"

"My age."

"*Your* age!" He looks at Barney again and something passes between them, an understanding. Barney leans against the door frame, drinking his Scotch in a deliberative posture. I want to ask, "Uncle Barney, are you going to arrest them?" But he isn't dressed like a cop, or even a detective. He's dressed exactly like my father, in a ribbed turtleneck and slacks, and like my father he's let his sideburns grow out and his hair curl over the collar. He doesn't take his eyes off my dad, as if awaiting an order. "Okay," my father says, as he pats my knee and stands up. "Let's go."

"Let's *go*? Let's go where?"

He answers only in body language. He stands in the doorway next to Barney, both of them throwing their shoulders back and hitching up their pants. They drink down their Scotches and head for the kitchen for another round, minus the ice. My mother is wringing her hands and belching. *"Lou,"* she says pleadingly. "Frances," my father says decisively. I follow them out to the Caddy, hitching up my own pants, sure that I'm going to witness a reckoning—that my dad is going to prove once and for all that he can lick their dads. He looks around, squinting like a cavalry scout. I figure he's going to ask where they live. Instead, he says, "Tommy, where is your bicycle?"

"My bicycle?"

"Yes, yes, the one I bought for your birthday. Where is it?"

"I left it," I say.

The two men stiffen. They stop what they were doing, stop

stretching and flexing and cracking their knuckles. They stand in front of me, side by side. "You . . . left it?" my father asks.

"But they were going to hit me with a *chain* . . ."

"You . . . *ran*?"

I nod, and stare at the ground.

"Go get it," he says, through pale lips that barely move.

When I reach the Chopper it is in a spindly heap, its front tire twisted around and its black cables tangled, evidence of how violently I jettisoned myself from it when the hoods were closing in on me. I walk the bent Chopper home so my father doesn't see that it lists and wobbles. But he is already waiting for me in the Cadillac, Uncle Barney sitting next to him in the front seat. My father swings the door open, and when I slip into the back, I offer him one last pleading look. He raises his eyebrows, and says, "I'm doing this for you, son. You ran. If you run again, you'll keep running the rest . . . of your *life*."

I don't argue. I climb in the back seat and he drives slowly down Britton Street without needing to explain what we're doing, the car silenced by shame. When we reach a cross street, he slows nearly to a stop, peering west to Wantagh Avenue while Uncle Barney peers east to the woods, both of them all business. Then we hear the motorbike, its band-saw call. My father does not speed up, but when we get to the mouth of a street called Silverton, he indicates a group of kids with his chin and asks, "Is that them?" I look and nod. My father barely touches the gas pedal. He just makes a left and rolls silently up to the boy on the motorbike. There is only one of them now, the one who was tossing his hair like a girl when he wasn't swinging the chain. He is still tossing his hair but girls surround him, girls with shag haircuts and their eyes Kewpie-dolled with dark makeup. His arms are stretched full length to the handlebars and his right hand is working the throttle with languid ease. Some of the girls put their hands over their ears as the lawn mower engine roars.

My father touches the chrome switch on the door and the electric window slides down, noise pouring into the car like a swarm. Though it's very loud, he doesn't raise his voice. "*Heeeeey,*" he says, and the girls back away, one of them turning on her heel and heading home. I hope the hood on the motorbike will see him and

Uncle Barney in the front seat and do what I did. I hope he will run. But he stands his ground, and revs the engine twice before taking it all the way down to a sputtering growl. "Hey, *Veronica Lake,*" my father says, and the hood immediately stops tossing his hair. "I hear you came after my son . . . with a *chain.*"

The hood doesn't so much as glance at me. "He beat up my friend," he says to my father. "My friend is, like, weak, and he hit him while he wasn't looking."

My father turns his head slowly and looks at me like he's discovered a stowaway. "Is that true, son? Did you . . . *coldcock* the boy?"

I want to plead my case and say that I hit Billy Knott because I wasn't about to let Billy Knott squeeze my balls. But I just shake my head.

"Okay," my father says. "Listen up, the two of you. We live at 1463 Britton Street—the house with . . . the marble steps. Do you know it?"

The hood nods.

"Then come by tomorrow morning at ten o'clock. You boys can put on . . . the *gloves,* and settle this like men."

"Dad!" I hear myself blurt. Now they're all looking at me, my father with embarrassment, Uncle Barney with affront and the hood with curiosity and something like sympathy. When our eyes meet, his ask questions. *Is he serious? Is he crazy?* In response I offer a clandestine shrug, barely moving a muscle.

"Okay," he says, and after revving the engine, he peels out. When he's gone, I say, one more time, "Dad"—but my father shushes me with a raised palm. "You can either fight him or you can fight . . . me."

When we get home, I don't tell my mother what happened or what is going to take place. That I'm scheduled to box a local hoodlum is a secret my dad and I share—a secret I can't tell my mother because then it will seem like I'm telling on Dad. He comes to my room and checks on me every once in a while, but I'm afraid he's going to put up his dukes and try to teach me the manly art of self-defense. Then both of my parents are asleep—I can hear the water-in-the-drain sound of my mother's snoring—and I am wide awake, experiencing the first sleepless night of my life. I don't fear what the hood will do as much as I fear what my father will do if the hood starts winning. Will he stop the fight? Will he give me tips? Will he revive me with smelling salts? Will he give the hood a beating? Will he hold the hood's hand up over me and tell him, "Good fight"? Will he even be on my side?

I finally fall asleep when the sun comes up, and wake up to the smell of steak frying in a pan. I go downstairs and the Everlast gloves the color of dried blood are hanging from my chair by their yellow laces and my father is jabbing a smoking steak with a long-tined fork. "When Joe Louis was training to fight Max Schmeling," he says, "he ate nothing but steak, every meal." He deposits the steak on my plate and gives me two slices of buttered toast, so I can "mop up . . . the *blood*." And then we wait. It's eight o'clock on a Saturday morning, and I'm thinking of the permanence of my father's edicts. *You're going to run for the rest of your life. You can either fight him or you can fight . . . me.* So of course I'm terrified of what's going to happen once the hood knocks on our door. But what if he doesn't? What if, instead of me and the hood, it's just me and my father, for the rest . . . of my life?

I puke up the steak at nine. Ten o'clock passes without a knock on the door, but when the doorbell rings at eleven I go *flying* downstairs like my brother's coming home from college. But it's just the man who delivers the dry cleaning, my mother's dresses and my father's suits sealed in plastic that billows in the breeze.

I hear the TV downstairs. I'm at the corner desk in my room, doing homework, and Mom is in the den, watching a variety show or a cop show or maybe the ABC Movie of the Week, which is always about what she calls "controversial subjects." I'm usually with her, when Dad is away; I usually finish my homework after dinner, and then join her in front of the TV, my mom in one of the white leather chairs and me on the floor. But tonight I have to write an analysis of a poem I don't understand and therefore detest. It has no punctuation. It has no capital letters. It is not only difficult; it tries to be, and I grow angry at the poem, at the poet, and at poetry in general, as if they were all mocking me. I keep saying, "This is stupid, this is stupid, this is stupid," and yet my bafflement in the face of its stupidity is what holds me in thrall. I try to figure it out for at least an hour, until at last I go downstairs and plop myself down theatrically on the carpeted steps, the offending poem printed in purple on the fragrant "ditto paper" my teacher at St. Francis distributed in class.

"What's wrong?" Mom asks.

"I have to write two paragraphs about a poem that doesn't make any sense. And I can't do it! Why would someone write something that doesn't make any sense? I hate it! I hate it! I hate it!" I'm so worked up I'm nearly in tears.

"Let me hear it," Mom says.

"I'll give it to you and you can read it."

"No, read it to me."

"Mom, that's the problem! I can't read it! It's all in small letters!"

"*Try,*" she says. "I'd like to hear it, and if you read it out loud, maybe you'll understand."

"It's so stupid!"

"I'm *lis*tening," she says, with a song in her voice.

"Okay," I say. Then I take a breath and read the nettlesome lines to my mother:

anyone lived in a pretty how town
(with up so floating many bells down)
spring summer autumn winter
he sang his didn't he danced his did.

Women and men (both little and small)
cared for anyone not at all
they sowed their isn't they reaped their same
sun moon stars rain

children guessed (but only a few
and down they forgot as up they grew
autumn winter spring summer)
that noone loved him more by more . . .

Halfway into the poem, she leans forward and folds her hands in her lap. At the end, the glistening in her eyes makes the dim room seem darker, as if the sun has started setting for a second time. She is very quiet, and I'm a little ashamed that I've read her something that made her sad.

"See?" I say. "It's stupid."

"I think it's *beautiful,*" Mom says.

"But what does it mean?"

"Did you listen?" she asks.

"Yes."

"Did you like it?"

"Well, it's not as bad as it I thought it was."

"It's a *love story,*" Mom says.

"But who is 'anyone'?"

"Anyone is anyone."

"Why doesn't he have a name?"

"Because anyone can fall in love."

"And who is 'no one'?"

"Someone who goes unnoticed, I guess." She squeezes her hands together and stares at them as if they do not belong to her. Then she looks up and says, "Maybe it's me."

Dad has a secret life when he goes away. But Mom and I have a secret life when we're home together, just the two of us. We're happier alone than we are with him, happy together with Mom free to be herself. I know she is smart because she wrote all Cathy's papers when Cathy went to college and I know she wants to be thought of as smart because she pronounces the word with a sigh that infiltrates her Brooklynese: "smaht." But when she tries to sound smart when Dad's around she sounds strained and snobbish, all her intelligence draining into her worried hands, her watchful eyes. She is smartest when she feels what she's thinking, and that's what she doesn't allow herself to do in front of him. We could never have had the conversation we just had with Dad home, and she never would have given me the lesson about poetry I would remember the rest of my life—don't just read it; read it out loud. Nor would I have seen how beautiful Mom is in the presence of beauty, how it warms her. I am in eighth grade and I have probably never read a poem that doesn't rhyme, and I suspect that neither has she. But E. E. Cummings makes her *shine,* there in the gloom of a room lit only by a twenty-five-inch color TV, there in one of the white leather chairs my parents bought as a pair but only occupy singly, one in the absence of the other. And I allow myself to think—I can't help but think—something that makes me feel sorry for him, and then for all of us.

He has never seen what she's like when he's not there. He has never seen her as I see her.

The master bedroom looks like it belongs to her—the furniture is French Provincial, like the furniture in the living and dining rooms, and after Cathy becomes Mrs. Ronnie Gustafson my mother sends it off to be "distressed," which is to say beaten with chains for rustic effect. Distressed French Provincial: if anyone asked me to describe my mom, I couldn't do better than that. But of course it's Dad's room; he controls vast swaths of territory, including the bathroom, the closet and the dresser. Mom is literally backed into a corner—the narrow space between her side of the bed and the wall—and, accordingly, has built a barricade in the form of a stack of women's magazines so tall it tilts and totters. *Woman's Day, Good Housekeeping, Redbook, Better Homes & Gardens*—she reads them at night, when her hair is netted and her face shines with cold cream. When we're alone, I stand outside the door and hear the pages turning.

I've never opened one. But one afternoon my fingertips are touching the polished wood of my mother's nightstand. It's strange—my father is a man of many secrets, but his hiding places are as familiar to me as my own. My mother has no secrets at all, and yet I've never so much as opened her drawer. It's not a forbidden place, exactly, but I've kept my hands off it for the same reason I've left her magazines unmolested—because I can't imagine that it's about sex, the great beating heart of the rest of the room. I haven't been curious about it until this moment, figuring that it's full of prayer cards and rosary beads. She's been spending most of her afternoons in Holbrook, helping out Cathy, who is having "a hard time" as a mother and a housewife. She probably won't be home for a while, so I decide to investigate her as I've investigated *him*.

The drawer slides out easily, as if on soaped tracks—so easily that I think it's going to slide straight out of the nightstand and spill on the floor. It is scandalously open, and the first things I see are . . . mass cards and a rosary. No, wait; several rosaries in cellophane bags, with gift cards attached to them. *To Fran . . . To my friend Fran . . . To Fran, from the Vatican . . . To Fran, from Lourdes.* Her friends have done what she won't do, they have traveled, they have "gone abroad" with their husbands and have sent her rosaries from the places of Catholic pilgrimage they have visited. But she hasn't opened them, and the rosaries are no different than all the bric-a-brac that fills the drawer—the ribbons of Green Stamps, the clipped coupons, the hopeful recipes, the rolls of undeveloped Instamatic film, the snapshots of parties and "functions" she has attended with my father that she has not put in photo albums, the smudged reading glasses swaddled in toilet paper along with their unattached arms. My mother is "put together," not in my father's sense of the term—she is not "stacked"—but rather in the sense that no one would ever look at her hair, her makeup, her clothes, and conclude she's disorganized and something of a mess. But I know that she has terrible trouble finishing what she starts, or even starting what she swears she's going to finish. She feels terrible pressure to be a perfect housewife. But in the drawer is the kit for the perfect housewife she will never get around to building.

There are two things that stand out, two blank manila envelopes, because I'm enough of a sneak to know that *these* are the ones to open. The first seems brand-new, pointed at the corners, the edge of the flap sharp enough to inflict a paper cut. It has not been licked and sealed, not even fastened with the clasp, and when I turn it over its contents spill right out on the comforter. Tied up in a silk ribbon is a set of official papers, dated July 6, 1947, and certifying that Frances Elizabeth Brandshagen married Louis Junod on this day at St. Edmund RC Church on Ocean Avenue in Brooklyn. They are artifacts, fossils, the past they signify so distant they should crumble in my hand, a treasure from King Tut's tomb exposed to light. But in fact they are unsettlingly well-preserved, not just unsullied but seemingly untouched, as crisp as a freshly minted dollar bill. I slip them back into the loop of the ribbon, afraid that I have already left my fingerprints upon them.

The second manila envelope is different, because so many fingerprints are already on it, presumably my mom's, that it looks like one of my dad's reflectors, his tanning oil finding an equivalent in my mother's cold cream. It also has more stuff in it, more papers, which spill out as haphazardly as Mom put them in. There is nothing official here, nothing sacred and wrapped in ribbon. There are just articles and columns clipped out of the women's magazines, along with some pamphlets distributed by Nassau County and the Diocese of Rockville Centre about mental health. I begin to read them with idle curiosity, as if they are just more recipes for "the roast with the most" and "the no-cook spaghetti sauce that tastes like it took all day." But the more I read, the more I feel I've stumbled upon my mother's diary, a compendium of secrets she has declined to share even with her best friends. I know I've hit the jackpot because I think of stopping, but don't; because I continue against my own best interests. Mom didn't write them, of course; they are written by doctors and psychiatrists who aspire to a tone of genial authority and take great pains to assure their readers that everything will work out in the end. What disturbs me is their unifying theme, the simple fact that Mom took the time to cut them all out. If the headlines all ask provocative questions, she, with her scissors and sometimes even her pinking shears, has already answered them: "IS YOUR BOY . . . A CRYBABY?" "IS YOUR SON . . . HIGH STRUNG?" "IS YOUR CHILD . . . TOO SMART FOR HIS OWN GOOD?"

And yet I don't catch on right away. My body does; my heart beats, my ears ring and my fingertips tingle. But I manage to read impersonally, almost objectively, until I open one of the pamphlets from the diocese, with advice on how to raise a Catholic family. Though it's not a comic book, it contains illustrations of a crew-cut boy in a striped shirt and his sister in pigtails. I flip right open to a page my mother has earmarked, the page where the pamphlet urges Catholic parents to present a united front in the matter of child-rearing. It must be good advice, because my mother has underlined a passage that says parents who argue about their children risk confusing them about their role in the family and "even society at large." In the illustration, the father, in a suit and tie, commands his son to go to his room while his mother beckons him with open arms. The boy is trapped inside a cocoon of elliptical lines that suggest he is spinning; he has multiple faces, and a comic-book-style thought balloon rises above his head in the shape of a cloud: "I wish they'd make up their minds! They make me feel like . . . a human football!"

I close the pamphlet, and stuff it back into the manila envelope along with the clippings. I put them back in my mom's nightstand drawer with the forensic care I usually reserve for my father's dirty books and magazines. I have always felt obliged to choose sides, when I enter my parents' bedroom or fall down into their bed, with a second sight for the invisible borders that crisscross the divided territory. I am a sneak who has fancied himself a spy or even a double agent, on my mother's behalf. But now I can claim allegiance to neither principality and find refuge on neither side of the bed. They *both* have secrets, and I feel both of them growing inside me, as my own:

My father's secret is, of course, sex.

My mother's secret is me, the human football.

There's a commercial that's always on TV. It's for something called Radio Free Europe, and it shows, in black and white, a kid on the other side of the Iron Curtain listening to "On Broadway," by the Drifters, a song from the free world that's otherwise forbidden to him. It stops me in my tracks, because I know how he *feels*—because I have secret songs whispering from my own radio in my own room, Radio Free Wantagh. I'm in the middle of discovering "free-form" FM radio and thinking myself too cool for AM, but I can't quite kick the habit of listening to WABC from New York City, with its antic deejays and fifty-two-pickup playlists that juxtapose the Carpenters and the Temptations, the Doors and the solemn stately divorced-woman reverie of "One Less Bell to Answer." When I listen to FM radio, I can hear the Doors and Led Zeppelin and Crosby, Stills, Nash & Young, but I can't hear the Temptations and "One Less Bell to Answer" and "Rainy Night in Georgia" and all the weird country songs like "Funny Face" and "Rose Garden" that my mother sings to herself while she's washing the dishes and that remind me of how lonely she is. But my "On Broadway" is a song I hear on both AM and FM, a song I seem to hear every time I turn on the radio precisely because it's telling me what I'm not supposed to hear—"Sunshine" by Jonathan Edwards. It sounds harmless enough, a catchy folk song with a singalong chorus. And yet in that chorus there's something contraband, an inkling of revolt and freedom. Could Jonathan Edwards be singing what I think he's singing? "How much does it cost? I'll buy it! The time is all we've lost—I'll try it! He can't even run his own life, I'll be damned if he'll run mine . . ." I can't precisely articulate the message but I find myself turning the song up when I'm alone, turning it down when I'm with my mom, and turning it off completely when my father's home. It's a summery song released in winter, so that I always seem to hear it when my room has grown dark and the radio feels more like a source of light than sound, and on one of those dark afternoons my mother comes into the room when "Sunshine" is playing, as if she too is drawn to it. She sits down on the bed next to me.

"You like this song, don't you?"

"Yeah, I guess so."

"I do too," she says.

How much does it cost, I'll buy it! The time is all we've lost, I'll try it! He can't even run his own life . . .

She takes my hand in hers, and pats it. "I know it's hard," she says.

I don't say anything. I just look at her, her blue eyes shining as the winter takes away the light.

"I know *he's* hard," she says, to clarify. But there is no need. I understood as soon as she said "I do too." She stops patting my hand and grips it instead. She has my attention; now she wants to hold it. She doesn't speak until I am looking directly into her eyes.

"He does the best he can," she says. "He works so hard and *he does . . . the best . . . he can.*" It's a plea on his behalf and a confession on hers, though I understand what she's pleading far more than I understand what she's confessing. And then it happens: I wince and so does she; my face crumples, and so does hers. We fall against each other, our shoulders heaving, the last two people in the world, the only two people in the world, the only two people in the world who *know.*

I have seen him make her sob. She has seen him make me sob. But we have never sobbed together, over him, over our common . . . well, what? Our common enemy? How can we call him that when we are both crying over our love for him, when we are both acknowledging for the very first time our helplessness in the face of it? And yet the gravity of the moment, the electricity of the moment, makes me realize something, makes me resolve something: I have to survive. I *will* survive, although my mother is telling me she can't help me.

8

Here's the one thing I believe about myself: I don't give up. I have been in love with the same girl from the moment I laid eyes on her freshman year. Her name is Maura, a two-syllable Dickensian plea. She is dark haired and Irish—like my father, I apparently have a type. Unlike my father, I am loyal, if only to an ideal. I strive for constancy . . . no, *fidelity.*

That I am in love with a girl, however, is not to say that she is my girlfriend. I have never had a girlfriend. I have never kissed a girl, and so I have never kissed Maura, never called Maura, never asked her out. I just follow her around. I memorize her class schedule so that I manage to run into her when the bell rings. I stay after school when she goes to volleyball practice and try to sit close to her at basketball games. I hold her phone number in my head the way the kids on the math team hold on to formulas and equations, and night after night I dial six of its digits and keep my finger frozen over the decisive seventh. That finger never moves.

Does she know about me—how I feel about her? She must, because of my dogged omnipresence. But I hide my lonely passion for her in the interest of preserving our friendship, which I regard as the commensurate achievement of my four years in high school. I can talk with her, as a friend. I can study with her, as a friend. I can even, as a friend, sign up with her for a religion class on the subject of "marriage and sexuality" without revealing myself as a stalker and a creep.

It is one of those classes that is a trademark of Holy Trinity Diocesan High School in the 1970s—a religion class that is the product of Vatican II, and so heavier on throw pillows and beanbag chairs than it is on Catholic dogma. The teacher, a fugitive from the seminary, wears ribbed earth-tone turtlenecks, plaid polyester slacks and Granny glasses; we sit on the floor, "in the round," and try our best to abide by the spirit of "the encounter group" as he asks probing questions and offers the terrifying assurance that he requires nothing of us but our honesty.

I lie. I lie the way I lie when I go to confession. I have to lie, because although I signed up for the class as an exercise in voyeurism, I also took it as a kind of anthropological study of my classmates. I am desperate to find out about them as a way of finding out about me—how abnormal I am. And what I have discovered, to my horror, is that I am the only student in the class who is not in a relationship. I am the only student in the class who has never had sex, much less never been kissed. I am a stalker and a creep, and so I make up a girlfriend, a doomed summer love from the beach in Westhampton. I even give us a song, our song, hoping that Maura will somehow realize the Spinners' "I'll Be Around" is actually *her* song, a profession of my stubborn and eternal resolve.

Then one day our teacher asks not about us but about *them:* "How do you feel about the fact that your parents are still having sex?" The question, he says, is meant to be provocative, is meant to make us feel uncomfortable, but as he makes his way around the circle, one of the boys says that he found his father's condoms in the sock drawer and one of the girls says that she has heard her parents, behind closed doors, "going at it." Maura says that while she might not like thinking about her parents' sex life, she accepts that they probably have one. "And what about you, Tom?" our teacher says.

"My parents don't have sex," I answer.

There is a slight rustling, a suppressed giggle, from the other side of the circle. "Oh, sure they do, Tom," the teacher says, with gentle understanding. "Listen, it's very hard to look at our parents as people, but really, they're just like you and me—they're human, and humans have sex. That's what we are, Tom, sexual creatures . . ."

"No, I don't think so," I say, the circle starting a queasy spin. "Well, maybe my dad does—" I stop short. Did I just say what I think I said?

"You don't know that, Tom. You'd be surprised at the lives your parents have when you're not around."

But of course I do know, because I know about the briefcase. I know about the dildos and the degrading porn and I know, with a sense of relief, that they have nothing to do with my mother. I just can't say what I know, what I've learned, what I've discovered, and so I just sit shaking my head until our teacher grows a little frustrated.

"Why are you so certain?"

I look at him. I look at Maura, I look at everyone. "Well, you see, my dad, he's this really charismatic guy, he's very flashy, he wears a gold dog tag, and my mom, she's very . . ."

"Conservative?" the teacher asks, with a smile.

"Yes, conservative. That's it."

"Well, just remember that looks are deceiving, and you never know what's going on inside a marriage from the outside." He claps his hands together and says, to the rest of the class, "And that goes for everybody . . ."

I can breathe again, because I think I've given him, and he's given me, the great gift of . . . an out. But after he dismisses the class, he's waiting for me by the door. "Tom," he says, "is there anything you'd like to talk about?"

Actually there are a few things. I'd like to talk about the fact that my sexuality, as it now exists, is determined by the contents of my father's briefcase. I'd like to talk about how when one of the old nuns brought a busload of Trinity students into New York City at the end of our junior year for a day of cultural enrichment, I snuck off with my friend Jack to watch *Behind the Green Door* at the World Forty-Ninth Street. I'd like to talk about how before I've even kissed a girl I've seen Marilyn Chambers suspended on a trapeze servicing four men at once, and how, even now, at this very moment, there's a matchbook from the notorious Jade East Hotel, with its daily newspaper advertisements of circular beds, mirrored ceilings and adult movies, stashed in the drawer where my father keeps his cuff links and his Sen-Sen, and I know this is true because I make it my business to *check*.

"No thanks," I say. "I'm fine."

"Well, if you ever need to talk . . ."

But by that time I'm already in the hallway, alone among the crowds of red-blooded Catholic school kids headed for class and well on my way to the parking lot, where I ready myself for football practice by getting apocalyptically wasted.

There are people waiting for me outside the locker room. I know this because my teammates tell me, and because I know who they are. My parents have come to all my games even as I dutifully sat the bench. My brother encouraged me to play quarterback even when I couldn't throw a football ten yards. My pal Jack caught passes from me all summer. They want to congratulate me, I know. But I just sit there in front of my locker. Most of my teammates have dressed and gone. But I'm barely out of my uniform. Maybe I just want to make this improbable moment last.

I've been playing football for Holy Trinity for four years. I play quarterback because I can throw a football, but I'm skinny and I'm slow and I can count my time on the field not in games but in *plays,* one in freshman year, five as a sophomore, thirty or forty as a junior. I began my senior year as the fourth-string quarterback, and the coach pulled me aside after a practice and urged me to quit because he was never going to let me play. I refused. But he is as good as his word, and the only time I have the occasion even to stand up during games is when I warm up the other quarterbacks on the sideline. It's a mixed blessing, because when I come home I have to listen to my father's advice: "Take your helmet off on the sideline! Let people see your face! What are you covering up for? Don't you want the girls to see you? I saw some beauties in the stands today—and take it from me, lad, I *know* . . ."

Then there's a surprise. We were supposed to be a good team. The surprise is that we stink. We're undersized and half the team shows up to practice high and we put up such scant resistance that the coach delivers unhinged halftime harangues comparing us to history's most notorious cowards and turncoats. With the season two-thirds over, we fall behind 35–0 in our homecoming game and in the second quarter the coach grabs me and says, "You might as well go in." I've thrown three passes in three and a half seasons at Holy Trinity but now I throw for a couple of touchdowns and I even scramble for a first down, and when the game ends the score is 43–12 but I'm the starting quarterback of my high school football team. I have been so depressed I have prayed to God not to let me commit suicide. I have been so deeply into drugs I have prayed for Him not to let me use heroin. Now I stay in the locker room wondering if my prayers have been answered but also discovering that my fondest hopes about myself might actually be true: I really *don't* give up. The people who love me are outside waiting but a part of me needs to be alone, if only to outlast them.

When I finally open the big steel locker room door and step outside, the field has cleared, and there's hardly anyone left, anywhere. But three people still wait for me. The first is a nun who taught me Spanish as a freshman and must have seen something in me, because now she's clutching her hands together and saying, "Oh, I've been waiting for this day!" The second is my brother, who says, "What did I tell you, when I took you to the field and you couldn't throw the ball ten yards? I said, 'Mark my words. Mark my words . . .' "

And the third is Maura.

The faucet runs behind his bathroom door. The hair dryer grunts and exhales. The tall black can of Consort hair spray hisses. The tiny chrome scissors snip and snap. He begins to sing "Peg o' My Heart," knowing the girl I'm taking out on a date is Irish. The door opens with a gust of steam and spray and fragrance. He's standing behind the sink in black bikinis and black socks and it looks like he's the one with a big night ahead, while I sit on the edge of his bed waiting to use his shower. The flag-sized yellow towel from the Diplomat Hotel lies in a crumpled pile at his feet.

"Son, I have a question," he says.

"Okay . . ."

"Have you ever . . . cleaned your navel?"

"My *what*?"

"Your navel, your navel. Have you ever cleaned it?"

"No, Dad. Why would I ever clean my navel?"

"You're becoming a man, Tommy. Next year you'll be in college. You're going to be with women, and you don't want to risk turning one off with an . . . offensive odor."

"Dad . . . ," I say, because once again I know he's not talking about my mother.

"Just watch." He finds a Q-tip and a brown plastic bottle. "This is witch hazel," he says. "All you have to do is dip the Q-tip in the witch hazel and then swab it around your navel for *a full minute.*" He proceeds to follow his own instructions to the letter, counting off the seconds on his wristwatch. "*Capisce?* Listen to your father. You'll thank me one day . . ."

It is my first date. I take my shower and dress in a sweater and corduroys, conscious that my navel remains criminally unswabbed. I listen to "Moondance" five straight times in my room, then say good night to my parents. My father cups his hand on my shoulder and walks me to the door. "This girl you're taking out . . . I've heard you mention her name. You like her, don't you?"

"I do."

He reaches in his pocket for his solid-gold money clip, the one he carries instead of a wallet. He licks his thumb, then peels off five twenty-dollar bills and presses them into my palm. "Here's a hundred dollars," he says. "Enjoy yourself."

It's another of those moments of truth my dad talks about. But I must get . . . the apple. Everything is a little off. Even gravity is a little off, because I can barely keep my feet—in Maura's presence I feel buoyant as the astronauts hop-stepping around the moon but at the same time I act like some sort of stumblebum. I spill the popcorn I buy her at a showing of *One Flew Over the Cuckoo's Nest* and not only spill my drink at the restaurant where I spend my father's money but also knock over my chair. She doesn't laugh; she smiles with a bemused tolerance, because she can't possibly miss that I'm off-balance from adoration. Now I'm standing in her kitchen—when I dropped her off, she invited me in—and leaning against the sink as I talk to her parents. I drink from a glass of orange juice and begin to relax just enough to shift my weight, just enough to uproot the little mat on which I stand. It goes flying, and so do I, executing a silent-movie pratfall of such perfection that not only do I end up on the floor, the liquid in my glass ends up on the ceiling. I look up at three astonished faces as OJ rains down on my head. And yet Maura must either feel sorry for me or find me harmless enough to be endearing. I don't get a kiss out of it. But I get a second date.

This time, I resolve to kiss her good night. My father has bought a brand-new red MG so that girls will like me but I leave it in the garage because I don't want Maura to think I'm on the make and I spend a lot of time on the joint I roll, getting it just right. I take her to a wine bar on the North Shore of Long Island and when we're finished with our fondue and Blue Nun and head out to my mother's Buick I light the joint with the Jade East matches. She takes a hit and she coughs as though she's inhaled a hornet and doesn't stop until tears fill her eyes. "That's strong *stuff,*" she gasps, and after a few minutes she begins to look at me funny, like I've slipped her a mickey. As I drive her home, she slides away from me on the bench seat and then she keeps on going, ending up pressed against the door and staring out the window when she's not looking askance back at me. The radio plays, but it offers only a soundtrack for the relentless waves of silence, and I begin to wonder if she somehow knows not only who but what I am—if I've said something in Marriage and Sexuality that revealed the terrible things I've seen in the tainted light of my father's projector. "Would you like to go someplace else?" I hear myself asking.

"No, I just want to go home."

"Can I walk you to the door?"

"No, I'll be fine."

I watch her walk up the little concrete path to her house and use a key to turn the lock and her hip to push the door open. I wait but she does not look back before the door closes. When I reach the parkway, I think for the first and only time in my life of driving off the road but instead I content myself with repeating "What did I do, what did I do, what did I do, what did I do, what did I do?" over and over again. There is no answer, and as soon as I reach Wantagh I pull into the little side street that leads to St. Francis de Chantal school. I park the car and turn it off. Then I squeeze my right hand into a fist and punch myself as hard as I can in the jaw. I beat my fucking face in, until I can taste blood where a kiss was supposed to be.

My father's good to my friends. He kids with them. He gives them advice. He's tolerant and easygoing. He takes an interest in their lives and he asks for their opinions. The same maxims he drills into me he repeats to them, all in an effort to make them men. They get a kick out of him. They all think he's a great guy. One or two even wonder why their dads aren't like my dad, as openly affectionate and fun, and try following his example.

And yet, at the same time, he's suspicious of them. He's not suspicious about their drinking and their drug use—what he should be suspicious about—but rather about their sexuality. When they come out to Westhampton and we go walking the beach after dark in search of bonfires and parties, my father will call out as we leave: "You boys better come back with some chippies or I'm going to start to wonder! You can't tell me that it's *normal* for three guys to be out on the beach alone at night!"

The one friend about whom he harbors no suspicions is Jack, because he not only has a lot of girlfriends but sometimes brings them to our house. He and my father talk like confidants, and one day when Jack visits the house and I'm out with my mom, my father takes him aside. "I'm thinking of buying Tommy a hooker for his eighteenth birthday. What do you think?"

"No," Jack says, almost involuntarily.

"No?"

"No—not *that*. He doesn't need *that*."

"So what does he need then?" my father asks in exasperation.

There is no answer, only a confirmation. My father likes my friends. He's good to my friends. He's only suspicious of my friends to the degree that he is suspicious of me.

On the weekend of my high school graduation, a car pulls into the driveway in Westhampton. It's full of friends. But they are not my friends from Holy Trinity, who for the most part are attending parties of their own. They're friends I've met in the woods of Wantagh, smoking weed. They're friends I've dropped acid with. They're friends who showed me where Wantagh's most selective drug dealer lives, just around the block from 1463 Britton Street. My parents are suspicious of them because, for one thing, they barely know them. My parents are *pissed* at them because they didn't just bring secret stashes of the drug dealer's high-quality product to our beach house.

They brought the drug dealer's girlfriend.

Her name is Kathy. She is twenty-four years old, studying to be a nurse. She dresses like a hippie—in a gauzy blouse, cutoffs and sandals—but she's an adult and she carries herself as such. She has a certain hardness about her, especially in regard to my parents. I know we are in trouble when my father doesn't flirt with her, my mother speaks to her in a put-on voice and she doesn't help my mother in the kitchen. All day long my mother and father exchange concerned glances and by the end of the day the glances my father exchanges with me are on fire, as the fundamental question in their minds stays unspoken but becomes more consuming by the second: where is this girl—this *woman*—going to sleep?

They stay up later than usual, putting off the inevitable. Then at nine o'clock my mom shows Kathy to the guest room inside the main house rather than to a bed in the bunkhouse, where I'll be sleeping with my friends. She uses her poshest voice to tell Kathy that there's a freshly made bed and a stack of clean towels and she sounds like a matron in a home for unwed mothers.

Kathy refuses. She comes out to the bunkhouse and says that she'd rather sleep in the car than sleep in a house with two people who look at her the way my parents do. She turns to me with a scornful laugh: "What do they think is going to *happen* if I stay out here with you guys?" I decide to go in and ask. It's late at night, I've been high all day and I'm tired. I go into my parents' bedroom. The black-and-white TV is on, its bleaching light finding the disconsolate image of my mom in bed, her face shiny with cold cream and tears. But my father is still in his clothes, his sweater and slacks, and he's jiggling a highball, alert and on the prowl.

"Kathy doesn't want to sleep in the guest room," I say.

"Where . . . does she want to *sleep*?" my father asks.

"With us."

My mother begins to sob.

"Look what you've done," my father says. "You've made your mother very upset."

"But I don't understand. What does she think is going to happen?"

My father puts down his drink on the TV table and moves toward me, just a step. "Don't play dumb . . . with *me*," he says. "What do you *think* she thinks is going to happen?"

It hits me then, the reason for their anxiety and their distaste. For a moment I want to laugh, but instead I plead with her. "Mom, it's not like that. I'm not like that. Not everyone is like *Dad*—"

He slaps me across the face. All my life he's been bragging he doesn't hit me—he doesn't have to—so now the lack of precedent is more violent than the blow. It's what makes me dizzy. It's what makes me cry. I go outside to the deck and want to run down to the ocean on the other side of the dune. I can hear it and I can smell it, the salty breath of the booming waves. I can also taste the slap, the taste proof that it really happened. Did he really hit me? Is it possible? I don't want to believe it but I also don't want to forget and I know I'll have to find the mental force to keep the memory from slipping away like a dream or like a secret.

I don't go back to the bunkhouse. I don't want them to see my tears and more than anything I don't want Kathy to know what my parents suspected. Then there's a creak, and the popgun sound of the screen door slamming shut. My father's outside. He walks up to me and I fall against him, his hand coming up behind my head, his fingers curling around the scruff of my neck. He pulls me toward him and holds me there until I stop crying and begin to breathe. "I'm sorry," he says. "But I couldn't let you talk like that to your mother." He puts both his hands on my shoulders and takes a step back, considering me in the dark. Then he pushes the wet hair that has fallen in my face off to the side, combing it with his fingers. "If your mother wasn't here I wouldn't give a damn what you did with that girl," he says. "You know I was a young man once too."

"But we're not going to *do* anything, Dad."

"Just promise me one thing."

"Dad, we're not going to *do*—"

"Promise me you guys all have . . . protection."

I'm not even sure what to say. I wonder if he's crazy. But I know for sure there's no budging my parents off their certainty that once they go to sleep a gang bang will ensue in the bunkhouse.

"Sure, Dad, we've got it all taken care of," I say, and, still dizzy from the slap, I kiss him good night.

Many years later, I will find proof of where my father goes in the summer of 1976, and the plans he was making to change our lives together. But all I register at the time is a change in how he treats *me*. My father and mother still spend time in Westhampton, but I stay home because I have a night job washing dishes at a restaurant in Jones Beach and I am not only doing a lot of drugs; I'm *reading* about drugs, spending day after day studying the impossible canon of Carlos Castaneda in the seclusion of my room in Wantagh. In the middle of July, Dad does something he generally only does in August, turning his back on the allure of 879 Dune Road and traveling to Florida. When he comes home, he drinks a lot, and one afternoon I hear him go down to the kitchen and fix himself a cocktail, maybe two, a couple of pops. Then he opens the door of my bedroom. He is shirtless and swaggering, wearing only his white ducks, his body scandalously dark. He is biting his lip.

"What are you doing today?" he asks.

"What am I doing?"

"You heard me. What . . . are you *doing*?"

"I don't know, Dad. Nothing, I guess."

"You *guess*?"

I sit up, something in his tone. "Yeah, Dad, I guess . . ."

"No, Tommy, I *know*. You're going to do nothing today. And do you know how I know?"

"No, Dad."

"Because that's what you do every day—nothing. And do you know why you do nothing every day?"

"No, Dad."

"Because you *are* a nothing. A big nothing. How do you like that?"

"I don't know, Dad."

"You don't *know*?" He begins walking around the room, touching things, my books, my magazines, my clock, my desk lamp, my stereo. I have a nice stereo, a monster. He bought me my nice stereo for my high school graduation and now he extends a brown finger and runs it along the plastic cover of the turntable. He stares offended at the dust on his fingertip.

"When are you going to clean your room? I bet you don't know that either."

"I don't."

"Do you know why?"

"Because I'm a nothing?"

He steps toward me now, a green glee in his eyes. "No," he says. "Because you're . . . a zero."

I don't answer.

"How do you like that?"

"I don't," I say.

"A big . . . zero," he says, with a leer.

I stand up.

"Oh," he says. "*Now* you're up."

We are both standing in the middle of the room. He assumes a kind of stance, cocky, with his shoulders at an angle and his chin thrust out. He bobs his head. "You want to hit me, don't you?"

"No, Dad."

"Zero," he says, wagging his chin at me.

"I'm not a zero," I say.

"Ze-*roooooo*," he sings, he croons.

"No!"

He closes the forefinger of his right hand upon the thumb, forming a circle. He offers it to me, right in front of my face, with the goading instinct of a matador. "Ze-*roooooo* . . ."

"No, Dad. You're wrong."

"Come on. You want to hit me, I can see it in your eyes. You can *taste* it. But you better make it good."

I am six foot tall and weigh 165 pounds. I have hung a heavy bag in the garage and every morning after I get high I go after it in a half-hour frenzy. I am in the best shape of my life. But I'm not angry at him. I feel something different, something new, something permanent, a discovery of sorts: coldness.

"I'm not going to hit you, Dad."

He shrugs his shoulders and waves a dismissive hand at me. "I didn't think so," he says. Then he shrinks. His shoulders slump as he turns his back and walks out of my room. For the last month he's had to live with hitting me out in Westhampton. He must have decided that I should live with hitting him back.

And then, a month later, he opens the door for the last time. He steps quietly into my room for the last time. He shakes my shoulder and wakes me for the last time. He sits on the edge of my bed for the last time, his shoulders hunched and his hands folded in front of him. It is the last time because I am leaving. So is he. I am leaving for college in a week. He is going to Florida for business and sticking Mom with the job of moving me. We are saying goodbye.

"So . . ."

I immediately perk up. His morning visits to my room have always been of consequence, whether he's dropping silver into the Paris fund or demanding that I swear on his life. But he will never visit me again in quite the same way or with quite the same ceremony and as soon as I open my eyes I realize that I've been waiting for this moment all week long, maybe all summer. I want him to say something and he has to say something—he's my father and he is under obligation to leave me with a parting word. But what will it be? Will he apologize for the fights we've been having all summer long? Will he leave me with some magic maxim that finally explains the secrets of manhood? Will he acknowledge that I'm not a zero after all? Will he give me his blessing?

"So . . . I guess this is it," he says. "My number two son is going to college. I'm sorry I can't take you. But I know Mom can handle it. She handles everything else."

"It's okay, Dad."

"I was never much of a student, so I don't know what to tell you about your studies and all that kind of stuff. You were always the brains of the family so you're going to do just fine. You're going to do just *great*."

"Thanks, Dad."

"But I have lived a little, so I want to leave you with some advice before I go."

My heart thumps involuntarily, like the tail of a dog whose master keeps speaking his name. After all these years and all those tears, here it is—the moment that will make it all worthwhile. He glances at the doorway to make sure my mother isn't standing in it. He lowers his voice and speaks to me man to man.

"Do yourself a favor and date a Jewish girl," he says. "They're all . . . nymphos."

I look at him, expecting a punch line, expecting him to laugh and tell me what he really means to say. But no. That *is* what he means to say. He tousles my hair and then kisses me hard on the forehead and when he stands up and walks to the top of the stairs and says, "Frances?" I know he's done with me. And here I've been thinking I'm leaving him. But he's been getting ready to leave me all along.

9

I'm so close. I'm almost there. I have just about everything I need. I have a firm handshake. I'm not afraid to look people in the eye. I have good manners. I open doors for women. I stay in shape. I can bodysurf. I can throw a spiral. I have a solid left jab. When some hood hassled my friend Chicky out in front of a bar, I stepped in and stopped him in his tracks with a right hand. Though I still don't clean my navel, I have absorbed my father's precepts about grooming and hygiene. I believe to my bones that a turtleneck is the most flattering thing a man can wear and despite the damage it's inflicted I believe there's almost nothing a little sun can't cure. I'm so close to becoming what my father taught me to be—a man. But I'm not a man, and not just because I'm still an eighteen-year-old boy. I'm not a man because I'm not my father.

I'm reminded of my failure every day, because now that I'm in college I'm also close to girls. I'm even close to Maura, my reward for never giving up. I kept following her even when I graduated from Holy Trinity and she went to the state college in Oneonta, New York. How close is she? By some force of miracle, she lives down the hall and at night I can see the girl I worshipped and adored in her striped pajamas. But then I see lots of girls in their pajamas. I also see lots of girls brushing their teeth or hanging out in the hallway with their hair in curlers, because I live in a coed dorm. I *live* with girls now, and they live with me, including the Jewish girls my dad told me about. They come to my room at night to smoke my pot and listen to my stereo. They sprawl out on my bed in their Danskins and hip-huggers and the clogs they dangle from their toes. I don't know if they're nymphos or not. I never find out if they're nymphos or not because instead of making a move on them I debate with them, I contend with them, I lecture them, turning myself into an entirely new incarnation—the late-night dorm-room mystic, proclaiming eternal verities from my beanbag chair with a bubbling bong between my legs.

The bubbling of my roommate's bong wakes me at seven in the morning. If it were dinnertime, I'd take a hit. If it were nighttime, I'd take five, and then start quoting Carlos Castaneda. But I got stuck with an 8 a.m. class, so I refuse his standing offer and use the bong as an alarm clock instead. I wake up, get out of bed, take a shower and then head up the hill for my survey course in American literature. The teacher is a skinny middle-aged man who wears the same greenish tweed suit every day, the same white button-down shirt, the same narrow black tie, the same Hush Puppies and horn-rimmed glasses. He has a long face and a twitchy smile, and though he speaks passionately about the stories and poems he assigns us, his passion also causes him to look away from us—to look beyond us, as if at some distant prospect—so that the more desperate he seems for connection the less he actually connects. About half the class attends any given morning, and about half of the attendees fall asleep. And yet he continues speaking with undimmed enthusiasm for Jonathan Edwards and Charles Brockden Brown and Bret Harte and Ambrose Bierce and Hamlin Garland and the quizzical vocabulary of Emily Dickinson, until it becomes clear that his love for American literature has nothing to do with us—that he is as immune to us as we are oblivious to him. He gains stature with each squandered soliloquy, and after a while I admire him even more than I feel sorry for him. He's nothing at all like my dad. But in his slightly ridiculous fashion, he's just as much a man, and I never miss a class.

I do my reading in the study lounge of the dorm, until I get bored and make my nightly announcement: "I'm going to get stoned and read *Walden*." My friends chuckle but there's a girl reading at a desk who neither responds to my remark nor registers my existence. She's there every night and she's not only an English major; she has a *reputation* as an English major, her nose always in a book. She's a sophomore, very blond and so tall she slouches. She wears no makeup or lipstick or earrings or any of the jewelry so many of the girls wear, their names hanging from their necks in gold. Her name is Janet, Janet Folk, and she is the most American girl I've ever seen, beautifully plain and plainly beautiful, hippieish in affect but preppy in style, given to wearing Top-Siders and painter's pants and scavenged T-shirts of secret provenance, so white-bread she's almost exotic. She restricts her communications to the literary quotations she writes on the whiteboard that hangs on her door and is otherwise almost theatrically secretive, huddling cross-legged in the hallway with Curtis Hall's most effeminate boy, whispering into his ear through a cupped hand. "Pssss pssss pssss," I say when I pass them by. The only indication that she knows of my existence is her habit of shaking her head at my habit of leaving my Kalsø Earth Shoes behind in the study lounge and then returning late at night to retrieve them, the mystified mystic. One night I come back for my shoes wearing my high school football jersey and she is sitting alone reading a paperback with a cover illustration of a man wearing a varsity letter jacket.

"Is that book about, like, an *athlete* or something?"

She smiles indulgently. "Not really. It's John Updike."

"Who's John Updike?"

"He's a writer."

"Who's Rabbit Redux?"

"That's him, on the cover. But 'Redux' is not his last name."

"Looks like he played basketball. I was a football player."

"I *see* that," she says.

"Could I take a look at it?"

She hands it to me, her name already printed on the inside of the front cover, along with the number of her dorm room and home address. "Don't break the binding," she says.

"The what?"

"The binding. I don't like books with broken bindings."

"Oh," I say, and give the book back to her. "Maybe I'll read it one day."

For a few moments, she holds me in her firm regard, her eyes full of frank assessment. I think she's going to laugh, so I ask a question:

"How can you read a book without breaking the binding?"

—

I start stopping every day to read the quotations on her door. But the door stays closed. She is unapproachable, I decide. She is a snob and she's intimidating. Then one night her roommates forget her birthday and go downtown without her. Her daunting self-possession disappears, and I am part of the coterie of freshmen who seize the opportunity to comfort her. My pal Willie asks her to get high, and to my bewilderment he closes the door behind him when she follows him into his room. Willie is an unlikely swain for this American flag of a girl, his 110-pound body a balsa-wood airplane balanced by a nimbus of wild Hebraic hair. But the very impossibility of their pairing is what draws me and my friends to eavesdrop on the action by crouching close to the crack under the door. This, then, is how I impress Janet Folk: I am on my knees with my ear pressed to the ground when Willie opens the door and says, "You *children*." I go inside to smoke Thai stick from Willie's Pyrex bong, and sit across from Janet on another bed. She takes a hit and coughs savagely and when she finally stops I notice she's staring at me, her cheeks red and her gray eyes turning blue and her face as vivid as a sunset. I am flattered, at first; but her shoulders begin heaving and tears start streaming down her face. I want to reach out to her, this poor heartbroken girl. But then I realize she's not crying at all. She's laughing, and pointing, at me.

"You . . . ," she says, barely getting the word out.

"Yes?"

"Have the biggest . . ."

"Uh-huh?"

"Head," she finally announces, before collapsing sideways in a song of stoned belly laughs.

And yet . . . I don't give up. I keep trying to figure out a way to elicit a response from her that's not simply amusement and one night, when I see her in the study lounge, I decide to show her something I've written on assignment for freshman comp. It's an obituary. My teacher gave us a list of people we could memorialize and I chose the actor and cynic George Sanders because I remember my father disparaging him: "He committed suicide because . . . he was *bored*. The man was married to Zsa Zsa Gabor. How bored could he have been?" I write in ambiguous defense of him and hand her the two pages that were assigned as one. I watch her read and await her verdict.

"It's very . . . *different,*" she says, and I promise myself to write three pages next time.

I have this idea. I've been dropping acid for the last six months and every time I do I see the world tilted at a different angle, spinning at a different speed. The first time I dropped acid the sunset seemed to last three hours and to leave everything I saw awash in beneficence. I feel not only free when I'm tripping, but free from what has bound me, in a very specific way. I have always wondered what I'd be like if I hadn't been my father's son. I have always wondered what I *was* like, before he made me cry. Now I know. A single dose and I feel like Adam before the fall, no longer the child of Lou but a child of God.

So my idea is simply one of magnitude. My father has a little hideaway in Florida, a little apartment in Hallandale Beach he shares with a divorced salesman. My brother lived there awhile, when he was a lifeguard after college. My father hasn't been making much use of it lately, so during Christmas vacation of my first year in college I decide to use it for a psychedelic sojourn with some of my friends. I've dropped a little acid and I felt better about being my father's son. My idea is that if I drop a *lot* of acid I might be completely cured of being my father's son.

It does not work out as I expect. I indeed drive with my friends to Hallandale Beach for New Year's. And I take plenty of acid. But I have a bad trip, and so does a dear friend. Instead of seeing God, we see the devil, and instead of feeling shriven, we feel damned. I go back to school; my friend does not and at the start of second semester, I am still trying to get the *sound* out of my ears, the infernal sound we heard in Florida. If I listen closely, I don't hear the wind and I don't hear the birds; I hear the sound of the universe eating a hamburger. To drown it out—to keep myself from going crazy—I make a ritual of meditating in my dorm room, pronouncing the divine syllable "om" as an alternative to the grumbling of cosmic peristalsis. It is a success, in that I don't lose my mind. It is a catastrophe, in that I wonder if I'm going to lose my friends.

One night, I hear them laughing on the other side of the door, so

I open it. I like them, but *they* didn't see the devil; I go to the phone to call the friend who did—who was there, who heard, who saw. But his mother answers. She's crying, and she immediately begins grilling me about the drugs we took in Florida. I hear panic in her voice, then bent notes of terror and grief. "What's happened?" I ask, and when she tells me I can hear her shaking. She has no control of her voice and I finally understand a word I've come across in English class, "caterwaul." While I went back to school, her son went mad. He tried to kill his father with a shotgun.

I stagger back to my room and my friends are all drinking beer and sitting around the great tall bong. And just like that, it's all over—my spiritual discipline, my psychedelic resolve. I haven't drunk a beer in months. I drink one now. I haven't taken a bong hit since I met the devil on a fishing pier. I take one now. I have no idea what happens next, only that I am out of ideas and excuses. I have to figure out a way to be a man by becoming a human being.

A few weeks later, when everyone on my floor decides to head downtown for St. Patty's Day, I go with them. It's a big crowd, drinking green beer at a bar called Abner Doubleday's, and I find myself talking to that tall blond English major from down the hall, Janet Folk.

I have nothing to say except what I'm afraid to—that I had a bad trip and a friend of mine tried to kill his father and then some cops—so out of habit I lay some of my old lysergic schtick on her. I tell her that if we look inside ourselves we will find a universe that is as infinite as the universe we see when we stand under the stars at night, and to my shock she doesn't get up and leave. She waits me out, listening even as the crowd starts to thin. But I see, and feel, a change: at first her friends are leaving for another bar; then they're leaving so that we can be alone. Finally the bar is nearly as empty as my head-shop platitudes, and we are sitting there with our knees touching and then pressing together. "What I want to know," she says, "is where the universe *ends*."

And that's how the universe begins.

We go to one more bar and another and then the bars are closing and the buses back to campus have stopped running and we might be the last students downtown. We have no choice but to walk, though we have already chosen, the quiet residential streets of Oneonta all ours. We don't hold hands, but we keep on bumping into each other, hip to hip. We are wobbling as we walk but not from the green beer. We walk waiting for the moment when we stop. Then a black cat emerges from an alleyway and crosses the street right in front of us and we both let out a breath—resignation, defiance—and start kissing. She smells like soap and her mouth tastes like spring water and her neck is long and the first place I touch is the virgin lobes of her ears and I kiss her so long and so hard that her blond hair grows tangled and wet. We have just a mile and a half to walk and a hill to climb before we are back to campus but our kissing is inexhaustible so our return takes hours, takes forever, just like a psychedelic sunset.

It snows the next day. I'm on a bus with her, in the back seat on the way home for spring break. The ride takes eight hours, and for some reason we try to hide from all our friends that we're an item. We play Geography with people from our dorm and she whispers answers in my ear when I'm stuck and though she has a high school boyfriend waiting for her at home I sound exactly like my dad when I think about him: He doesn't stand . . . a chance.

The bus pulls into Roosevelt Field in Westbury, Long Island, past midnight, and the only cars still in the parking lot belong to the patient parents who keep the engines running to keep themselves warm. Their headlights ignite as soon as the bus makes the turn and knots of moms and dads greet their returning children from a line that forms informally about ten feet away from the bus's door. There is, however, one man who doesn't wait, who ignores the other parents and stands right in front of the door, practically stepping inside. He's wearing ski pants and a ribbed mustard-colored turtleneck that forms the backdrop for his twenty-four-karat-gold dog tag and I can hear the intonation of his voice from the back of the bus—"Where is he? Where is . . . my *son*?" His effrontery blocks traffic, and as we stand stuck in the aisle Janet says, "Who is *this* guy?" I don't answer; I just walk up to him and register the shock on Janet's face when I say, "Hi, Dad."

—

I see her every day and every night. I see her every day because I'm working for my father in a handbag showroom on Fifth Avenue between Thirty-Third Street and Thirty-Second and she's working for a jeweler right around the corner. I see her every night because she's a South Shore girl who lives in Baldwin, four towns away from Wantagh on Sunrise Highway. I eat lunch with her in the city and then make out with her on park benches and in empty churches before I have to go back to work. I eat dinner with my parents on most nights but then I drive either my father's red MG or my mother's orange Camaro five miles to Baldwin and we play tennis together and make out until the car windows are opaque with steam.

All our friends call us "clingy" because we start kissing and pawing each other every time they turn around, and one day we're caught clinging in the lobby of 330 Fifth, where most American handbag companies keep their showrooms. The lobby is small but stately, with brass-faced elevator doors and marble floors and architectural columns lining the walls. I pull Janet into a little nook formed by one of the columns and in a second our tongues are in each other's mouths and the lobby falls away until we both register a shadow close by. We open our eyes and a woman is standing in front of us with her hands on her hips. It's my father's favorite showroom girl, Muntu, with her imposing height amplified by her Afro and her expression of amused disapproval. "*Tommy,*" she says. "This is not the place for that, this is a place of business. Show some respect!" She walks off, looking back and shaking her head as she enters the elevator. About an hour later, my father returns to the showroom after an extended lunch and summons me with a curled finger. "I hear you made quite a spectacle of yourself in . . . the *lobby,*" he says.

"Who told you?"

"Never mind who told me. I *know.* And I have a tip that'll save you a lot of trouble."

"What's that, Dad?"

"Be *discreet,* my son," he says, and then chucks me in the cheek with the edge of his hand, so I can feel his pinky ring.

But I'm not discreet, not about Janet—I want everyone to know. I have a girlfriend and that changes everything, even my relationship with my mother. For so many years . . . for just about all my life . . . I have been her comfort and confidant and she has been mine. But now I can't wait to get away from *them,* which means I also can't wait to get away from her, and she can see it, my recalcitrance, just as I can see her resignation. I catch her trying to be brave when I leave the house, but I can see her shoulders slumping, just as they do when my father mistreats her. He sees it too. "Hey, why don't you stay in tonight," he says one night after dinner. "We've hardly seen you since you came home from school."

"Dad, I see you every day. I work for you."

"That's not what I mean and you know it. Look at your mother. She cooked for you special and you don't even say thank you. Why don't you stay tonight and watch TV with us. It would mean the world to Mom."

"I'm going to see Janet."

"Oh, I know where you're going. But one night's not going to kill her."

"Lou," my mother says, a warning and a plea, and though she's trying to make peace my father's lips tighten and his eyes flare.

"Stay out of this, Frances," he says, and when he turns back to me he looks oddly boyish and eager. "You come and go like you rule the roost. You take the car, you don't even ask."

"Mom, can I take the car?"

"Sure, Tom," she says, but with a quaver in her voice.

"You're going to be a wiseass now?" my father says. "I don't like wiseasses."

"That is well established."

"What did you say?"

"I said you don't like wiseasses."

"And this is what I say: you're not going anywhere. You call up your girlfriend and you tell her you're staying home tonight with . . . your mother and father."

I stand up and look at my mother, the big tears about to spill from her eyes. "I'm sorry, Mom, but I have to go. I'll see you—" But I don't finish the sentence. She reaches for my hand and my father says, "You sit back down or I'll knock you down."

I fall back into the chair, as if on command, as if suddenly I weigh four hundred pounds. There is a terrible weight on every bone in my body and I feel that even if I get up I'll move in slow motion. The only way to escape that weight is to speak. But when I open my mouth, my voice is not heavy, it's light and fast and furtive—it's *high*.

"Why are you so mean to Mom?"

"Mean to Mom? What are you *talking* about?"

Nothing sounds as it should. My voice, his voice—they're not coming from our mouths, it's as though the room itself is speaking and I am watching myself from a slight remove.

"Look at her! You're always mean to her! You're always mean to me! You're mean to everyone!"

I am suddenly where I have never been. I expect him to hit me—I expect to be blown to pieces by the forces I've unleashed. But his eyes are cold but docile, and his hands stay put, and I cannot stop the words from coming, they pour from me in a spill of salt and snot and tears. I have been thinking about this moment since I was born but now that it is upon me it is nothing at all like I imagined. I have neither dignity nor eloquence; I am shrieking and blubbering, and my voice is a lapdog's bark.

"You treat me like dirt! You've treated me like dirt all my life! You treat Mom like dirt! You treat us all like dirt!"

Like *dirt*? I hear the words I'm speaking and a part of me knows I'm missing my chance, it's not what I wanted to say. But I can't stop saying it and I can't stop crying and my mother's face is wet and my father hasn't moved and I stand up and I snatch the keys from the hook and I kiss my mother on her forehead and I turn my back on them and I hear my father saying "Come *back*" but it's not an order, it's a plea, and I run to the car and I drive to Baldwin in a single sobbing sprint along Sunrise Highway, making all the lights. Janet is at the door when I arrive, and she meets me on the sidewalk with her arms extended and I fall into her, saying, "I hate him, I hate him, I hate him, I hate him, oh God, I *hate* him." She is kissing me; I feel her hands on my shoulders and my back, and though I am crying so hard my face is *bubbling* I can hear the words she's whispering in my ear: "Oh, you love him—you love your big bad daddy."

I come home late, hoping to return to a house dark and silent. But I can see from the street that a single light burns somewhere inside, and when I open the door my father is sitting at the kitchen table in his striped bathrobe and glasses, reading a newspaper under the light hanging from the chain. He looks up when I enter and watches me walk straight to him and he accepts a silent kiss before I head upstairs. I am at the bathroom sink, brushing my teeth, and he opens the door and steps inside. "I have never treated you like dirt," he says. "I have *always* loved you."

"I know, Dad," I say, and with that he is never able to make me cry again.

I take Janet to my parents' bedroom when they're away in Westhampton. The yellow shag carpet, the multiple infinity signs of the ornate headboard, the wall-unit air conditioner the size of a Volkswagen, the Sony Trinitron that allows my parents to laugh together watching *The Honeymooners* before they sleep, the drawer in my father's dresser where he keeps his cuff links and his Chiclets and his matches, the photograph of Raquel Welch on the mirror of my father's closet, the brown Samsonite briefcase still lurking under the shelf like a giant snapping turtle, silent and secret and seething—I can't tell her what they all mean to me and I don't want to. We make love on the vast acreage of the bed, our bodies naked on the quilted satin comforter garish with purple, green and indigo orchids. I feel free in a way I never have, and when we are done we step into my father's shower. We stay under the water for a long time and then instead of drying her off with the yellow Diplomat towel I kiss every single drop of water from her long and golden body.

My parents surprise me the next day by coming home early. Janet is back in Baldwin, but I hear my father open the taps on the shower through the wall. He is singing. Then he stops. He goes through his ablutions and after a while he appears in my room, dressed in slacks and his cream-colored shirt with epaulets. Just a year ago, he walked into my room and called me a nothing and a zero. Now he seems ready to engage me again—but not to fight me. Something has taken the place of the anger he displayed that day, although he still makes the room feel very small, like a fighter adept at cutting off the ring. "There was some hair in the drain of the shower," he says. "*Blond* hair."

I don't answer. I wonder if he's going to congratulate me, shake my hand and welcome me into his fraternity.

He looks at his loafers, then back at me, imploringly.

"I know you like this girl," he says.

"I do, Dad. I think I love her."

"Well, I'm a little more experienced in these matters and there's one thing that I need to tell you."

"What's that, Dad?"

"Chicken tastes pretty good until you've had . . . *steak*."

Janet is preparing to leave for college. She's not returning to Oneonta; she's transferring to Albany, and so as July turns into August I begin to understand that suddenly we are both facing the unknown. On a Saturday I take her out to dinner, and afterward we wind up going to the grounds of an old Gold Coast estate that has been transformed into a public garden. It's closed, but the gates are unlocked and we grab an army blanket from the trunk of the car and sneak onto the vast rolling lawn. We're scared. The sky is very dark and full of stars, and we spread out the blanket under the twinkling barbed canopy. Then something happens. The stars begin to move. They move, they dance, they put on a show, they fall. We have no idea what's happening, because we've never heard of the Perseid meteor shower; we just know that the sky looks full of fireflies, except they're stars, and they leave silver streaks that dissolve in the dark. At first we count them, but then we can't keep up and I hear Janet's involuntary "oooh" when there's an especially spectacular one, and as they leave tracks in the sky they also leave tracks on our bodies—we can feel their tingle, and on this night, they belong to us as we belong to them. *Where does the universe end?* Janet had asked, but now the universe is putting its signature on us, and after Janet falls asleep in my arms, I speak out loud, a prayer and an imprecation:

"Dad, you can eat all the steak you want. But you've never had a night like this, not once, not ever, not in your *life,* and you never will."

10

It's him.

Just as I knew as a small boy when he was up and about in the mornings, I know now that he's waking me up with a phone call. The phone in my room sounds the same as the rest of the phones in the house; there is nothing unusual or coded in the ring. But as soon as I hear it I know who's on the other end. True, I'm not going on anything more than a hunch. But he's not just calling; he's calling for *me,* and so the ring is somehow rife with insinuation, just like his voice.

"Did I . . . *wake* you?" he asks, when I pick up the phone.

"What time is it, Dad?"

"Ten o'clock. And here I was worried you'd already be at . . . the beach. What time did you come home?"

"Oh, about one o'clock."

"You dirty dog. You dirty stay-out. I hope you're not too tired to come into the city and spend the night with . . . your old man."

"Come into the city? Um . . ."

"What—you have to ask . . . the Boss?" He means Janet.

"It's not that, Dad. It's just . . ."

"You like Woody Allen, right? Isn't he . . . your *idol*?"

"Well, I don't know if I'd call him my idol. I just think he's funny."

"On Monday night, he plays jazz clarinet at a joint in town called . . . Michael's Pub."

"I know all about Michael's Pub, Dad."

"Your father has a table."

"Really? When?"

"What day is today?"

"Um, Monday?"

"Never underestimate your old man, son."

"Gee, Dad."

"Come to the showroom and we'll go out for a drink." He

pauses. "Just you and me. A night on the town, like . . . a couple of *bachelors*."

"Okay."

"Do you think Janet will . . . approve?"

"Dad."

"All right then. I'll see you at five. And, son?"

"What?"

"*Dress.*"

I see him before he sees me. I've come to town on the Long Island Rail Road, and walked from Penn Station to my father's showroom at 330 Fifth Avenue, just down the block from the Empire State Building. I spent the previous summer in that showroom, so its modesty comes as no surprise—the smell of cows and chemicals, leather and Scotchgard; the handbags hanging by their straps from the chrome wall fixtures; the stacks of order pads on the simulation butcher-block tables; the prints; the potted ferns. But then I peek around a corner to one of the small ancillary offices and stop short to behold a man in a pin-striped suit sitting at a desk with a pencil in one hand and a drink in the other. His legs are casually crossed, his pencil is moving over the racing pages of a newspaper, the ice in his drink is making alluring music, and his presence in this familiar place is what never fails to pack a wallop of surprise. My father is the only celebrity I've ever met, and yet he makes his living selling handbags.

"Dad . . ."

"Tommy!" he says, standing up and straightening himself, brushing off his lapels and adjusting his tie in a single autonomic gesture. He embraces me and kisses me so hard I can feel his knees quake and I can smell the amalgamated fragrance of his Lubriderm, Jean Naté and Consort, though not—though never—his sweat. Then he pushes me away by the shoulders and says, "Let me have a look at you." He studies me up and down, his white teeth set on edge. "I thought I told you . . . to dress."

"I am dressed."

"Where do you think I'm taking you—the library?"

He has a point. I am not dressed like him. I am dressed like my English teachers at Oneonta. I want so much to be hip I am willing to dress like a square. "I'm wearing the blazer you bought me," I protest, pulling at the lapels so he can see the brass buttons against the navy blue fabric.

"Yes, and it looks *great*. But what's on . . . your feet?"

"Shoes, Dad."

"What . . . kind of shoes?"

"Hush Puppies."

"Hush Puppies! You look like . . . a farmer. Well, when we get back to the hotel, you can try on a pair of *my* shoes. What's your size, eleven Charley?"

"I'm not going to wear your shoes, Dad."

"Tommy, Tommy, Tommy. I wanted you to see Woody Allen. I didn't want you to dress like him."

I don't have to ask the name of the hotel. He used to come home with hangers and towels imprinted with the names of many different Manhattan hotels, but now there is only one. The Essex House, on Central Park South, is where he stays whenever he goes to the city. It's where he . . . entertains. It's where the staff, according to my mother, "makes a big fuss over him," and where, now, they make a big fuss over me. The doorman, the bellman, the woman at the front desk—they all greet me not only as though they already know me but as though they already knew I was coming. There is something professional about their smiles, some sort of winking steeliness that makes them look like palace guards. They are kind to me. But they are in on it, I think. They know more about my father than I do. My father's briefcase comes with him to the Essex House. My mother doesn't, and never will.

Our room is on one of the upper floors, overlooking the park. I walk immediately to the window and sway, not simply because I am pressed up against the sky and the June-green rectangle of Central Park opens the horizon all the way to Westchester. I feel a little dizzy because all my life I've wondered what my father sees when he stays by himself in New York City—what it might be like to see the city through his eyes. Now I've found out, and its enormity knocks me back on my heels, like the ocean. He stands next to me, our shoulders touching. "Not bad, eh, son?" he says, then yanks me around to face him and drapes one of his wide ties around my neck. My head tilts back, and he begins tying the knot, with commentary. "The full Windsor is very *in,* but I'm just going to give you a regular four-in-hand. You can't wear a full Windsor with . . . a blazer."

"Why do I need a tie?"

"To get *in,*" he says, then stuffs a handkerchief in my breast pocket and lightly slaps each of my cheeks twice "to bring up the color." He studies me with his green gaze, and says, "Look at you! You look like a million bucks—you're going to knock 'em dead!"

We are both walking toward the door when he says, "You sure you don't want to change those shoes?"

We have gone from light—the 6 p.m. walk on Central Park South, with the sun blazing in the sunglasses of the beautiful women walking west—to dark, because right before we reached Fifth Avenue my father swung open an enormous oak door and nudged me inside. We're now in a bar, struck blind by the change. "Where are we, Dad?"

"You've heard of . . . the Plaza?"

"I think so."

"Well, you're in the Oak Room. What are you drinking?"

"I'll have a vodka gimlet."

He winces. "That's a *woman's* drink."

I don't want to tell him that he's right, that I never heard of a vodka gimlet until I met Janet. "Okay, how about a vodka tonic?"

"A vodka . . . tonic?" he asks, with a dash of disapproval. But he's just teasing, the way he used to tease at the dinner table. "You know, I was going to order a martini. But I'll have a vodka tonic with you. A great drink . . . for summer."

I watch him go to the bar. My eyes still have to adjust to the gloom, but he's returning to his natural habitat, and moves like a fish restored to the sea. Everything about him works in the dark. His tanned skin shines, his green eyes glow, his teeth match the white of his collar, his face seems to show only in profile, and the blue suit that appeared pedestrian in the daylight turns as black as the onyx on his pinky ring, its pinstripes deserving of the word he unfailingly uses to describe them—"chalk." "Hey, buddy," he sings to the bartender in a soft conciliatory accent that sounds almost

Southern, and returns with two astringent vodka tonics that smell, even here, like Westhampton.

"Salute," he says, and we touch glasses.

It is just as he promised: We are two bachelors, out on the town. And like two bachelors we act in concert, our heads simultaneously turning as we watch two women make their entrance. They are middle-aged, and both wear their hair up, revealing their necks and their baubled earlobes. Their hair is the same color, a rich chestnut with hints of red that pick up the flickering luster of the room like fine wine. Their cocktail dresses are complementary, the taller of the two wearing eggshell and the more demonstrative wearing black, with a tiny black shawl over her bared shoulders, like the plumage of a flightless bird. The dresses are tight and the women, standing very straight, possess what my father likes to call "great builds." They each carry a small glittering purse in both hands and nudge each other as they scan the bar, whispering secrets. A hostess approaches them, but they look past her until they see my father. Then they collect themselves, and begin to walk, as if aware they are being watched, being studied. They take small steps, keeping their tiny purses in front of them, but they also prance and sway, a motion within a motion. I watch them helplessly, and watch my father watching them, his movements growing formalized as he issues, from the back of his throat, a sound that is the vocalized version of a wolf whistle:

"Heeeeeey . . ."

I stare at him, in a small thrum of panic. "Dad, who are they?"

He spares me only a swift and brightly colored glance.

"They're our dates," he says.

They are the women—the *ladies*—I have always heard about, wondered about. They are buyers. They are the Friedlanders, the woman in black named Peggy and her companion in eggshell named Ann. They look like sisters, but they are sisters-in-law. They are from south Georgia, where their husbands, two brothers, own a department store and a small chain of specialty shops. They are in New York for Market Week, and it is my father's duty to entertain them. "And you must be Tommy," Peggy Friedlander says, after my father releases her hand. "I've heard so much about you!" Her familiarity is beguiling, because it makes me the center of attention. And yet it puts me on alert, like the smiles of the palace guards at the Essex House. She speaks as though she has gone out with my dad as an excuse to meet *me,* but the fact she knows me serves as a reminder that I don't know her—that I am a spectator to something I can't possibly understand.

We step back outside into what's left of the sunlight and then into the limousine my father has hired to take us to Michael's Pub. It is my first limousine, and from their excitement it might be the Friedlanders' too—as my father discourses from the little seat that faces them, I see Ann give Peggy's hand a quick squeeze. I wonder about it, even when we are seated at Michael's Pub, even when I watch my father try to get a better table with a fistful of green and the captain refuse the offer, the entire sequence carried out at hip level and meant to be sub rosa. That squeeze, *their* squeeze—was it a gesture of excitement, encouragement, or comfort? Then Woody Allen comes in off the street and walks right past us on his way to the stage, dressed as I wish to dress, in a tweed jacket and a button-down shirt, symbolically smart. He stops at a table in the front and I crane my neck to see if his cinematic sidekick Tony Roberts has shown up, or even Diane Keaton, whose resemblance to Janet Folk—her preppy clothes, her "la-di-da"s, her pink cheeks, her small pointy nose, her crinkly eyes, her scrubbed Protestant beauty—helped me fall in love the summer before. But no; he simply takes the stage with his band and begins dourly playing the Dixieland jazz that in his movies works as a kind of laugh track. I wish he would crack a joke, or simply smile, and when he takes a break, Peggy Friedlander reaches for my hand and asks, "Tommy, what do you *see* in him?"

"He always gets the girl," I say.

"Well, so does your *father,*" Peggy answers.

And then I know.

We are standing on the corner of Fifth Avenue and Central Park South, saying good night in front of the Plaza Hotel. I can hear the horses nickering from the carriages parked alongside the curb; I can smell them too, but on this night even the smell of straw and horseshit is invested with the lure of romance. I have no doubt that but for my presence my father would be hiring a carriage and disappearing with Peggy into the dark of the park—I have no doubt that they've gone once around the park already, and that I should hate this woman on my mother's behalf. But I don't; I remember the squeeze Ann gave her, and I find myself rooting for her even at the risk of betraying my mom. I shake Ann's hand, and try to do the same with Peggy, but she's been drinking all night long and she's wobbly. She steadies herself with her hands on my shoulders, and considers me from arm's length. "Oh, Tommy," she says, "you're going to be a writer one day—I just know it. I can just feel it. So you have to promise me something. Promise me you're always going to follow your dreams. Do you promise?"

"I promise."

Then she draws me to her, with whirlwind strength and power, and kisses me hard on the mouth. She pulls me close to her and presses herself against me, and I feel everything, her body, her breasts, her breath, her heart, her throttled eroticism and her thrilling desperation. She holds me until my head spins, and then releases me. She takes off her high heels and puts her arm around her sister-in-law's shoulder and my father watches them walk back to the Plaza, her shoes dangling by her side. She has not said good night; she has said goodbye, and I somehow know I will never see her again.

The lobby of the Essex House is empty around midnight. I am waiting for my father to check his messages at the front desk when a man and a woman come in from the street. He is tall and regal, and she is small and radically fine boned, with her hair tightly knotted. He wears a jacket and a tie, she a full-length dress, but about them both is a sense of austerity, even renunciation. I look at them, once, twice, and when my father returns I am bug-eyed from trying to stifle the cry in my throat. I whisper, "Dad, Dad!" but he gives me a scolding glance and if he recognizes the man who has just walked across the lobby he doesn't let on. We go to the elevators and see one with open doors and when we step inside we are alone with Muhammad Ali and his new wife, Veronica.

No one speaks. Ali stares straight ahead, his hands folded before him, while she stays close to him, turned away from us. I avert my eyes, staring at the floor and comparing the architectural construction of his leather shoes to my dust-colored Hush Puppies. When the elevator stops at our floor, I exit without saying a word, but my father says, "Good night, Champ," and then nothing else until we reach our room and I go back to the window and its view of the park, its secret immensities. He stands next to me, as if we're both straining to see what's taking place on those snaky paths, and says, "Stick with your old man, kid." I don't answer, and after a while he says, "I bet you can't wait to go home and tell Janet." But that's not what I'm thinking, and that's not what has silenced me. I will go home and tell Janet I saw Woody Allen and Muhammad Ali on the same night. But I will not tell her what made the night so romantic; I will not tell her—any more than I will tell my mother—about Peggy Friedlander.

It's his phone this time, the business phone, the secret phone with the secret number, the one that sounds different from any other phone in the house, the one we all hear but only he is allowed to answer, usually behind closed doors, as if the calls that come through on it concern matters of state. His door is closed now but I can hear not only the ringing of the phone through my bedroom walls; I can hear him, his movements. My mother is out shopping on an afternoon in late summer; I am alone with him, and so even as I try to read Thomas Pynchon's *V,* I listen by habit to him taking a shower, undergoing his ablutions, whistling and humming and singing, and then at last answering his phone, its furtive bleat. I hear his voice, the baritone greeting, and then I hear it drop so low I cannot make out what he is saying. And then he hangs up, and I hear a sound I've never heard before.

It is a gasp. It is the sound of a man who has been underwater breaking the surface. It is loud and it is desolate and it is followed by loud repetitive breathing that turns into an even more troubled sound—like a fit of coughing, violently suppressed. I don't hesitate. I get up and I go to his room to see if he's all right and I find him sitting shirtless on the edge of his unmade bed with his head bent and his back heaving and his fingers pinching the bridge of his nose. I sit next to him, the room dim with the shades down. He doesn't respond. "Dad, are you okay?"

He turns and stares slack-jawed, uncomprehending. He doesn't recognize me. I put my arm around him, and he says, "Tommy?" I begin patting his back and he begins shaking his head and saying, "Tommy, Tommy, Tommy . . ."

"Is everything all right? What happened? Did something happen to Mom?"

He turns to me, with no words in his open mouth. He keeps shaking his head in barely perceptible disagreement, like a fighter who has decided to stay on his stool. I keep my arm around him and at last I feel the return of his normal breath. "Do you remember that nice lady we took to dinner in New York? Mrs. Friedlander?"

"Of course I do, Dad." That nice lady. I saw her just two months ago.

"Well," he says, with his brow knitted in concentration and confusion. "Well, she . . . killed herself. She . . . committed suicide." He presses his knuckle into his cheek and his mouth opens in horror. His eyes open in horror.

I give him a squeeze. "Dad," I say.

"She . . . shot herself," he says. "She put a bullet through her head." He begins rocking in place, as though davening. "How could that be?" he asks. "She had so much life. She was so . . . *alive*." He keeps repeating, "How could that be, how could that be, how could that be?" until I feel I've failed him by not having an answer.

A half hour later, my mother comes home, with her own sounds, always the sounds of return. The car idling in the driveway; the robotic thunderstorm of the automatic garage door opening; the music of her car keys disappearing into her handbag as she walks into the den and calls for me to help with the groceries. I go downstairs as if on a chute, and after I give her "a hug and a love" I begin carrying the brown paper bags from King Kullen to the kitchen. By my last trip my father is at the table, dressed in slacks and a polo shirt. My mother is speaking, and I hear that other familiar sound, her nervousness. I have come upon them in the middle of an argument.

"She really was very beautiful," she says, in her most conciliatory voice.

My father's lips tighten, grow pale.

"What? What did you just say?"

"I was just *agreeing* with you," my mother says, chastened. She is not sitting with my father; she is putting the groceries away. Then her tone changes. "She was beautiful, *all right*? She had everything going for her, *all right*? I was wondering how she could do something like that."

They are talking about her, about Peggy Friedlander. My father lets go of the newspaper in his hands and stands up with his black reading glasses sliding to the end of his nose. He watches her until she turns from the refrigerator and faces him. Then he says, "Oh, Frances, you don't understand. You don't understand *anything*." I watch both of them standing together; he is growing, as if fed by anger, and she is shrinking, because he has her cornered, and she is cowering. Then I watch him gather himself, and go. He turns his back on both of us, heading out of the kitchen, then across the living room foyer and out the front door, disappearing down the marble steps. The Lincoln starts in the driveway, and I hope he is just going to the OTB to lose some money. But he doesn't return for dinner and he doesn't call, and so instead of driving to see Janet, I stay at home with my mother, waiting for the dark to bring my father home.

My mother has one power, in her ongoing engagement with my father. It is not the power of seduction. It is not the power of a sharp eye or a sharp tongue. Though it has financial implications, it is far more fundamental even than the power of the purse. Not long after my parents moved to Wantagh from Levittown, my father wanted to move from Wantagh to Old Brookville, on Long Island's posh North Shore. When he began spending a few months of every year in Florida, he wanted to buy a condominium on the Hallandale beachfront, in a high-rise tower with black marble floors in the lobby. When he discovered California, Las Vegas, Puerto Rico and the Bahamas, he told my mother to hop on a plane and meet him. At night, when he came home from work, he'd tell her to have a drink—"live a little." But she would never drink a cocktail with him, looking down as she did on "women who drink." She would never fly, citing her claustrophobia. She would never accede to the condo in Florida, claiming it was "too Jewish." She would never go see the house in Old Brookville, insisting she was happy with her friends on Britton Street. She said no, and keeps saying no, because against the onslaught of my father, her only power is the most basic of all—veto power.

Nothing has ever changed inside the Westhampton house in the fourteen years our family has owned it. The dartboard still hangs from the pitted door, the rocking chair still has the letters "JFK" stenciled on its back a decade and a half after the assassination, the little iron monkey dangles from a nail on the mantelpiece, the collection of eccentric beach hats still clings to the beams in my parents' bedroom, and a fishing net full of seashells still ensnares a piece of driftwood nailed to the wall over the down-filled couch. What has changed, what keeps on changing, is the shoreline. The beach used to be so large that arguments would break out over who would have to trudge back to the house for refreshments. But the ocean kept nibbling away at the beach and then it began gobbling. There is no dune anymore, and at night we can see the froth of the waves from the back window. It is only a matter of time before the ocean devours the house itself, and it is a stroke of luck that, in the summer of 1979, my father has been able to sell it.

He does not look at the sale as lucky, however. He blames my mother for forcing him into it and on July 15, our last day at 879 Dune Road, he never stops waxing sentimental over every stick of furniture or stray decoration we're going to leave behind. "Hey, Tommy, you always loved this couch . . . Hey, Tommy, remember you and your friends playing darts . . . Hey, Tommy, I used to make you clam sauce in this pot . . ." My mother keeps working, folding linens and towels, and when she doesn't respond to his litany of lost glories he tells me, "See? Your mother doesn't care. She's tough, your mother, with a heart of stone. She never liked the place anyway . . ." Then he starts singing a song from the 1920s, "Hard-Hearted Hannah," and my mother shakes her head as she toils, saying, almost to herself, "Oh, you S of a B." And yet she seems able to shrug him off until I join in. I don't blame her for this day. But my father is right—she didn't like the house, especially when she had to feed Uncle Chip, and when my father grew dangerous with drink or disappeared down the road to the Dune Deck.

"Hey, Dad, there's a phrase I learned in French class, *'Partir, c'est comme mourir un peu.'* It means 'leaving is like dying a little.' " My father repeats the phrase to himself, and then, when he's not singing "Hard-Hearted Hannah," he repeats it to my mother. She endures his needling for a while, in silence. Then she sobs, "I'm not Hard-Hearted Hannah," and with her composure cracking, and her face slick with tears, she looks straight at me, because I'm the one with the power to break her heart.

He sells the Westhampton house for $100,000 and at the end of that summer he has an opportunity to do something with it. "The Essex House is going . . . condo," he announces when he comes home from the city, rubbing his palms together because he has the chance to buy one of the new units for $150,000. He is in the living room with my mother, and I am upstairs and, as always, listening. He explains that not everyone has the opportunity he has; that not everyone has been *given* the opportunity he has. He is not some schmuck off the street; he can buy a condominium in the Essex House because he's been invited to buy one and he's been invited to buy one because the people at the Essex House *like* him . . .

"Forget it," my mother says.

"Forget it? Frances, in five years it will be worth a half a million dollars! I *have* to buy it!"

"So you can use it for your *affeahs*?" my mother says. "How dumb do you think I am?"

I stay in my room, but one thing—my relationship with the word "affair"—is changed forever, even the sound of it. I will never be able to speak or even read it without rhyming it, as my mother did, with "yeah," or without the certainty that she knows my father has them. And my father never mentions the condominium in the Essex House again.

11

I know what I want to do but I don't know *what* to do. I followed Janet to the State University of New York at Albany, against my father's wishes; now I have a degree in English and professors offering to write letters of recommendation if I want to go to grad school and telling me that with the papers I've written I can probably go anywhere I want. But I don't want to be a scholar, I want to be a writer, because I can't imagine doing anything else and besides, if I don't write, I'll never be able to write about . . . him. I just don't think I can write enough to make a living—I write by the inch instead of the yard—so I begin to think about making a living so I can write. I have an idea that I can be like Wallace Stevens, one of those writers who takes some kind of drab day job so at night they can write whatever they please. But what kind of job can I get that won't kill the writer in me? And what kind of writing can I do, when I have no confidence in my ability to write a novel, a poem or even a newspaper story?

I'm standing in Janet's Baldwin kitchen, drinking a glass of orange juice with her mother, Helen. The phone rings, late, and Helen picks it up. She listens and says, "Hi, Fran." She's a nurse who specializes in sangfroid but when she hands the phone to me I know something is wrong.

"Mom?"

"Your father fell," she says.

"He *fell*?" It's like being told the enormous beech tree in our backyard has come toppling down.

"He stepped right off the marble steps. Oh, it was terrible, Tommy—you could hear the crack. He thinks he's broken his leg and we're on our way to the hospital. Can you meet us? You know your father—he doesn't do well in these kinds of situations. He's gotten himself very worked up."

Janet and I drive to a hospital off Hempstead Turnpike and wait for my parents in an empty lobby that feels like a ballroom in a hotel closed for the season. We see the Lincoln pull up to the curb, and my parents get out, my father using two golf clubs as crutches. He's hobbling, and he's bent over, but he's grinning, and it doesn't matter that there's not a living soul on hand—he might as well be sitting in the back seat of a convertible during a ticker-tape parade. And yet when I embrace him, I feel that sudden surrender, that familiar shudder of necessity, and for the first time in my life I realize I have to take care of him.

Two days later, my father has a plaster cast from his hip to his toe and I have my first job since graduation. It's Market Week, and I chauffeur him to the city in the Lincoln and show the bags to buyers while they sign his cast with a felt-tip pen, some of them bringing it low to the ankle, others daringly, salaciously high. One evening, on the way home, he says, "You know, I've been watching. You don't think I do, but I don't miss . . . a trick. You're pretty good at this."

"At what?"

"*This.* Sales. You know, everyone loves Michael—how could they not? But sometimes he's *too* good, too honest. I say, 'Michael, bullshit 'em a little.' But he's so straight. You're more like me. We both have a little larceny in our souls."

"I don't know about that, Dad."

"I'm *telling* you. And I want to tell you something else: Phillippe is hiring. I saw Bobby Kaden today and he asked me if you wanted to interview. That lucky SOB can't order a hamburger without spitting all over himself and he makes a million dollars a year."

I know about Bobby Kaden—my father has known him since the war and calls him "Mumbles," insisting that "he has . . . an affliction." And I know about Phillippe, because my father talks about it—because it's revolutionized the handbag business and threatened his brand of salesmanship. Based in downtown LA, it's run by Michael Greitzer, who inherited the company while still in his twenties and became known as a "genius" for kicking buyers out of the showroom when they didn't buy enough. "He doesn't charm them, he treats them like shit—and they love it, they love it! They can't wait to come back for more!"

I've never met a genius. I ask my father to set up the interview, and the next week I find myself in Phillippe's New York office, in the first conference room of my life. Bobby Kaden sits on one side of a long table, with a tan and silver hair and such an abundance of dried spit in his mouth that he appears to have to have binged on Elmer's glue. Michael Greitzer sits on the other, in leather pants and a dress shirt with the insignia of a polo player on the pocket and a knit tie with a fist-sized full Windsor. One of them is known for the mileage he's gotten from his one intelligible utterance—for being able to call any handbag he's selling "a license to steal"—and the other for a volatile cocaine cool that makes him seem more like an A & R man from Warner Bros. or a tyro trader from Goldman Sachs than a handbag manufacturer. And me? I'm twenty-two years old and I'm known for one thing and one thing only: being the son of Lou Junod.

I'm aware of this as soon as I start talking, and so is Greitzer. "Guys like your dad, they've had a good run. But the business is changing. It's getting harder and harder to make a sale on a smile and a shoeshine. I grew up in the handbag business, just like you. But I'm going to level with you: I don't give a shit about handbags. Handbags are just a means to an end. The only thing I care about is capitalism."

He drums his fingers on the tabletop and I answer by sliding him my résumé. He keeps drumming, neither touching the sheet of paper nor looking at it. "Hey, I know you're smart. You got the good grades. *Good for you.* What I want to know is, what makes you think you can sell?"

I have never sold anything. I have never even done what my father insists is the precondition for both sales and life: "Sell yourself first." Most of my stories are actually about him, except for one. "The last two summers I worked at a drunk tank in Nassau County. I think if I can convince alcoholics to lay off the sauce I can convince little old ladies to buy handbags."

It's a lie. I was a clerk. I didn't help the patients I encountered; I checked them in and then took out my notebook and wrote about them. But Greitzer stops drumming his fingers. His little O-shaped mouth broadens into a smile and he looks at Bobby Kaden. "Didn't I tell you?" Mumbles says. "The kid's a license to steal! A license to steal!"

I walk to the parking garage and retrieve the Lincoln. I pick up my Dad at 330 Fifth, as usual, and he hoists the big white log of his leg across the front seat. He is quiet until I pass through the tunnel. Then he looks at me. "Well?"

"Well what?"

"How . . . did it go?"

"I guess okay."

"Okay? That's not what I heard. Mumbles called. He told me . . . what you *said*."

"What I said?" I think back to Greitzer's comment about my dad having a good run. Did I agree with him? Am I in trouble?

"Where did you get . . . that line?"

"What do you mean, Dad?"

"The line, the line! About working with alcoholics! That's a hell of a line! And I thought *I* was a bullshitter!" He reaches over, pats me on the head. "You're in, son. You got the job. Mumbles told me. I'm . . . *bursting my buttons*."

I drive. I grow quiet for a while. I wait until we cross into Nassau County to release the sigh I've been saving up, thinking about what happens when we get home. I've made my mother two promises in my life. I can still keep the first. I can still get married without eloping like Michael and Cathy; I can still give her a wedding in a church. But now I have to go home and tell her I've broken the second. I've become what I've promised never to be.

I've become a handbag salesman.

I have been in Dallas for a month. I have a showroom at the Apparel Mart. I have a beige Chevy Impala that cracks my father up when he's visiting—"Tommy, it's a *doctor's* car!" I have some new suits and I have some sample cases and now that Phillippe has shipped the merchandise, I have to prepare myself to go on the road at least five days a week in my vast territory of Texas, Louisiana, Oklahoma and Arkansas. It's something I've never done and when I leave the Mart and make it back to my apartment I have to make a momentous decision. I have, in the kitchen, the answering machine my sales manager Burt Phillips instructed me to buy before I started traveling. I have to decide the outgoing message. More difficult still, I have to decide how I will pronounce my last name on the message I leave.

It should be easy. My name is Tom Junod. My father's name is Lou Junod. It's a French name, but my grandfather supposedly Americanized it decades before, and though my father didn't think much of the man who raised him, he thinks highly of the name itself; he has told me since I could make out words, "You're a Junod," putting a fist-on-the-table emphasis on the second syllable: juh-NAHD. It's a brand, his brand, and now that I'm in his business it's an asset, maybe my only one. Nobody in my nearly seven hundred thousand square miles of territory knows who I am, but plenty of people in my business know about Lou Junod, if only by reputation. I am his son, and I should be proud to carry his name like a declaration.

But then, I took two semesters of French in college. My teacher pronounced my name joo-KNOW without asking and I began using the Gallic variant. It was pretentious, yes, but so was I. I didn't know if I could become a writer, but I sure could become writerly, and I changed the pronunciation of my name instead of wearing a beret. It was my brand, not his, and besides, Janet liked it better.

Now I'm a handbag salesman, like my brother a chip off the old block in the family business, and so I should simply change the name back, and become Tommy Junod, son of Big Lou. All I have to do is record an outgoing message that says, "You've reached Tom juh-NAHD at Phillippe . . . ," and accept my fate. But I can't. I don't want to be a chip off the old block. I don't want to have a little larceny in my soul. I don't want to have . . . a reputation. I want to be as good and straight and honest as my brother, Michael, but I also still want to be a writer. I want to prove that I can make my living selling handbags and be good and honest and be a writer and, above all, remain faithful to Janet. I want to prove that I might be a handbag salesman but I will *never* be Lou Junod. So I record my message and go out to buy some supplies for my travels and when I come back to the apartment the red light on the answering machine is blinking. I have received the first message of my life. I hit "play" and hear my mother's voice, soft and sweet at first, then full gun moll:

"Tom joo-KNOW, this is your mother speaking, and I've known you your whole life as Tommy juh-NAHD—so don't *think* you can put the *Ritz* on *me*!"

—

I have driven to San Antonio and Austin and Waco. I have driven to Little Rock and Hot Springs and Tulsa and Oklahoma City. I have driven to Shreveport and Texarkana and El Dorado and Natchitoches and Nacogdoches and Lufkin and Temple and Tyler. I have driven to Waxahatchee and Denton and Wichita Falls, Amarillo and Borger and Midland and Odessa and Big Spring. I have driven to Fort Worth and Abilene and Sweetwater and I have driven to Lubbock and then to El Paso by way of Carlsbad, New Mexico. Today I'm driving to Houston to visit one of my father's accounts. Her name is Monica Haig and she owns Pickpocket, a handbag store in the Galleria that cultivates a wealthy clientele from Central and South America. She carries handbags ranging in price from twenty-five to five thousand dollars, but she doesn't carry Phillippe because she doesn't like my boss, Burt Phillips. She likes my father, though—likes him so much that he often stays with Monica and her husband when he visits Houston. Indeed, she likes my father so much that she's invited me to come visit her at the store and has let it be known that she's ready to buy some handbags.

I don't know if this is such a great idea. I have gotten in trouble with Burt for visiting department stores he considers his accounts and I know I am risking his ire even if—especially if—I reopen the account with Monica Haig. But she's a formidable woman, a square-jawed and square-shouldered German with short blond hair and a disregard not just for Burt but for the prospect of letting a man like him stand in the way of what she wants. I go to work as soon as I walk into her store, and when I am done showing the line she hands me the biggest order I've ever received. "You still zink Burt will be angry?" she asks, releasing the paper with an airy flourish of her fingers that suggests he is not worthy of my concern, let alone hers.

I take her to an outdoor restaurant at the Galleria to show my appreciation. But that is not the only reason; that is not even the real reason. I begin talking about Burt Phillips, complaining about Burt Phillips, as a way of inducing Monica Haig to talk about my old man. It doesn't take long. When I ask her to compare how my father and Burt Phillips do business, she says, "Your *fahzer* wouldn't *work* for Burt Phillips, that's for sure."

I nod. "They hate each other."

"Your fahzer hates Burt Phillips because of how he treats you. Burt Phillips hates your fahzer because your fahzer is a legend and Burt is just a *money grubber.*"

"But Burt makes so much money," I say.

She lets go a soft snort that crinkles her face into a squinty smile. She leans in, relaxed and confidential. "Ah, yes. Burt has money. But of course your *fahzer* had Zsa Zsa Gabor."

"What?"

She leans back and crosses her legs. "You did not hear zis?"

"No."

She spoke so offhandedly, making the rumor of an impossible conquest sound like common knowledge. *Of course,* she said. Now she knows she made a mistake. She lights a cigarette and flutters her hand dismissively. "I don't know if zis is true. People say lots of things, and salesmen are like washerwomen."

But her retreat from what she stated so confidently is the clincher. I know it and she knows it, and I shake my head. I inhale. "My father," I say.

She exhales for me, a stream of smoke off to the side. "Your fahzer," she repeats, but wistfully, in a sigh. And then for a while neither of us say anything.

I have come a long way for this. I have come from Wantagh to Dallas, and then from Dallas to damned near every town in Texas. I went from college student to aspiring writer to handbag salesman. But I am back to where I started, back to where I have always been. I am supposed to be following in my father's footsteps. But once again I am hot on his trail.

My father drops me off at my hotel after I meet him for dinner. It's March 23, 1981, and he is sixty-two years old. I had a nice night with him, celebrating his birthday in the middle of Market Week in Los Angeles. But he is not at all pleased by where Phillippe has put me up. He is staying at the Bonaventure, along with some of Phillippe's senior salesmen. I and the other fledglings who got their jobs when I did are staying at a place called the Gala Inn Towne in downtown LA, a couple of blocks from Phillippe's office and factory. "I can't believe that cheap son of a bitch Burt Phillips put you in this shithole," he says, making a face. "It's . . . a hot-sheet joint."

"It's fine," I say.

"You sure you don't want to stay with me? I could get you a cot."

"Happy birthday, Dad." I kiss him on his creased and oiled forehead and walk into the lobby as he drives reluctantly off. I step into the elevator and press the button for the second floor. As the door begins to close, a man slips just inside. He is the color of tobacco, with a wide face and dimples. He has a pointy mustache, broken at the philtrum, and he is sweating so profusely his skin gleams. He presses three and slouches against the back wall. When I say hello, he nods.

The elevator stops at the second floor. "Good night," I say, remembering the way my father talked to Muhammad Ali in the Essex House, how classy he sounded. I walk down the hall to my room and insert the key in the lock. The cylinder doesn't turn. I wrestle the key out and slide it back in. A shadow appears on the wall in front of me, and it alerts me to the presence of someone just over my shoulder, standing very close. I try turning the key again and it doesn't budge. "Shit," I say, and the man at my shoulder walks on down the hall. It's the sweaty man from the elevator. I figure he's lost.

I go down the hall and knock on the door of Steven Grossman's room. Steven is one of the salesmen Greitzer hired when he hired me. He is also another legacy, another son of a legend, Hy Grossman. "*Tommy,*" he says when he opens the door, as if in relief.

He goes back into the room, plops down on the bed, and resumes the task of rolling joints from the big bag of weed on his nightstand. I sit next to him and he passes me a bottle of Jack Daniel's. I swig from it and take a hit from the joint he's already burning. I watch TV for a few minutes and then swing my legs off the bed and head to the bathroom off the dark and narrow hallway that leads to the door. I switch on the light and undo my belt. I hold up my pants with one hand and my dick with the other. I'm starting to pee when my head twists three inches to the right, the result of a small but very pointed act of violence. There is a gun pressed hard against my temple and it's pinching my skin. It hurts.

I see neither the gun nor the man, because the pressure of the barrel angles my head and face away from them. But I know a few things. The gun is made of metal, an enormous shadowy machine in the strained periphery of my vision. The man who is pressing it into my skull is the man from the elevator and the hallway, with his drenching ammoniac sweat. I flinch from the gun, and he relieves the pressure from my temple only to slide the barrel into the notch at the base of my skull.

"Put your hands up and walk," the man says as I hear the last trickles of my piss in the toilet, a sound already in the past. I do as I'm told and my pants fall down around my ankles and I toddle as if shackled. When I see Steven, he sees me and recoils from the sight. His legs move like he's pedaling a bicycle but then his back hits the headboard and he stops. His wide-open mouth goes slack, and he says, "Oh shit."

The man orders us to lie face down on the bed. Steven turns over; I have to climb in next to him, and as I do we sneak a glance at each other. Steven's face is simultaneously antic and frozen, a face from a movie still.

"Stick your faces in them pillows," the man says. "Don't look at each other. And don't let me catch you looking at me." I follow his orders. I don't see anything but what I can *feel* with the radar of furtive glances and the sonar of my ears: me on my belly on a hotel bed, my pants around my ankles, my thighs bare and my ass swaddled in white underwear while the man roams the room, doing as he pleases, with the run of the place. When he begins stealing, he's selective, choosy, as if he has all the time in the world. He snatches Steven's wallet and flicks through the wad of bills in the billfold as he would the pages of a paperback. He takes Steven's hands and removes the wedding ring from the left and the signet ring from the right. He slips the watch from Steven's wrist and says, "I hate to be doing this, but you see, I have a monkey on my back."

He walks to my side of the bed. What's the worst that could happen? I ask myself, and it's not a rhetorical question. It has an answer. I am helpless. I am afraid of him touching me. But the worst thing that can happen is not him touching me; it's him killing me. I make a decision that I will have to live with, but it helps me live. I will accept anything short of dying.

"Where's your wallet?" the man says.

"In my pants," I say.

He reaches into the fabric twisted at my ankles. He opens the wallet and says, "Thirty-eight dollars? That's all you got?"

"Yes."

"You sure about that?"

"Yes."

"How about you?" he asks Steven. "You got anything else?"

"No."

"You're not lying to me, are you?"

"Mister, I swear . . ."

"You better not be. Because I'm going to search the room and if I find any money I'm going to kill you both." Then he chuckles. *"Mister,"* he says to himself, and begins searching the drawers, which are empty and make booming sounds as they open and close. He is as methodical as he is meticulous, and time splits in two. On the one hand, each moment becomes an extra moment—a reprieve. On the other, each moment gives him another opportunity to find an excuse to kill us.

When he opens the closet, the wire hangers sound like wind chimes. "Well what do we have here?" he asks, and sweeps his arm along Steven's wardrobe. "I'm going to check all your pockets, so if there's anything in them it might be a good idea to save me the trouble." Steven stays silent. "What was that?" the man asks.

"I told you I don't have anything," Steven says.

The man whistles. "Well, what you do have is a nice wardrobe. I could use some nice clothes. So I can get myself a job, you know—so I can look good in an *interview.*"

He takes too much time and too little and finally I lose track altogether. I try counting the seconds, and wind up calculating instead our likelihood of survival, based on his movements and tone of voice. I tell myself many times that his chattiness bodes well for us, that as long as he's talking he's not going to shoot us. When he pilfers Steven's bag of pot and says, "I'm going to leave you boys a joint for when I leave—you gonna need it," I want to thank him.

Then everything changes, and I have no idea why. He orders us off the bed. He orders us onto the floor. He says, "Now crawl. Crawl to the bathroom, with your noses on the floor."

"You don't have to do this," Steven says.

"You do what I tell you to do," the man says. "Crawl to the bathroom, and don't fucking look at me. If you look at me, I'll blow your fucking heads off."

We crawl to the bathroom. We keep our noses to the floor and discover the locker-room stink of the carpet. My tangled pants catch on my shoes, but we make it to the bathroom, where I'm still hoping he'll shut the door on us and leave. "Get in the bathtub," he says instead.

I have been trying to follow his orders. I have been trying to keep my eyes on his shoes so that I don't give him any reason to blow my head off. But now I can't help it. I look up and see him standing over us with the gun angled at our heads. It's a .45 automatic, endlessly black and ludicrous in its overkill. "I told you not to look at me," he says, and there's a softness in his voice, a terrifying reasonableness and regret.

Steven and I try to climb into the tub, but it's as if we're trying to board a tiny rowboat tossed by slapping seas, me at the stern and Steven at the bow, by the taps. We are kneeling and crouching and trying not to fall down and the sad-sack pessimism on Steven's face hardens and turns into the look of someone going under. The man reaches down to turn the taps and Steven, with his hands folded before him, says, "Oh Jesus Christ please don't kill us."

He is begging for his life, for our lives, and I worry that it's going to give the man ideas—that the plea will stand as a suggestion. But the man changes the angle of the barrel ever so slightly, so that I'm no longer staring into the hole. "Don't Jesus me," he says. "I'm a God-fearing motherfucker myself."

He closes the shower curtain on us and says, "Don't call the police for fifteen minutes. I can always come back, you know. I know your room number. You don't *want* me coming back." He returns to the room and takes Steven's clothes from the closet, the sound like the conveyer at a dry cleaner's. Steven and I crouch in the tub and I hear the television again. "Do we wait?" I whisper, and Steven, his mouth all agog, reaches out for me with both arms. "Tommy," he says, and embraces me.

I pull my pants up and call the cops. When they arrive, the first thing they want to know is how the man got in, and that also becomes the first thing Steven wants to know. "I went up in the elevator with him," I say. "Then I saw him in the hallway."

"But how did he get in here?" Steven asks.

"I think I left the door open," I say.

"Jesus fucking Christ," Steven says.

"Jesus fucking Christ," one of the cops says.

My father arrives when we're giving our statements. Steven told me not to call him until the officers were done with their work—"What can your father do?"—but I wanted him to know I am alive, as if already there was a wild rumor afoot that I was dead. He looks like a mourner when he steps through the door. He looks diffident and composed, and even more than Steven's busy and jittery hands, it is my father's funereal aspect that tells me something didn't *almost* happen in that room at the Gala Inn Towne. Something did happen.

"You got lucky," the lead officer tells us when we trace the path we took from the bed to the bathtub with our knees and noses on the floor. "Putting you in the bathtub—that's an execution scenario. It's a power thing, and usually when things go that far someone's going to get killed. There's not a lot of doubt in my mind that he had decided to kill you. What I don't get is why he changed his mind. Maybe it was the mention of Jesus Christ. Maybe that touched something inside of him." He looks at my father, not at us, and says, "You're a very fortunate man, Mr. Junod."

We walk down the hallway together to my room, the last custodial gesture of the cops before they leave. We stand around the door, and while I dig in my pockets for the key, one of the cops draws his gun, "just in case." I tell him he doesn't have to worry, there's no one in the room, I couldn't get in, the lock is broken. "Give it a try," he says, and I slip the key past the teeth of the cylinder, without a catch. I give it a turn and the door swings open to a room that is untouched, preserved, like a museum for a world now gone for good. "Go in and pack your bags," my father says. "You're not staying another night in this dump. From now on, you're staying . . . with me."

We follow him to his car. So does Steven, because his room has been cleaned out. But all I can think of is the lock in my hotel room door—how it was broken and then it wasn't. There is no doubt in my mind that if I had managed to open the door the man at my shoulder would have pushed me inside, and I would have been alone with him—there is no doubt in my mind that I would be dead. But it didn't open. It didn't open when ingress would have been fatal. Then it did. And all I know, all I believe, to the very bottom of my soul, is that the lock was never broken. I wasn't lucky. I was spared.

We go to the Bonaventure. My father calls the desk for a roll-away cot; Steven, still angry that I almost got him killed, says no, he'll sleep downstairs in the lobby. "Don't be an ass," my father snaps, and when the cot arrives Steven sleeps fully clothed, without even taking off his shoes. I lie down, next to my father in his bed, and do something I've never done, even once in my life:

I fall asleep holding his hand.

My father is a salesman at a linguistic level. He can't say "steak" without making me hungry. He can't tell me to go out and "get a little sun" without convincing me to angle my face to the sky. He can't speak of . . . *Raquel* without simultaneously inciting lust and making me feel sorry for my mother. But of his entire lexicon of desire, there's nothing he says with more spin than . . . "Balboa Island."

It is a tiny island that sits in the middle of Newport Bay, a ferry ride from Newport Beach and about an hour and a half south of downtown LA. My father first visited there in the mid-seventies at the invitation of one of my brother's college roommates, Skipper. But he fell under the sway of Skipper's friend, a guy named Ray Vincent, or "Vinnie," and his girlfriend Mikie. They all shared a small house that convinced my father that Balboa Island was the modern equivalent of Shangri-la and even though Skipper moved out in fractious circumstance my father has kept staying with Vinnie and Mikie every time he travels to California, in the same way he always stays with Frankie Klein when he travels to Florida. He stays with them because "they treat your father like . . . a *king*," and now, he says, they are prepared to do the same for me. Two days after I faced execution in a hotel bathtub, he repairs to Balboa and the obliging company of his two friends, and then begins calling upon me to join him.

I take a bus from LA to Newport and they're waiting for me in the kind of Jeep–turned–beach buggy I've never seen outside California. My father, with two days of sun, is as brown as steak sauce, and so lavishly anointed with oil and iodine he smells like a salad. I can *taste* him, and when I reach the house he says, "I bet . . . you're hungry."

"A little," I say.

"A little? I bet you're starving. And I have something for you."

"What's that, Dad?"

"Your favorite—clam sauce. Vinnie wanted me to make it last night. He said, 'Lou, you can't leave here without making your spaghetti and clam sauce.' I said, 'Oh no, we're waiting . . . for *Tommy.*' "

He pours salt from a box of Morton's into a pot of water, then reaches into a cabinet for two cans of Progresso clam sauce. He says what he always says—"*better* than homemade"—and when the water begins to boil he dumps a box of Ronzoni into the big pot and then reaches for another box. "How many do you want?" he asks. "You want two? I told Vinnie you'd want *two*. I bet you can eat a whole box . . . by *yourself.*" He slides the second box of spaghetti into the pot and pours the cans of clam sauce into a small saucepan. "Hang around," he says, "and I'll show you some of my tricks, my son."

"Oh, Lou," Mikie says. "I've been telling everyone about your clam sauce." She pronounces "Lou" with an extra breath, like a blown kiss, so that it rhymes with "coo." Her real name, her given name, is Michael, because her father wanted a boy. But Vinnie calls her "Bunky," and the exiled Skipper calls her "the Bear," and she is the furthest thing from a boy. She is lean and twisty, with dark skin and dark eyes and dark hair and lips so thick they seem flattened, as if she were trying to kiss you through a pane of glass. She wears ankle bracelets and belly chains, but she is quiet and spends a lot of time reading paperback novels bloated by exposure to the elements, to Vinnie's annoyance. "She reads too much," he says, when I ask Mikie what she's been reading. "That's how we met. Did I ever tell you that, Lou? I saw her on the beach reading a book and knew she wasn't getting fucked enough. It's a law of nature: any woman who reads at the beach isn't getting fucked enough."

My father shakes his head and bites his lip, resembling my mother in one of her hopeless flinches of disapproval. But he doesn't disapprove; he admires. "Oh, the things he says—the things this man gets away with. Listen to him. He's like . . . a Nazi."

He is. Raymond Carl Vincent is a special education teacher who doubles as a bookmaker. He is a former small-college linebacker and Vietnam vet. He works out in front of a mirror on which he's written, in lipstick, "What doesn't kill you makes you stronger," and keeps a blowgun in his tiny fenced yard for killing small animals. He has a long face as red as a rash, gray-blond hair combed in Beatle bangs, and a big matching mustache that makes him look like a butcher. He demands absolute obeisance from Mikie, brags about bringing "the retards and troublemakers" at the high school to heel, and relishes the atrocities he committed in Vietnam, claiming to keep a necklace of human ears in his room upstairs. He fetishizes masculinity in general, spouting as many maxims and aphorisms as my father does, but what's unsettling is that he fetishizes my father's masculinity in particular, speaking his name reverentially, the holy syllable *Lou*. I want to tell my father that he's better than this bully and his bullshit, this Orange County Übermensch. But my father falls for it, for him, and, especially, for *them*.

When I wake up in the morning, it's late, but my father is in the kitchen, waiting for me over a sizzling frying pan. "I'm making you . . . some *eggs*," he announces, dressed in a pair of Ocean Pacific shorts and a singlet. I sit down at the table, hungry almost against my will. I haven't spoken to him yet about what happened in the Gala Inn Towne. I haven't spoken to him yet about the decision I've made to leave the handbag business—my realization that if I'm going to die, I don't want to die on my knees in a cheap hotel room.

I sit down at the table and he slides the fried eggs onto my plate, tinted with burnt butter. Astringent California sunlight fills the room, and I ask where Vinnie and Mikie have gone.

"Vinnie's out buying *steaks* for tonight," he says, "and Mikie's at her apartment. She's got a little place of her own, you know. She's there right now. You ought to pay her a visit. She'd *love* to see you."

"Visit Mikie?"

"She's right in town."

"Why?"

"You've seen Mikie. You need . . . a reason?"

I leave after breakfast, with the familiar tingle of excitement and apprehension. I've been alone with Mikie before. On a previous visit I was in the house with Vinnie and Skipper away, and Mikie came home from work. She changed into denim shorts and a tube top. She poured vodka to the top of a juice glass and put a 45 on the record player. Then she stood in front of a full-length mirror and go-go danced to Brenda Lee's "Sweet Nothings," pointing a chiding finger and singing along in a growl. Nothing happened. But I sure didn't tell Janet about it.

I go upstairs and knock on her door. She answers in shorts, and asks if I want a beer. She pours me a glass and sits down on the couch with her legs drawn up. There's a book on the table. She's wearing glasses. She asks me how I'm doing and I tell her what I wanted to tell my dad—that I want to stop selling handbags and start writing. She sighs. "I wanted to be a writer," she says. "I used to write poems. They were all about boys. I don't think they were very good." She smiles, her lips riding up on her gums. Then she says, "I heard about what happened to you, Tommy. Lou told me. He was very upset. Are you okay?" There is a little shimmy in her movements, but it's just the natural physicality she brings to everything, even the task of listening. But she listens, so I tell her the story—I have to tell her the story, and when I'm done, she stays put, considering me through her glasses. "Oh, that must have been awful, Tommy," she says. "But do you know what? You're going to write about it one day. It will just be something that comes out of you, and you'll be on your way."

When I go back to the house, my father is drinking his own beer, making a quenched noise with each sip. I am unable to resist the inducement, so I go to the refrigerator with him watching my every move. At last he says, "So?"

"So what?"

"Did you go to see Mikie?"

"Of course I did."

"And?"

"And what?"

"What happened?"

I bring a bottle of beer to the kitchen table. "I don't know. We talked."

"You talked? What about?"

"Mostly books and writing."

"That's it?"

"Was something supposed to happen, Dad?"

He drinks from his glass. "I know how much she likes you."

"I like her too."

"I thought you might get to know her a little better."

"Dad . . ."

He studies me from head to toe. Then he issues his pronouncement. "Mikie," he says, "knows how to make a man feel like . . . a *man*."

12

My family convenes at another beach house. But it's not in Westhampton—the Westhampton house is gone for good. And it's not ours—we're renting it. It's in Nags Head, North Carolina, and my entire family is waiting for Janet and me to make the drive from Dallas in the Impala. Before we leave, I call to say we're on our way, and my mother answers. "I want you to be prepared for something," she says. "Cathy's sick."

"What do you mean, she's sick? What's wrong with her?"

"She's just sick, is all. She's lost a lot of weight, and she doesn't look good. I don't want you to be shocked. And I especially don't want you to say anything."

I lower my voice, as if I'm already keeping a confidence. "Mom, does she have cancer?"

"No, no, nothing like that. She's just sick, all right? She's just sick."

We reach Nags Head in the dark. It is all so very familiar—the modest wooden house poised against the dune, the briny air and the concussive music announcing the presence of the unseen ocean, my family greeting us at the door—that our arrival feels like a staged return. "Heeey," my father says. "You made it!" He kisses me hard, then grabs me by the jaw and turns my head around. "Let me have a look at you. You're a little pale, my son. But a few days in the sun will fix you right up!"

I look around, at my parents; at Michael and his wife, Pat; and at Cathy's children, Stacey and Scott. "Where's Cathy?" I ask, and my parents share a glance. They don't share glances unless they are also sharing secrets, so I resolve to search for my sister and am pushing my way past them when Cathy appears in the dark hallway, her face lit by the protrusion of her smile.

I have been studying her face for as long as I can remember, trying to find evidence of what she's thinking and feeling. And so when I see her, my eyes stay past their welcome, and she flinches even as she keeps smiling. She is gaunt, yes, so gaunt that her face has been narrowed and slightly rearranged, her white teeth and her green eyes gaining prominence under the multilayered bonnet of hair that is as thick as my mother's but has always been a source of friction between them—my mother is never happy with my sister's hair. But Cathy is also the only one of us with a touch of my father's dark skin, so she's already deeply tanned, and Stacey and Scott move to hide against her, peering out protectively from behind her hips. She certainly does not look sick, at least not in the way I imagined. She just looks different, and the difference registers in her smile, which is defensive and evasive and at the same time conspiratorial, and in her eyes, which turn wobbly at the height of their color, as if her pale green irises are made of some shuddering jelly. The difference is that she is onto me, that she is aware of my scrutiny and doesn't want to be scrutinized any more than Blanche DuBois did. Cathy generally doesn't give me, or anyone else, a kiss; she just offers her cheek, accepting whatever tokens of affection come her way. I step forward to kiss her but as I do she whispers, in the gruff Brooklyn voice she sometimes puts on, "Whaddaya think you're looking at?"

It's late. Cathy retreats to her bedroom, followed by Janet, who might live with me but is not allowed to sleep with me for my mother's sake. I stand in the kitchen, hungry, and soon enough Mom finds cookies. "How do you think Cathy looks?" she asks.

"She looks okay," I say. "I mean, she doesn't look sick . . ."

"She's getting a divorce from Ronnie," my mother says. And that's when I understand that my sister has had a breakdown.

We hit the beach in the morning, and my father, in a Speedo, frets as I throw the football to Janet—"Watch the bubs. You're going to hurt . . . the bubs." But it's hot in Nags Head, and by noon the beach is unbearable. Janet and I go back to the house to read, and even my father follows, the first time in my life I've seen the man seek shade. He goes out to buy a newspaper, and when he comes home he starts reading a review of a new movie, *Endless Love*. "Listen to this," he says. "Some kid is told he can't see a girl anymore, so you know what he does? He burns down her family's house. That's a sickie. No wonder there's so much trouble in this world, with Hollywood making sickies like that."

I'm curled up on the couch with Janet, and show him the book I'm reading. It's a paperback copy of *Endless Love*. I wonder if he already knows that.

"That book's probably a sickie too," my father says.

"It's not a sickie, Dad. It's written by Scott Spencer . . ."

"Scott Spencer? Another sickie."

"Dad, you have no idea what you're talking about."

"Well, I know a sickie when I see one. You have to be a sickie, to write a sick book like that."

"I would give my right arm to write like Scott Spencer."

"Hold on to your arm, you might need it one day," he says, and then goes back down to the beach.

I return to the book and in a few minutes Cathy emerges from her bedroom. "I hear you're writing a book," she says. "What's it about?"

"Prairie dogs."

"Tommy. What do you know about prairie dogs?"

"I used to think about them driving through West Texas. I thought I was going nuts so I figured I'd write about them. But what I wrote is not really about prairie dogs. Do you want to hear it?"

"Sure, I'll hear it . . ."

"Well, then let's go to your room," I say. "I don't want Dad to butt in . . ."

The book—the beginning of a book—fills about fifteen pages of a long yellow legal pad. I wrote it at night, in hotel rooms, in my ransom-note print, and it's about the power struggle between two prairie dogs, father and son, for control of a vast underground colony. The son is indulgent of his father's brutal exercise of power until he goes after the son's beloved and then issues an edict calling for the subordination of all females. I read it straight through, to the bitter and bloody ending, and Cathy is quiet for a moment.

"Did you have to kill the father?" she asks.

"I didn't kill him," I say. "The character did."

"Oh," she says. "I see." Then she gives me a peck on the cheek.

The next morning, I'm sleeping on the couch like a doghoused husband, and Cathy creeps out of the room she's sharing with Janet. She shakes me by the shoulder and I wake up to late light and a mostly empty house. My mother, Michael and Pat, the kids—they've all gone out, and Janet is still asleep behind a closed door. The only sound outside of Cathy's whisper comes from the shower, the sustained chordal note of rushing water. "Shhhh," she says. "I want to show you something." She leads me to my parents' room, where she stops in front of the nightstand. It is my father, in the shower—I know that, from the magnitude of the roar. But on the table is a set of false teeth. At first, I think that they're a practical joke my sister is playing, a novelty item set out for shock value. But they shine, even in the shadows. Their engineering is extravagant, and they look alive, as if freshly extracted. "What are they?" I ask.

"Whaddaya think?" Cathy says.

"Who do they belong to?"

"Whodaya think?"

I stare at the closed door of the bathroom, listening to the tidal swell behind it. My father has been mourning my teeth ever since they grew in brown. He has been singing the praises of the teeth he beholds in the mouths of both men and women, as the final stamp, "the capper," of their beauty, and I have been staring at his own teeth, his own white choppers, in awe and shame. He cannot possibly wear dentures. In all the times I've searched his bathroom I've never encountered any evidence he wears dentures, never uncovered any Fixodent or Polident or Efferdent, much less the dentures themselves. Now they are sitting out on the table like an ashtray. How does Cathy know? And why does she tell me? Then the sound of the water stops, and my sister and I make our escape, fleeing him and, most of all, fleeing them, our father's false teeth.

I put on my suit. I bought it at Macy's with Michael in a two-for-one sale. The suit he picked was double-breasted and charcoal gray; mine, single-breasted and navy blue. It's from a secondary line, the department-store variation of a designer collection, but it's the nicest suit I've ever worn, as well it should be. I'm getting married in it, and today is my wedding day.

I'm in the house at 1463 Britton Street in Wantagh. My parents are down the hall in their bedroom, preparing for the first public wedding of one of their children. My father stands at my door for a few seconds, silently adjusting his pose, and then he says, "All right, let's see . . . how you *look*." He takes me in, top to bottom. "Do you have a handkerchief?" he asks, a word he uses instead of "pocket square." I shake my head no, and he produces one in white silk and slips it into the breast pocket of my suit jacket. "A lot of men like to fold them into points," he says. "But that's for squares. I like just a little . . . puff of fabric, myself." He finishes his work, then takes one last look and makes a face. "You gotta get out of those shoes."

"What's wrong with my shoes?" I'm wearing shined lace-ups I bought at Florsheim.

"*Never* wear black shoes with a blue suit," he says. "You look like a . . . *policeman*."

"What color shoes am I supposed to wear with a blue suit?"

"*Blue* shoes," he says.

He drives me to the church and waits with me for Janet to arrive in the limo he hired. I go into a vestibule and on my knees pray that I can *do* this, that I will not betray my wife, that I will not make Janet as unhappy as my father has made my mother, that I will not turn out to be . . . him. Then the organ music starts, and he comes to get me . . . to retrieve me. I ask if he remembered the ring. He better have. He's my best man.

I asked Janet to marry me when I was twenty-two and selling handbags. Phillippe gave me some days off over Christmas and I took her for a ski weekend up in Vermont. We stayed at an inn, and one night, after we had gone out to dinner, we pulled into the parking lot, surrounded by nothing but the deep New England darkness outside. We talked, we made out, we held each other close, and suddenly I felt the darkness deepening as my heart swelled. I felt the keen and keening difference between the world outside and the world here, with Janet, and that awareness just kept deepening and rising until it got *loud,* until my ears rang and my tongue thickened and I heard myself say the only thing left for me to say: "You wanna get married?"

She did. Then we both got scared: "Did that just happen?" We were both just kids, and we promised each other we would remember this swaying, vertiginous moment of commitment. We didn't mention it again, not for years. But it's always there, the love and the commitment and also the fear of what the dark world has in store for us when we are not together. She joined me in Dallas right after I survived the Gala Inn Towne. We moved together to Atlanta right after Michael Greitzer fired me, and Janet toiled in the corporate world while I tried to write. One spring we were doing our taxes and one of us said, "Remember that time we talked about getting married?" But neither of us will remember the second time I ask her, the time that leads to our actual betrothal. We will just remember the wild, terrified first, out there in the iron New England dark.

I didn't even have to think about my choice for best man. My brother, Michael, had been my protector, my guide, my mentor, my role model and my best friend since I was born. I moved to Atlanta with Janet to be with him. I stood as godfather to his first child. I only asked him as a formality. He said, "I'm honored to be asked, Bro—you know that. And I'll do it if you want me to. But how about Dad?"

"Dad?"

"It would mean so much to him."

I nodded. I deliberated for a few moments. I had some qualms, but I couldn't bring myself to mention them. The time my father told me the difference between chicken and steak, the time he introduced me to one of his girlfriends in New York City, the time he tried to set me up with Mikie in California so that I could recover my manhood: I couldn't tell Michael about any of these things now because I had kept them from him when they happened. I have always wanted to be as good as my brother, as honest and genuine and sweet and kind, and in order to achieve that goal I had to agree to love our father in the same innocent and unqualified way he did. "Okay," I said. I never really considered saying anything else, and the next day, when I called our dad and asked him to be my best man, he choked up and had to put the phone aside, the occasion of my wedding turned into a gift from both his sons.

All my life I have heard of him singing at weddings. The story is always the same: he's not the singer in the band, just a guest; he sings only by acclamation, by people demanding that he take the stage, and then he has to be careful not to show up the hired singer. Of course, that's exactly what he does, singing "I'll Be Seeing You" or "My Buddy" or "Where or When." I hear about his performance from him and sometimes from his friends, never from Mom.

I want to hear him sing at *my* wedding. I want him to sing almost as the fulfillment of a promise, the legend at last come to life in a way I can actually talk about. When the band summons him to the stage for the toast to the bride and groom, I wonder if he's going to say, "Hit it," and go into his own version of our first-dance song, "Strangers in the Night." But he's too nervous to sing. He's too nervous, for that matter, to give a toast. For all his sophistication and savoir faire, he doesn't appear to know that giving a toast is his obligation as best man, and has nothing prepared. He is surprised and he is baffled and he is drunk and when the guests shout their encouragement he wobbles to the microphone and speaks in a small and meandering and terribly plaintive voice: "When Tommy asked me to be best man, I said, 'No, son—*Michael's* your best man. Michael, your brother, he's the best man.' But Tommy said, 'No, Dad, I talked to Michael, and we agreed—*you're* the best man.' I didn't know what to say. I don't know what to say now. I . . . I . . ." He reaches into the inner pocket of his suit jacket and when he finds a big pair of sunglasses to hide his tears he looks like a mob boss in mourning. A note of sympathy rises from his audience, a soft but contagious "Awwwwww." He sways and his shoulders begin to shake and Millie, in a brawling Brooklyn bray, cries out, "Come on, *Lou*!" Michael comes to his rescue, wrapping his arm around our father's shoulders and stepping to the microphone to toast the newlyweds and thank the guests.

I wanted something from him—greatness. Instead I realize that at sixty-five my dad is growing old. It is one of the first times I've seen him fail, and yet it makes me love him all the more, love him in a way that is at odds with his sins, the love and fear that once held me in his thrall giving way to love and pity. I receive the dose of innocence I wanted when I made him my best man, even when Janet and I go to the hotel room he bought for our wedding night, and it's in the Essex House.

I shouldn't be so terrified. My father has been talking about taking me to Paris since I was in eighth grade. He's been saving up for the trip, first by dumping fistfuls of "silver" into the big plastic Ballantine's whiskey bottle in my closet, then with a savings account dedicated to the purpose. He's been so dead set on taking me to Paris that he believes I changed the pronunciation of my surname as preparation for our journey, and every time he sees me he says, "*Comment allez-vous,* Mr. joo-KNOW, *ça va combien merci beaucoup,*" a greeting that doubles as a rundown of all the French words he knows. He's been so dead set on taking me to Paris that I felt a little guilty to be taking Janet there on our honeymoon, until I promised that I wouldn't spoil his dream, that the trip I was taking with Janet would serve as prelude to the trip with him. He's returning to Paris after forty years; me, after twelve months. And yet on the way to the airport Janet and I are entangled in the back seat, holding hands so tightly our knuckles turn white, staring into each other's eyes with both longing and desperation, certain that if I board the plane we'll never stare into each other's eyes again.

At first, my father thinks it's funny. He's always been amused by my displays of public ardor, my unabashed uxoriousness. "Who knew what . . . a *lover* you are?" he'll say, when he sees me and Janet together. "It's a beautiful thing. But don't you think it's a little much? Don't you think you might be laying it on a little . . . thick?" Now, with Michael driving, he begins throwing glances at us from the passenger seat. They're worried glances, and they're guilty glances, and occasionally they're annoyed glances. After all, he asked Janet for her leave before we left, and she gave it; he's been thanking her ever since for her generosity, because he knows that she's making a sacrifice and that it's for him. But now she's on the verge of tears, and instead of engaging in the usual public affection we're indulging in a kind of anticipatory mourning. "You know," he says in a downcast voice when Michael pulls the car up to Departures, "we don't have to do this, we can cancel. Jesus, I feel awful that I ever brought it *up* . . ."

He's not saying it for show or to show me up. He means it, and his sincerity snaps me out of my despondency. I don't really think we're going to crash. I don't really think I'm going to die. I just think I'm provoking the gods who vouchsafed my happiness by spending the first anniversary of my marriage with my father instead of with my wife.

It's another story I have known all my life and barely know at all. There was the photo on our basement wall of my father looking like every other father who served in World War II, posing from a pup tent; then, a few photos away, there was another of him looking like he served in an entirely different war, singing in front of a big band in his dress uniform. How did he jump from one photo to another? How was he like everyone else and then like no one else? I have accompanied him back to France to let him revel one last time in those days when he really was a star, and, as always, to find something out for myself.

I planned the trip and I drive the car and on the first day we get lost. My father landed on Omaha Beach a month into the invasion but we wind up on Sword Beach, where the British expeditionary forces established their foothold. We're walking around, our futile maps catching the breeze like umbrellas, when a man in pajamas calls to us from the balcony of a little house not far from the water. He speaks English; he is English, with a ruddy face and haphazard teeth, drinking gin early in the day. He offers us a drink and then a woman wearing colorless clothes and her hair pulled back in a severe bun brings them to us. She does not speak any English, and he speaks very little French. I figure, at first, that she's a housekeeper for a place he's renting as he returns to his own past. But as we drink he tells us that he's a married man back in England but that every fall he comes back to Sword Beach and stays for two weeks with the woman he met during the war. They are both in their early sixties and they don't speak the same language. But they have been lovers since 1944 and they will be lovers as long as he can make the trip across the channel.

We go back to the car and my father can't stop shaking his head. For one thing, he can't believe that a man and a woman who look . . . like *that* are capable of such sustained passion, such an epochal romance. For another . . . "That could have been *me.*"

He was not true-blue when he went off to war. He didn't marry Frances Brandshagen before he enlisted and then become one of those soldiers for whom "Don't Sit Under the Apple Tree" or "We'll Meet Again" was written. He broke up with her, so that he could be a free man. He was a soldier in World War II, an infantryman who was seriously wounded in the hedgerows of Normandy and received a Purple Heart. He was a singer in World War II, who performed in Paris after the liberation and sang "Silent Night" close to the front in Bastogne during the Battle of the Bulge. But he was also . . . a lover, and now, after we meet the couple in Sword Beach, he begins to confide in me. We drive to Omaha Beach, where he landed. We drive to La Haye-du-Puits, where he was wounded twice. We drive to St.-Lô, where he was hospitalized, and on those drives I hear about not only the war but the women whom the war made hungry and free.

I hear about the coterie of married women who invited some of the soldiers from his traveling show, *For Men Only,* back to one of their homes, served them dinner and Calvados, then took off their clothes in unison and said, "Now we make love." I hear about the woman who took my father up to her garret and plied his "privates" with Mennen Skin Bracer and I hear about all "the pros" so readily available on Place Pigalle—"We called it Pig Alley." I hear about the many and also about the one, a woman he fell for in Paris, a married woman who cried when he left for the States and begged him to stay. When I ask if he considered staying, he says, "Sure—I had a chance to get on with the American Theatre Wing. And one night I sang with Django Reinhardt, the Gypsy with . . . a withered hand. We went back to his place. He sat on the bed and played guitar while I sat on the floor and sang surrounded by . . . three women.

He offered to train me. But you know me—some schmuck. I wanted to go home. And besides, I missed your mom."

On the last day in Normandy, we go to the big cemetery, and he stands with a tear in his eye among the endless headstones of soldiers who were not as lucky as he was. We head for Paris and when we reach our hotel I ask if remembers the name of the woman he loved. "Her name was Yvonne Polita," he says. "She was French but her husband was Italian." I pull out the phone book from the drawer of the nightstand. "What do you think you're doing?"

"I'm seeing if Yvonne Polita is in the phone book."

"Tommy . . ."

Sure enough, there is a "Y Polita." I dial the number and a woman answers. She sounds old. I speak English and she begins yelling, squawking. I hang up.

"Well?" he asks.

"She sounded like . . . an old washerwoman," I say.

"An old . . . ?" Then he laughs until a tear comes to his eye.

I talk to the proprietor of a jazz club in St.-Germain, Le Bilboquet. I tell him who my father is—that he was a soldier in the liberating army and also a singer in Paris. He's come back, after all these years. Would it be possible for him to sing?

The proprietor is a bleary-eyed man with a pointy beard but he brightens at the prospect of an American GI singing at his club. He goes to our table and talks to my dad, telling him that he can join the band at the end of the second set. He puts his arm around my father's shoulder as if he's posing for a photo and assures him that he'll let the band know and come back to the table when everything is ready.

My father begins to drink. "Dad . . ."

"You sound like your mother," he says, and after a few drinks he points out a young woman sitting at a table against the wall. "You see her?" he asks.

"Yeah, I see her."

"She's gorgeous," he says.

"She is."

"And she can't keep her eyes off . . . you."

He is right. She has long jet-black hair parted in the middle and kohl-lined eyes and a pout. She's wearing a burgundy sweater that shows off her . . . physique, and under the sweater she's moving her shoulders almost imperceptibly but also unmistakably, as if she's dancing so only I can see. She's staring at me so brazenly that I suspect my father has tried to set me up with her, that she's in his employ. But she's with a date. She's imperiously ignoring her date, and now my father starts giving me advice on how to handle . . . the situation. "You stay here after I leave. You stay if she leaves with him because she'll come back. Listen to me, son—I know a thing or two about these things . . ."

I protest. I am married to Janet. I am celebrating my first anniversary, and Janet gave us her blessing. "*Jesus,* Dad—"

But a part of me wonders if this is the moment we came for, the moment we've been waiting for since he first started saving for the trip. Then the proprietor comes to the table and tells my father that the band's second set is about to begin and my father goes upstairs to the bathroom. He is gone for a long time, and the young woman doesn't back off her stare or her slither and I think for a moment that she's going to abandon her date altogether and visit our table. But instead I feel a tap on my shoulder. "Your father . . . ," the proprietor says.

I look at him.

"Your father is on the floor of the bathroom. He fell."

"Oh God." I stand up instantly and head up the stairs but a crowd has formed and he's on his way down, his arms hooked around the shoulders of strangers. The proprietor says give him some air and opens the door and then suddenly we're out in the street. The door of the club closes behind us and it's just me and my father all alone in St.-Germain under a morbidly black sky. I say, "Dad," and reach out to him, but he turns and looks at me blankly, uncomprehendingly. "Tommy?" he asks. "What are you doing here?"

"Dad, we're in Paris. Together. I'm with you."

"Where?"

"Paris, Dad. We're in Paris. You must have had a—" And then I stop, because I don't want to say he must have had a blackout.

"Oh, thank God," he says, and falls against me.

—

Janet is waiting at the airport with my brother and we hug each other as if I'm returning from the front. I've made it home, and I have the chance to stare into her eyes again. But I had a close call, and I got lucky. I'm not relieved I'm alive; I'm not relieved that the plane didn't go down. I'm relieved that I went to Paris with my father and didn't betray my wife.

Book Two

NOW I'VE REACHED THAT AGE I TRY TO DO ALL THOSE THINGS THE BEST I CAN

13

It was the oldest story in the book—even the newspapers said so. An older man fell in love with a younger woman, and aroused the ire of his devoted but plain wife. What made it a story that raised eyebrows was that the young woman lived with the man and his wife, as a houseguest of the man's daughter from his first marriage. What made it a newspaper story—and a tabloid newspaper story, at that, in the lurid heyday of tabloid newspapers—was that one night the man professed his love for the young woman in front of his wife, and his wife reached into her purse for a gun and shot the young woman dead.

The killing occurred on the night of August 14, 1935, and stayed on the front page of New York City newspapers for months, until the case was adjudicated right before Christmas. In those days, New York had dozens of newspapers competing for readers, and the bloody sacrifice of an ingénue with bee-stung lips and a permanent wave gave readers all they wanted. It was a "crime of passion" that resulted from a "love triangle" in which a combination of innocence, anger and betrayal exploded in secrets, sex and violence. And it had twists and turns, not only in the fickle course of justice, but in the sympathies the story elicited. The victim, twenty-three-year-old Virginia Seigh, started out a hussy and became a paragon of innocence, the fact that she died "intact" attested to by the medical examiner. The killer, Etta Reisman, began as merely jealous of a rival younger and more attractive than she was—"a girl killer"—and ended a symbol of wronged women everywhere. And the man? Well, it was the man whose illicit desire set in motion the destruction of a young woman who had come to New York from a small town outside Pittsburgh, and so it was the man who could only redeem himself by losing everything he owned.

His name was Arthur Reisman, and he had style. He had money too, as the proprietor of a fifteen-store chain of what were called "twenty-five-cent" beauty parlors in Queens, Brooklyn and Manhattan. He had a house on the water in Queens, before the bridges and parkways were built, and a wooden speedboat he'd pilot in vests and knickerbockers and a white yachtsman's hat that heightened the effect of his deeply tanned skin. He had a big nose undergirded by a trim mustache and a shiny bald scalp that added to his sleek allure. He also had an eye for the ladies, and with dozens of ladies in his employ he had, in the middle of the Depression, something of an empire. He wanted only for an empress, a woman with pizzazz equal to his own, and so when his daughter Annette invited her friend Virginia to live in the big house in Beechhurst he must have believed he'd found an adornment for his arm suitable to his station.

He ended up making a fool of himself, like so many older men who think they can keep the upper hand when they fall for much younger women. On a summer night, on his front lawn, he swore his love for Virginia for an audience of his wife and his daughter and begged Virginia to do the same. According to the newspapers, he said, "Tell her the truth—tell her it's too late, and you love me too!" Etta shot Virginia before she could finish her answer; in the struggle that ensued, she also shot Annette in the hand, the bullet snipping off one joint of her stepdaughter's middle finger. Eli, Arthur's nine-year-old son with Etta, stayed in the house and never saw the carnage that changed the course of his life.

Arthur's devotion to his children—and particularly to Annette—was what kept him from being written off as just another cad. He was a cad, sure. But he was a particular *kind* of cad, the betrayer who had been betrayed, a divorcé whose first wife had left him to raise their daughter on his own. Annette's mother became part of the story too, when the tabloids tired of vilifying Arthur Reisman and instead set out to win him some sympathy. He might have been an inconstant husband but his first wife was an inconstant *mother,* and so one day the *Daily News* sent a reporter and photographer to the apartment where she lived on Coney Island Avenue in Brooklyn with her son and four daughters.

The newsmen knocked on her door, and one would think that, knowing why they had come, Bess Junod would present them with the spectacle of her entire brood, from her eighteen-year-old daughter, Marie, to the infant, Mildred, not even old enough to walk, not to mention the handsome teenage son. But she didn't. She made a choice. She shooed Ellie into the back room with Mildred and possibly her son Louie and told them to stay there until the men had left. She brought Marie and Elizabeth out front and sat for a photo with them, the proud matriarch dressed in black. And when the reporter asked about her daughter Annette, she told a lie that was taken as truth and circulated, by means of the newswire, all over the country.

It was a lie about love.

My grandmother died when she was about to turn eighty. At least, I thought she died. I was in her room with my father. I was almost sixteen but felt much younger. I had no idea what was killing her, since what was killing her hadn't been properly diagnosed and now went unmentioned. The room was dark, and he had parked a chair next to his mother's bed. He sat hunched over, already in the colors of mourning, his nose pinched between his fingers, his broad back shaking with his silent sobbing. He offered a desperate hand to the dark and I grabbed it. At my touch, my dad abandoned himself to his grief, taking big whooping breaths that prompted me to rub his neck the way I rubbed my mom's. He regained control of his breathing and reached around to pat my hand. "What am I going to do?" he said in a desolate singsong. "What am I going to do?"

I was certain that I had witnessed the moment of her death. She was a large woman shrunken by her unspoken illness, and I could see as never before the underlying ferocity of her face, as if the jolly mask had finally fallen off. On her dresser, next to the photo of Louis Augustus Junod—the man who stared in quizzical judgment at the son who bore no resemblance to him whatsoever—stood a portrait of her own father, Martin Schmeckenbecher. He was an old man when he fathered her. He had been born in the Black Forest of Germany in 1828, and had been in his late sixties, a widower who remarried, when my grandmother drew her first breath in the Bronx. In the photo, he looked more like a historical personage than an ancestor, with his white hair and white mustache, his imperial nose and pale prepossessing eyes and implacable sense of himself, but as I stared at him and then at my grandmother and father, they looked like one another and *only* like one another—a race unto themselves, a royal line about to be undone. I was not only watching my grandmother die; I was watching, for the first time in my life, my father weep.

I tried to cry along with him. It should have been easy—after spending my whole life as a crybaby, I finally had the chance to let the waterworks come without shame. My father's tears were manly tears, *appropriate* tears, tears of real feeling, and I wanted nothing more than to join him in his grief. But I couldn't. No matter how much I squinted and grimaced, I remained dry-eyed.

My mother didn't cry either. Nor did she comfort my father when she came into the room. She fretted at the fringes, unable to find a place in the tumult at 112 Old Farm Road, and after a while I stood up and joined her. I could tell she was disgusted by what she saw happening around her, all the Junods trying to outdo one another in their histrionics while the matriarch of the family died without proper care. A doctor came to the door with his leather satchel and attended to my grandmother with the resignation of a coroner, checking her vitals and uttering a word not only unmentionable but forbidden—"coma." He told my father she had to go to the hospital and my father, tottering as he stood and mumbling as he spoke, surrendered to his professional judgment. Grandma had been unconscious for days. There was nothing else to do.

And that's when the house erupted. "Over my dead body," Aunt Ellie said with bobcat fury, and as I huddled with my mother I witnessed something I had never seen and could scarcely imagine—my father deferring to her. I always knew Aunt Ellie wasn't afraid of him; now I understood why. She was stronger than he was. He was afraid of *her,* and so as he shrunk into his grief, she expanded into her authority. She kept saying, "This is my house and my mother and she's gonna stay right here with me. She's not going to die with strangers in some . . . *hospital.*" As punctuation she spat on her own floor in pantomime.

My mother was appalled. I believe to this day that my mother managed to sneak down to Aunt Elizabeth's house and call the ambulance, which arrived in front of Ellie's house with the baleful ceremony of a siege engine. The siren whooped and hollered, and when the red light poured through the slatted windows Ellie responded as if her home had been fired upon. She had vowed that Grandma would only go to the hospital over her dead body and now as the emergency technicians rolled a gurney over the concrete pathway to her door she prepared to sacrifice herself. She stood athwart and astride the doorway like some segregationist governor, her short arms and legs extended to the corners of the frame, and bellowed at the technicians, "If you try to come into this house, I'll kill you. You hear me? I'll kill you, so help me God!"

They stalled and huddled on the pathway, one of them speaking into a walkie-talkie; then they withdrew, loading the gurney back into the ambulance, extinguishing the red light, and slinking away with a single whoop of the siren. Ellie closed the door and locked it behind her. The house grew very dark and quiet, and I saw the face of Martin Schmeckenbecher manifested in her own while her diminished mother continued to breathe.

Michael and I took the train to New York for the funeral because Michael was afraid of flying. It was 1989. Grandma had lived fifteen years after Ellie barred the door to the ambulance, a foolhardy gesture that time had turned heroic. In the family mythology, Ellie had saved her mother by keeping her out of the clutches of not only medical personnel but death itself, and since then Grandma's endurance had become something of a parlor trick, a source of double takes when visitors walked through the door. "Grandma, you're still *alive*!" exclaimed one of my cousin Billy's scruffy hippie friends when he came to Levittown one Christmas, and though he risked my father's ire, he wasn't speaking only for himself. Plenty of people were as old as Grandma, but only Grandma could make her survival seem scandalous. To anyone who would listen she announced her goal of living to one hundred and participating in the parade sure to be organized in her honor, a noble aim that she made sound like another of her vices. Indeed, she sought out her own perpetuity by *indulging* in her vices, particularly the unabated consumption of Scotch. She might not have been Levittown's oldest woman but she was surely one of Levittown's oldest drunks, a shrunken sinner who clung to her bottle of Johnnie Walker Black as tenaciously as some elderly smokers drag around their canisters of oxygen. It was, so far as I knew, her only medicine, one that banked but did not extinguish the flame in her eyes and freed her to speak in a soft gibberish that sounded like tongues. She did not live so much as hibernate, but when I married Janet in 1984 she roused herself for our wedding, showing up on a walker and declaring, with a gift for emphasis that rivaled her son's, "Ninety! Ninety! *Ninety* years old . . . !"

She made it three days past her ninety-fifth birthday. When she died at Ellie's home, of an illness unspecified, in the bed next to the dresser adorned with photos of her father and her wayward husband, there were no histrionics and barely any tears. My father and mother had sold the house in Wantagh and moved to Florida and when Grandma entered her last days they were summoned but because my mother did not fly they did not reach Old Farm Road for her last breath. Fifteen years earlier, I had seen my father brought to his knees by the anticipation of his mother's death, and I feared that his failure to make it to her dying bed would add another regret to what was turning out to be a life of them. But he was already a different man than the one I saw at wit's end in 1974. That man had been invincible. That man had shocked me by coming undone, by not knowing what to do in a time of crisis. If the man who showed up at his mother's funeral in 1989 seemed to have regained his self-possession, that was because, a week short of turning seventy, he seemed to have so much less to lose.

We buried her the next morning at the Lutheran cemetery in Queens. It was a crowded place, with a sprawl of gravestones tilting along narrowing paths that forced us to abandon our automobiles, and yet the great shock was the crowd—the invisible throng—at the family plot. Martin Schmeckenbecher had bought it a century before, and so it was already populated with members of his first family. A black granite obelisk rose from the uneven ground, and on all four of its polished faces was a scribble of strange names in Gothic lettering. Who were these people? They appeared to be our ancestors, except that we were Junods, and so we didn't *have* any ancestors—we didn't have any history at all. Our lineage didn't begin until Grandma gave birth to our father, and so Michael,

Cathy and I kept exchanging sidelong glances, as if there had been some mistake and we'd stumbled upon the wrong interment. There was the name of a boy whose birth came within a few years of Grandma's and who must have been her brother. There was a tiny gravestone that had a place of its own near the edge of the plot and on which was written one word: "Baby." These were our people, but since they did not exist in our stories they existed only as scratches on stone.

I stepped forward with the eulogy I had written on the train—the eulogy I had written because at the age of thirty-one I was finally starting to work as a journalist and was now "the writer in the family." I repeated what I knew, all I knew, about Elizabeth Schmeckenbecher, the survivor, the heroine, the matriarch, the rock. She married a drunk. She had four daughters and one son, all Junods. She fed the family by playing piano for silent movies. She was easy with a buck, and during thunderstorms she soothed her terror by gathering her children in her bedroom and entertaining them with dirty limericks. She was born in the Bronx, married in Brooklyn, and wanted a parade in Levittown. My last line: "She might not have gotten the parade, but by God, she got *us,* this crazy, wonderful family, and as long as we keep gathering together she'll always be there with us, with a Scotch in her hand and a song in her heart."

It was a eulogy of platitudes. It was also the last time I was able to believe in either the platitudes or the details of the story I had told. Nobody said much when I was done but Aunt Marie waited for me in her black dress and the white veil she sported on top of her head, the size of a cocktail napkin. She'd always figured me for a writer, even before I'd started writing; whenever I showed off my vocabulary, she'd say, "Listen to him, with the *words.*" Now she pulled me hard by the sleeve, and whispered urgently through the barbed wire of her teeth: "If you ever want to know the truth about your grandfather, you come and see . . . your aunt *Marie.*"

I promised her I would and followed the funeral train back to Aunt Liz's house in Levittown. There, waiting on line for the *terlet,* I encountered my cousin Billy, Liz's son, whose temperament required him to make encounters of the most casual meetings. He was a guidance counselor at a high school, big on bear hugs and bomb-dropping.

"I have something for you," he said, and thrust into my hands a folder of old newspaper clippings copied from microfilm. "I've been doing some digging about the family and I think I have a story for you."

"A story?" It was the first time I understood how being a writer changed my status. I opened the folder and saw one tabloid front page after another, the headlines all the more lurid for how they were printed, the microfilm palette of white on black. They were from the thirties, and they referenced a murder that had been the result of a "plain wife" driven to kill by her husband's love for his daughter's "pretty blonde" best friend. The victim was named Virginia Seigh. The rest were Reismans—the "girl-slayer," Etta; the inconstant husband, Arthur; the daughter who lost the tip of her finger in the shooting, Annette.

"What does this have to do with us?" I asked.

"Arthur Reisman was Grandma's first husband. Annette was her daughter."

"Did Grandma have anything to do with the murder?"

"Yes and no. She didn't pull the trigger. But the papers blamed the whole thing on Arthur, and he blamed Grandma."

"How did he blame Grandma?"

And this is where Billy flushed in triumph, as if he'd found that Grandma had buried a treasure in the backyard, or he found that we, all of us, were the beneficiaries of royal blood:

"He said that Grandma had destroyed him . . . as a *man*."

She was what my father said she was. She was a wreck. She was a ruin. She lived in Selkirk, in upstate New York, in an apartment pressed so close to the road that stones and cinders spattered the windows as trucks went by. She had diabetes. She was nearly blind, her eyes magnified to the size of decals behind her glasses. She could barely walk. She sat on a couch with ankles as big as buckets, tilting in on each other in wrinkled flesh-colored stockings. Music played from a radio the size of a Victrola, one of those "Music of Your Life" stations that still remembered Connie Francis, Perry Como, Kay Starr, and of course, Frank, "It Was a Very Good Year," the startling cataclysm of those final strings. She was a shut-in who had received a visitor, and a sense not only of happiness but of victory had settled into her tangled smile, as though, now that I had shown up to talk, she had all the time in the world.

It had taken me ten years to take her up on the offer she made at my grandmother's burial—ten years to come and see . . . my aunt *Marie.* She had promised to tell me the truth about my grandfather, and I wanted to hear it. But I kept putting off the trip to Selkirk until on one of my visits to Old Farm Road my uncle Harry told me that if I really wanted a story I should talk to Marie. When I asked him why, he stopped stirring the pot of stew that was a fixture on his stove and glanced around as if to make sure we were out of earshot. "Marie," he said, "was used and abused."

I didn't register what he was trying to say so much as how he said it. He liked to feign agony when he tested my grip, and after I told him that I didn't quite understand what he was trying to say I figured that his grimace was part of his playacting. But he leaned into me, and spoke in a lowered voice through furiously clenched teeth. "To make rent, her mother made her ride in the back seats of cars with *men,*" he said, making me remember what it felt like when I was a boy, and his fist squeezed my hand like a python.

"Uncle Harry, are you saying that Grandma pimped Aunt Marie?"

"I'm saying Marie was *used and abused,*" he repeated, and returned his ladle to the stew as my father appeared at the threshold of the kitchen. Dad's interest in food extended only to his stomach, and he had been sitting with Aunt Liz in her living room. Now he looked at us and said, "Caught . . . in the *act,*" as if we'd been talking about him. Of course, we hadn't been; of course, we had, in that any discussion of my grandmother also pertained to her son. When Uncle Harry answered by turning up the heat, my father found a spoon and stepped toward the pot. "Forget it," Harry said with a smile, intercepting him without looking up from his work. "Out of the kitchen. I'm trying to teach your son how to cook a stew."

"Oh, yeah?" my father said. "What are you telling him?"

Where Harry had grimaced he now grinned, and he swirled the ladle around the pot with the flourish of an artist with a fancy brushstroke. "That it's all in the *wrist,*" he said, and when he elbowed me gently in the ribs I understood that he had entrusted me with a secret—something my father either wasn't supposed to know, or wasn't supposed to know I'd been told.

Aunt Marie hadn't ruined herself, after all.

She had been ruined.

She was born in 1917. She married a man named Ernie Peters in 1934, when she was sixteen. Five months later she had a child, my cousin Vivian. Though she and her husband divorced in Miami Beach in 1941, she was Marie Peters the rest of her life. She lived in Brooklyn not far from her mother on Coney Island Avenue, and was the last of her siblings to move to Long Island, where she had an apartment in West Hempstead.

She was eighty-two years old, and when I first sat down with her, her body was sagging under its own sprawling weight. But she had a lifetime of stories to tell, and the opportunity to tell them had restored her, had straightened her, had given her an air of calm and bedraggled majesty. "And that's your father for you—that's my brother Louie," she said, as she counted all his slights. "If he don't like it, it don't exist. But there are certain things in this life you can't wish away, and one of them is *family.*" She began to strain against the pronged cane she had been grasping like a tiller, until she managed to stand up and begin tottering across the room. She bent over and began digging under the couch. "Could you help me, Tommy?" she asked, between grunts and stertorous breaths. "I got something I want to show you. Something that might be . . . of *interest.*"

I got on my hands and knees and felt for the treasures Marie had stashed away. Then I began extracting, one after another, elaborately framed portraits of unsmiling strangers, all of them posed and formally dressed, the sepia tone of the photographs itself a kind of attire. "You see?" Marie said. "That's your *family,* Tommy. I keep them pictures hidden away because they're so precious—even the frames must be worth a fortune. But I wanted to show them to you so you know where you *come* from." Marie sat down and when I stacked the photographs between us I could hear the old glass grinding at the corners, as if turning into sand. From the top, a balding man with a small officious mustache and a prim and unforgiving mouth eyed me suspiciously. "That's your great-great-grandfather Count Robolsky. He was from Hungary. See, Tommy, that's what I wanted to show you—we got *royalty* in our blood. You and me, we're aristocrats."

She showed me one generation after another, the story ending with Louis Augustus Junod, in the same portrait that had adorned Grandma's nightstand. "Oh, he was a stern-looking man," Marie said, with a certain thrill. "But he wasn't so stern. He wasn't so bad unless he drank. Then he beat my mother. But she was no saint! She drove him to it, with her shenanigans. He wasn't perfect, but then who is? I'll tell you this—I was the apple of his eye, just like Louie was my mother's. I felt bad about what happened later on, after we moved to Coney Island Avenue. There was a man who used to stand in front of the candy store across the street, in a suit. His name was Schmidt, John Schmidt. Oh, an elegant man—but I made the mistake of introducing him to my mother. He moved in, my father moved out, and that was it—it was all over. My father lived in Bushwick and stayed there the rest of his life, even when the neighborhood got bad. He died in 1968 and is buried in Evergreens Cemetery in Brooklyn. I went to the burial. You know who else did?"

"No," I answered, though I had my suspicions.

"Your *fatha,*" Aunt Marie said. "We were the only ones. Me and Louie, we were the only ones who came when they laid that man in the ground."

We ate spaghetti and meatballs for lunch, from cardboard takeout trays delivered by the local pizza parlor. She wouldn't let me pay, and tipped the deliveryman extravagantly. They knew each other. "Thanks, Mrs. Peters," he said, and left us alone—left me alone, with the burden of what I had to ask.

"Aunt Marie, when I visited Levittown back in December, Uncle Harry told me something I wanted to ask you about. He said that Grandma let you be used and abused. It was very vague, and so I wanted to ask you what he meant."

"Grandma let me be . . . abused?"

"'Used and abused' is what he said."

She paused a few seconds. "Well," she said. "Grandma was never my friend. She was never the kind of mother a girl should have—a mother a girl could ask questions. She was like that to Elizabeth, but never to me. I think it's because I looked like her grandmother and she never liked her grandmother. I don't know."

"But what does that have to do with being used and abused?"

"Well, Grandma used to like to go out with men, and the only way she could get out of the house was to say she was taking me, you see. So she'd be in the front seat with a man, and I'd be in the back seat with another."

"How old were you?"

"Well, I was at the age of attainment. Fourteen, fifteen—somewhere around there."

"That must have been awful."

"I was too young to know what was really going on. And when I did—well, I'll put it to you this way. One day you have respect for someone and then one day you don't. That's the way it was. I still loved her, she was my mother. But something went away."

"Who were these men?"

"Oh, men, you know. We'd drive around, go out to eat. Nothing happened. I can assure you of that—nothing happened. I remember the ones who went with my mother more than I remember the ones who went with me. She was seeing a half cousin of hers. We even lived for a while over where he lived, in Springfield Gardens."

"Where's that?"

"In Queens."

"My father has never told me anything about living in Queens."

"Well, like I said—that's your *fatha*. If he don't like something, he just walks away."

The day was nearly over. Marie's daughter Vivian lived nearby in Albany, and was supposed to stop by and take me out to dinner. Vivian was my first cousin, but she was born in 1934, and until I went to college I'd called her "Aunt Vivian" when I saw her in Levittown. I was looking forward to seeing her, but now the sun was setting, and Marie's apartment had grown dark without either of us thinking to turn on a light. I didn't believe what she had told me—that nothing happened in those cars. I asked her again: "Aunt Marie, were you used and abused?"

And this is how she answered:

"When I was a girl, I used to buy expensive handkerchiefs for my mother and leave them under her plate at the dinner table. I just wanted her to say something—'Thank you,' 'That's nice,' 'I love you.' But she never did. It was always like that, Tommy. When she lived in Levittown, I used to take her out every weekend, anywhere she wanted to go and anything she wanted to do. But she never said anything about it. She never said thank you. And she never told me she loved me. Never. Not once in my whole life. She loved Elizabeth. She loved your father and God knows she loved Millie. But I would have done anything for that woman. I *did* do anything for her. Oh, Tommy," she said, with her magnified eyes shining in the waning light, "why didn't my mother love me?"

My father was sixteen when it happened—when his mother's first husband witnessed the murder of his girlfriend by his second wife. He had just moved, with his mother and his sisters, from Gerritsen Beach to Coney Island Avenue. His father, his namesake, didn't come along. After the murder, reporters came to the apartment, knocked on the door. He had never mentioned any of this to us, and so I figured I wouldn't mention it to him until I found out more about it.

In 1998, I went to the public library on Forty-Second Street and Fifth Avenue with a pen and a stenographer's notepad, my resources as a researcher limited to the *Readers' Guide to Periodical Literature* and the big bound ledgers of stories that had run in *The New York Times.* I had nothing to go on except what my cousin Billy had told me and what Aunt Marie had said when I asked about Grandma's first husband:

"His name was Reisman. But we called him 'the Jew.' "

And yet, in the research room at the public library, in the pancaked drawers of microfilm spirited away in their dingy cardboard boxes, the story existed and endured and was available, beyond the uncertainties of memory. I searched for a microfilm machine that was not out of order, then wound the film into the plastic sprockets and hit the power switch. The light went on with audible breath and tangible heat, and there, right in front of me, in the burning sunlamped square, was the story of the straying husband, the wronged wife, the dead girl—of Arthur and Etta Reisman and Virginia Seigh. What I didn't find, at least in *The New York Times,* was my grandmother, or the destructive sexual power that Billy had attributed to her. What I didn't find was Arthur Reisman, with his own character on trial, pleading to the public that he had cheated on his second wife because his first wife had "destroyed him as a *man*." I was disappointed at first, because I had thought that the story was *about* Grandma, until I realized something that filled me with optimism and purpose, something that I could share with my father.

He was visiting Levittown with my mother, staying with Liz and Harry at 106 Old Farm. I took the Long Island Rail Road train from New York and he picked me up at the Hicksville station. I loved this routine, the reversal of the roles we played when I was a boy and went with my mother to meet the 5:19, the implied recognition that I was now the man of the house. He was parked along the curb in the car that I had bought him, a gold Mercury Sable, and when I opened the door he swept the old newspapers, betting forms and lottery tickets off the passenger seat and sang, "Heeeey, buddy boy . . ."

"Hey, Pop."

"Let me look at you. You look a little tired, my son. You must have been out late in the city, burning the candle at both ends. You see any *celebrities,* in your travels? You see . . . Tony?"

I had written a profile of Tony Curtis for *GQ* a few years before, and ever since my father had been of the belief that Tony and I were friends and saw each other whenever we could. "No, Dad, Tony's in LA. I was in New York doing some research. On the family."

"Oh yes?" The formal note was a warning, the verbal equivalent of a man straightening his posture after someone makes a remark.

"Yes. At the library on Fifth Avenue."

"May I ask . . . *what* you were researching?"

"A few years ago, Billy told me the story of Grandma's first husband getting caught up in a murder that made the newspapers. I went to the library today to read about it. I didn't find much about Grandma. But, Dad, I realized something when I was reading all this stuff—you have another sister!"

I was trying to tell him that he had finally gotten lucky—that his ship had come in at last. But he was unmoved. He remained still as a carving, and I found myself having to sell him on his own jackpot. "Dad, she's seven years older than you. But she might still be alive!

We might be able to find her! I can look for her! I know people who do that sort of thing . . ."

"It never happened," he said.

"What do you mean, Dad? It happened—today I found *proof* that it happened. There were articles in the *Times* and the *Daily News*. Grandma's husband was Arthur Reisman. And her daughter's name was Annette. Your sister's name is Annette."

He did not move a muscle. But his countenance changed entirely. His face contracted. His nose became a predatory beak; his lips tightened as if stitched; his eyes flamed green. It was the face that had terrified me as a child—the face I'd never expected to see again. "Now, *you* listen to *me*," he said, raising his forefinger. "It never . . . *happened*."

I did not return to the research room of the New York Public Library on Forty-Second and Fifth until ten years after he died.

14

He was never supposed to grow old. He was never supposed to go broke. He was never supposed to lose his hold over women. He was never supposed to live in a rented home. He was never supposed to stop calling me up and asking me who I like on Saturdays and Sundays. He was never supposed to *yield*, to surrender his standards and accept his diminished prospects. He was like nobody else, so he was not supposed to become like everybody else. I didn't *want* him to become like everybody else.

But look at him now. He's not that old, for God's sake. He's just sixty-eight, in 1987. But he's out of the bag business because he couldn't adjust to how it changed—the tide of imports, the advent of computerization, the cuts in commission, the young college-educated buyers he could no longer seduce or even charm. He's out of Wantagh, too, because he had to sell the house on 1463 Britton Street to pay off his gambling debts. He got a good price for it, $270,000 for an aluminum-sided split-level, enough to satisfy the bookie who wrote Janet and me a check for our wedding, enough to invest $100,000 in Treasury bills, and enough to buy a modest condominium in Florida. But that never happens. My mother doesn't like any of the condos they can afford, and exercises, one last time, her veto power. They rent a condo in Jupiter—the development is called the Bluffs—and drive a white Mercury Marquis tricked out by an after-market custom shop to look like a Lincoln Continental.

My father still has a talent for making pronouncements with a dramatic—even a musical—flourish, but his subject has changed. Instead of issuing definitive judgment on what makes a man a man or what makes a suit . . . flattering, he bemoans what has led to his own reduced circumstances, his own unmaking. He repeats, in a register of comic fatalism, the Italian word for old age, *"la vecchiaia."* He confides that "the only thing that grows when you get old is . . . your nose." He warns that "losing your confidence is like losing your hair—once it starts going, it's gone, man, and once it's gone, it's not coming back." And when he's getting dressed to go out, he observes me observing him, and, as if to beat me to the punch line, he says, "How the mighty . . . have fallen."

For years, he has taught me that clothes make the man, and I have taken him at his word. He so fervently believed that clothes mattered then that I believe they matter now, when for the first time in his life he's wearing what everybody else wears. He wears pro-shop knockoffs, even though he's a hapless golfer. He wears a ball cap on his head and running shoes on his feet. He wears khaki shorts out to dinner. He doesn't look any worse than anyone else, but that's the problem—he was a man who made his suits and his ties and his custom shirts into a uniform all his own, and so now uniformity itself is ill fitting. He doesn't even buy clothes anymore. He either wears them to death, like the blue jeans that are faded to the color of skim milk and worn to the texture of cheesecloth, or he accepts them as handouts, like the polo shirts his friend Vinnie sends him from . . . Balboa Island.

Ray Vincent married Mikie in 1984. He was arrested for running a large bookmaking operation four years later, but he still calls my father to flatter him as the only real man left in America and my father still extols the singularity of . . . his vision. Before anyone else did, Vinnie saw a nation dressed in personalized clothing and the *fortune* to be made in monograms and insignias. He invested in industrial sewing machines and now not only does he handle the embroidery for companies interested in brand extension, he sends the spares and seconds to my father. They become all my father wears. When I visit the Bluffs, I see the man who wouldn't allow me to ask celebrities for their autographs—"they should be asking for *your* autograph"—sporting polo shirts embroidered with obscure nomenclature, and when I ask what they actually *say,* he gives me a look and a ready answer: "Who cares? I get them . . . for nothing."

Then the traffic in secondhand shirts comes to an end. On December 13, 1994, Vinnie goes to a supermarket in Newport Beach to buy food for his attack dog, Schotzie. The bag of kibble is still in his car when the police begin to investigate his disappearance. There are half-hearted rumors that he is on the lam or in witness protection. But Raymond Carl Vincent, fifty-two, is never seen again.

My father takes it hard. "He was a *genius,*" he says, shaking his head.

"He was a bookie," I say.

"A bookie! You never listened to him talk! The things that came out of his mouth!"

"I heard plenty. A genius is not what I'd call him."

"He was . . . a genius businessman," my father says, with an insistent thump of his fist, and I can't help myself. I usually let my dad utter his own tragicomic epitaphs. But now I look at him in a shirt emblazoned with the logo of a club to which he never belonged, and I remember a line from *Prizzi's Honor:*

"Oh yeah? If he's so fucking smart, why is he so fucking dead?"

There is no house. There is no dune. The sand is smooth and white, with just a few tufts of beach grass by the road and a few pebbles shining in the sun and the glare off the endless ocean stinging our eyes. My father is standing in the sand, his hands clasped behind his back, moving something with his toe, maybe a shell. He's wearing his polo shirt and his ragged jeans and he looks as drawn and depleted as a former president.

I've brought him here, my idea, my plan. I want him to see this, the final erasure of what used to be. He's been kicking himself for selling the Westhampton house since he cashed the check, and I hope I can make him understand there is no Westhampton house *left,* that the ocean swallowed 879 Dune Road entire, without so much as a burp. But the last time I drove down Dune Road, I went with Janet in the immediate aftermath of the storms of 1992, and there were ruins as guideposts—slumped houses with seawater pulsing in and out of doors, drifts of scattered siding, hanks of wiring, Ozymandian chimneys. Now it's all gone, and in the vast beachfront clearing I can't find 879. But my father sure can. *"Here,"* he says. I stop the car on the sand shoulder of the two-lane asphalt and now with proprietary regret he's inspecting a lot that's been cleared for sale.

"You sure this is it, Dad?"

"Yeah, I'm sure," he says, biting his lip. "Now let's get the hell *out* of here."

I give the sand a kick on the way to the car, sending it up in a farewell spray. Then I turn the car around on the empty road, and take my father back to the Dune Deck.

I have gone to the Dune Deck on assignment. I write for *GQ*, and have already written profiles of a son like me and of a father like him—I have written about Frank Sinatra Jr. and Tony Curtis. Now I am writing about my father himself, his authority in matters of style and hygiene and, yes, masculinity. I have brought him to the Dune Deck to remind him of the way he was so that he can pronounce definitively on the way all men have to be . . . and I can write the story I've pitched to my editor as "My Father's Fashion Tips."

He is seventy-seven and he no longer abides by his own rules and maxims. "Who's going to listen to fashion tips from an old man like me?" he asked when I first proposed my idea to him. But that's the point of the story—that's why the story is much more than a story, at least to me. I am writing it as a gift to him. I am writing it so that he stops thinking of himself as a loser. I am writing it to let him know that as his son I have put so much of what he has taught me into practice. I am writing it to show him that I am finally successful, and to make him understand I owe much of my success to him.

But I didn't have to stay a weekend with him at the Dune Deck to write a story about my father's fashion tips. I grew up with them; I could write from memory about his proselytizing for turtlenecks, suntans, and the advantages of witch hazel as an omphalic antiseptic. I have brought him to the Dune Deck to do something I have wanted to do since I was a little boy and watched him *go* to the Dune Deck on late summer afternoons in his alpaca sweaters and his white ducks. I want to ask him questions. I want to interview him. I want to find *out* about him, and the people he used to go meet, Chip and Valerie Schocket and even Zsa Zsa Gabor. They were once all right here, but now it's just me with a tape recorder and my father with no place left to go.

The joint still has some pizzazz. It still has the red carpet on the wide steps that ascend to the entrance, and a chandelier that hangs down over them. It's still painted white with its name in lowercase black type that was the last word in class to me as little kid. It still has the sprawling eponymous deck, painted gray now, and the wait-staff serving drinks on the beach. The ocean my father wanted to *drink* when we lived down the road is less than one hundred feet away, but we don't go swimming. We didn't even bring . . . trunks. It's cool, one of those days in mid-August that used to send a message from fall, the sun strong and the sky clear but a touch of melancholy in the breeze, the suggestion of an ending. Other patrons are wearing jackets and sweaters. My father and I find a couple of chaise longues near the pool and we put our faces in the sun, as much for warmth as for color. He closes his eyes and I think he might be dozing off, but then a server comes for a drink order and I say, "Gin and tonic," and my father is wide awake, regarding me with a raised eyebrow. "It's a little . . . early, isn't it?"

"We're on vacation, Dad."

He nods, and holds up a finger to the server. "I'll have what he's having," he says, then specifies . . . *Tanqueray,* like it's the name of a song.

I find a little table where we can face each other. When the drinks come, he starts talking. He doesn't say much about his fashion tips, and I don't ask. We're together at the Dune Deck, and I'm preparing to ask about everything from the secrets of masculinity to the secret of Valerie Schocket. I figure I'll start with a question I consider comparatively innocent, the kind of question young men ask their fathers in duck blinds or in the clubhouse after a round of golf. I'm only guessing, of course, since neither of us hunt or care about golf, and it's not until much later in life that I discover it's not a question a single one of my friends asked *their* fathers. It's not an innocent question at all, and in any case my father doesn't have an innocent answer:

"Dad, when was your first time?"

He was fifteen, he says. He already knew how to take care of himself and he was already the man of the family. His mother had a friend who lived close by in Brooklyn. She needed something—a cup of sugar, or perhaps just a strong young man for help around the house—and his mother dispatched him to her friend's apartment. "She was waiting for me with a drink in her hand," my father says. "She poured me one too, and took off her dress. Then she took off . . . her wig."

"Her wig?"

"She had a condition," my father says. "An *affliction*."

"What do you mean, Dad?" I ask, about to learn yet again that his family differed from other families—that our family differs from other families—not in matters of wealth, or class, or education, or religion, or country of origin, but rather in matters of sex.

"Tommy," he says, with a wince that passes over his face and then disappears like a shadow. "She was . . . hairless."

Down at the Bluffs, he has his cronies by the pool, the fellow codgers who are his new audience. "They can't believe my stories," he says, but with a few of them he has a problem—they *don't* believe his stories. They think he's a bullshitter and when he starts talking about the wine and women and songs of his glamorous past there's one of them who stands up and says, "Oh, here we go again," and leaves.

"People will think I'm *crazy* if they hear me talking like this," he says now.

"What do you mean?"

"I'm telling you my true emotions here, my true feelings. I used to walk . . . on a *cloud* when I walked down Fifth Avenue. Like I owned it. I'd walk down the street with the other salesmen, and they couldn't believe it. They'd say, 'Look at the way the women are carrying on—we've never seen anything like it. Every place we go; it's unbelievable!' And it was, it was. And I used to feel, oh, so good. And that was enough to satisfy my ego. I didn't have to go any further than that. Any aspirations I might have had, about being theatrical, about being a singer, I was. *I was.*

"I used to go to the El Morocco. Have you ever heard of the El Morocco? They used to have a room called the Champagne Room, where they used to put all the celebrities. Against the wall was the place to be, and I used to get a table right there, with Jackie Gleason and the rest of them. I used to reach over and shake their hands. I would come down those stairs and people would look at me like . . . a bride at a wedding. I couldn't believe it! I couldn't believe it. And that satisfied me. All the things I wanted to do, all the things I might have done . . ."

For a moment, I wonder if he's going to try to say that all the attention made it unnecessary for him to be unfaithful to my mother. But that's not what he says at all. "I used to get on a plane and the stewardesses would sit with me—you know, try to date me. Unbelievable. And of course Chip used to come on something terrible. He'd say to Valerie, 'Look at him. Two drinks, and look at his eyes! Look at his eyes—they're beautiful. Look at his eyes!' I used to think he was crazy. But she would agree with him. It was amazing. To me, it was amazing . . ."

I remember the photograph hanging on the wall of the basement, the framed photograph of Chip Schocket and Lou Junod convening over a cigarette in the ashtray of the Harwyn Club. They were in suit and tie, and Chip was pointing out something, explaining something, telling my father something he needed to know. I always wondered what it was, the nature of his tutelage, and therefore the nature of his hold on my dad.

"Dad, why did Mom hate Chip so much?"

"Well, Chip was a troublemaker. He was always getting me in trouble . . ."

"What kind of trouble?"

"You see, everybody wanted a piece of me back then," my father says. "The handbag business had never seen anyone like me, and all the manufacturers wanted me to rep their lines. Chip had been after me, and one day he invited me up to his apartment on Sutton Place. I think I was bringing him a bag I thought he should copy—that was the reason for my visit. I knocked at the door, and three . . . showgirls answered, with nothing on but high heels."

"What did you do?"

"What did I *do*? I serviced them. All three."

"What did Chip do?"

"He watched. He was a *voyeur*—I don't think I even knew the word back then. But that's what he was."

"Did you . . . take the line?"

"Eventually he told me that if I took the line he would let me date his wife. He knew I had a thing for Valerie."

"I can see why Mom hated him."

"He used to needle her about it. If he saw Valerie and me together at a party, he'd go over to Mom and say, 'Look at the way she looks at him! Look at the way they look at each other! I'll bet there's something going on . . .' And your mom, you know, she wasn't that way. She was no swinger. She was very old-fashioned, and she couldn't stand him . . ."

Am I done? I should be done. That should be it. I've gotten what I've come for—not the fashion tips, but rather the truth I've wanted to know since I was three years old and my mother wouldn't let me call Chip's wife "Aunt Valerie." I should be satisfied. I should take my dad out to dinner and go home. But there's another question, always another question, the interviewer becoming a confidant.

"What about Zsa Zsa Gabor?" I ask him.

He responds with . . . the wince. "What about her?"

"I hear you had a relationship with her."

"Me? With Zsa Zsa Gabor . . . ?" He throws his head back and crosses his legs, considering the question like a guest on a talk show. "Who told you that?"

"Monica Haig told me, when I was a salesman and visited her in Houston."

"Monica Haig told you . . . ?"

"Yeah, Dad."

He has all the body language of a man lighting up a cigarette and looking for time, with no cigarette in sight. "I don't know if I should talk about this," he says uncertainly, almost in a mumble. "I don't want this in your article!"

"It won't be in my article, Dad. This is just between you and me."

"How about Mom? She's very sensitive, you know. And still on the ball!"

"You and me . . ."

"Well, if you must know, I met her in New Orleans, at the Fairmont Hotel. She was still married to George Sanders, so this must have been the early fifties. He was there. I was onstage. I used to like to sing with the piano player. And I was good, then, as good as anybody. I still had a lot of confidence. So I was singing, oh, probably something like 'Embraceable You'—that was one of my songs. And she came out and began dancing under a spotlight. Her husband was right there, but she danced all by herself, and . . . she *took her shoes off*."

"That's it?"

"That's it."

"Monica Haig said you . . . had her."

"She did, did she?"

"She did."

"There was another time, in New York. I was at a bar, a . . . watering hole on Fifty-Second Street. Her mother saw me. Jolie Gabor, God help me. She invited me to a party. I took a cab to an apartment that Zsa Zsa shared with her sister Eva. There was no party. I walked through the door with Jolie Gabor and she looked at her two daughters and said, 'Do I have a present for you!' "

"Really, Dad?"

"Really."

"Both of them?"

He doesn't answer the question. He looks away. When he turns back to me, a hardness has touched his face, and his green eyes are on fire.

"Anything else you need to know?"

It's the morning after. We're drinking Bloody Marys—"a couple . . . of *Bloods*"—outside, eating breakfast in the sun, seagulls flying close to see what kind of chances they have. We went out for dinner last night, and ate well, ate expensively, the waitstaff paying extra attention because *GQ* made the reservation. We went to the bar afterward, and my father insisted we drink grasshoppers, "the *in* drink at one time." We returned to our room and I put him to bed, kissing him on the forehead, which unruffled itself as he fell asleep.

I am as relaxed with him now as I have ever been. He told me the story I wanted to hear and now all that's left is to figure out what to do with it. There's an unspoken understanding between us: I know everything; I will say nothing. What I have learned would still blow up his marriage, so I won't tell my mother. It would make Janet uncomfortable, so I won't tell my wife. It would disappoint Michael, so I won't tell my brother. And, of course, I won't put any of it in the pages of *GQ*. I will just work to layer it between the lines, letting the secrets inform my story by going unsaid.

My father is looking at me, thoughtfully, ruefully. He's become a sentimental man in his old age, but his softened gaze is still arresting. "I just want to thank you," he says. "For this, for dinner, for the whole thing. That restaurant we went to last night—I never thought I'd have a meal like that again in my life. I never thought I'd have a night like that again. I thought those days were all gone, man. But you brought them back to me. I don't know how to repay you. I haven't felt this good in years."

"You don't have to repay me, Dad," I say. "This weekend is payment enough."

And I mean it. I got what I wanted from the time I spent with him and I gave him what he needed. There could be nothing better. I have no idea my life is about to change.

We are almost done with breakfast, each on our second Bloody Mary. An impatient seagull swoops and squawks, waiting for us to clear out. We say hello to a woman on a walker who last night noticed my father at the restaurant and asked for his phone number. When she passes by, I ask him a question.

"Dad, what that woman did last night—was that what it was like when you were my age?"

"Well, sure—but the women weren't . . . eighty! The only thing that old broad did was remind me of how good your mother looks!"

"You know what I mean. Her walking over and asking for your number. Is that what would happen?"

He regards me, then fixes me with his stare. "Oh, Tommy, you have no idea. I'm telling you the God's honest truth. There was a time I couldn't walk down Fifth Avenue without being propositioned. I couldn't board a plane without the stewardess sitting in my lap. I couldn't eat at a restaurant without the waitress giving me her number."

I feel those words in my face, in the heat that comes to my cheeks. "Gee, Dad. Did you take any of them up on it?" I have been trying to talk to him as a journalist. But now I can hear in my own voice the hopeful naïveté of a son.

"Not *all* of them," my father says.

And there it is, another opening that turns into an obligation.

"How many?" I ask.

My father puts his brown hand on the table, where it sits between us. He backs up a little bit, and sits at an angle. "I'm not telling *you,*" he says. "I'm . . . a gentleman."

"Okay, Dad. How about a percentage?"

He frowns as if he's doing arithmetic. His shoulders rise in a theatrical shrug and he takes a big breath through his big nose. "I don't know," he says. "Twenty-five percent?"

"Twenty-five percent!" I say this loud enough for people to hear.

"Is that . . . too little?"

"No, Dad. That's a lot. That's a *huge* number. Twenty-five percent!"

He doesn't respond. He doesn't say a word, and there's only one question left to ask him.

"Did you fall in love with any of them?"

It is still early. The sun is still rising over the ocean, so its light has not quite separated itself from the charged salt air. What's left of our food is cold, the seagulls insolently squawking. I watch my father as much as I listen to him, everything that happens happening in slow motion. He does not answer right away. But he raises his right hand, as if under oath, and unfurls a single brown digit, his forefinger. He holds it there, for inspection. I stare at it.

"One," he says.

He keeps the finger extended, one, two, three beats. Then he withdraws it, puts it away. But the ghost of it lingers. One.

"Who was she?"

"A woman I knew in Florida. In Hallandale."

"What happened to her? Is she still alive?"

"She . . . died. She . . . fell. She . . . fell down the steps of her home. She . . . fractured her skull."

"Dad." I want to hold his hand. But I don't. "She fell? Was she drunk? Did she commit suicide? Was she pushed?"

"I don't know. I could never find out."

"Dad, what do you mean, you could never find out? How could you not find out?"

"Her husband was a big man . . . at the Diplomat."

I know about the Diplomat. It was the fanciest hotel in Hollywood, Florida, the city next to Hallandale. Frank Sinatra sang there, as well as Liza Minnelli and Tina Turner. My father went to the shows. My father sometimes stayed there and the long yellow bath towel with a Diplomat insignia hung from his shower door in Wantagh, like a flag from a foreign country. "A big man at the Diplomat"—when I was growing up, that was *him,* that was my father. But now he's used those words to describe the husband of the woman he loved. He's used them to explain why he never found out how the woman he loved died.

I'm shocked, because if I know anything about myself, it's that I would have found out. My father didn't, and when he displayed his forefinger, it was a gesture biblical in its force, in its reckoning of loss. I brought him back to Westhampton because I thought the turning point in his life, the incident that led him to a life of regret, was the sale of the house on Dune Road. But now, at the Dune Deck, he turns his face away from my scrutiny, so that all I see is his profile against the endless ocean. The turning point in his life turns out to have been a tragedy. But it was not just a tragedy. It was a defeat. My father might have loved and lost. But he had also gotten scared.

On our way back to Levittown he tells me how he met my mom. It's an offhand revelation, although, like everything he says, it strikes me as a confidence. He is talking to me about his sartorial inspirations—Cary Grant, who wore ties of grenadine with simple suits; Fred Astaire, who danced in a tux with a sash tied around his waist instead of a cummerbund; Walter Pidgeon, "although he was . . . a little gay"—and I ask him how he got his start as a man of fashion. He pauses and says, "Mom's not going to like this—

it's a good thing that machine is not on. I was eighteen when I first met your mom. I was working at a haberdasher's on Flatbush Avenue. She was twenty-one. So you see, I was always interested in fashion . . ."

He is wrong about the tape recorder. It sits between us, and it's on. But that hardly matters, because now that he is finally sharing his fashion tips, he seems out of dangerous secrets, other than the perpetual one about my mom's real age. He has a startling memory for what he wore and when he wore it, and when he tells me to buy my shirts from a custom shop instead of off the rack, he summons up a lost world. "All my shirts were custom," he says. "I bought them from Seewaldt & Bauman, in midtown. I'd get them two-tone, with the high collars, and a little monogram on the French cuff . . ."

"I don't own any shirts with French cuffs," I say.

"You can't wear cuff links without French cuffs."

"I don't own any cuff links."

"Oh, Tommy, you work for *GQ*, how can you not have a pair of cuff links?"

"I'd like to borrow your cuff links one day," I say.

"I'll give you a pair of mine, with diamonds," he says. "Will you take them?"

"Sure. And then I'll buy a shirt with French cuffs."

"These are very plain," he says. "You're going to love them. They're not overdone. They're not busy. They're about . . . yay big. And in the center of the gold—they're fourteen-karat gold—there's a diamond."

"Where did you get them?"

He pauses. "Frankie gave me those, and the money clip . . ."

The money clip—yes, of course; it's made of solid gold, with a solid-gold bas-relief of the Oscar statuette, and it's his trademark. On the back is an inscription: "The Greatest." I have wondered where he got it from the moment I saw it, and now he tells me it came from a man.

"Frankie Klein gave you the Oscar money clip? Is it on you right now?"

"No, it's in my vault. That and my cuff links. You want them, you got them. They're very close to me. I . . . treasure those things."

I know how much he treasures them. I know he treasures them

more than any of his other possessions, more even than his gold dog tag, because they're gifts. The ferocity of his attachment to them has always been a mystery to me, but now it's beginning to make sense, the way that the Diplomat towel makes sense. As soon as he says that they're in his vault, I know Frankie didn't give them to him. I know he's talking again about the One, the love of his life.

I say goodbye to my father on the sidewalk in Levittown, with Aunt Liz, the eternal sentry, looking out the window. "When you get home, thank Janet for me," my father says. "Thank her for letting you do this. It was wonderful."

"I will, Dad."

"What time is your flight?"

"I don't have a flight."

"What? You're not *driving* back to Atlanta, are you?"

"No, Dad. I'm going back to the city. For work."

We are standing in front of the rental car I've parked along the curb. My father cocks a shrewd eyebrow at me, his canny gaze snapped to attention. "You know," he says, "if I didn't know how deeply in love you are with Janet, I'd say you have something . . . on the side."

"Dad."

He reaches out and grips my shoulder, turning me, forcing me to face him. "What you and Janet have, it's a beautiful thing. Your mother and I never had that."

"I know, Dad."

"Well . . . *don't blow it*."

When I kiss him goodbye, he captures me with his extended arm and we fall into a clinch, where I can feel the power of his entreaty. I have to free myself, and when I finally drive off I watch him in the rearview mirror, an old man in a yellow polo shirt and khaki shorts and sneakers, with a little glow from his weekend in Westhampton. I begin speaking into the tape recorder, dictating notes, and one of the things I say is this: "Me coming into town and feeling like the old man."

I make Manhattan by about four.

And then I blow it.

—

I have to call my mother. It's late, I'm in New York City, but today, September 26, 1996, is her birthday. She's turning eighty, so I have to call no matter what. I'm in a hotel room in Manhattan; I step into the bathroom and close the door. I sit cross-legged on the floor, huddling in a corner. I speak very softly. When she answers, "Hi, Tom," the familiarity and constancy of her voice is like a drink of water. We talk for a few minutes, my father carrying on in the background. I say, "Happy birthday, Ma," and then I walk back into the room, where a woman who is not my wife is waiting for me.

I've been in the hotel room writing "My Father's Fashion Tips" and the next morning, after the woman goes home, I finish. I take a taxi to LaGuardia, where I meet my father, in town for the *GQ* photo shoot. I escort him to the studio of a fashion photographer in downtown New York. There are clothes waiting for him, tuxes and turtlenecks, and a stylist to help him choose. He dons a black Paul Stuart tux, and drinks a martini from a crystal glass. The photographer shoots him sipping it, his legs crossed nonchalantly and his eyes aflame with defiance and command. The portrait is a restoration of sorts, a reminder of why once upon a time I lived in fear of him. I haven't seen him look that way in years. I will never see him look that way again.

When the photographer finishes with the shoot, she shows him the Polaroids she took, rough approximations of the final image. He studies them, and once she steps out of earshot, he says, "I don't think these are very . . . flattering."

"Not flattering! Dad, how good-looking do you think you *are*?"

The phone rings at ten thirty sharp and yes, I know it's him. I've been waiting for the call since I sent the first-bound copies of the December 1996 issue of *GQ* to him, with Tom Cruise on the cover and "My Father's Fashion Tips" inside. I pick up the phone, heart beating.

"You . . . killed me," says the voice on the other end.

"Dad, what do you mean, I killed you? I made you a hero! The story's a love letter!"

"You . . . killed me."

"I don't know what you're talking about," I say.

"He's . . . still *alive,*" he says.

"Who?" Was he talking about the big man at the Diplomat? I never mentioned the big man at the Diplomat in the story. For that matter I never mentioned Chip or Valerie or Jolie Gabor. I kept all my promises to him. I kept all his secrets.

"Sinatra, that's who. He's still alive!"

"Sinatra?" I begin to laugh, in part from relief. "What does Sinatra have to do with anything?"

"Go ahead, laugh. Easy for you. But you put it in your story that Ava had a thing for me. He's a very jealous man. He could have his goons rough me up."

"Dad . . ." I don't know what to say. I keep waiting for a punch line but no punch line is forthcoming. He's dead serious and he sounds a little bit—the word he uses instead of "crazy"—*cuckoo*.

I have published a story about my father's secrets—the occult secrets of how to dress and carry oneself . . . like a man—without revealing any of his, well, secrets. I have honored him but also honored that, the omertà between fathers and sons, and every day I tell myself that no one who reads it will be any the wiser about what kind of man he really is . . . and what kind of man I've become. But I'm kidding myself. My father reconciles himself to "My Father's Fashion Tips" when B. Altman posts his portrait in its window on Fifth Avenue. But there's one person who knows exactly what's in the story, exactly what I wrote on and in between the lines, and with each day that goes by without her call, the more I know that I'm busted.

I call her at the condo in Jupiter when a week passes.

"Hi, Mom."

"Oh, hi, Tom."

"Did you read the story?"

"I did."

"Well, what did you think?"

I have to wait. There is a pointed silence, and it's like listening to her chew gum. Then come the first and last words she will ever utter on the subject:

"Don't forget who *raised* you, kid."

15

When my father turned fifty, his sister Elizabeth gave him a keepsake photo album, burgundy leatherette with black pages. "This is your life, Lou Junod," she wrote across the first page in silver marker, and then kept on going, annotating every photo along the way in her swirling hand. The photos capture his heyday, that charmed span of time when he and Bess's brood lived in Gerritsen Beach and he acquired his taste—his hunger—for sunshine. In half the shots, he's with "the guys" and in nearly as many he's with "the girls," a cascade of young women in bathing suits who inspire Liz's double entendres and saucy commentary before my mother makes her entrance, all alone.

I was eleven when I first saw the album and I was scandalized by it. The "girls" didn't bother me; they just happened to be young when my father was young. But the album also contained a series of photographs that were taken when my father came home from the war. In 1946, when he was twenty-seven years old, he had taken "the guys" to Miami, and met a woman arresting enough to be shot by a professional photographer—a long-legged woman who wears a turban. She could be an actress; she could be a dancer; she could be both. But in these photos she's working as a bathing suit model and my father is working with her, a little stiff before the lens. He doesn't loosen up until he turns up with her in a series of snapshots in which they're clearly intimate, just a year before he marries my mom. The other young women in the photo album can't compete with Frances Brandshagen, but for a certain kind of man Frances Brandshagen can't compete with a turbaned bathing suit model with a talent for standing en pointe. I was a kid and these were the first photos of my dad I was sorry to see, even though Aunt Liz cracked wise in the caption: "On your toes Lou!"

I found it again when my parents moved to Florida and brought their old photographs with them. One afternoon when I was paying them a visit I came across the old "This is your life" album from

Aunt Liz, the string that bound the pages together loosening and Liz's handwriting so faded that the silver sentences looked like slug trails. But when I opened it there she was, in her turban and swimsuit, and I asked my father about her. "Oh, she was a dancer I met," he said, and left it that. But my mother walked over and took his place. She rested her elbows on my shoulders and peered at the artfully composed portrait of her husband and another woman who was part of the past and at the same time prefigured many of the other women to come. She snickered, then said, casually but confessionally, as an aside meant for my ear and mine alone, "There he is, True Blue Louie."

She didn't cackle, as she often did when she attempted a joke. She just let her words sit, unsoftened by amusement, until she went to the kitchen to fix dinner. I was left with the sound of her voice, that note of distaste, and wondered what she was asking me to think of him. Then I flipped through the book and came to the end. There, slipped between the last black page and the back cover, was a studio portrait of my mother, Frances Brandshagen, before she dyed her hair platinum. She is dirty blond, naturally so. She is very young, in a pale sweater and pearls, with a hopeful and yet wary smile. It's an eight-by-ten photograph, with tiny holes at each of its upper corners, for it must have been tacked on my father's wall, somewhere, around the time he went off to war. In the lower right corner, in pen, is a simple inscription in my mother's handwriting. I read it, and then I stare at it in relief and heartbreak. It says, "I love you, honey. Fran."

A few months later, I visited Levittown and Aunt Liz slipped me a prize. I was beginning to write "My Father's Fashion Tips," and she wanted me to read the letters her "bruddah" had sent her when he was in the army. There were three of them, each on a single page of army stationery, all written from Camp McCoy in Wisconsin, between October 1943 and February 1944, and all wrapped in a blue ribbon. I undid the ribbon as soon as I got in the car and read his familiar left-handed print. In each letter, he wrote tenderly and affectionately to his favorite sister, sounding at times like a street tough who's gone soft. He congratulated her on her engagement to the man who became my uncle Harry and reported that he was singing at dances at the service club. And then he mentioned the job she had gotten in the typing pool at the military contractor Sperry, courtesy of my mother, the Queen of Sheba:

"Very happy to know Frances got you the job. Please take care of it, you got a good start. I never liked the place but the girls that work there are nice and some highly educated and it will do you good to mingle with them. Take care of yourself. You always did and you were very clean so never neglect personal hygiene and buy some nice clothes. I guess I don't have to preach to you but it doesn't do any harm to take some advice from your big brother. Be especially nice to Frances, she sure is a swell kid and though we broke up, confidentially I'll always love her. Don't say anything to her. You got to promise me that."

Aunt Liz shared the letters with me on the condition that I return them to her when I was done. I never did. I kept them and when my parents moved away from the condo in Florida, I took the "This is your life, Lou Junod" photo album. I have them all to this day, the only documentary evidence that Louis Junod and Frances Brandshagen were once in love.

The call comes when it always does, in the dark, in the wee hours. I don't have to check the time and I don't have to figure out who's on the line. It's about 4 a.m. and it's my sister, Cathy. She's sick—or sick again. She's alone at her house and she needs my help. She and Ronnie didn't divorce, back in 1981; they stayed together. But he's still up on Long Island, working construction, and Cathy's moved to Georgia to be close to her brothers. I try talking to her, calming her down, asking her if she can go back to bed and to sleep. That's when she says that she can't breathe, that she thinks she might be dying. I put on some clothes, kiss Janet goodbye and go.

She's waiting for me when I arrive, sitting on the couch with an overnight bag already packed. I squeeze her shoulder and then slide my hand down to her wrist and try to take her pulse. She pulls her hand away and begins using it to fan her face or else spread her fingers over her chest when she's belching. She's belching a lot. I stand up and pour her a glass of water. "Cathy, are you okay?"

"I've never felt like this before," she says in a quavery but at the same time emphatic voice. "I woke up and there was a terrible weight on my chest. I couldn't take a *breath*. It kept getting worse and worse. I wouldn't have called you but I felt like I was gonna die."

"Do you still feel that way? Are you in pain?"

"It's worse than pain," Cathy says. "It's *pressure*."

"Do you think it might be indigestion?"

She stares at me, with eyes that see but dislike being seen. "I wouldn't be calling you if I had *indigestion*," she says. "It's my heart. I know you don't believe me, Tommy, but you have to. It's my *heart*."

I pick up her bag and walk her to the car. I drive her in the dark to the hospital emergency room. I've done this before—I've been doing it, in fact, ever since Cathy moved to Georgia from Long Island. So has Michael; so has Michael's wife, Pat; so has Cathy's son, Scott, who's attending college in Athens, Georgia. We've all risen before daylight and taken Cathy to the hospital in answer to her insistence that something terrible is happening and something still worse is about to. Her back, her neck, her sinuses, her breathing, her heart. She's been admitted, she's been tested. No doctor has found a cause, in her body, for her symptoms.

I wait with her, for her, and when she's discharged I ask if she wants to eat breakfast at Waffle House. We both love Waffle House. But she's angry at the doctor, at his incompetence and lack of urgency—he wouldn't admit her and he couldn't say what's wrong with her. We're driving under a blue sky, the light with an artificial tinge after a day that started so deep in the dark. I take a breath. "Cathy, I love you. But I won't take you to the hospital again. The next time you call, I'll only take you to a psychiatrist."

"You think I'm faking it," she says. "But you don't know what kind of pain I'm in. Nobody does."

"I don't think you're faking anything, and I don't think the pain isn't real. I just think the source of the pain is here and here." I touch my head and I touch my heart.

She wakes up many more mornings in panic and pain. She calls Michael, she calls Pat, she calls Scott. But never again does she call and ask me to take her to the doctor.

She's back. It is the summer of 1968, and Cathy's home from college, with an associate's degree in fashion merchandising and a job at the A&S department store in Hempstead. She is twenty years old, and has returned to the dark room with the door closed at the end of the hall. She goes out a lot and my parents fight with her and over her and the two years she spent away from Britton Street seem more like a pause in the life she was living rather than a prelude to the life to come. Even Ronnie Gustafson comes back, on leave from his tour of duty running track at an army base in Germany. It is a summer of televised tumult, but neither of them have been touched by either war or student unrest and when I go out driving in Ronnie's car and he turns up the Moody Blues' "Ride My See-Saw" on the radio, Cathy turns it off. "I hate that psychedelic shit," she says.

I have even returned to my old place at the dinner table, the chair I have to squeeze into with my back against the wall. Cathy is back facing me, until one night at the end of summer I sit surveying the kitchen and see that Cathy is cooking. My father, to my right, is drinking enough that his eyes light up and my mother, to my left, is nervous enough that her palms are sweating and she's softly belching and getting up occasionally to help my sister fry the meatballs and stir the red sauce. I can see that Cathy is nervous too, and that when she confers with my mother she whispers, just out of earshot. I wonder if she's nervous because she's dressed up for dinner and is afraid of staining her clothes. Then I wonder why she's dressed up in the first place and why she's cooking dinner and why for once I'm the only one in the family who's not nervous until I realize that she's dressed up and cooking dinner for *me,* and I get as nervous as everyone else.

I am the first one she serves. She puts a plate in front of me piled high with spaghetti thickened by overcooking and sauce red as the seal of a letter. I start winding noodles around my fork and normally I'd wait for my parents to be served but I see that they're waiting for me and so I shove the fork in my mouth. "Whaddaya think?" Cathy asks, in her funny tough-girl voice.

"It's good," I say, though the sauce has a sharp taste and the meatballs are a little dry.

She's smiling but her eyes are jumpy. "*That's* good," she says, and sits down across from me. "And do you know why I'm cooking tonight?"

"No."

"Because I have to *learn* to cook. And do you know why I have to learn to cook?"

"No," I say, slightly irritated by the singsong voice she's using.

"Because I'm Mrs. Ronnie Gustafson."

She does not let go of her smile. My parents do not let go of their silence. I do not let go of my fork, which is suspended between my mouth and the plate.

"You're *married*?"

She exhales, her shoulders sinking in relief, and allows her amusement to alter her smile. My sister always looks beautiful when she's about to laugh.

" 'Fraid so," she says.

"When was the wedding?"

"*Well* . . . we eloped. On July second."

"Wow," I say. And that's all I say, because I don't know what else to say. I guess I should say "Congratulations" but the occasion is as solemn as it is festive and there's no champagne or even ginger ale. My parents don't take their eyes off me and I don't take my eyes off Cathy's hands. I keep waiting for her to show me the ring but the only ring she wears is the opal ring that belonged to my mother's mother, who died before any of us were born. I keep staring so expectantly and intently that she withdraws her hand from the table and puts it in her lap. Then we're all nervous again, and the only person who doesn't belch before we start eating is my father.

It's Mother's Day 1996, but my father is the one I hear. My mother is speaking softly, hesitantly, and the diminuendo of her speech just encourages him to turn up the clamor of his own. He's crowding her. He's growling, in the background, and I keep expecting him to take the phone out of her hand.

"Mom, what's going on? What's Dad saying?"

"Oh, he just—Lou! Please! I'm trying to talk to Tommy!"

"Mom, just tell him it's *Mother's Day*. I'll talk to him in a second, right after I talk to you."

"Tom, I wouldn't even ask you if he wasn't carrying on so . . ."

"Ask what?"

"He wants to know . . ."

"*What?*"

"He wants to know why you're picking on Cathy."

"Picking on Cathy? How am I picking on Cathy?"

My mother's voice becomes smaller still. "Telling her that her back pain is all in her head."

"I'm not picking on her, Mom," I say. "I'm telling her it's all in her head because it's all in her head. And if you put Dad on, I'll tell him the same thing."

But Dad doesn't come on. They both grow quiet, and I finally have the chance to tell Mom what I called to tell her in the first place: Happy Mother's Day, Mom.

I forget how old-fashioned my mom is. I forget how unsophisticated my mom is. I forget how unadventurous my mom is, especially about food. On the one hand, she loves restaurants because she hates cooking. On the other, she's suspicious of ethnic restaurants to the exact degree she's suspicious of the restaurant's particular ethnicity, and so it turns out I've made a mistake taking her to the Persian restaurant that's opened near our home in Marietta. I figured we couldn't go wrong with shish kebabs, but I was mistaken. She doesn't just pick at them, with the tines of a fork turned upside down; she gets nervous picking at them, glancing around the dining room with a stagey smile.

At least she went with us. My father refused. He's stayed back at Michael's house instead, so now Janet and I have the chance to spend some time alone with my mother. My brother and my sister and me, we all live within a few miles of one another and I mention to my mom that Cathy and Ronnie are just about to celebrate their thirtieth wedding anniversary on July 2. I was ten years old when Cathy made dinner and announced that she was "Mrs. Ronnie Gustafson"; now I'm forty, and perhaps because I can never forget the shakiness of Cathy's manner when she made the announcement, I try to remember to observe her anniversary. When I was a boy I sent her cards, and although these days I just call her up, her anniversary never comes as anything less than a surprise to both of us.

"Now, they eloped, right?" Janet says.

"Yes," I say, with certainty.

"But there's that photo of Ronnie and Cathy getting married in a church—what's that?"

"Well, after they eloped, Cathy went to Germany, and they had a priest marry them, so they could be married in the Catholic Church."

"Huh," says Janet. She is Protestant to the bone, and has never lost her skepticism about Catholicism and its rote mysteries.

"I think that happened in October," I say.

"I remember talking to Ronnie about it one day and he said their *anniversary* is in October," Janet says.

"I'm sure he meant the anniversary of the church ceremony. Right, Mom?"

But when I turn to my mother, her eyes fill with tears. I look at Janet, and after she takes a breath she reaches across the table and holds my mother's hand.

"It's *okay,* Fran," she says. "Everything worked out. They've been married for a long time, and they gave you beautiful grandchildren."

Then she gives the old gnarled hand a squeeze, and my mom's tears don't so much fall as splash, drenching her crumpled face. I don't know what's happening, and I sit with my jaw slack. I turn to Janet and she explains, almost in a whisper, "They didn't elope. Cathy was pregnant when they got married."

I reach out for my mom's shoulder but she pays no attention to my touch because something else has come over her, an uncoiling in a woman I've never even seen coiled. She balls her hand into a fist, and brings it down hard on the table. "That son of a *bitch,*" she says with a clenched fury, and only then, when the sound of the blow has become the sound of a secret revealed, does the grief overcome and overwhelm her. I have seen my mother cry many times. But I've only seen her cry like *this* once before, when I accompanied her to a funeral at the Dineen family plot in New Jersey, and she fell to her knees in front of her mother's grave and teardrops spurted from her eyes. She is like that now, again, so naked in her bitterness and shame that I almost forget what I've just learned:

Everybody knew the secret of Cathy's pregnancy but me.

He calls from a phone booth on the way to Atlanta. My mother has passed out in the car. He drives her to an emergency room and calls back an hour later. He's ebullient, from the hospital room.

"Here, let me put your mother on."

"Ma, how are you? You okay?"

"Oh, I'm fine—just a little sleepy. But you know your father. Everything's a big deal. Here, you talk to him."

He returns to the phone. "Your mother, she's unbelievable. I brought her in here, worried sick. I thought she was *gone*. But she was just a little bit dehydrated. You know your mother—she snaps right back, then all she wants is her lipstick. Very vain, your mother. But you should see it here—I'm in the room with her, and the doctor says he wants to bring in another doctor. I said, 'I don't like the sound of *that*.' A second doctor comes in, then another and a couple of nurses. I say, 'What's going on?' They say, 'We're looking at her chart. Is she really eighty-two years old?' They couldn't believe it! *Couldn't* believe it! I said, 'Don't let her hear you, she's very sensitive about her age.' Ah, *now* she's listening, because she knows I'm talking about her. Right, Frances—isn't that what they said? Unbelievable, your mother—unbelievable. Eighty-two years old! Oh, she doesn't like that—now she's giving me . . . the *look* . . ."

A year later, I'm sitting alone on the balcony of their condo in Florida, facing the great black expanse of the Atlantic Ocean. It's a week after Thanksgiving, but the breeze is still thick and warm and I've gone outside just to feel it, and also to spend some time alone. I used to love Florida. It belonged to my father and yet it always beckoned, the softness of the air and the proximity of the moon promising some kind of perpetual permission. Now I visit out of filial duty, and two times I've come to be with my mother when she's undergone surgery. Back in 1985, she slipped getting out of a Jacuzzi at a Holiday Inn in Cape Canaveral and broke her hip. The surgery left one leg an inch and a half shorter, and eight years later I sat with her in the hospital after a more competent surgeon evened them out. But none of those operations were like the one she has to endure tomorrow. She kept feeling faint and then she grew short of breath and she's not driving anymore because she momentarily passed out behind the wheel of their car. A week ago, she called me with the news that she has three blocked arteries and needs bypass surgery. She is eighty-three years old, and she asked me to come to Florida to be not with her but with my father.

She didn't have to ask, of course, and even as I'm listening to the hissing fountain in the swampy pond dug between my parents' place and A1A and then the high and low notes of the ocean beyond, I can hear her in the condo, the brave small talk she's making to my father as she packs her clothes and he watches TV. I listen to her—for her—in the little laundry room and then in the kitchen and I listen to her push the sliding door open a little wider so she can join me on the balcony. She stands with her hand on the railing, breathing through her nose, and then sits next to me without a word, the webbed beach chair scraping against the concrete as she settles in. We are both breathing now, as if we are trying not just to inhale the ocean breeze but to calm ourselves down. I was sure she had gone to the kitchen to bring me cookies—my mother always tries to feed me cookies in Florida—but no, she has come to the balcony empty-handed. My heart starts beating, because I know what is happening, I know she has come outside to tell me something. I don't know what she is going to say, only that she thinks she is going to die in the morning, die on the operating table as her father did, and wants to leave me with the last word, something she believes I need to hear. And I want to hear it, desperately; I've wanted to hear it my entire life. And yet I don't wait for her to start talking; I can't. I begin talking, blabbing, to break the awful poise of her silence. "I've always liked Florida," I say. "There's something special about it—"

She cuts me off, not just her words, but her tone. "I know you idolize him," she says.

My shoulders relax, or slump; I exhale, or simply surrender my breath. "Mom, I don't *idolize* him; I just—"

She stops me with a raised palm, a gesture I associate with him, not her. "No," she says. "You do. And that's okay. You're his son. He's your father. But he's not who you think he is. He's a mean, nasty, *little* man. And he's *no one* to idolize."

And then she goes back inside to finish packing her bag.

We all wake up early and head to the hospital in the dark. My mother went to the hairdresser for the occasion and the sight of her heading for a triple bypass with her lipstick freshly applied and her spun coiffure restored to its tensile strength reminds me of her special brand of pluck—her essential defiance. And yet I have never seen her so afraid. She prays out loud, which is something she rarely does, and then before she has to change out of her clothes, she lingers in my father's embrace, which is something she has never done in my presence. "You look great," he finally says, patting her between the shoulders. "Look at her, Tommy. Look at your mother. Doesn't she look great?"

"She looks great."

"People can't get *over* how young she looks. We went to that hospital in Georgia and she drew a *crowd*. They couldn't believe it! They couldn't believe it when they found out her age! They thought there was some kind of mistake!"

"I might look young," my mother says. "But I'm old." She looks at us, past us, through us, her eyes cornered, everything now the subject of a sidelong glance. "I don't want to die on the table," she whispers, as though confessing a secret.

I step away from the bed and so does my father. The curtain closes with a rasp. I want to say, "Dad, go in there and help her—she's your wife!" But he tilts into me, slumped, with his dangling hands balled into useless fists. He takes a sharp discordant breath and I pat him between the shoulders and when the curtain screeches back open my mother's lipstick is wiped clean and she's goose-fleshed in the scandalous miniskirt of her hospital gown. "Tommy, can you get me an extra blanket?" she asks. I am relieved for the request, to be of use, but when I return with the folded square my father is standing bereft in the space left by her departure, a hand over his eyes. I run past him and catch up to the cortege of her gurney. She doesn't see me; flat on her back, she is staring up at the ceiling, her brave hairdo sealed in a surgical cap. But I reach for her hand, and give it a squeeze; she squeezes back. "Don't leave me," she says, with the smile of the blind. But I'm an interloper in an accumulating crowd, and I have to trot to keep up with her acceleration. The masked surgeon, nurses, technicians—they shrug me aside, and I feel my fingers coming undone, surrendering my mother's hand as we approach the ceremonial doors of the operating room. "Tell Michael and Cathy I love them," she says just as she is being stifled, just as other hands reach for her and the doors close behind her and in front of me and I'm standing there with a blanket in my hand, worrying that she's cold.

I find my father standing where I left him, like a mourner. He is not crying, just stunned, agog, his familiar outfit—the brown leatherette Members Only jacket with zipper parted to reveal his butter-yellow turtleneck and his gold dog tag—pressed into ceremonial duty. At first he seems surprised to see me; then, with a whirl of force, he grabs me, and holds me, and presses his mouth sloppily against my cheek and then into my ear. "She told me last night she *hated* me," he says. "She told me several times. Of course I didn't believe her. But . . . do you think . . . ?"

I have devoted my life to keeping my father's secrets. To protect my mother I have protected my father, either lying outright or earning compounding interest from the sin of omission. Now it falls to me to keep the truth . . . from *him*.

"She's just frightened, Dad. She's just scared to death."

16

He's a desperate man. He sells the MG he promised me. He sues people. He asks me to pay him back the money he gave Janet and me when we were putting together a down payment for the house—"If I don't need it, it was a gift; if I need it, it was a loan," he says. When we buy him the one-year-old Mercury Sable, he asks if we can give him the cash instead, as a down payment on a Lincoln. He urges me not to buy a house in Shelter Island and to buy his condo in Jupiter instead, promising he'll pay us rent. He runs up enormous credit card bills and when we pay them off and cut up the cards, he simply applies for new ones—"How can I resist free money?" When he buys some profitable stocks during the first tech boom of the last millennium, he writes himself checks from his margin account; when the market crashes, he loses all he's made and then some, and my mother asks me to talk to him again.

"Dad, how much do you have left?"

"Oh, only about twenty-five thousand dollars."

"Get out of the market now! You and Mom can survive on that for a while!"

"Who said anything about just . . . surviving?"

"Think of Mom, Dad."

"I got a tip on one of those startup companies you read about. I have . . . an in."

"Dad . . ."

"I'm thinking of putting it all in . . ."

"All of what?"

"What's left."

And that's exactly what he does.

My mother still has a sweet tooth. That it has ruined her teeth—that she has few teeth left, and that her ravaged mouth occasionally makes her look like a glamorous madwoman—has not stopped her from pursuing and indulging it. She has always liked cakes and pies and cookies and exotica like éclairs and charlotte russe. But now she mainly goes for the hard stuff, which is to say the soft jellied candies already responsible for so much dental damage. Chuckles, Jujyfruits, and Dots: she carries boxes of them in her handbag and pops them like medicine in the late afternoon when her blood sugar craters and she endures what she calls her "slump," their bright kindergarten colors flashing in her mouth's black shadows. She used to go out for them herself but now that she has stopped driving she waits for my father to stop for gas and she has to step inside the gas station to use the bathroom. That's when she sneaks the candy and stashes it in her bag, along with her pills.

They are in Hicksville, Long Island. They have to drive back to Levittown, because they have come back to where they started—come back home, although they are homeless. They lost their condo in Florida and Aunt Liz invited them to live in her house, in a spare room with a foldout couch. For all her devotion to her "bruddah," his sister is not happy. Neither are my parents, and on this day they're driving around Long Island just for something to do. When they stop at the gas station, the rack of candy is to the left, and the ladies' room is in the back, to the right, on a raised platform. My mother has to take a step up to reach it and on the way back she forgets to take a step down. She goes flying, and lands in a sprawl near the candy. She goes to the hospital in an ambulance, my father following in the Sable. Michael and I both fly up from Atlanta for another operation.

Michael is weeping. It is late at night and all the lights in his town house are blazing punishingly bright. He is upstairs, in his office, going through his financial records and apologizing to his daughter Brittany. She doesn't know what he's apologizing for and is just trying to make him feel better. She's trying to tell him that she loves him and everything is going to be okay. But he doesn't believe that everything is going to be okay because he can't—because his brain won't let him. His thoughts are coming too fast and he can't stop them. All he can do is go over his papers and blame himself for the condition of his finances and weep so loudly that my father opens the door of the room where he and my mom are staying and comes out to see what's wrong.

It is December 27, 2004. My parents have been staying with my brother because they had to *move in* with my brother—because Aunt Elizabeth asked them to leave her house in Levittown and they have nowhere else to go. They arrived about two weeks ago, and their arrival has coincided with the deepest and most dangerous crisis of Michael's life. It started when he went into debt but it gained a devastating momentum and has turned into a cyclotron of negative thinking. He is in agony, and the spectacle of his suffering has been terrifying to his two daughters and to me. Tonight, we are all staying with him, because we are afraid of what might happen if we don't.

It began in the summer when my brother broke up with his girlfriend. He had managed to endure an open-heart surgery at the age of forty-eight and a divorce two years later, but this time he couldn't shake the despondency. He went to a doctor who prescribed Paxil, which broke something in him. He didn't sleep for days. The doctor told him to stop taking the pills, but now that his thoughts had begun speeding up, they never slowed down. They seemed to accelerate day by day and even moment by moment. He not only obsessed over his precarious finances; he obsessed over his precarious finances in the belief that obsession was his only way out and repetitive thinking his only way to find answers. "So what are you going to do, Bro?" I asked one day after listening to him spend hours on the phone with creditors and debt counselors.

"I'll be okay. I'll just sell a million socks."

"That's a lot of socks," I said. "What if you can't sell a million socks?"

He considered my question, then looked at me as though I weren't there. "I'll just sell a million socks," he said.

I did not think my brother was mentally ill. I refused to think he was mentally ill. He was fifty-six years old and had never received a diagnosis of mental illness. He had never been treated for mental illness. He kept himself in great shape and even when he was down in the dumps about money he was always my big brother and I could always depend on him. When two days before Christmas I took him to a hospital emergency room and the doctors wanted to admit him, I was outraged: "What do you mean 'admit him'? My brother is not mentally ill. He just needs the right medicine."

What convinces me in the end is the relentlessness of his mania. It doesn't just change the way he thinks. It changes the way he eats, the way he bathes, the way he looks, the way he looks *at* you and responds to being looked at. His eyes bounce around. He whispers to himself. He is no longer made of just flesh and blood and bone and muscle. He is made of flesh and blood and bone and muscle and mania, as if his every molecule has become subservient to the million socks in his brain.

Does my father see what's happening? He does, in that he's told me he's worried about Michael. Does he *understand* what's happening? He doesn't, in that he thinks all Michael needs is money and wishes he could write him a check. He either doesn't see or doesn't permit himself to see that something none of us can even identify is taking over Michael. Indeed, as my brother's condition grows worse and worse, both of my parents spend more and more of their time behind the closed door of the spare bedroom. And so when the door opens and my father finally steps into the tumult, he arrives at the worst possible moment and says the worst possible thing. Brittany is crying, begging her father to tell her what's wrong. Michael is crying, pleading that he doesn't know. My father sees the tears and doesn't know how to respond except to say that enough is enough—it is time for my brother to "be a man."

It is Brittany who defends her father, a nineteen-year-old college student standing on the narrow walkway that connects Michael's office to the spare bedroom on the second floor of his town house. "Stop it, Pop-Pop!" she says sharply, through her tears. "Stop it! Stop talking to him like that! Can't you see what's happening?" Her grandfather's expression changes immediately, which is not to say it softens. It stiffens and it sharpens and he seems almost to welcome Brittany's challenge. "Don't you *dare* talk to me like that," he says in a voice that makes a stranger of his own blood, and then he advances on her with his hands balled at his sides. He looks as lethal as he looked when I was nineteen, but Michael is on him in a rippling instant, all three of them now squeezed into the walkway, eight feet above the floor. I am not just afraid of the possibility of an accident. I am afraid of the possibility of violence.

I manage to get between them and to turn my father back to his bedroom. Brittany leads Michael downstairs. I find him pacing in his room, and he gives me his BB gun for safekeeping.

It is a long night. It doesn't even feel like night, since there is no possibility of sleep with Michael up and about in the darkness. Every so often I leave the big leather couch in his living room and check on Brittany and Kim, and find the two sisters huddled together with their eyes wide open, like waifs. Nobody is sleeping, nobody can even conceive of sleeping except my parents, whose door is closed and whose room is silent.

It is still dark when we leave the house for Michael's early appointment with the psychiatrist. The light is just coming up when we get there, but the waiting room is already crowded. We find a place to sit. We find a place to talk. We are sitting close, practically against each other, our shoulders touching. "Bro," I say, in the casual, offhand voice I sometimes use on my job. "Last night, when Dad and Britt were having that fight and you advanced on Dad, what were you going to do?"

"I was going to kill him," Michael says, in a voice as casual and offhand as my own, as though he said he was going to give Dad a cookie.

"I thought so."

The psychiatrist calls us in. The appointment lasts less than five minutes, and when it ends I take Michael across the street to the psychiatric hospital that occupies the center of the grounds. My big brother is not mentally ill. My big brother can't be mentally ill. He just needs the right medicine. He's a salesman and he just needs to sell a million socks. "Do you believe that he is a threat to himself or others?" the intake nurse asks.

"Yes," I say, and in that single word, that single syllable, I hear myself saying goodbye. It is irrevocable. I can't change it even if I want to, and now all that's left for me is to kiss him, hug him, squeeze him and leave him. There is paperwork. There is an interview. But there is also the inevitable moment when his arms are outstretched and his face is folded in a rictus of agony and I have to turn my back and walk out the door, knowing I have just committed my brother for an acute episode of what turns out to be bipolar I.

It is the shock of my life. No: it is the end of my childhood, the collapse of my belief system, the one ingrained in my DNA. When I go to my car and find myself alone, I turn up the radio and then I raise my own voice even louder. So much of my life seems behind me now but an utterance comes to my mouth about what I need to do next—a vow. I have never said it out loud. I have never *allowed* myself to say it. Maybe I shouldn't say it now—bipolar I, after all, is an organic condition. It's nobody's fault. But now I nearly shout it, radio on:

"I will survive this. I swear to fucking God I will survive this. I will survive my family and I will survive my fucking father."

I am a father. Janet is a mother. My parents come often to our house for Sunday dinner so that they can spend time with the family—our family. When dinner is over my father does what he usually does, repair by himself to the living room. He sits on a the big couch, facing the wall filled with CDs and books, and I pour him a drink and select the music for him. I play a CD of Harry Nilsson singing American standards. He knows the words to every song, and listens closely and critically to how the singer navigates all the hard turns.

My daughter, Nia, appears while I'm searching for the next CD. She has been in the kitchen, playing cards with my mom, whom she calls "Po Po," Chinese for "grandmother." Now she is climbing on the couch with my dad, who says, "Why, *hello,* tiger." Nia is a climber, whose first word was "up." But she is also something else.

There has never been more than one singer in my family; the one singer has never really permitted another. Neither my brother nor my sister would sing so much as "Happy Birthday" as a kid. But Nia can sing, and when she climbs next to him on the couch she sings to him what she sings to us, to Janet and me, in the car:

"Moon wiver, wider than a mileah, I'm crossing you in stylah, someday . . ."

"Heeey," my father exclaims. "Listen to you! You're pretty good! You're . . . a singer!"

"Oh, dweam-makah, you old heart-bweakah, wherever you're going, I'm going your way . . ."

They share a birthday; they were both born on March 23, he in Brooklyn in 1919 and she in Jiangxi Province in China in 2003. She is heading for her third, he for his eighty-seventh, and as I watch her climb the couch and listen to her sing to him, it strikes me that his loss of power, his declawing and defanging, is a kind of triumph. His granddaughter is afraid of any number of things. But she is not afraid of him.

He begins to bleed a few weeks before Christmas. I take him to the emergency room, where a nurse reads his blood pressure and immediately admits him to the ICU. His heart is racing and his blood pressure is cratering because he's overdosed on blood thinner. He is assigned a room in the hospital and a nurse comes in, frank and saucy and knowing. She talks to him as if she has a history with him, as if, at the very least, she can see what kind of man he's been, and when she tells him she has to install a catheter he begins to flirt with her. She gets him out of his clothes and into a hospital gown; then she opens his gown and reaches for his penis and he says, "I know it gets smaller with age, but this is *ridiculous*—I'll never look at a woman again." She laughs, and without warning stabs the head of my father's downcast dick with a spool of clear tubing. He recoils as if he's been harpooned, shivering and gasping with his eyes and his mouth wide open and his back arched and his skin turning as pink as a squalling baby's. I never thought he had any pink in him. I never thought I'd see him so mortified or in so much pain.

After the nurse leaves and we're alone together, he asks me a question that is really a question for himself:

"And what do I do tomorrow if they come back in here and say, 'Mr. Junod, we've done all we can do'?" He gives my hand a squeeze of assurance. "I guess then there's nothing *to* do. I guess then I try to be the man I always thought I was."

He does not die. But that doesn't mean he's not dying. He returns to the hospital a few weeks later for a CT scan. His heart is a wounded leviathan, vast and sprawling and yet decisively diminished. It's a wreck, literally—it looks like some fabled dreadnought, some vessel of war and plunder that after too many battles has found its home on the ocean floor, not only submerged but surrendered to the deep. "It's *huge,*" I say to the radiologist, hearing in my voice the echo of boyhood awe.

"Yeah," he says. "That's not good."

My father has a late-stage congestive heart failure, and when the scan is done, he doesn't bother looking at it. He just reads my face.

"How long do I got, doc?" he asks.

He's still sneaky, because he still has his credit cards and he still has his keys. He's using the credit cards to buy food at the supermarket and take my mother out to eat and he's using the keys to get into accidents in the Sable. He doesn't report the accidents. He doesn't admit the accidents. He lies about the accidents, because they take place in parking lots, and so he blames the accumulation of dings and dents and sudden stripes of alien paint on the infamies of others. He even reports one of his sideswipes to K-Mart, hoping the corporation might be moved to pay him off for the perils he faces when he parks in their handicapped spaces: the Death of a Salesman, the Birth of a Plaintiff. I call a few times and tell him that he has to give up his keys before one of us, Michael or I, takes them away.

"Oh yeah? I forgot more about driving . . . than you'll ever *know.*"

"The forgetting is the problem, Dad."

"Just you try to come over and take my keys. Just you try."

But pain is even sneakier than my father. It catches up to him in the spring of 2006, a few months after he receives his terminal diagnosis, and it's sneaky because it's unconnected to his failing heart. He has shingles, and I try to explain to him that he did nothing to cause it, that the chicken pox he had as a boy has just been hiding away and waiting for the opportunity to reemerge. But he is consumed not just by the pain but by the conviction that he is being punished. A man who has never prayed or even mentioned God turns suddenly into Job, clutching the sheets and blankets that provide him no comfort and repeating over and over again, "What did I do, what did I do, what did I do, what did I do . . . ?" It's a question I can't answer, because I can't clear his conscience, I can't assure him he's done nothing wrong.

The pain lasts for weeks, for months, despite the antivirals. My mother sleeps in a separate room and tends to him in perfunctory fashion, since even the lightest touch can reduce him to trembling. They still fight; their neighbors in the complex report on his yelling, the awful things he says. But if nothing has changed, so has everything, for instead of living in fear of him, she seems on her way to living without him.

In June, I drive him to the VA hospital. He is stubbly and disheveled and when he steps on the scale he weighs 143 pounds. The weight shocks him—"I was two hundred when I was discharged from the army, and now my mighty riveter's arms look like . . . corncob *pipes*"—and so does my attitude. "Do you drink?" the doctor asks.

"No," my father answers.

"He does," I say.

"Are you depressed?" the doctor asks.

"No," my father answers.

"He is," I say.

"Do you suffer from any memory loss?" the doctor asks.

This time my father doesn't bother to answer and instead looks at me.

"Yes, he does," I say, and now my father narrows his eyes and holds his gaze on me, its ice-cold assessment.

"You must really want me *gone,*" he says.

I stare back at him, in a kind of awe. *The old man is still throwing haymakers.* He's wrong—I certainly don't want him gone. But I am, indeed, *going;* I'm heading up to Shelter Island with Janet and Nia for the summer. I tip the brim of his hat back and kiss him on the furrows of his forehead, without any inkling that this might be the last time I ever do so.

The phone rings on a Friday morning in the middle of September. It's Michael, in Atlanta. "I'm driving Dad to the VA to get his pacemaker checked," he says. "He's not doing great—his ankles have really blown up. Do you want to talk to him?"

He hands his cell phone to our father. "Dad?" I say, into the little blurt of silence.

"Tommy," he says, with something I haven't heard in a while, that note of desperate relief.

"How are you doing, Dad?"

"Not too good, son. I can't believe I'm not going to see the baby again."

"Dad," I say. "Will you just stop? We're leaving on Monday or Tuesday. We'll be home in less than a week. I'll take Nia to see you as soon as we get there."

"Well, you better hurry up then," he says, and gives the phone back to my brother.

It is the end of summer. It is the most beautiful time of year on Shelter Island, and on Saturday we go in the evening to the beach for a farewell dinner with our friends. One of them sees me walking the sand with Nia on my shoulders and says, "Tom, you are *besotted.*" And I am, and it crosses my mind how lucky I am that my father is too. We'll return to Atlanta in a few days. She'll sing him "Moon River" again.

It is dark when we go back home. Janet and I put Nia to bed and then go downstairs to clean up and drink some wine. At 12:30 a.m., September 17, 2006, the phone rings. It's Michael.

"Dad's gone," he says.

Everything turns black, and I go right down. I hit the ground with a thud. I'm staring at the ceiling. The room has turned over, the floor going out from under me like a piece of carpet. My eyes roll back in my head. I cover my face with both hands, with no idea of how I got here—how I ended up flat on my back, my father's body a thousand miles away.

Book Three

NO MATTER HOW I TRY, I FIND MY WAY INTO THE SAME OLD JAM

17

There is a black-and-white photograph of my family, taken at a bar in Wantagh two years after my father died. It is a photo he'd be proud of—a photo of a family that looks happy and handsome enough to carry his name. Indeed, the photo is so celebratory that it belies its occasion, which happens to be the death of my mother and his wife, Frances Brandshagen Junod.

She had died on October 25, 2008, at the age of ninety-two, and we had just attended her memorial service at Charles J. O'Shea Funeral Home on Wantagh Avenue. The service was very similar to the one we had given my father in the fall of 2006, in that I planned it, wrote it, picked the music and delivered the eulogy. And yet it couldn't have been more different, and not simply because I made sure there was no Sinatra on Mom's final playlist. I had tried giving Lou Junod a state funeral, speaking for him to imagined multitudes, bargaining with posterity. At Mom's service, I spoke to *her*—"You were my first love," I said, and those words, spoken to a small crowd comprised primarily of family, released me from worry. I didn't have to sweat the turnout. I didn't have to be defensive about the inescapable factuality of cremation or about the size of the urn. I didn't have to be vigilant about the possibility of being surprised by some dimly remembered figure from the past. I didn't have to worry about putting on a show. All I had to do—all we had to do—was say goodbye to a woman we loved.

It's an oddly crowded photograph, given the closing-time emptiness of the bar and given that Janet and Nia stayed back home in Atlanta. Eight of us are squeezed into the frame, as if pressed on all sides by thickets of people, when in fact we're all there is and all that's left—from left to right, my nephew Scott; my brother-in-law, Ronnie; my niece Stacey; my sister, Cathy; me; my brother, Michael; and his two daughters, Kim and Britt. Michael wears the most serious expression, because the camera does him no favors, and Ronnie the most *satisfied* because he, the son-in-law, could never satisfy my mother. But even if we tried none of us could hide the shared sense of survivorship and giddy relief. It wasn't that my mother was gone. It was that both of them were, and the orphan air we breathed was like a strong spirit.

The next day, we drove Mom's ashes to the national cemetery in Calverton, Long Island, way out east, where Dad waited for her in the cold ground. There was a brisk ceremony in a bleak concrete "committal shelter" where Cathy—who rarely if ever cried—shocked me by staying behind and weeping alone over Mom's urn, the patient attendant waiting to take it away. Before we left, I walked over to the little administration building near the entrance, where I had to finalize the paperwork. It was a veterans' cemetery, and I had to confirm that Private Louis Junod had received a Purple Heart for wounds incurred during World War II and wanted that honor to be noted on the bronze plaque that marked the location of his—and now Mom's—ashes. "Would you like the plaque to say anything else?" the administrator asked.

"Anything else?"

"Something to personalize it. Were your parents married a long time?"

"Almost sixty years."

"Well, people write things like 'Together forever' or 'Together in heaven,'" she said. "You know—something nice."

"'Mom and Dad,'" I said.

"'Mom and Dad'?" she asked.

"Yes, that's who they were to us," I said.

She smiled. "All right then—'Mom and Dad.' That's nice."

In silence I watched her enter the words on a form, then felt compelled to add: "They were a good mom and dad."

"I'm sure they were," she said. "They were together a long time!"

I walked out. Seven years passed.

Then Michael had lunch with Muntu Law.

—

It was the summer of 2015. Michael had come up from Atlanta to stay with us in our house on Shelter Island, New York, which Janet and I bought in 2000 at least in part to recapture the summers my family had at the house in Westhampton Beach. He was doing better, my brother, still Big Mike. He'd suffered an episode of bipolar illness when Mom and Dad moved down to Atlanta in 2004, and then again a year after Mom died, in 2009. He had not been cured, no, but on most days it was hard to tell he had ever been sick. Though born ten years apart, my brother and I had been dedicated to each other since I was born, and the onset of his illness made no sense to me. He had always taken such good care of himself, fetishizing his body no less than my father did his own, practicing the fundamental tenets of Dad's faith with such zeal that Michael wound up exemplifying their more radical corollary. Dad believed—and instructed us to believe—that "if you look good, you feel good." Michael believed that "if you look good, you *are* good," and was so kind, so decent, so good-humored and caring, that he very nearly validated my father's ethos while demonstrating his own. Dad's teachings were materialistic to the point of frivolity, but with Michael they worked, and so after his bouts of illness he tried to get better the only way he knew how—by getting into "great shape." In 2015, he was three years shy of seventy, but he posted videos of his improbably rigorous exercise routine on an Instagram page that drew a large number of female followers who described themselves as personal trainers. When I suggested that Dad might have described some of them as "pros," he characteristically took offense not on his behalf but on theirs: "Come on, pal," he said. "That's not nice."

He did not expect his lunch with Muntu to be of any great consequence. He kept in touch with her on Facebook, and though he disliked her politics, he used to work with her in the bag business and he considered her a friend. Besides, she was Dad's friend, and Michael therefore felt an obligation to keep the friendship going as a way of keeping his memory alive. She lived in Westbury, with her *man,* her *dude,* and now her husband, Bob Law, and one day in August Michael borrowed my car and drove two hours to meet her. He called me from the road as soon as they finished.

"Hey, pal."

"Hey, Bro."

"Did you know that Dad had an affair with Muntu?" he asked without preamble.

"Yes," I answered immediately.

"I did not. Why didn't you tell me?"

"Because I *didn't* know."

"You didn't? You just said you did. I'm confused."

"I did and I didn't. I mean, you remember Dad's memorial service—how could they not have had an affair? But I never saw them together. And I never heard about it until right now."

"Muntu said that it lasted eleven years. That's a long time!"

"That's a long time."

"I told her, 'I had no idea.' She said, 'Michael, how could you not know? It's not like we tried to keep it secret.' I said, 'I just didn't look at my dad that way.' "

And that was the difference between Michael and me. We had very similar experiences as Lou Junod's sons. But Mike didn't look at Dad "that way," and I did. Mike looked at him as a colorful man who was a paragon of virtues both masculine and familial, and I looked at him as . . . well, how did I look at my father? It was hard to say, hard even to admit. Michael loved and admired Dad as a good man. I loved and admired him while knowing he might be a bad one. And so when Michael asked me a simple question, I didn't know what to say, because both of the things I told him were equally true. I knew. I didn't know. I had lived my entire life between those two answers, subpoenaed and compelled to testify even if on taking the stand I inevitably took the fifth. And yet it was at that moment, late in the summer of 2015, when I still felt my father pulling me in two simultaneous directions—in other words, pulling me apart—that I decided to give Muntu a call.

I met her in Brooklyn, at the health-food store she started with Bob Law. It was still morning, and she stood behind the counter, dispensing cups of "Muntu's Drink." It was a concoction of apple cider vinegar, turmeric, cayenne, garlic and powdered ginger, and she served it mostly to the aging men who walked in from Atlantic Avenue, and obediently drank down their daily doses as if to render tribute. She would ask what ailed them, and after she heard out their lovelorn confessions she prescribed herbal cures for their exhaustion, depression, stymied libido, diarrhea, baldness, corns, piles. She was near eighty, and the fanaticism that my father found so bewitching was still very much in evidence as she dispensed nostrums and advice validated by the miraculous endurance of her own magnificence. "Look at you, with your gray hair," she said to me, when she had a break. "That's because you drink coffee. Stop drinking coffee and start drinking my drink and it will come back brown."

We went out to lunch at a place that sold bean burgers and tofu, since she was still as adamant a vegetarian—"Adamant! Adamant!"—as my father said she was when he met her. I had called her on the phone shortly after my brother told me about my father's affair with her and I finally decided to reckon with the mysteries that had haunted me all my life. She did not hesitate to answer my questions. She was happy to answer my questions, proud to answer them, because the days she spent with Lou Junod were the happiest of her life. She was not making a confession; she had nothing to confess, no sins and no guilt. She did, however, lay down terms, not for my access to her but rather for my understanding of my dad: "You're just going to have to accept that your father was a Casanova, Tommy."

It wasn't even his fault, she said now, as we took our table near the window, the pale Brooklyn sun pouring through. "He was so good-looking and had such style and such charisma that women wouldn't let him alone. How could he turn them down? We'd be walking down Fifth Avenue and he'd say, 'Look at the way they're looking at me.' At first I thought they were looking at *us*—'What's that old man doing with that young woman?' But no—it was more like 'What's he got?' Well, he had plenty. Almost had too much."

Their affair started in 1974, during Market Week, the showrooms crowded with buyers who had come to New York from all over the country. My father had lent her $100, and when she tried to pay her debt in cash in the Valeri showroom, he refused it. "Why don't we take it out . . . in *trade*," he said, and invited her to his room in the Essex House that night.

She went. He was twenty-one years older than she was. He had a wife and she had a boyfriend and so she thought she'd humor him.

"I had no intention of doing anything," she told me. "But he had a table set up in the room. He had steaks under glass, and a bottle of champagne on ice. He was just so suave—and so *nice.* And after fifteen minutes, I was laying in the bed and getting the best head I ever had in my life. And that was it for me. He was absolutely insatiable, Tommy. We'd make love, eat dinner, make love again. I should have been able to keep up with him because I was so much younger. But I couldn't. Your father, he was the original Energizer Bunny. Lord have mercy."

They had, she said over and over, "big fun" together. When he was in New York, she stayed with him at the Essex House, and he took her out to restaurants where he didn't bother with reservations. "It didn't matter how long the line was," she told me. "Your father would walk right to the front with a fistful of money and when the maître d' asked, 'Name, please?' he'd say, 'Mr. Cash.' The maître d' would say, 'Oh, right this way, sir,' and we'd go right to the best table, in front of everyone." He loved spending money on Muntu, in the most public way, flaunting her presence on his arm. He bought Mom furs, jewelry, fancy dresses and housewares, often to make up with her after one of their fights. But Muntu he took to La Grenouille, and spent three hundred dollars—three hundred 1975 dollars—on dinner. Muntu he flew to Nassau, in the Bahamas; Puerto Rico; California; and, most frequently, Las Vegas. "We both loved the sun," she said. "We'd spend all day by the pool, with me drinking piña coladas and him drinking whatever it was he was drinking. We'd lay out there until we were both the same color and then at night we'd go to the casino. Your father wouldn't even gamble. He'd just watch me gamble. He'd give me a hundred dollars to play roulette, and then when I lost it all he'd give me another hundred, all night long. He'd just stand and watch, and then we'd go back to the suite—and it was always a suite, at Caesars Palace. Later on, he said, 'I wish I had all the money I spent on you.'"

In all their years together, they had only two fights—the first because of her jealousy, the second because of his. In the first, they were in Vegas, and my father wanted to have a ménage à trois. He hired a blond prostitute for both of them to share, but when they went to bed, the sight of him having "big fun" with another woman incensed Muntu and she fled in tears to the casino, refusing to talk to him for days. In the second, he found out that she'd had lunch with another man, and so waited for her in the lobby of 330 Fifth Avenue, the epicenter of the handbag industry. When she walked in through the revolving door, he summoned her with a curled finger and the incandescence of his angry green eyes. "Oh, he was jealous, he was *pissed,*" she told me. "He was saying that he owned me, and, technically, I guess he did."

It wasn't just about the sex—"though the sex, Lord have mercy"—or even just about the money. It was about how he treated her. "He was just so good to me, in so many ways," she said. "He treated me like royalty." He was almost old-fashioned in his gallantry, and when she needed him he showed up. When her car broke down at a friend's house in Great Barrington, Massachusetts, he drove there in the middle of the night and picked her up. When she needed a car, he gave her the car he loved, the car that was symbolic of his velvety extravagance, his white 1973 Lincoln Continental with the white vinyl roof and the little American flag on the back of the trunk. He even asked Uncle Johnny to deposit $2,000 in his checking account, so that he could tell Mom that Muntu bought the car from him at market price, that it was a purchase instead of a gift. She drove it for years, until it became as representative of her as it once was of him, with a custom license plate that acknowledged its ludicrous dimensions. "I called it the SS *Muntu,*" she said.

The details of my father's liaisons, graphic though they were, didn't shock me. They didn't even surprise me. They filled me instead with a kind of relief, because at least I wasn't crazy. My father was the man I always thought he was, the man he tried to be. What did surprise and shock was the power of some details to sadden me—the details of his kindness. My father, with Muntu, was something even those who worshipped him never said he was; he was *nice.* He treated her like a queen. He treated her exactly as he didn't treat my mom, which made me sad for both of them and made me wonder if I knew him at all.

"How well did you know my father?" I asked Muntu.

It was the only question that seemed to unsettle her. "How well did I *know* him? Tommy, we were together for eleven years. What was there left to know?"

"Well, my father could be very prejudiced, in the way he talked about Black people."

"Not with me he wasn't. I never got that from him. Do you think that I would have gone out with a racist?"

"What did you two talk about?"

"We didn't have to do too much *talking*."

"Did he ever talk to you about how he grew up? About his mother? About his father?"

"I never met his mother and we never talked about her."

"How about my mother?"

"I might have met her once, at some handbag industry function. That was it."

"Did he talk about her?"

"He never mentioned her. Not a word. Not one mumbling word."

I thought of asking if he ever talked about me, but I didn't want to risk hearing her answer.

Muntu didn't think about my mother when she decided to go to my father's memorial service in Wantagh—she didn't worry if Fran Junod was going to attend Lou Junod's farewell, didn't give it a second thought. She didn't go to funerals, or for that matter even weddings, "none of that mess." But there was no way she was going to miss *this* one, her last chance to honor the man who had bequeathed her the SS *Muntu*. "I had to go," she said. "That was my man. That was my *man*."

Was she his woman? She was, in that she was his type, and she was his type in that he'd met his match in her, not so much his equal as his reflection. They had a looking-glass compatibility, both of them vain, fanatical, imperious, willing to live entirely in their bodies, with nothing between them and the blazing sun. They didn't ask many questions of each other, so when I asked questions of her, about him, I realized I had come to the wrong place. Muntu spoke without compunction about sleeping with him but knew nothing of his dreams, because he hadn't told her. He was a scrupulously superficial man, believing so fervently in the magic of surfaces that his fervor almost passed for profundity and he was able to wear his soul quite literally on his sleeve, like cuff links.

They never talked about getting married—"that was never on

the table." They never considered leaving the lives they had because they were living the lives they wanted and having big fun. That was enough for eleven years, and besides, Muntu had a creed of her own, a belief that they were each true to the other in their fashion. She knew very well that there were other women—that there had *been* other women. "But once he started seeing me, that was it. He gave up all that. After me, he did nothing and was with nobody else. Just me."

Muntu knew my father as I couldn't—as a *man*. He had seduced her, pleased her, pampered her, spoiled her and showed her consideration even as he showed her off, often out in the open, often in front of men who, like Uncle Johnny, had been friends with my mother for almost as long as they'd been friends with him. And yet he never let her get to know him, and now, for all her candor, I had something on her, information she didn't have. She had been naïve when she trusted my father's ability to be exclusive to her and her ability to keep him in line; what's more, she *sounded* naïve now, in the restaurant, because I knew that she was mistaken, that she'd gotten it all wrong when she said there was nobody else. I knew, that is, for a *fact,* and yet I didn't tell her, didn't disabuse her of . . . her innocence. I keep his secrets, even from his lover.

18

There is still a little of him left over. Half the ashes went into the ground and half went into the sea, scattered from the public beach a quarter mile from where our house once stood on Dune Road. And that was that—almost. I've kept a last ounce and a half of him in a shot glass, as a reserve. I did this in answer to a request from my father's best friend in Florida, Frankie Klein. He wants the last of Lou. He still lives in North Miami, in the little house on a little lake where my father often stayed. Before we surrendered the ashes to the elements, he called and asked if he could have some. He was going to have his own ritual, his own scattering and his own goodbye.

It was my idea to use a shot glass. My father used one word and one word only to make toasts—"*salute.*" I kept the shot glass in the Ziploc with his ashes as a salute, as a way to preserve some of his brio and significance, proof of his singularity.

I held on to them for a year and a half before I had the opportunity to bring them to Florida. We were taking a spring break vacation as a family, at a beachfront hotel in Hollywood, not far from where the original Diplomat Hotel once stood. And yet I felt not just an obligation to deliver the ashes to Frankie but also a compulsion. My father had died ten years after telling me about "the one"—the woman in Florida whom he had fallen in love with and who had herself died in a fall. I had never asked him about her again, and he had never told me anything more. But what he told me had stayed with me, had haunted me. It gave his life a tragic dimension because I knew for a fact he had never found love at home.

What would his life have been like—what would my life have been like—if she had lived? The way he raised his finger when he told me about her, the way he intoned that single syllable, "one"—there wasn't just another story in that syllable, there was another life. Now he was dead a year and a half, and when I thought about the woman in Florida it was as though I was waking myself up in the middle of the night in order not to forget a dream. In his long life of loving women there was one woman my father loved, and I didn't even know her name.

I drive to see Frankie Klein on April 8, 2008, the day before I turn fifty. I bring the ashes with me as well as the certainty that this is my last chance. My father is dead; so are most of his cronies. I am bringing the last of my father to Frankie because Frankie is the last man who can tell me what I missed. He was not merely close with Lou Junod; there was something confidential between them, perhaps even a pact. Back in the fifties, my father had helped Frankie get back on his feet when his wife ran off with another man. At the Apparel Mart in Miami, Frankie rebounded by courting a tall blond model from Virginia named Dolores Lewis. He wasn't the only one: Dolores had fled to Florida as a divorcée with two children, and all the salesmen who styled themselves lady-killers came after her. But my father—at least as he told the story—said, "*Hey . . .* she's Frankie's." That was enough; nobody dared make a move on her, and my father, with a show of his own manhood, helped salvage the manhood of his best friend. Frankie *owed* my father for his marriage and his family. But what did my father owe Frankie?

He is waiting for me at a bagel joint in North Miami. He sold handbags and other accessories, but he would have been just as convincing as a racetrack tout or a Broadway song plugger or a candy-store bookie or a sidekick in *Guys and Dolls* who's so light on his feet he got his own number, wearing a pin-striped suit adorned with a diamond stickpin. He has curly hair and a big pitted knob of a nose behind which hide his soft, forgiving, mirthful eyes. As my father mass-produced a photograph of me and him, Frankie mass-produced a photograph of him and my father, standing together in their bathing suits on the sand in Miami Beach, Frankie's body pale and plucky and a little paunchy, my father's in the deep oily stain of his tan. I hand him the Ziploc with the ashes and he shakes his head as the grains of the friend he worshipped shift inside. "He actually looks better than the last time I saw him," Frankie says. "He wasn't meant to grow old, and those last few years were tough on him. I went up to see him in Jupiter and I was shocked by how much he had wasted away. I came home and told Dolores, 'That was the first time in my life I ever looked better than Lou Junod.' "

He thanks me for the delivery and looks at me from across the table, my father still there between us, ashes to ashes, as in play as a stack of chips. Frankie used to call the house when I was a kid and if I answered the phone, he'd always ask, "Who do you like?" He was easy to talk to even then; he was not intimidating and my mother laughed at his jokes and didn't hate him. But now I have a question for him. "Frankie," I say. "Can you tell me about the woman my father had a relationship with in Florida?"

He doesn't blink. He breathes and does something with his hands, something with his fingers. "So you know," he says.

The words hit me like the snap of the locks on my father's briefcase did thirty-five years ago. I nod. I know, sure. I've always *known*. But I sure as hell don't know what he knows—the knowledge that has changed his voice and his posture and the look in his eyes.

"Because if you didn't already know I would never tell you," Frankie says.

"I know," I manage to say out loud.

He nods, as much to himself as to me. He has made a decision. "Her name was Peggy Monahan," he says. "They were very, very close."

"How long were they together?"

"I can't say exactly. Many years. A long, long time. In fact, they were going to get married. You had gone off to school, so they were going to leave their spouses and be together. She was married to the guy who ran the Diplomat, John Monahan. Then Peggy died. No one knew what happened, no one could say. I went to the funeral with your father. It was very, very tough. He was beside himself. I had to hold him up."

I ask if Peggy had any kids and Frankie says yes and that's my last question. He stands up and I walk with him to the parking lot and he tells me he'll see if he can find a photo of Peggy back at his house. She swam in that lake, too, he says. They both did. Now he is heading home and when the sun starts going down he will sprinkle my father's ashes in the water and offer a toast to both of them, to the memory of Peggy and Lou.

Salute.

I've never told anyone.

I've never told anyone what I know.

I've never told anyone what I know . . . about him.

About Chip and the showgirls.

About Chip and Valerie.

About the woman he went to visit when he took me for a sundae.

About the briefcase.

About Peggy Friedlander.

About Mikie.

About Zsa Zsa.

I've never told my mom. I've never told Janet. I've never even told Michael.

But I tell my brother when I come back home from Florida. I tell him her name, and the general time frame of the affair. I can't say when it began, only what Frankie said about its duration. I can, however, offer an approximation of when it ended, because they were supposed to go off together after I went to college, and I went to college in 1976. I also show Michael a photograph that Frankie put in the mail.

"That's her," Michael says, with the ring of recognition.

"What do you mean? We just found out her name."

"When I was a lifeguard in Florida after college, I lived in Hallandale with Dad's friend Ira."

"Frankie says Peggy lived in Hallandale."

"Dad sometimes stayed there too. And one day, I was going back to the apartment with my girlfriend and I saw Dad with a woman. They were in a car in the parking lot. He had his arm around her. He was kissing her and she was crying. I was shocked. I didn't know what to do, so I guess I just stood there, and Dad saw me. He introduced me to her. He called her Mrs. Rudolph."

"Like our neighbors in Wantagh?"

"He told me she was a buyer and she had lost a member of her family and he was consoling her," Michael says.

"And you . . . believed him?"

Michael looks at me and nods. "I was twenty-four years old," he says finally. "And it was *Dad*."

I have always been proud when people recognize me and Michael as brothers—proud when they say we look alike, proud when Nia came off the plane in Atlanta after her adoption in China and, just ten months old, pointed at my brother and then pointed at me. But his plaintive use of the phrase "It was Dad" reveals his unwillingness to follow where I need to go. It might even be a warning.

To Michael, those words acknowledge our father's enduring authority—they mean that Dad is a great man, deserving special consideration and at the very least the benefit of the doubt. To me those same words carry an obligation to ask questions. Whenever I took it upon myself to scrutinize him—okay, to snoop on him—I always discovered something shocking and at the same time crucial about him and our family and myself. I solved mysteries that had unsettled me all my life. And when I asked Frankie to tell me about the woman in Florida and he responded by revealing my father's relationship with Peggy Monahan, I didn't just find out more corroborating evidence about incidentals such as the Diplomat towel hanging in the bathroom or the provenance of the solid gold Oscar money clip.

I found out who I serenaded in the summer of 1964, when my father put me on the phone in Westhampton with a woman in Florida and she said, "I hope I can meet you one day."

I found out why my father treated me as he did in the summer of 1976—why he slapped me and called me a nothing and a zero and did whatever he could to put distance between us.

I found out that when my father introduced me to Peggy Friedlander in the summer of 1978, she was the second Peggy in his life, and when she died by her own hand that August she was the second Peggy in his life to suffer a tragic end.

And I fear I found out something else, about the morning he made me swear on his life. I swore then, and I lied, even though he told me he was flying to Florida. I prayed all day long that my lie hadn't been a curse, that my small act of cowardice hadn't doomed him, and when he arrived in Miami safe and sound I told myself that I had gotten away with it. But as soon as Frankie told me how Peggy Monahan died, I began thinking that maybe I hadn't gotten away with it after all. And neither had my dad.

I look up John Monahan as soon as I'm back home. He's dead. He died in 2004, two years before my father and four years before I search his name. He was seventy-seven, and he shows up in my first searches only as a face in the crowd—as a name that appears in the minutes of city council meetings in Hollywood, Florida. So I call Hollywood's former city manager, a guy named Sam Finz, and ask if he remembers a guy named John Monahan. He does. "He hung around city hall," Finz says. "He knew a lot of the local politicians. The old Diplomat had been demolished and they were trying to build a new one with union money. He had something to do with that. I think one of his kids was in prison."

I don't know anything about the politics of Hollywood, Florida. I don't know that there is an old and a new Diplomat—that the Diplomat my father frequented is as much a memory as the house at 879 Dune Road, and that the Diplomat erected in its place has been financed from the Plumbers and Pipefitters National Pension

Fund. I don't even know how many kids John and Peggy Monahan had, or what their names might be. But as soon as I hear about one of them going to prison, I remember one thing about them: they lost their mother. And I ask myself what my life would have been like if my mother died when I was heading for college—if I didn't have her, only him. I wouldn't have *had* a life. I wouldn't be here, doing Google searches on another family; I'd be in jail, or God knows where else. And I arrive at my first characterization of the Monahans before finding out even the barest details about them: they are our tragic reflection. They are the Junods without Fran, only Lou. I want to search for them, I want to find them, I want to meet them, I want to reach out to them. But I don't. Instead, I write this in my journal:

"My father helped destroy this family once.

"Do I propose to do it twice?"

Seven years will pass before I look up John and Peggy Monahan again.

She complains about the food all the time so at first she just seems a little more picky than usual, making a face when the servers come to the table. She turns up her nose at the fish, because of the smell, then at the mashed potatoes, because they're so starchy, then at the pot roast because it's too tough. It all happens very quickly. One day, she's the most beautiful woman in assisted living, dressing for dinner in what's left of her fancy clothes, smiling with what's left of her teeth. Six weeks later, she swoons from lack of nutrition, and breaks her shoulder in a fall.

My mother didn't go to the funeral on Long Island. When Muntu Law stepped up to the lectern and declared my father's manhood in Wantagh, Mom was in the apartment she'd shared with him in Roswell, with Janet checking in on her to see how she was doing now that she lived alone for the first time since 1947, or perhaps just my father's last road trip. It was a Sunday, and Janet came by with Nia, who was three years old. They brought food, and then said good night, leaving my mother content on the couch in front of the television. But the next day, she didn't answer the phone, and when Janet went back to the apartment she was still sitting on the couch, urine-soaked. She hadn't moved, and she was so ga-ga with dehydration Janet was certain she'd suffered a stroke.

I found an assisted living facility as soon as I returned from New York. She didn't want to go, she pleaded with me not to go, tears streaming from her eyes as I kissed her good night and goodbye. She was sitting on the edge of her new bed, and I couldn't help but remember the tears we'd shed together on Britton Street. But something happened at her new home. She never called it home; she called it *the* home, or occasionally, the "place," as in "My kids, they put me in a place." But then, they all called it that—all the superannuated widows who sported Ultrasuede pantsuits and had their hair set weekly and became her friends.

I'd always wondered what my mother would be like when she got out from under my father's boot heel. Now I found out. She painted. She wrote a little bit, even a few encouraging letters to politicians. She was an attentive and easygoing "*po po*" to Nia, and when she came to our house for dinner she never failed to match memories with her in games of Concentration. And she laughed. She was well-known in our family for not having a sense of humor around our dad—we joked with her about not being able to take a joke. But people at "the home" were drawn to her sharp wit, and sometimes when I joined her table for lunch she and her friends would suddenly clam up as I sat down. "What are you ladies talking about?" I'd ask, and my mother would say, "Oh, nothing," and all of the ladies would laugh, cats who were on familiar terms with canaries.

She entered assisted living when she had just turned ninety.

She stopped eating two years later.

The fall does more than injure her shoulder. It presages her end. She suffers a stroke in the hospital after surgery. She suffers seizures after the stroke. She can't go back to "the home," because she's no longer ambulatory, so she goes to the rehab wing of a large nursing home. She does not really receive any rehab and once her insurance runs out she'll be moved to a "care floor" and right now all Janet and Michael and Cathy and I can do is show up at lunchtime each day and try to feed her, congratulating ourselves when she eats five spoonfuls of cottage cheese instead of two or an entire individualized serving of applesauce.

—

The look that snuck into her eyes when she first stopped eating has become more pronounced; there are days she might be a madwoman. But today is not one of them. She's dressed nicely and her hair has been done and I want to show her off, so I push her wheelchair onto the elevator and take her down to the lobby of the nursing home. It's unexpectedly fancy, in country club colors—dark green and burgundy, matched with dark wood. It's also empty, and its emptiness surrounds us like the seats in an amphitheater, with both of us right in the middle.

"Am I dying?" my mother asks me, when I've put the blanket on her lap and I'm sitting across from her.

She is my first love. And now this is my last lie.

"Everything's going to be okay, Mom," I say.

Then I ask her a question. It is my only chance.

"Tell me about Dad."

"Who?"

"Dad. Your husband."

"Oh. Him."

"He wasn't easy to live with."

"No," she says shyly. Then she looks at me and offers a little shrug. "But he was a good egg."

I can't believe it. I can name the people my mother called good eggs. Her brother Harry, HB. Joe McGarty. The fellow who delivered dry cleaning to the front door and did odd jobs around the house. They all had a softness, and a twinkle. I never once considered my father one of their number.

I take her hand and squeeze it and I realize right then and right there she is getting ready to go.

They give us a bed. It's a spare in the back of their RV. Michael and I share it. It's not comfortable, but its availability comes as a surprise. The deaths of our parents, along with Michael's troubles with his bipolar illness, have strained the family ties, me and my brother on one side, Ronnie and Cathy on the other. I figured Michael and I were going to have to split a hotel room. But now we're splitting a bed in the RV Ronnie and Cathy bought for their retirement, and it's the first time all the Junod children have slept in the same place in years. It is a fitting rapprochement, since we have all come to Jersey for the funeral of a man everyone in my family loved—HB, the good egg.

He remained a young man most of his life, a kid brother. He was thirty-six when he married a woman ten years younger, and together he and Aunt Ceil seemed different from any other married couple I'd ever met—they drew youth from each other, instead of age, Aunt Ceil with her auburn hair and soothing voice, Uncle Harry with the dash of the only entirely successful mustache I'd ever seen this side of Tom Selleck. He stayed slim, he stayed upright and smiling, and for many years time only exacted its cost by way of color, the frost that snuck into his hair and mustache that otherwise stood stalwart against change. I figured that being a good egg would always rejuvenate him, and even when he no longer recognized me—even when I heard he had Alzheimer's disease—I imagined his illness as a kind of grace, as a kind of extended innocence that allowed him to forget the world before the world forgot him.

I knew very little about Alzheimer's disease.

He died on August 26, 2012, and now here we are, in an RV parked in front of the Brandshagen home in Middletown, New Jersey, watching Cathy zoom around with a rag in her hand, cleaning up after her brothers, dabbing the clutched cloth any place we've touched. I try talking to her, but that's never been easy and it's only gotten harder over the past few years. She talks. She talks a lot, to the extent that I've occasionally left her talking on the phone and then returned to find her still speaking, in an oblivious unbroken stream. But she's averse to conversation, and after talking for an hour she can still leave me with the impression that she's been fending me off, that something crucial has gone unsaid.

"Hey, Cath, it's good to see you," I say. "Too bad the timing didn't work out. Too bad you and Ronnie weren't able to come out to Shelter Island when Michael was there."

"Oh, we came out to Shelter Island," she says.

"*Cathy,*" I say, scoldingly.

"We did," she says. "We had a nice time on Shelter Island."

"Cath, we were out on Shelter Island all summer. It's a tiny place. Are you saying you came out in the RV and didn't let us know?"

"I went with———," she says, naming a high school friend. "We went to that little place by the water."

"What little place? Cathy, why didn't you call?"

"You know, that cute little place . . ."

"Why are you trying to tell me something that's not true? You don't have to do this. What's going on?"

But she goes back to puttering, dabbing with the rag where my hand has just been. I don't say anything more, because I tell myself this is just the way she is. Whether she is in the grip of psychosomatic illness or making excuses for not doing something she's promised to do, she seems, at some basic level, unable to tell the truth. I decide that it is simply a matter of character.

And once again, I am dead wrong.

19

One day, I am a person who has said goodbye to his mother and father and is living in the peace of their absence. I miss them and I especially wish that Nia could spend more time with them. But I have to admit that life is easier without them, because chaos followed them everywhere they went. I am, in the summer of 2015, three years short of turning sixty. It is time to live free of their spell, though they still often visit me in my dreams.

And then, in the course of a single afternoon, indeed a single instant, all that changes—that tentative peace. Michael has his lunch with Muntu and she tells him of her affair with our father. He calls and asks if I knew. I tell him I did and tell him I didn't. It is not confusion; it is something more fundamental. I feel it, a pang of the unreconciled and the irreconcilable. I have always believed it was dangerous to try to find out about my father's love affairs and the families they affected. Now I believe it's dangerous not to.

When I visit Muntu in Brooklyn and she tells me I have to accept that my father was a Casanova, I suspect she's also suggesting I have to accept something else—letting go. But can I? Should I?

She informs me that her affair with him started in 1974 and ended eleven years later, when she got married. But it's a timeline that deepens my sense of unease, because it overlaps with my father's relationship with Peggy Monahan. She was supposed to be "the One," and Muntu, for her part, insists out of deep conviction that once my father started in with her, there was no one else. She is fiercely possessive of him even now—posthumously possessive of him. But Peggy turns out to be the only woman to whom Muntu Law yields. She considers herself "the One" but never says that she loved my father or that he loved her. She uses the word "love" only when talking about the woman who preceded her, shaking her head with a sigh and speaking in a singsong:

"Your dad, he sure loved him some Peggy."

And so Muntu hasn't given me a final answer after all.

She has given me my last chance at a beginning.

His full name was John Francis Monahan, and all I know of him is that he was married to a woman my father loved and was a big man at the Diplomat. When I check my old Dune Deck notes, I find a comment my father made that suggested he and Monahan had met—"good-looking guy, very conceited. I didn't like him." I also remember that, according to Frankie, his wife, Dolores, had known Peggy since they both modeled in Miami, and suspected Monahan pushed her down the stairs.

But there is something else, of course. I know nothing about John Monahan but the one thing he perhaps didn't even know himself: that he was a cuckold, and that when Peggy Monahan fell, she was preparing to leave him for my father. For the last seven years, I have abided by the vow I made after meeting Frankie, and have not investigated her death out of respect for her children. But after I speak with Muntu, I realize that my father lived and loved a long time ago, and his story is slipping away. I decide to look for whatever information I can find, if not about my father then about the people in his orbit, his inescapable gravitational pull. I spent most of my life looking at my dad and asking, "Who is this man?" Now, nearly ten years after his death, I resolve to ask, "Who *was* this man?," and with that question comes the resolve to start asking who were these men and who were these women.

I start with John Monahan, because he played a role in the central tragedy of my father's life and also because I figure I have a better shot at finding something out about him than I would, say, about Chip Schocket or Irwin Friedlander or even Vinnie on Balboa Island, missing since 1994. Like those men, Monahan had a wife whom my father took as a lover. Unlike those men, he had a public life in the heyday of 1960s and '70s South Florida, and shouldn't be hard to find.

It's not as easy as I think. I plug his name into a search engine and discover that being a big man at the Diplomat doesn't mean he's one on the Internet. At first, I can't even find his obituary. Then his name begins to come up, and I experience the same feeling of simultaneous arrival and departure that accompanied my father raising his finger and saying, "One," at the Dune Deck and Frankie Klein looking at me across the table at a bagel restaurant and saying, "So you know." I have a hunch that my life is about to change, because although the information is fragmentary, it also defies belief. No, there's not a lot about John Monahan online. But when he does appear, he's not alone. He's in the company of another John, John Walsh from *America's Most Wanted,* and not as a villain but as a hero.

He is, in fact, a character in Walsh's book *Tears of Rage.* The book tells the story of how John Walsh, a young businessman from Hallandale, responds to the abduction and murder of his son Adam by becoming the outraged and avenging host of a pioneering American true-crime series. But as soon as I receive my copy, I open the book and discover it tells another story, one that touches on my own.

John Walsh is from upstate New York. In the early 1970s, he heads to Florida and gets a job at the Diplomat Hotel as a cabana boy. One day, he saves the son of one the Diplomat's executives from drowning, a boy named Johnny. The grateful executive sees a spark in his employee and when he leaves the Diplomat to go to work developing hotel properties all over the country and in the Bahamas he makes John Walsh his right-hand man. The executive, described as "an erudite Irishman"; his "beautiful" wife, Peggy; their four children, Johnny and Michael and Lizanne and Tommy—they become family to John Walsh and his wife, Revé, and when six-year-old Adam

Walsh disappears from a Sears store in 1981, the executive is central to the search. John Monahan has been steeled by Peggy's death, and is given to talking "about how hard it had been, and about God and faith." He also owes John Walsh a favor for saving Johnny's life, and so when law enforcement finds a child's head floating in a canal in the Everglades, he volunteers to make the identification to spare his friend and protégé the pain and the horror.

And that's what I learn when I begin the task of learning about my father: John Monahan, the big man at the Diplomat, was the man who identified Adam Walsh as the victim of one of the most infamous crimes of the century.

The young girl my father used to talk about when he returned from his long stays with his friend Frankie is a woman now. She is fifty-seven years old when I call her in the fall of 2015. But she remembers *her,* which is to say she remembers *him*. How could she ever forget? Kelly Lewis was so very young, "a little girl from Virginia," and she hadn't seen a man like Lou Junod before. "God, he was just someone who took my breath away," she says forty-five years later. It wasn't just that he was "a beautiful specimen of a man." It was that "he paid attention to me. He treated me so wonderfully, treated me like a woman, before I was a woman. Plus, he was funny, because he was insecure. I could tease him about taking over the bathroom. Like, 'Are you gonna leave space for my toothbrush?' But he was special to me and I think I was special to him. I'd lay in the sun with him. He'd go to the beach. We'd go to the beach together."

Kelly can't recall exactly how old she was when Peggy Monahan began coming to the house in Miami, only that her mother, Dolores, had married Frankie Klein, and she was old enough to be in love with her stepfather's "marvelous" friend—old enough to be jealous. But even then she was able to learn from him, even then he was able to give her a glimpse of the adult world that she wouldn't forget. "It would be Lou and Peggy," Kelly says. "And I was very young, but there was something to it. It was a little secret thing. I remember sitting in the family room and watching them. My mother had a love seat, and they'd sit in it—it was where they always sat together. I didn't know so much about forbidden love at that age. But that was my first lesson in forbidden love, because I knew they were both married, and I knew how dedicated your father was to your mother. But then again—well, I don't know exactly how to put it. There was no marriage or religion or anything else that was going to keep those two apart."

Frankie and Dolores are gone. But their children and stepchildren are the first people I call when I decide to learn about the romance between Lou Junod and Peggy Monahan because they might be the only people still alive who saw Lou and Peggy together. They grew up with my father in their house. He had a room and a bathroom. He had a pool and a lake and then he had Peggy. After Frankie told me about Peggy for the first time, I used to wonder how he felt speaking to my mom on the phone and making her laugh and how Dolores felt about chatting up my mom when the four of them, the Junods and the Kleins, went out to dinner in Florida. They were family friends; they were also go-betweens, and like so many others they protected my father by betraying my mother. How did they live with themselves? Their children tell me how: "Frankie and my mom, they were just safe haven," Kelly says. "Their house was where Lou and Peggy could go and relax and just be together. They were in love, and they made love."

And so they were all invested in it, the entire household invested in the doomed love affair taking place right before their eyes.

When I first call Kelly, I mention my father's name and she says instantly, "Lou Junod is my love," and tells me that she still dreams about him.

When I call Kelly's brother Rick, he remembers Peggy coming to the house in 1964, right after Dolores and Frankie were married. "She came with the Beatles," he says, and she stood out right away as a complementary figure to my father. "He was statuesque, with a hell of a body on him. You just had to look at him twice, and women had to look at him more than twice. And she had an Indian look to her—almost Native American, with dark complexion and dark, dark hair. She was very pretty." But what distinguished them as a couple, what he remembers them by, is "that little word, 'love.'

"It was a true love affair," Rick says. "I would ask him how Peggy was doing, and he'd say, 'Fine.' But I was a teenager, so I would always say, 'Man, she is hot.' And once I asked, 'Do you really love her?' And he said, 'Yeah, I do.' And you could see he teared up a little. He really did love her. But he said, 'We both have families, we both have children, we don't want to hurt anyone, so this is the way it has to be.' "

And when I call Frankie's daughter Nancy, she remembers the time she met Peggy at the pool—how she came to the house to visit her dad and surprised them all, how she knew she wasn't supposed to be there, and how later, after Peggy died, she would look at photos with Dolores, and they'd say, "And that's Peggy," as if not to forget.

Then, a week after that first conversation, Nancy calls me back.

There's something she has to tell me, she says—something she's been thinking about telling me, agonizing about telling me, but something she doesn't quite know how to say. Finally, she asked her husband, and he said, "He needs to know, so just come out and say it."

I am closest to Nancy, of all the Kleins. She's an aspiring reporter, and she sends me copies of her sharp-eyed work. She's the one who found me to tell me that Frankie died back in 2011, and she's the one who reminds me of her father, with his irrepressible dash and pluck. At first I think she's calling to tell me what they all have told me from the first time Frankie spoke her name—that Peggy died suspiciously. But that's not all, that's not it, that's not what she's been carrying around since Dolores Klein died in 2003.

Nancy grew very close to her stepmother in the last years and days of her life. They confided in each other, and not long before Dolores died she told Nancy that she believed Peggy had been pushed.

"And that same night," Nancy says, "she talked about Peggy's children, and how one of the boys was Lou's."

Margaret Madeline Sheehan doesn't look directly at the camera in her high school yearbook photo. Her head is tilted, as if she's just heard her name being called, and she's glancing off to the side, as if she's trying to see who called it. She doesn't appear distracted so much as alert to possibilities outside the frame, and open to suggestion. The accompanying commentary says as much: She's "a pretty, high stepping twirler" who "can dance to anything" and a "promising stenographer" but romantically "she likes to keep people guessing." She's known to her fellow students at Cathedral Academy in Camden, New Jersey, as "Peggy."

She's seventeen years old in 1948, the lace collar of her white dress emphasizing her long neck and the dark hair falling in wavy tendrils to her shoulders offsetting the girlish bangs that are cut straight across her forehead. She lives with her mother, father, brother and sister in Pennsauken Township, but by the look on her face in the photograph—singular in its simultaneous serenity and restlessness—anyone can see she's not going to hang around New Jersey for long. The fifties come, with their lonely and halting liberations, and she moves to Miami to work as a stewardess for National Airlines and as a model. In 1955, she appears in *The Miami News* in a leopard-skin bathing suit, displaying her gams to promote the movie *Daddy Long Legs*. A year later, the *Miami Herald* uses a photo of her in a white bikini to illustrate a story about her apartment being burglarized and the thief making off with $1,008 "in small bills" she won at the racetrack. The next time she shows up in the public record she's obtaining a license for her marriage to John Monahan in May 1959.

Monahan was born in Chicago and is four years older than his wife. He was a young soldier in World War II, and after the war he went to the University of Miami. He became sales manager for the Hollywood Beach Hotel in 1955, and by the time the Diplomat opens in December 1958 he's a man on the move and on the make, adept at getting his name in the paper. When he marries Peggy Sheehan, she's two months pregnant.

Over the next decade, they become the kind of couple whose parties and travel plans and milestones are covered in the society pages of the local newspapers and whose modern home, built on Diplomat Parkway in 1966, garners a multipage photographic tribute in the Sunday supplement of the *Miami Herald*. They have a 1934 Packard they use for special occasions and a show dog, a giant schnauzer named El Lobo Duque. They also have four children, John Jr., born in 1960; Michael, born in 1961; Lizanne, born in 1964; and Thomas, born in 1970. They are sixteen, fifteen, twelve and six years old when their mother dies, and by the time I begin looking for them in the fall of 2015 they have been without her for thirty-nine years.

There is no investigative act less dramatic than trying to find people by peering into their Facebook profiles, especially when their name is as common as Monahan. As hard as it is to get the information you need, it is harder still not to get the information you don't—harder still not to spend so much time at other people's birthday parties, class reunions, tropical vacations and Saturday morning soccer games that your search barely counts as voyeurism, much less an investigation.

And yet the possibility that what Nancy Klein told me might be true . . . the possibility that one of the Monahan children might be one of my father's children . . . that I might have an impossible sibling somewhere out there in the vast surfeit of faces . . . that there might be one more Junod . . . makes the routine task of sifting through the mundane moments of complete strangers feel as dangerous as anything I've ever done. I stare at face after face, at Monahan after Monahan. But how am I supposed to know which one belongs to my father? And what am I supposed to do when one of those faces stares back?

Michael Vincent Monahan is not on Facebook, perhaps because he did five years' hard time in federal prison for his role in an extortion case in Florida. Neither is John Francis Jr., though some of his exes have profiles. But Thomas Matthew Monahan posts frequently, and though he is the youngest of the children he turns out to be the family curator. The first thing I find on his page is photos of Peggy in a white bikini splashing in the waves of Miami Beach with a beachball—pinup Peggy, turning the frothing surf into an inviting bubble bath. Then I find a photo of John Monahan, deeply tanned, in white slacks and a beige Members Only jacket, the bomber-style windbreakers that middle-aged men made their uniform in the 1980s. Of course, my father was also deeply tanned. My father also wore white slacks and Members Only jackets. And it hits me for the first time—the bewildering fact that they were the same kind of man . . . that Peggy chose the same kind of man, and then chose *from* the same kind of man. I find myself growing defensive on my father's behalf, saying things my father might have said, calling Peggy's husband "a knockoff," assuring Dad's jealous ghost that he makes John Monahan . . . look sick.

Eventually I am able to study photos of all surviving male Monahans, the three boys that are now men. I think of what Nancy told me, that one might be Lou's. But which one? Tommy, as people call him, is thin and dapper, with a long unlined face and thin lips and a grudging, suspicious look in his brown eyes, which are pulled down at the sides, like John Monahan's. Michael is thick necked and pink faced, the most obviously Irish of the bunch, the family muscle, who looks almost jolly when he's smiling, menacing when he's not. And Johnny, on the flank of every group photo, is gray and gaunt, with a beard and eyes that are both arresting and tentative within their deep sockets. Is he the one? Maybe, but I can't see beyond the uncertainty in his gestures. In truth, any of them could be my brother, and any of them could be just another face on Facebook, this universe of familiar strangers.

I see Lizanne last, because it's not until I find the obituary of John Monahan from the Miami newspapers that I discover her married name is Searing. She's dark, with her mother's hair, the tendrils over her shoulders. She is, in just about every photo, smiling—no, grinning, mugging, the camera's favorite. She has smile lines. She has a chin, but not much of an upper lip. She has a notable nose, and beneath her dark arched eyebrows, there's something going on, eyes that flash green and brown by turns. I can't help meeting them when I stare at them and they can't help staring back.

I show the photo of Lizanne Searing to Janet. "What do you think?" I ask.

"What do you mean?"

"I don't know. Do you think she might be . . ."

"Your sister?" Janet looks back at me skeptically, then fidgets with the photo, covering the top half of Lizanne's face with her hand, then the bottom. She's a great student of faces, breaking them down to their constituent parts.

"I don't know," she says. "Maybe the smile lines."

I hadn't even known Peggy had a daughter until I read John Monahan's obit, but I'm already somewhat possessive about the photo of Lizanne. I do not think of it in terms of resemblance. No, what I feel is *recognition,* the whole much greater than the parts, as if I've been waiting for her, this stranger, my whole life. The emotion is so strong I caution myself against it. But if I am subject to wishful thinking, I am also liable to something else. A year before, my sister Cathy was diagnosed with Alzheimer's disease. I am losing her, we are losing her. The pull I experience when I look at Lizanne Searing's photo is as mysterious as attraction, in that it just exists, in that it's just . . . *there.* I exit out of Facebook, close my laptop. But my fears turned out to be well-founded. There's no going back.

From that moment on, not a day passes when I don't think that Dolores is wrong and Dolores is right, that Peggy and Lou might not have given me a brother, but that not so far away from me, in Connecticut, working from a food truck she owns and married to a guy from, of all places, Wantagh, I have a sister.

Peggy Monahan falls down the stairs at eight o'clock on a Sunday morning. The police arrive at the house on Diplomat Parkway five minutes after they are called, but they cannot help her. She has fractured her skull. She is bleeding from her nose and from a deep wound in her scalp and she is bleeding also in her brain. She goes to the hospital in an ambulance and though she lingers on life support for four days she never regains consciousness. She dies five minutes past noon on Thursday, October 21, 1976, and her body goes to the Dade County medical examiner for an autopsy.

She is forty-five years old. She has dark hair and hazel eyes. She is five foot six inches tall and 133 pounds. She is wearing a religious medal. The medical examiner scrutinizes her brain, her heart, her liver, her kidneys, her spleen. He concludes that the primary cause of death is cranial injury due to blunt trauma. He determines that the secondary cause of death is fatty cirrhosis of the liver. She is an alcoholic, he writes. She "uses barbiturates & Valium."

He rules the death accidental, and there is no further investigation by his office or by the Hallandale police. His report, with its repeated implication that the decedent died drunk or stoned, is the last word on the last four days of Margaret Madeline Sheehan Monahan.

—

It has been gnawing at me for nineteen years. Back in 1996, when my father told me that the woman he loved died falling down the stairs, I asked if she slipped, or was drunk, or committed suicide, or was pushed. He didn't know, and I've never forgotten the look on his face. I'd never seen him so defeated, and right then I knew I wanted to find out the truth on his behalf. I'd spent so much of my young life fighting against my father and his influence. The days I spent with him at the Dune Deck commenced the years in my life when I began fighting for him.

I search for the police report. There is none. It "met retention"—the bureaucratic term for "was destroyed"—on March 20, 1987. I search for the medical examiner's report. It has not been digitized and it is not in the database. But the Dade County medical examiner's office finds a record of the paper copy and orders it from storage. On October 29, 2015, I am able to read about the death of Peggy Monahan, eight days after beholding for the first time the face of her daughter, Lizanne.

The report both tells a story and has a theory—and indeed, the story and the theory are one and the same. Before the medical examiner began his work on Peggy Monahan three hours after she died, he called the Hallandale Police Department. He took notes on what he was told, and the notes begin with this sentence:

"Dec [decedent] has hx. [history] of alcoholism—her two children (one an 18 yr old boy) were leaving for Church 10/17 when dec tripped & fell down some inside stairs."

The two children are Johnny and Lizanne, who were in fact sixteen and twelve, and the only witnesses listed in the report. And yet someone had to have told the police that Peggy drank, because the police told the medical examiner before he started his work. Someone had to have told the police that she popped pills. All of the children were home, but it is unlikely they were the source, given their shock, their trauma, their grief and, of course, their youth. John Monahan was home, too, the husband of the decedent and a forty-nine-year-old man—but neither the police nor the medical examiner mentions his name.

ME reports are generally not widely circulated, because their gruesome catalog of individual organs weighed and considered reminds us of how unprotected we are once our lives are over. But the story contained in the medical examiner's report—the theory of Peggy's death—has gained the currency of rumor and the authority of gospel. Her children will come to believe she fell down the stairs at eight o'clock on a Sunday morning because she was drunk. Friends and associates of John Monahan will remember him repeating over and over, "It was those pills, it was those pills, it was those pills!"

Which is why every time I read the report I have to read it twice. It is confident in its narrative—Peggy Monahan is a doomed woman because of her alcoholism. But the toxicology report it provides almost as an afterthought on page 5 tells a different story. It is negative on the presence of alcohol in her blood. It is negative on the presence of drugs in her blood. She might have been an alcoholic. She might have popped pills.

But Peggy fell down those stairs stone-cold sober.

Her ashes are buried in Hollywood, inland between Fort Lauderdale and Hallandale. When I visit Florida in 2016, I go to see her marker, and I also go to see if he is there with her—if they are, like my own ill-matched parents, side by side. I go to the office to find the location and the attendant takes out a map. I see the plot and see something that moves and disconcerts me. There's a place for the two of them. Peggy and John Monahan. But there's also a place for their daughter, Lizanne. The plot is across the street from the office, close by, and when I bend down to examine Peggy's plaque, dated October 21, 1976, I realize she's already spent forty years in her scrub-grass corner of the cemetery, most of them all alone. The sky is darkening and the air is thickening and a Florida rain is about to come sweeping through, and I am standing in front of the final resting places of two people I've never met and when I imagine a third person joining them—Lizanne, the only one of their children so provided for—my job gets harder. I don't know exactly what I plan to do next. But I do know the woman I believe might be my sister was loved by the parents who raised her.

I'm done. I'm closing the bin. It's been open for a week, its contents spread all over the kitchen counter. I've been bagging, tagging, occasionally summoning Janet or calling Michael to share what I've found. Some things I remember, and they inspire a pang of nostalgia or even regret. Some things I discover, and they perplex me and entrap me once again in the mysteries of my father and my family. It's taken longer than I thought, but now it's Father's Day 2016, and I'm getting ready to drive up to Shelter Island for the summer with Janet and Nia. The hundreds of photographs stuffed into the big plastic bin finally obey at least some kind of organizing principle. On the bottom is a layer of loose snapshots and random slides and envelopes full of negatives undeveloped and doomed by now to permanent obscurity. Next comes a layer of the photos I've ziplocked along with sheets of lined loose-leaf paper Sharpied with the names of the subjects—"Mom," "Dad," "Michael," "Cathy," "1463 Britton Street," "Westhampton," "Family Friends," "Women," and then me, "Tommy." When I finish carefully stacking the photos I know best—the framed photos that once hung on the wall of our basement and my father's bar—on top, I'll snap the latches shut on the cover and slide the bin back into storage.

My parents used to argue about the photographs as they argued about everything else. They both lacked any semblance of executive function, but my mother also fell prey to the lie of good intentions, convinced that if she expressed a desire to put photos into an album it was as good as done. It never was, and when she bought yet another disposable camera and stuffed yet another fat envelope from the Wantagh Fotomat in the bottom of yet another dresser drawer, my father would put his hands on his hips and intone, "Why don't you just throw them . . . *away*?" But she didn't, and neither did he. The photos traveled with them to Florida and then to Atlanta and when they died I salvaged them as if determined to salvage the golden dream that informed every last frame. I am not much more organized than my parents were. But simply by looking at the photos one by one I can not only see my parents again; I can hear them, I can smell them, I can be in awe of their innate beauty and glamour, I can love them, and in the very chaos of the collection, I can feel the discord that somehow kept them together.

I also find pictures of *them*—my father's women. I find pictures of my father in swim trunks flexing his muscles with girlfriends in Brooklyn. I find pictures of my father with the dancer he met in Miami after the war. I find pictures of my father hamming it up in the showroom with buyers young and old. I find pictures of my father with Valerie Schocket in her green dress. I find pictures of my father dancing with a curly-haired woman whose eyes are closed in erotic transport—the woman I remember as the woman my father visited when he took me for a sundae. I find a picture of my father with a woman I believe is Peggy Friedlander and I find pictures of my father flirting with women I haven't seen before. They are all there, all in a bin that yawns open like a plastic ravine, along with pictures of my mother when she was young and the prettiest and most photogenic of them all.

I don't want to be finished when I finish. I don't want the deep dive to end when I am layering the last fragile framed photos on the surface of a vast assortment of images from the last century. Father's Day has something to do with it—I don't want to say goodbye. But there is something else, a disappointment. I've seen photos of women I recognize and women who will remain forever strangers. For God's sake, I've seen a photo of Valerie among the family photos, shameless as ever. But I wish I saw—I wish my father had tucked away—a photo of Peggy Monahan, because she was the one I was looking for when I opened the big box in the first place. Now there's nothing I can do about it, except be careful with the photos that have become heirlooms to me and me alone. I place the black-framed photo of my father and my mother on their wedding night in the bin—"Please! *Do Not . . . Disturb!*" I do the same with the color photo of my family on Westhampton Beach, my mother's hair wrapped in a blue chiffon scarf and me with a scowl on my face. I do the same with the photo of Jayne Mansfield posing on the diving board at the Fontainebleau and the photo of Frankie Klein in the company of Sammy Davis Jr. I even do the same with the photo I know my mom must have hated, the shot of my father absorbing Chip Schocket's tutelage at the Harwyn Club, his cigarette burning in the ashtray.

I am down to the last of them, the one that will go on top. It's the mysterious photo of Lloyd Bridges attending some kind of press event, sitting next to a tanned brunette I always mistook for Valerie Schocket. I take a look at it, at the woman dressed oddly like my father used to dress on holidays, in a red V-neck sweater, a white button-down shirt and a black knit tie. Then I stop. Everything stops, and I say, "Holy shit," out loud.

It's not a photograph of Lloyd Bridges at all. He was just an excuse, just a beard. It's a photograph of Peggy Monahan and it hung from the wall of my father's bar in Wantagh for twenty years and it followed my parents everywhere they lived, hidden in plain sight, the love of my father's life dressed in my father's clothes. I lay it on top of the other photos not just carefully but tenderly, patting it before I close the bin as if I'm saying good night. Peggy might be gone. But the Monahan children are all still here, and I decide there and then that I have to contact them.

20

In the early summer of 2016, I go with my cousin Betty Ann to the Schmeckenbecher cemetery plot in Queens. I have not visited it since Grandma died, and I am startled how much story fits on the shining face of the old marble obelisk—startled that my great-grandfather Martin Schmeckenbecher was born in Germany in 1828, and that after he came to America he sired his first brood of children before the Civil War. Elizabeth Junod was the last interred and the most recent name etched in the stone, but when Betty Ann and I walk to the office, we find out that the plot isn't filled up. There is a vacancy, space for one more of Martin's descendants in a place of eternal rest whose ancient obsequies were written in high German. "Well?" I ask Betty Ann.

"Not for all the tea in China," she says with a shiver.

Betty Ann Feldman is Aunt Elizabeth's daughter, and she is a gentle, caring person, with a voice as soft as a purr. But she is not discreet, and a few weeks later, my phone rings. I answer and hear a voice that is rude, commanding and still somehow pleading. "Hello, Tommy, this is your cousin Vivian, I hear you're writing . . . a *book*. About the *family*."

"I am," I say, fearing hellfire. She is the oldest of my cousins, by a considerable margin; the daughter of Aunt Marie, she is also the roughest and the toughest.

"Well, don't you write any book until you talk . . . to me. Your *fatha* was a great man and a war hero. I loved that man. But Uncle Louie, if he didn't want to see it, it didn't exist. He thought his mother was the *Madawna*. Well, I lived it, Tommy. I was *there*. Our grandmother was *not* the Madawna. And your *fatha* was not her only son."

The microfilm room in the New York Public Library on Forty-Second Street hasn't been updated since the last time I visited. It's still a refuge from modernity, as seedy as it is scholarly, with an unwholesome Times Square air—solitary men hunched over the few precious machines that don't have Out of Order signs taped to them, the wheels turning faster and faster until the film jumps the reel and punctuates another journey into the past with a futile slapping sound. It is, in other words, a perfect place to learn more about the scandal that enveloped my family in the middle of the Great Depression.

I have known the bare outline of the story ever since my father told me that the story never happened: my grandmother's first husband's second wife killed my father's first sister's best friend in a love triangle that would have confused Euclid. But I have sought the details in all the wrong places. I have studied old editions of the *Times* and the *Daily News,* newspapers too squeamish to revel in the squalor of what happened on the night of August 14, 1935. I need to sink lower. I need to crank my way through microfilms of Randolph Hearst's afternoon tabloid, the *Daily Mirror,* which still looks like it could leave ink stains eighty-five years after the fact. I need to understand the scandal as it was understood then, in inescapable black headlines, each lurid seventy-two-point letter about the size of a cockroach:

SUICIDE GUARD FOR GIRL KILLER
REISMAN JURY BATTLES OVER GIRL KILLER
DEMAND CHAIR FOR GIRL KILLER

The "girl" was Virginia Seigh, born and raised in a small town outside Pittsburgh and twenty-three years old when she died. The "girl killer" was Etta Schmier Reisman, who had lost her first husband to another woman and, at thirty-five, was desperately afraid of losing another. They both lived in the same well-appointed Tudor home in Beechhurst, Queens, Etta as the wife of beauty-parlor magnate Arthur Reisman and Virginia as the best friend and guest of Arthur's daughter from his first marriage, Annette, nicknamed Sissie. Etta was, according to the *Mirror,* "plain" and "plump" and "aging"; Virginia was "pretty" and "blonde" and "vivacious" and "sophisticated" and on the night of August 14, Arthur professed his love to her at the foot of his driveway in front of his daughter and his wife. When Etta took the stand in her own defense at the trial, she didn't just tell the jury what happened next; she sobbed it and screamed it and when she was done she had to receive medical attention.

"They had a secret! They had no room for me! They didn't want me! I went and got Arthur's gun!

"I told Virginia, 'Tell me everything!'

"My husband said, 'Yes, tell her—everything!'

"She said, 'I have loved him for a long time!'

"I had always known they cared for each other. I'd known it since after the first year she came to live with us. But I hadn't heard about it from her own lips . . .

"I said, then what's the use. I'll end it all. I put the gun to my head. Virginia jumped at me. The gun went off. She stepped back and then Sissie came at me. I said, 'Get back, I don't want to hurt you.' And then I emptied the gun."

At which point Arthur Reisman, seated in the courtroom, stood up and cried: "You've killed the only woman I ever truly loved!"

Damn.

I can see why the story dominated New York's yellow press for so many months. The murder of an innocent young woman was no less talismanic then than it is now, especially when the murderer is an older woman characterized as her "rival." But the story of what drove Etta Reisman to become a girl killer is still incidental to the story I am looking for, which is the story of what—and who—drove Arthur Reisman to his ruin. The *Daily Mirror* had portrayed him as a heartbroken victim and then as a heartless villain, as an American success story and then as a common heel. But none of its reporters succeeded in investing him with pathos until one of them found out about Elizabeth Becker.

She was his first wife. She married Arthur Reisman in 1910, when she was sixteen and he was seventeen. Two years later, they had a child and named her Annette. They lived in Brooklyn, in Bedford-Stuyvesant. He worked as a contractor; she played piano in movie houses, where she met an electrician named Louis Junod. A reporter with the *Girl Friday* name of Erskine Gosling told what happened next in a story headlined "Records Reveal Reisman's Past." It ran on page 4 of the *Mirror* three weeks after Virginia Seigh's murder and attempted to account for what it called "the strange conduct of Arthur Reisman in failing to step forward as the champion of his jailed wife." He wasn't "missing from the courtroom" because he was so angry at the second Mrs. Reisman slaying his beloved young secretary but rather because he was so ashamed of the first Mrs. Reisman making him a cuckold—because "a record of early marital misfortunes culminating in . . . the birth of another man's child is the one which Reisman may be hoping to conceal."

Erskine Gosling revealed Reisman's "old secret" by going to the Kings County supreme court and finding records of the divorce proceedings he initiated in 1916. Reisman didn't only have ample evidence for his claim that Elizabeth Becker Reisman had been unfaithful; he had "the accused wife's own mother, the widow Marie Becker of No. 79 Church Street, Brooklyn, furnishing the testimony which named her daughter as a faithless wife whose misconduct with the correspondent Louis Junod of 149 Winthrop Ave., Brooklyn, gave Reisman his absolute divorce and custody of baby Annette.

> On the stand, the erring wife's mother admitted:
>
> "Yes, I kept house for my daughter and Mr. Junod. They were living as Mr. and Mrs. Junod."
>
> "They lived, had their meals and slept together?" she was asked.
>
> "Yes."
>
> "You often saw them in bed together?"
>
> "Oh, yes."

—

The testimony of Elizabeth Becker's mother wasn't the only revelation Arthur Reisman brought to the judge. Justice Walter Jaycox "heard remarkable evidence by an eye-witness to the actual birth of a child born to Mrs. Reisman and Junod. Mrs. Dorothy Davenport, neighbor of Junod, took the stand and declared:

"'One night last year, Mrs. [Marie] Becker roused me out of bed in the middle of the night and asked me to help her daughter, who was sick. I saw at once the "illness" was the imminent birth of a child and helped summon doctors and nurses. I remained and helped in the delivery.'"

And there it was—or, rather, there *they* were, in the *Daily Mirror.* Elizabeth Becker was, of course, my grandma Bess, who Americanized her name from "Schmeckenbecher" in the same way her husband Aaron Reisman Americanized his to "Arthur." Annette Reisman was her daughter and my aunt. Mrs. Marie Becker was my great-grandmother Marie Hanfman, who married Martin Schmeckenbecher in 1888, when he was sixty. Louis Junod was the phantom who gave my father his name and, much later, came to our home to ask for money.

I had grown up in a family that barely acknowledged the existence of the past, much less a history. But I had finally found the secret history of my family in the pages of New York's most notorious tabloid newspaper, as well as conclusive proof that my grandmother was not the *Madawna*. But who was—and what happened to—the child born one night in an apartment on Winthrop Street in Brooklyn?

I call my cousin Vivian. She was born just a year before Etta Reisman emptied her gun into Virginia Seigh on the lawn of the Tudor home in Queens. She grew up with her mother, Marie, on Coney Island Avenue in Brooklyn, down the block from Grandma. When I ask her what she knows about the first child born to Louis Junod and Elizabeth Becker, she says, "I just know there was a boy involved—a boy child. He was put up for adoption. His name was William Hayes. I don't know why, Tommy, but that's the name I remember hearing. Don't forget, I'm older than anyone else. So I heard things. Once in a while, Grandma would say something like 'I made mistakes' or 'I did some foolish things.' I tried to get her to say more, and she'd clam right up."

"But you remember the name . . ."

"William Hayes—I never forgot it. And I saw him once, I swear to God. I was riding a streetcar on Flatbush Avenue and I looked out the window and saw a man who looked exactly like your father, the spitting image. I said, 'Stop this car!' I got out and looked all over for him but he was gone. Oh, I never rode that car again without looking for him. But I never found him."

Once upon a time, my father had four sisters and he was the man of the family. His sisters worshipped him and lived in fear of him, and he believed that he embodied masculinity itself and had earned the right to preach its principles. Now I discover that he not only had a sister named Annette—Sissie—who had the tip of her finger blown off in the murder of her best friend by her stepmother; he had an older brother, born in an apartment in Brooklyn with his grandmother and a neighbor as midwives. Was his name really William Hayes? Did my cousin Vivian really spot him through the window of a streetcar? I can't say. But the questions I keep turning over in my mind have less to do with his identity than with my father's.

What kind of man would Lou Junod have grown up to be if he'd shared his dominion with an older brother?

The girl killer didn't get the chair. The jury found her guilty of manslaughter the week before Christmas 1935, and an association of women from her neighborhood appealed to the judge for holiday mercy. She was a wronged woman. She was trying to preserve her marriage and her family. She had been in tears nearly as long as she had been in jail, and she had suffered enough.

She walked.

Virginia Seigh was buried in North Braddock, Pennsylvania, where she had grown up. Etta Schmier Reisman returned to her husband, Arthur; her son, Elias; and her stepdaughter, Annette. They moved away from Queens and the unsavory attentions of the scandal sheets and lived in the Catskill Mountains, in upstate New York. There were no more beauty parlors, and no more pretty secretaries. There was only a bungalow, and if not peace, then quiet.

But that wasn't the scandal's only happy ending. On September 10, 1935, the *Daily News* found the notorious adulteress Elizabeth Reisman Junod at home in her third-floor apartment on Coney Island Avenue. A reporter and a photographer knocked at her door, and she let them in. She talked to the reporter and sat for photographs with two of her children, Marie and Elizabeth. She wore a black dress like a woman in mourning and her black hair swept her forehead like the wing of a crow. She was forty-one years old, and looked at once commanding and affronted. She looked, as she always would, just like her son Louis, who is not in any of the photographs.

The next day, her story appeared in the *Daily News* under the headline "'Dead' Daughter Lives, Reisman's Ex Finds" and wire services spread it all over the country. Millions of people read Mrs. Junod's shocking account of how the death of Virginia Seigh somehow resurrected Annette Reisman—how "through the grim message of murder, a Brooklyn mother learned that her child, whom she believed dead for 15 years, was still alive."

It was an audacious claim in 1935, and remains so now. "I married Arthur Reisman in the Bronx in 1911," Mrs. Junod told the reporter. "He left me two months after Annette was born. I supported the two of us as a piano player in a movie theater for two years, then my mother told me our marriage had been annulled on account of our ages." Here, she said, she "married Louis Junod in 1914 and bore another child. Then Reisman appeared with a lawyer and claimed there had been no annulment. He persuaded me to return to him. But in 1917 he quit me again, announcing he was going to war. Annette was sent to his sister. I remarried Junod and we have lived happily."

The story ended by alluding to what the *Daily Mirror* had reported days before: "Investigation revealed that [Arthur] Reisman had obtained a divorce in 1920, naming Junod." But the *Daily News* did not brand Mrs. Junod a "faithless spouse," as the *Mirror* had; nor did it question the chain of events necessary for her to have lost and found her first child—twice. Indeed, the wire service version of the story came with a caption that suggested Mrs. Junod had believed her daughter Annette dead until she recognized her photograph in newspaper coverage of Virginia Seigh's slaying. Anyone reading the story would have assumed that Mrs. Junod, my grandma Bess, had raised the second child she bore in 1914, and that a joyous reunion with her first was already in the offing.

I try to find her after reading about her in the papers, after studying the photographs of her attending the murder trial of her stepmother on the arm of her father, both of them in long fur-trimmed black coats, he defiantly dapper and she defiantly stylish, as if they had both slipped into the equivocal and somewhat sinister roles the newspapers had assigned them. They looked, indeed, like a couple, a gangster and his moll. He was trim and tan, wearing a small mustache and a hat that covered his bald pate; she wore lipstick and a small black hat, peaked and plumed, that gave her a jaunty military air. I recognize her immediately, for with her "strong profile" and her grandiose nose and her black glare of imperious disregard, the Annette Reisman of 1935 looks shockingly like one of my Levittown aunts.

She is gone, of course. She was born so long ago, and if she were still alive when I begin searching for her in the summer of 2016 she would be 104 years old. She was also not the twentieth century's only Annette Reisman, not even the only Annette Reisman born in New York City around 1912, and if she were not lost among history's erasures, she might easily get lost among its crowds. My family—Grandma's surviving descendants—can't help me because they know her only as they knew *of* her, by rumor. My father himself has been dead ten years, and when he was alive, he not only never met her; he refused to meet her when he had the chance. And yet it is my father who leads me to her. I cannot find any obituaries for an Annette Reisman that match what I have gleaned of her history. But in the Social Security Administration's lists of the deceased, I come across an Annette Reisman Goodman who died on March 23, 2001. Is this possible? March 23, 2001, was my father's birthday. It was the day he turned eighty-two, and only a few years after I told him that somewhere out in the world he had another sister, and he responded that "it never happened." Is it possible that the woman who died that day in Boca Raton at the age of eighty-nine was the sister his mother abandoned?

All I have to go on is an image of her headstone, courtesy of the website Find a Grave, with the name Annette Goodman, in both

English and Hebrew, engraved between a menorah and the words "BELOVED WIFE MOTHER GRANDMOTHER." They fill me with hope, those words—hope that Annette enjoyed a life beyond abandonment and scandal. But they don't give me the name of any of those children or grandchildren, just a hunch. Annette was not the only child of Arthur Reisman who endured the scrutiny of the tabloids. Elias Reisman was nine years old when his mother killed Virginia Seigh at the foot of his driveway. I look up his name and find out that he went to Cornell and became a physicist who pioneered the use of lasers in industry and defense for the Ford Foundation. I look up his name again and find out that he died in 2002, a year after Annette, and was survived by a wife, Leorita, and three children, Art, Joanne and David.

I call Dr. David Reisman, a research oncologist. Does he know the story? He does. He grew up with it in Orange County, California, as well as with her—the girl killer. Etta Reisman was his *bubbe,* his grandmother. She babysat. Annette was his aunt, but she was accorded a special place in his household, because she protected Elias like a mother while his mother was on trial. "She was always trying to hide and take care of Elias when the newspapers were saying all these terrible things," David says. Neither Etta nor Elias liked to talk about that part of their past. Annette was more forthcoming, except about her mother, Elizabeth Becker.

"Your grandmother is one sentence in the family history," David says. "She was the floozy."

Then he gives me phone numbers for Steven Goodman and Vicki Oglesbee, Annette's two children. They are his cousins. They are also mine.

I make a living out of calling strangers and asking them for their secrets. I grow nervous before every call, wondering what right I have to make it. Sometimes I overcome my trepidation by telling myself that I'm providing the people on the other end of the line a chance to tell their stories; sometimes that I will get information I need in exchange for information they might want—that I know their stories better than they do. But now, not quite a year after my brother's fateful lunch with Muntu Law, I am calling strangers who are also blood relatives and blood relatives who are also strangers. I am presuming some kind of familiarity with them. But they have managed to live their entire lives without hearing from me, or for that matter knowing I exist. I am not simply calling them from out of the blue; I am calling from out of the past, from more than one hundred years of abandonment and estrangement.

I call them one after another and they couldn't be more different. Steve is a lawyer in Chicago, nearing retirement. Vicki is, in her brother's description, "a vagabond" traveling the country in a motor home. But they have something in common, with each other and with me. They both have wondered and they both have wanted to know. The shock of talking to people with whom I share DNA—of talking to the children of a sister my father refused to believe he had—gives way to the solidarity of talking to people with whom I share a secret and a story. It is another excavation, but for once I am not the only one digging.

There were details that my grandmother left out when she spoke to the *Daily News* reporter about how she lost track of her daughter. According to Reisman family lore, Annette was in the room, in the crib, both victim and silent witness when her father caught her mother in bed with Louis Junod. She was two years old when her parents split; she was four when her father won custody. He tried to raise her, but he was just twenty-two and he wound up sending her to live with his sisters on a farm in New Jersey. They were not kind to her. They did not treat her as a full member of their family. "When they had chicken, they gave her chicken feet," Vicki says. She was just a child but they put her to work, perhaps as a moral corrective for her tainted birthright. "You're gonna grow up to be a tramp just like your mother," the sisters would say when she misbehaved. She still waited for her mother to come and get her. Only her father came, after World War I.

He met Etta Schmier at the office of his divorce attorney and married her in 1923. Annette wanted Etta to step in as her mother but the first time she addressed her with that word Etta said, "Don't call me that. I'm not your mother." So, as Vicki says, "she called her nothing."

The three of them, Arthur and Etta and Annette, lived together as Arthur made his way in the world, finally moving to the house in Beechwood when he opened a chain of "twenty-five-cent beauty parlors" built on his belief that even in the depths of the Depression "women care about how they look." Then Virginia Seigh moved in, and Etta filled her full of lead.

Annette did not move to Sullivan County with Arthur and Etta and Elias, not at first. They had their bungalow, then their bungalows, which Arthur rented out while working as a "radio repairman," according to the 1940 census. Annette lived in the city, "a career girl" with a past. But then she went to visit and a young man who worked on a chicken farm picked her up at the train station. His name was Albert Goodman, and "once she saw his blue eyes, that was it," says Steven. He was a careful, considerate man, and he set about delivering her to the normalcy she craved. They married right before the war and had their first child, Steven, in 1945, when they still lived in the bungalows. Steven has never forgotten Arthur and Etta—Arthur as the grandfather who "shrieked" at him when he touched his car; Etta as the grandmother whom he "definitely thought capable of killing someone." Annette never trusted Etta with her children; perhaps that is why they moved to Elgin, Illinois, after Vicki was born.

Annette was a happy woman in Elgin—"merry," in the memories of her children. She loved to sing and dance, though she had no talent for either; as a member of Elgin's Jewish community, she was a doer, an inveterate volunteer, and very much a *balabusta*. The one time she pulled her children aside to confess a "dark secret," she told them that she was three years older than their father; when they asked about her bent finger, she explained it was the product of a car accident rather than a stray bullet. She was proud of her looks, and even when her beloved husband had a heart attack while taking a walk, she made sure to put on her makeup and primp her hair before she went to see him in the hospital. It was after Albert died in 1978 that Steven and Vicki obtained her birth certificate and read the name of her mother as Elizabeth Schmeckenbecher. They asked who she was and Annette told them that she was the woman who abandoned her; they asked if she wanted them to try to find her, and she answered no, "because she never tried to find me." Both Steven and Vicki use almost the same words when describing their mother's "emphatic" response: "She wanted no part of her."

At last I have the answer to the question that has tugged at me since I read the article from the 1935 *Daily News* and saw the photo of my grandmother and two of her daughters taking in the joyous news of Annette's survival. Grandma thought she lost Annette in 1914. She thought she lost her again two years later. But she thought she *found* her in 1935. It is possible that she tried to contact her, and was rebuffed by her ex-husband and his family. But by the time Annette became a figure in a public scandal she was twenty-three years old and no longer under Arthur Reisman's control. Surely, Grandma could have written her, called her, or shown up at her door if she wanted to—if, as she told the *Daily News,* she was driven by the force of an entirely unexpected revelation. Annette had no memory of her doing so. She remembered Elizabeth Schmeckenbecher as the mother who abandoned her once and for all time. Grandma told any number of lies to the *Daily News;* the final one, the conclusive one, is that she never stopped thinking of her first child. She lived in Levittown until 1989; Annette lived in Boca until 2001. The last documented time they saw each other was in 1914, when Arthur Reisman caught my grandmother in bed with the man who gave me my last name.

> *JUNOD—Louis (former embalmer). Husband of Elizabeth. Father of Marie E. Peters, Louis, Elizabeth Nolan and Elsie Peragine. Survived by six grandchildren and three great-grandchildren. Brother of Elsie. Reposing at J. Carotozzollo Funeral Home, 178 Irving Ave., until Tuesday, 1 PM. Interment. Evergreens Cemetery.*

He was a Brooklyn boy. He is in a different place on every relevant document Ancestry can produce, but he lived and he died solely between Bedford and Bushwick Avenues. He shows up first in the census of 1900 on Lexington, living with his father, August, born in Switzerland, and his mother, Emmy, born in France. Five years later, he's on Patchen, thirteen years old and in eighth grade; by 1915, he's living on Gates Avenue, a block away from the apartment where he carried on his affair with Elizabeth Reisman.

Thus begins his career as a family man. My dad always marshaled the addresses of his years in Bedford-Stuyvesant and Bushwick—the flats on Gates Avenue and . . . Quincy Street—as evidence of his humble origins, shaking his head and cringing with distaste. But the documents reveal that the fractious Levittown clan we drove to see practically every weekend of my childhood was formed there, with Louis Junod Sr. so much the paterfamilias that he sought an exemption from the draft in 1917 as the sole means of support for his wife and two children. But who were *they*? My aunt Marie had been born earlier that year. But my father, whom I grew up knowing as Grandma's second child and first son, was still two years away from drawing his first breath. Perhaps the other child was the baby rumored by my older cousins to have died. Or perhaps the child was the son who preceded my father and became William Hayes.

In any case, my father is not the first son to have lived in the home of Louis Junod and Elizabeth Becker Reisman. Better to call him the first son to be kept, or to have survived—better still to call him something that can be confirmed, the first son of my grandmother to be named on a census. He makes his debut on the New York State census of 1925 as six-year-old "Louis Junad Jr," and if the ancient misspelling is not a surprise, the suffix is. Louis Junod . . . *Junior*?

It's a name that he never used in my earshot and that never makes its way to another public record, but still a name that suggests Louis Junod "the undertaker" was proud to claim him as his own. My father appears again in the 1930 federal census, which documented an iteration of his family that was very nearly whole, very nearly nuclear. There were Louis and Elizabeth Junod, the parents. There were Marie, Louis, Elizabeth and Elsie, the children. They all lived together on 623 Quincy Street, apartment 18, just as later they all clustered in Levittown. They were all Junods.

It is the last published census on which Louis Junod Sr. appears. He has thirty-eight more years of life, but he cannot be found on the federal census of 1940, nor of 1950. Grandma is on both of them, but with another man.

Marie used to see him at the drugstore across the street from their apartment, at 457 Coney Island Avenue. She used to go there for candy and cigarettes and he would be leaning against the brick wall in the sun, watching the world go by. He was a much older man, the hair on the sides of his bald head turned white, and he struck her as an idler, with nothing much to do. But he was tall and he was elegant and she never saw him wear anything but a suit with a vest and a watch on a gold chain. She would ask him the time and he would flip her, and later her child Vivian, a piece of candy. She wound up introducing him to her mother. She always regretted it.

His name was John Schmidt, and he moved in with them in the middle of the Great Depression. He paid rent, and insisted on ironing his own shirts. There were five Junod children once Mildred came along in 1935, and he is listed on the census from both 1940 and 1950 as nothing more than a "lodger," albeit a longstanding one. In 1952, Aunt Ellie married Frank Peragine, and when they moved to Levittown, Grandma left Coney Island Avenue for good and made the Peragine home her own. John Schmidt did not follow her, but in the days preceding Millie's wedding to Jack Thimons the Junods took him in one last time, in a manner of speaking. It was 1955, and Millie was twenty years old. Marie was thirty-eight, and her daughter Vivian was twenty-one. Marie had always envied Millie, for if nothing she did could win Grandma's love, nothing Millie did could lose it. Millie hadn't even learned to read or write, because Grandma insisted she stay by her side all day and wouldn't let her attend school. She was, as she always proclaimed, "the baaaaaaby." And so before Millie married Jack, Marie revealed a family secret, told her the truth and got her revenge all in one stroke: "You're not my sister," Marie said.

She meant Millie was not a Junod. She had obtained her marriage license as a Junod, but her birth certificate listed John Schmidt as her father and one "Elizabeth Becker" as her mother. She married Jack at a bowling alley in Levittown, with the reception on the village green, with John Schmidt, the lodger, eighty-four years old but still tall and elegant with his three-piece suit and his watch on a gold chain, walking her up the aisle and then turning around and giving away the bride.

Did my father attend Millie's wedding? He did. Did he know John Schmidt? He had to—he grew up with him on Coney Island Avenue. My father spoke frequently of the jobs he held as a boy and as a young man, because they helped *create* him, because his job at a haberdasher in downtown Brooklyn helped mold his sense of style and his job driving rivets at the Brooklyn Navy Yard helped mold his magnificent body. But the 1940 census gives him a job he never talked about. John Schmidt worked as "a packer" at the Whelan drugstore where my aunt Marie first encountered him, and my father, with one year of high school listed as the conclusion of his formal education, worked in the same place as a "general underling." He was twenty-one years old, and I take the liberty of imagining that he was humiliated by the man who paid his mother rent also fathering his mother's youngest child. This is not because Dad said something about it later on; it's because he didn't. Indeed, once he left home in Brooklyn he went the rest of his life without ever so much as mentioning the name of John Schmidt.

On April 30, 1930, an undertaker named Arthur E. Alden died. He was thirty years old, and not long after he was buried, another undertaker named Louis Junod moved in with his widow. Although he disappears thereafter from the census records, he surfaces once more, in the draft card he had to fill out for the Second World War, living with Olive Alden on Monroe Street. He also shows up in patents for an embalming machine he and another partner invented in 1939. He lived in Bushwick with Mrs. Alden until she died in 1964, and when he died four years later he was buried in the Evergreens Cemetery, at the eastern end of Bushwick Avenue. His obituary is an exercise in wishful—or even willful—thinking, reading like a posthumous attempt to restore a king to his throne and to make a family broken for at least three decades whole. The list of survivors is pointed in its exclusion of the woman who thought her name was Mildred Junod until she got married, and to this day I can't look at the obituary of Louis Henry Augustus Junod without wondering who wrote it.

Probably either Marie or Elizabeth—his children.

But I'm also wondering if it was someone who was obsessed with appearances, and wanted to give himself the father he claimed he never had.

I have a question. At the start of the summer of 2016, my cousin Betty Ann gives me Grandma's Bible and a framed photograph of her as a teenage girl. In the photograph, she wears white, as if for a wedding; the Bible is in German and in between its pages I find her marriage license, like a bookmark. The license is not for her first marriage to Arthur Reisman but rather her second; indeed, when she married her lover Louis Junod, she did so as Elizabeth Schmeckenbecher, as if her first marriage never happened. But it did happen, and my question concerns when it ended. In his *Daily Mirror* story about her divorce, Erskine Gosling wrote that Arthur Reisman won full custody of Annette on March 4, 1916, but he also wrote that the divorce ran into obstacles and wasn't final until 1920. Elizabeth Schmeckenbecher married Louis Junod on June 1, 1916, in of all places Greenwich, Connecticut. How was that possible?

To find out, I go to family court in Brooklyn, where Gosling discovered the scandalous testimony of the Reisman file. The clerk indulges me, her eyebrows slowly rising. "I'm checking to see if my grandmother was legally married," I say, and pull from my notebook a Ziploc snack bag containing the one-hundred-year-old marriage license. "Well, actually I'm checking to see if she was divorced before she did this. I mean, her husband had caught her in bed with another man and won custody of their daughter but I'm just trying to figure out when the divorce was final . . ."

"Sounds like your grandma was Kick-Up-Her-Heels *Sally,*" the clerk says with a conclusive shake of her head, and then she begins searching the pages of ancient ledgers that have been reduced to microfiche. She can't find a record of the divorce in the ledgers of 1916. She can't find it in 1917 or 1918 or 1919. At last, her chin swings the other way, beckoning me over. "Case number eight seventy," she says, "filed by Aaron Reisman on January 27, 1916. Is this the one?"

It is. He was born Aaron Reisman and changed his name to Arthur after he untangled himself from my grandmother and started his new life. The clerk points to a line on the page, the judge putting his name on a "final decree of divorce" as though he were signing the Magna Carta.

"This is 1920," she says.

"But she married Louis Junod in 1916 . . ."

"That was no wedding," she says. "That was just an expensive costume party. Oh, these old people—young people today got *nothing* on them. Your grandma was living in *sin*."

I wonder, for a moment, if Grandma made an understandable mistake when she married Louis Junod in 1916—if she thought that the judge's interlocutory decree had dissolved the legal bonds of her marriage to Aaron Reisman. But she had gone to Greenwich, Connecticut, to get married, when a judge had yet to finalize her divorce in Brooklyn. And she was still legally "Elizabeth Reisman" when she signed her Connecticut marriage license "Elizabeth Schmeckenbecher," as if her first marriage had never happened.

So she had schemed and plotted, she had covered her tracks. My grandmother wasn't just, as the Reismans had it, a "floozy," or, as the clerk said, Kick-Up-Her-Heels Sally.

My grandmother had never legally married Louis Junod.

My grandmother was a bigamist.

I go to the basement of the family court building to request the file, case number 870. I fill out a form with the name of the case—*Aaron Reisman v. Elizabeth Reisman*—and Eric Spruiell, the clerk of the court, asks me which one was my grandparent. "Elizabeth Reisman," I say, and then watch him disappear into the endless serried ranks of file folders as if disappearing into the past itself. When he reemerges from the deep shadows of his personal domain, the resignation in his voice has found its way to his face. "There is no case eight seventy here," he said.

"Is it lost? Disposed of?"

"No, we don't dispose of court cases. We move them. Yours was probably moved to a warehouse in Brooklyn. I'm sorry."

"Can't we find it?"

Eric Spruiell looks at me from across the counter, a sigh in human form.

"Have you heard about the fire?" he asks.

There was a warehouse on the Brooklyn waterfront. Then there was a spark from a broken light fixture. It started a small fire, which the automatic sprinkler system put out. But the warehouse stored so many ancient files from its main clients—the state courts, and the city health and hospitals administration—that concerns arose that water would destroy them. The sprinkler system was shut off, the doused fire turned out to be a smoldering one, and just before sunrise on January 31, 2015, on what would turn out to be one of the coldest days of the year, the warehouse began to burn. It contained

1.1 million square feet of space, and most of the space was given over to paper and photographs. The seven-alarm fire burned for days, and the warehouse disgorged its secrets. It spewed so much paper that the intake valves of the fire boats in the East River clogged; it revealed so much forgotten information that people who lived in the Williamsburg neighborhood began collecting it from the streets and the rocks that lined the river. They collected old X-rays, old medical photos, old court cases once sealed in the interests of privacy. By the end of the day, the curious posted their collected curios on Instagram, and the gutted warehouse, while still ablaze, was coated with ice.

I decide to join Ancestry after I learn about the fire. I send the company my spit in the hope that once I surrender my DNA no documents will be necessary—that case 870, likely lost to the flames, might still be found in my saliva. But Ancestry turns out to provide documents as well as DNA matches; it proves more effective at protecting and promulgating precious information than New York City's family courts, and soon I find an index of all live births in New York City from 1910 to 1965. I find Annette Reisman there, listed as Anna. I find my aunt Marie and my aunt Elizabeth and my aunt Elsie. I find my dad, birth certificate number 12273. Then one day I decide to go looking for someone I never knew. I search the list for everyone named Junod from 1910 on. I find a Maurice Louis Junod born in 1921, but I discount the possibility that he's a relative when I discover the names of his parents. And then I find "Wm. M. Junod," birth certificate number 43100, born on November 6, 1914.

Erskine Gosling opened Case 870 and in his article for the *Daily Mirror* he wrote that Grandma had given birth to a baby in an apartment in Brooklyn in 1914 with the next-door neighbor serving as a midwife. Was November 6 the day the baby was born? My cousin Vivian insisted that Grandma's first son's name had been William Hayes after his adoption. Had he been born as "Wm. M. Junod"? I still have Eric Spruiell's number and decide to call him. I no longer entertain hope that he can rescue case 870 from the ashes in the East River. But he has been kind and diligent and I wonder if he might have the original birth index right there in front of him. I wonder if he can tell me where I can find the birth certificate for "Wm. M. Junod."

He answers the phone and I tell him my name. Months have passed since I saw him over the summer and I start trying to explain why I'm calling. He cuts me off.

"You're the guy who was researching his grandma's divorce, right? Case number eight seventy?"

"That's right. It burned in the fire."

"No, it didn't. I've been waiting for you to call. I didn't have your number. I didn't even know your name."

"It didn't burn in the fire? Then what happened to it?"

"I have it."

"Where?"

"Right in front of me."

"You found it?"

"I'm looking at it right now."

"Wait—case eight seventy?"

"It's in my lap," Eric Spruiell says.

You need a miracle, when you're sniffing around your past and turning upside down the legacies of the people you grew up loving most. You will lose heart; you will want to stop, and in order to keep on going you will need to benefit from some impossible happenstance that not only lights your way but eases your conscience. My first miracle was the discovery of my cousins, Steve Goodman and Vicki Oglesbee. My second is the preservation of Grandma's divorce file. I don't know what I will find once I open it and look inside; it almost doesn't matter. What matters is that Eric Spruiell happened to be reading it the very moment I called him, and told me that whenever I came back to family court it would be waiting for me.

I come back in the first month of 2017. Eric Spruiell isn't there—he has taken a sick day—but the case file is, bound in a burgundy ribbon. It is one hundred years old, and it sheds little flecks of itself with every touch. I untie the ribbon, and there are three documents folded into oblong rectangles, the cursive on the 1920 divorce decree—Aaron Reisman against Elizabeth Reisman—so elegant it might be able to find a home on a wedding announcement. I take great care unfolding them, and then begin reading the testimony into a little tape recorder. I have encountered some of it before, in Erskine Gosling's article. There was the damning witness of the defendant's own mother; there was the judge's disgusted response. But here, in the little reading room at the courthouse, I come across something that counts almost as a visitation of the dead. Louis A. Junod was also subpoenaed and he also testified under direct questioning by Aaron Reisman's lawyer. I read both parts out loud, the questions of the lawyer and the answers of a man familiar to me only as an unyielding absence, as an inveigling stranger and then at last as a furtive and forbidding presence at the front door—the father who wasn't a father. I have heard his voice once in my life, asking, "Is your *fatha* home?" Now his voice is my own.

LAWYER: Where do you reside?
WITNESS: Number 922 Gates Avenue in Brooklyn.
LAWYER: Do you live there with the defendant, Elizabeth Reisman, under the name of Mr. and Mrs. Junod?
WITNESS: Yes, sir.
LAWYER: Were you at 4090 Fulton Avenue, Woodhaven, Brooklyn?
WITNESS: Yes, sir.
LAWYER: That was between the first of March 1914 and the first of December 1914?
WITNESS: Yes, sir.
LAWYER: Describe the premises there at 4090 Fulton Avenue. Is it a flat?
WITNESS: Yes, sir. A flat in a two-story house.
LAWYER: Did you have a furnished room there?
WITNESS: Not at the time. She was living with different people at the time.
LAWYER: You went to see her there?
WITNESS: Yes, sir.
LAWYER: Did you ever have intercourse with her there?
WITNESS: Yes.
LAWYER: You were in bed with her there?
WITNESS: Yes, sir.
LAWYER: Did you ever live with her at Number 61 Ralph Avenue, Brooklyn?
WITNESS: Yes, sir.

LAWYER: Did you have a furnished room there?
WITNESS: Yes.
LAWYER: Under what name?
WITNESS: My name.
LAWYER: And did you live there with the defendant Elizabeth Reisman and have intercourse with her there?
WITNESS: I did.
LAWYER: Did you live with her at number 247 Winthrop Street, Flatbush, between March 1, 1914, and the first of December 1914?
WITNESS: Yes, sir.
LAWYER: And you slept with the defendant there?
WITNESS: I did.
LAWYER: And had intercourse with her there?
WITNESS: Yes, sir.

The lawyer pauses his questions and produces a photograph. He asks the court to show the photograph to the witness. The transcript does not specify the nature or the subject of the photo, but what the witness sees on the stand may be inferred from the lawyer's next statement: "I show you this picture and ask you by what woman was this child gotten."

"By Elizabeth Reisman," Louis A. Junod responds, and what has to have been the photo of his child—his first son, born five years before my father and now remembered only as "Wm. M. Junod" on the New York City birth index and as "William Hayes" in the collective memory of my family—is offered into evidence.

My first cousin Vivian is eighty-three years old when I visit her at a rehab center in Albany, New York. She had a heart attack a few months ago and her body is filling up with fluid. She's always been a big woman like her mother, Marie, but now her ankles are almost too thick and heavy for her to move. And yet she's happy to see me, because she loves talking about the family—she loves *gossiping* about the family, especially about my dad. Did I know that he had an affair with the band singer Helen O'Connell?

"I did not," I say.

"Oh, yes, she used to write your father letters. They were beautiful. And that song of hers, 'Green Eyes'—she told your father that when she sang it she thought of him."

"Well, he definitely had green eyes."

"But he didn't stay with her," she says. "And do you know why?"

"Why?"

"Because he said she had body odor."

I've been listening to this story as another entertaining tidbit about my dad. But this one detail, perverse in its particularity, rings true, because my father was preternaturally sensitive to matters of hygiene. Vivian knows the truth. She knows what no one else knows, as she has told me many times since her first phone call. But here's the thing: She's not just a person who tells stories. She turns out to be a person with a story to tell.

She was born in 1934, when her mother was seventeen and married, for five months, to a man named Ernest Peters. He had nothing to do with his daughter and divorced Marie in 1941. Marie and Vivian lived on Coney Island Avenue with Bess. They had to move out when Bess took John Schmidt as a lodger. They found temporary refuge in the precincts of the Brooklyn Democratic Club and Marie found a married man who took care of her. His name was Joe Laura. He was a meat inspector. Every Friday he bought his girlfriend Marie a pound of veal—"he got a pretty good deal," Vivian says. "For a pound of veal he got the mother *and* the daughter." He began molesting Vivian when she was seven. She told Marie but Marie never took action; she had been prostituted by her own mother and now she left her daughter unprotected. "No one will ever know the fright of hearing that man's footsteps coming to the door," Vivian says. A much older man, Joe Laura used to drive to the orphanage and assure her that this is where she would live if she told anyone; then he'd park in the dark at a school and molest her. It lasted eight years; when she was fifteen, she finally told him that if he touched her again she would kill him. He stopped. But Marie stayed with him, as his lover, until she finally left Brooklyn and joined the rest of her family on Long Island.

It's a terrible story. But it's not the only story, and it's not the one that has kept Vivian intrigued, against her better judgment, with the possibilities of taking an Ancestry test. I have always wondered why the disappearance of Wm. M. Junod—and her subsequent identification of him as William Hayes—has meant so much to her. Now she tells me. She was not an only child. She was simply the only child raised by her mother. She already had a sister when she was born. Her name was Joan. Marie gave birth to Vivian at seventeen; she must have been very young when she had Joan. She was living with Grandma and when Marie came home from the hospital with Vivian, Joan was gone. "She was *sold*," Vivian says. "Grandma didn't think my mother could handle two. So she sold her." It's why she wanted to stop the bus when she saw a man who she believed looked like her grandfather. It's why Joe Laura's threat of putting her in the orphanage had such power. It's why she named her second daughter Joan and went through life with her presumed sister's date of birth in her wallet. And it's why she wanted to make sure I knew that Grandma was "no Madawna"—why she tells me now that Grandma was nothing less than a villain.

"Her apartment on Coney Island Avenue was a house of ill repute," she says. "But I guess it's in the genes. We're all a bunch of swingers, Tommy. But Grandma, she was the head swinger."

21

He was one of the young guys.

I have to remind myself of that, not only because he's not young anymore—he's pushing eighty when I meet him on a hot summer day in 2016—but also because like all the young guys, indeed like myself, he looked up to my father. He saw my father as a role model, as a mentor, as a teacher, and as an inspiration, but also as something harder to define: the fulfillment and personification of his own dream, the man whose presence let him know he *had* a dream. My father was who Mike Adams wanted to be.

Mike was a handbag salesman, back in the seventies. My father was *the* handbag salesman. It might not sound like much now, but back then, Mike tells me, the top guys in the business were making more than guys on Wall Street. They were making so much money, and Lou Junod was making more than any of them. He had an aura about him, a glow, and it wasn't just the tan he worked on every day of his life—"Your father used to take a reflector to Fifth Avenue at lunchtime, and sit with it on the fire hydrant." It was what happened when you were around him, and he was around you.

He took an interest in people, especially young people, especially young men. He was a big shot, but he never acted like a big shot, at least not one-on-one. He couldn't stand it if everyone in the restaurant wasn't looking at him. But when you were alone with him, it was different. He told you things, taught you things. Mike was in his early thirties when he began working for one of the lines my father represented, but still a kid from New Jersey. He had some ideas, but he didn't have any class. My father gave him class, just by letting him hang around, by letting him watch and learn. "Your father taught me how to dress, how to order in a restaurant, how to act. Your father changed my life."

I first met Mike when I was a teenager, and he was not only a salesman for Letisse but a designer, a knockoff artist adept at buying luxury items in Bergdorf or Bonwit Teller and translating them into handbags my dad could sell to department stores by the dozen. He had wiry black hair that sprouted from a widow's peak, skin that shined like a glass-top table, and lips so naturally red they gave him a leer. His hair is white now, and the shiny skin is spotted pink, but the widow's peak still points to lips as deeply colored as a clown's. I was supposed to meet him in a diner. But I am meeting him in a strange place, because something strange happened on the way—my old car began misfiring on the George Washington Bridge and I'm lucky to be sitting here with him in the waiting room of the BMW dealership in Teaneck, New Jersey. It's not crowded, but no conversation that takes place in it can be private. He seems to wish for privacy, and glances around even when he's giving "Louie" a compliment.

I tell him that he is not the only one who cites my father as an influence—that almost every male I've spoken to has done the same, in almost the same words, some of them salesmen who met my dad coming up and some of them friends from Wantagh or the sons of family friends. He would take them out to lunch in New York and encourage them to talk about life and then just listen to them. It was a side of my father I didn't know existed, except in terms of his own family, in terms of me and Michael, but it turned out to have a lasting effect on people who wished their own fathers would talk to them that way, with so much interest and respect. Some, I tell Mike, even wished he *was* their father, because their fathers told them many things but never that—never how to be a man.

"Well, that's because your father was the real thing," Mike says. "He didn't just talk tough—he was a genuine tough guy. I know, because I've seen it. And he didn't just talk like a ladies' man. I've seen that too. Even the stories that were too good to be true turned out to be true. One time, I went with him for the California market. Your father loved California—that was his place, and I spent a lot of time with him there. Well, one night we're taking some buyers out to dinner. We have a whole big table, and across the restaurant we see Eva Gabor. Now, everyone knows about your father and the Gabor sisters. But none of us believe it—we think it's just another of his stories. So we start kidding him. 'Hey, Lou, there's your girlfriend—why don't you go talk to her?' He waves us off. Then, when we see her leaving, we start in again. 'Lou, Lou, you're missing your chance.' But she sees him, and I'll be damned if she doesn't walk over and begin talking to him. 'Oh, Lou, Lou, Lou, you didn't tell me you were here! Why haven't you called me! You need to call me!' I think he was embarrassed, to tell you the truth. But we were in awe. He was our hero."

It was what I had to understand about my father. "He had his faults," Mike says. "But he wasn't a bullshitter. His problem was that he liked bullshitters, he fell for bullshitters. He had this friend, in California, this guy Vinnie. Do you know about Vinnie?"

"Yeah," I say. "I know about Vinnie."

"Well, your father was very impressed by him. Vinnie wound up wearing cement shoes, but your father couldn't stop talking about him. One time he came back from California and told me this story. Vinnie was a bookie but I guess he also taught special ed, if you can believe it."

"He used to talk about bringing troublemakers and retards to heel," I say.

"The story your father told was about that. They were on the beach one night, and they were with a bunch of young girls that

Vinnie taught. He took out a switchblade and flicked it open. He pointed to your father and told one of the girls, 'Suck this man's cock, or I'll cut your tits off.' "

I look around. There's nobody in the waiting room but me and Mike, though it's the summer of 2016, and the TV is blasting the news of Donald Trump's doomed campaign against Hillary Clinton. Nobody can get away from it, and now I can't get away from the image of Vinnie and the knife.

"Your father told this story," Mike says. "I wish it was bullshit. But I don't think it was."

I stop at the metal gate to see if it's locked. It isn't; the hinges are just stiff and the latches are just stubborn, but even when I manage to open it I hesitate before crossing the threshold. I don't think I'm breaking the law, but that doesn't really matter. I'm not supposed to be there. Green tarnish covers the gate, and bristling overgrown vegetation swallows the stone hinge posts. On a sun-blasted afternoon I am standing in a place set apart by shadow, a haunted place that wasn't created for me or for that matter any other stranger. It's private, it's family. But it's so different from the world outside the concrete wall that it has an irresistible pull. I step inside through a spiderweb to look for the grave of Peggy Friedlander.

I am in Moultrie, Georgia, a meatpacking town halfway between Albany and Valdosta and untouched by an interstate. I am in Pinecrest Memory Garden, a vast clearing of low gray and white stones and thistly grass bereft of any semblance of shade. And now, past the wall and the gate, I enter the inner circle, a private cemetery inside the public one, a kind of oasis identified by a long horizontal stone engraved with a declaration: Friedlander Family Gardens. A single bird is singing from one of the magnolia trees. I am otherwise alone, the gravel around the gravestones crunching underfoot, the big spilled leaves of the magnolias turning black in the elements. I walk straight ahead, and read the inscription on a bulwark of gray granite: "Wife, Mother, Friend, Lover." I sink to a knee. It's Peggy.

She's not from here, not from the South, any more than I am. She was born Peggy Weinberger on Long Island in 1922. She met Irwin Friedlander—Friedy—in New York City during the war. They were married in 1944 and she followed him to Georgia, where he was the son of a rag merchant who eventually built an Art Deco department store on the Moultrie town square, not far from the requisite monument to the Confederate dead. They opened stores of their own in Columbus, where she met my father and, in the summer of 1978, shot herself. She's here now, next to Friedy, whose inscription—"Father, Husband, Friend, Lover"—complements hers, and in the same plot as her son and two of her three daughters.

I came to visit them as much as I came to visit her, because I heard that her suicide was not an isolated tragedy—that the single gunshot she fired into her skull rippled and reverberated across her entire family. I read their names now, each gray slab dressed with a Star of David. There is Kenneth Mark, who died of cancer just a year before my visit. There is Judy Rita, who died of her addictions in 2001, and whose inscription says, "You were the wind beneath our sails. Fly high angel." And then there is Jill Leslie, a buyer for the family business who shot herself not long after her mother did, with less efficiency. She lingered for years, paralyzed, and died in 1990, buried now under a flat stone engraved with the words "You were only waiting for this moment to be free."

Thirteen years before, when my parents had to move to Aunt Liz's spare bedroom in Levittown, my mother fell and broke her hip. I flew up for the surgery, and that night, when my father and I left the hospital, we spoke about Peggy Friedlander for the first time since her suicide. I told my father I'd be headed to the city when Mom recovered and he asked why I didn't stay more often at the Essex House. I mentioned the night I met Peggy. He shook his head wistfully rather than ruefully and said, "Peggy Friedlander—she had a little *crush* . . . on your old man." I turned and studied his face. "Dad, she killed herself a few weeks later. She shot herself . . ." But he kept staring straight ahead, a faint yet insistent smile cracking his lips. "She had quite a little *thing* . . . for your *father*."

Her gravesite is quite a thing as well, for suddenly I feel as though I haven't arrived there so much as it has pursued me. It returns me to the question I had when I saw my father crying after he heard the news of Peggy's death. "She was so . . . alive," he said in disbelief, and I remembered how she said goodbye, the power of her embrace when she pulled me close to her. But I also wondered if he had anything to do with her death, if the chemistry and attraction they paraded right in front of me ended up breaking her heart.

There was a time when I believed the deaths of two lovers named Peggy over two years' time ennobled my father, turning him into some kind of tragic hero. Do I still believe that now? Do I still feel that way staring at Peggy and Jill's mute stones, a mother and a daughter buried just a few feet apart? I have no idea if Lou Junod played a part in Peggy Friedlander's unhappiness. But I do know that Peggy's successful suicide played a part in Jill's unsuccessful one. And I know that what my father said about Peggy—his boast, twenty-five years after she died—made him sound not tragic at all, but simply heartless.

The email is done. I've written it and I've contemplated it and edited it. I've shared it with Janet and incorporated her corrections and I've shared it with my editor and incorporated his. I've even settled on the subject line, the first thing that will be read when the message lands in a digital mailbox.

"My Father. Your Mother."

And then I sit on it. Days go by, weeks. Some days I read it ten times, some days not at all. But I never stop thinking about it, the itch never lets up. I have found email addresses for two of the four Monahan children, the youngest, Tom and Lizanne. Tom works for a media company. Lizanne owns a catering business. Tom is in his forties, Lizanne in her early fifties. They both—they all—lost their mother. I am about to tell them that she had an affair with my father.

"My Father. Your Mother."

The email sits in Apple Mail, a draft in a folder of other drafts. But it's the one that clamors, it's the one that's always there and can't be undone.

> *My name is Tom Junod and I'm a writer, mostly for magazines . . . I would like to talk to you about the relationship between my father and your mother, Peggy.*
>
> *I have hesitated many times before writing you this email; I hesitate even now, because I realize how difficult it might*

be to receive such news out of the blue. But I have decided to go ahead with it, because although I have known for 20 years that my father was involved with your mother, it is only after researching my father's life that I have come to understand your mother's primary place in it. She was, I am given to understand, the love of his life.

Every time I read it, I wonder how to make it better—how to defuse it, to how to lessen some of its potential for pain. I try changing the words, their order, their emphasis. I try adding words and I try taking words away. But words aren't what make the email dangerous. The email's very existence makes it dangerous. For all the care of its language, it gives itself—I give myself—permission to change the lives of the Monahan children forever.

I imagine that this must be hard to read, and I apologize in advance for any pain I cause . . .

Three weeks go by. The only way to improve upon the email is to delete it, and I can't do that. I won't do that. I can't send it and I can't not send it. Then one day I read it and something changes. I decide that the only thing worse than action is inaction, the only thing worse than sending it is not sending it. I have to send it in order to breathe.

"My Father. Your Mother."

On October 26, 2016, I hit "send" and then I hear the "whoosh," the sound of the digital great beyond. The email is now irrevocable.

Four hours later, there's a ping from my laptop, and an email with a new subject line:

"Peggy Monahan."

It's from Tom Monahan. It says, "Well, I must say this was a weird email to open on a Wednesday morning at work . . ."

And then, at last, I take a breath.

"Your story checks out."

That's the message I receive from Tom Monahan two days before I am supposed to meet him face-to-face. "My mother's best friend is still alive and I spoke to her today. I actually made a mistake and was referencing your father as Tom. Aunt Vern said the only person she knew my mother was close to was a Lou. And she confirmed that Mom and Lou had a long term relationship over the years."

It takes me by surprise—not the news that Tom has been able to confirm the story with a woman named Vern Winick but that he felt the need to. I know the story of the affair from my father, from Frankie, from Frankie's family, from Muntu. It has become my story, but now someone is asking questions about it, fact-checking it, as I have done so many times with so many stories over the years. It is not holy writ; it is a claim, made by the son of "a Lou." In the cold light of Tom Monahan's skepticism, my father is not a tragic hero, just an unwelcome first name.

I meet him on the morning of the last day of 2016, near his home in Queens, at an Irish bar he suggested "called Saints and Sinners (appropriately)." I park in the rattling shadows of an elevated train station, and stop for a coffee, since I am early and I am nervous and I am cold. I open my phone and find a new email from Tom Monahan, delivered four minutes ago. "Something for you to read before we meet," Tom says. "I have a feeling one of the biggest insights we will have today is both of our fathers might have been cut from the proverbial same cloth."

I read the attachment, and it's his story, written from the point of view of a six-year-old boy on the morning he loses not only his mother but the world of love and safety she created for him. One moment, he is in the kitchen, eating breakfast with the maid; the next he hears "a thump," and when he runs to the living room he sees his father at the top of the stairs "screaming 'Jesus Christ!'" and his mother at the bottom, bleeding "in her white robe with the red, white and blue sash."

He is not my brother. I know this as soon as I meet him—I know he's not the Monahan child of whom Dolores spoke before she died. He not only doesn't look like me; he's not built like me, or anyone in my family. His narrow face is matched by his narrow shoulders, and his green eyes, shaded by flaps of skin at the corners, narrow when they focus, like a croupier's. When he tells me he looks just like his dad, I take his word for it. But there is something else we are, if not siblings. We are counterparts.

We were both created in the same circumstances, and for the same purpose. He is, he tells me, "a love baby," a late child who was intended to keep his mother and father together but who wound up gravitating toward his mother's love and protection and also her need for an ally. He became her sidekick as well as a witness to her pain in a marriage he was supposed to rescue. His parents were beautiful, they were stylish, they were glamorous, they turned heads wherever they went, they aroused envy and inspired awe—and Tom turned out to be incidental to their lives together and essential to their lives alone. I have never met anyone outside my family who was raised like me. But if Lou Junod and John Monahan were cut from "the proverbial same cloth," then so were my namesake and I.

It's fun, at first, finding out what we have in common. I mention the warning my father used to give me—"Don't bullshit a bullshitter"—and Tom answers that his father used to say the same thing. I tell him that my father's philosophy of life was best expressed in the maxim "If you're going to be a bear, be a grizzly," and Tom brings his palms definitively down on the table. "Holy shit, that was my mom's!"

"It was the title I used for my father's eulogy."

"Now this is freaking me out a little bit," he says.

And yet the similarities extend only so far—or, more precisely, they lead to a place Lou Junod couldn't go. John Monahan had the life my father could only dream of, the life and then, yes, the wife. He owned a DC-3, a plane Peggy could also fly. They dressed in matching outfits. They traveled around the world and made the newspapers. They had Buddy Hackett and Lee Iacocca and Linda Evans and Connie Francis over to the house on Diplomat Parkway for dinner. They had a suspended staircase at the entrance of their home, fourteen steps up, with an M at the bottom. And then Peggy fell down those steps and Tommy saw her blood on the M and from that day on became what he calls, again and again, "damaged goods."

I cannot claim kinship here. I cannot claim equivalence or commonality, and in any case, Tom won't let me. I can only drink beer for brunch in the gloom of an Irish bar in Queens and try to imagine what my life with my father would have been like with my mother brutally subtracted from it. And then, just like that, there's just one question in my mouth and I'm sitting across a table from someone who might be able to answer it.

"Do you think your mother fell down the stairs on her own or do you think . . ."

And he laughs. He throws back his head theatrically, and he laughs. "I knew you were going to ask that question," he says. "Everybody asks me that question. I'd be the first to indict my father but I don't think he did it. I think she tripped on her robe and it was a freak accident."

But the question in my mouth reminds him of the question in his. "How are you going to handle that, if you write about it? How are you going to handle any of it? I don't really care what you write about my father—he was an asshole. But I want you to know my mother was special. The way she treated people, the way people responded to her—everybody wanted to be with her. To this day she is the only thing I truly respect in this world."

I knew I was going to ask about his father at the top of the stairs. But now my heart begins to beat and the tips of my ears begin to burn, as if I've heard someone talking about me. I have another question that's not a question at all. It's a confession.

"There's something I have to tell you," I say. "It goes beyond what I'm writing. It's the reason I'd be trying to meet with you even if I wasn't writing anything at all."

He stops. I think he's going to laugh again but he begins looking around Saints & Sinners as if cops have just barged through the door, as if we've been found out. He turns his face in profile and releases a whistling breath before regarding me with narrowed eyes and a level stare.

"I know what it is," he says. "But I can't talk about it here. I won't talk about it here. I need to go outside for a cigarette."

I step first into the noonday winter sun, blinking. He follows, in his black puffer jacket, his blue jeans, his Nikes. He stands framed by the bar's big front door and pulls a Parliament from the pack and lights it. He exhales the same way he did inside, this time releasing a stream of smoke and reminding me it's New Year's Eve. He says, "It's my sister, isn't it?"

"It is," I say.

His face narrows and clenches, eyes and mouth.

"I knew it," he says. "But here's the thing. Lizanne *is* my mother. She's the strongest of us all and also the most fragile. She lives in her own little world, her own bubble, and this would destroy her. You can *never* tell her."

My mother was too vain and too concerned with appearances to tell even her closest friends how her husband hurt her. She never would have told Rita McGarty, Marie Mule, Jeanie Labella—she would have been mortified to tell her pals in Wantagh. And she never would have volunteered any information to my father's sisters. There is only my aunt Ceil, and three days after I meet Tommy Monahan at Saints & Sinners I drive to her house in New Jersey to have lunch with her.

Aunt Ceil is eighty years old and has been widowed for four years. She was married to Uncle Harry Brandshagen, the original "good egg," and watched Alzheimer's nibble away at him before it devoured him in a few cruel gulps. She is a good egg herself, and when I knock on her door, she's watching a television show with her sister's daughter, who has an intellectual disability and comes to Ceil's house most days for care. She is cooking me lunch, generously, extravagantly, rosemaried pork tenderloin and penne alla vodka made from scratch. She cooks for everybody, and my father expressed his admiration for her by extolling her admiration for *him*—"Ceil loves to cook for . . . your father. She loves . . . how I eat."

She was twenty years younger than my mom, ten years younger than HB, and despite her age and the hardship of her husband's dementia, she is still disarmingly youthful, the frost just starting to encroach on her auburn curls, the lines just now beginning to pinch her smooth pale skin. And her voice has lost none of the softness and shyness that gave it such powers of consolation—that made me think, when I was a boy, that she was the kind of movie star who showed up in melodramas as the hometown girl who takes back the rapscallion hero after a big-city temptress breaks his heart. I still remember that voice; I remember that voice because it changed my mother's voice. The phone would ring, and when my mother picked up and heard Ceil Brandshagen on the other end, she'd say, "Oh, hi, Ceil," in the same way she'd say, "Oh, hi, HB," sounding suddenly younger, almost girlish. My mother mourned losing her mother at a young age and also never having a sister. But she had Ceil, and now I am trying to see if she had a confidant.

I am certain my mother knew that my father had affairs—*affeahs.* But ever since Tom Monahan told me about Vern Winick confirming the substance of my email, I've been wondering if my mom had a Vern Winick of her own. Peggy Monahan told her friend about the presence in her life of a man named Lou. Did my mother have someone she could tell about the presence in her husband Lou's life of a woman named Peggy? Did she know about Peggy and how far that particular affair went? And did she have anyone to talk to if she did? I hope so. I hope she wasn't all alone all her life. And I hope that if Ceil was her confidant, she'll confide in me.

I sit across from her and as soon as she talks about meeting Harry for the first time, she talks about meeting my dad for the first time on a visit to Westhampton Beach. "Your father, he left an impression. I thought he was some big businessman, the way he spoke. But then he'd start hollering, and I was a little afraid of him, to tell you the truth."

The hollering was the first thing she noticed, she says—the first thing that made her suggest to her new husband that "something wasn't right" in his big sister's marriage. "I always just felt so bad for your mom. Because your father didn't care where he was or who was there—if he wanted to holler, he would start hollering at her. And it had to be very humiliating for her. I told Harry, 'I don't think your sister has it easy.' But he had blinders on. He would say, 'Oh, that's just Lou,' or 'She's got it made.' He was just that way. He wanted everything to be peaches and cream."

"It definitely wasn't," I say. "They were good parents, and I didn't feel unloved. But they weren't great to each other."

"It was kind of sad, because it was just the way they were," Aunt Ceil says. "I remember something your mother told me, early on, when your dad was traveling. He used to go on these trips, these sales trips, and he would be gone for such a long time. And your mother said to him, 'I don't care how long you're gone. But when you come home, make sure you have my mink stole.' And he did. I never forgot that. I guess that was just the kind of life they lived. He was away so much, wrapped up in his business so much. And it had to be a major priority for him, because he did do well. He worked himself up from nothing, let's face it."

"There were a lot of different reasons for how they treated each other," I say. "And one of them was . . . well, he was a first-class philanderer."

"Well, he was a born salesman," Aunt Ceil says.

"He had a lot of girlfriends," I say. "Did you know that? Did my mom ever tell you?"

"She did. She knew about it, because she knew that when he went on these trips he . . . and that he had all these different . . ." Aunt Ceil doesn't speak the words.

"I've always wondered," I say. "They used to argue about it. But I wondered if she ever told anybody."

"She knew about it. But I guess she just accepted it at some point. She liked . . . she liked her lifestyle at that time. There were certain things she wanted, and as long as he gave them to her . . ."

"But the situation was pretty serious," I say, thinking now of the Monahans. "I mean, it wasn't just . . . casual. I've even wondered if I have other siblings out there."

"I think your mom realized that," Aunt Ceil says. "But she wouldn't talk about it. She knew he was out there. And that he had girlfriends out there. That's all she said." Aunt Ceil stands, replenishes my plate, and sits back down. "But that's all in the past, you know? They stayed together for how many years?"

"They were married for fifty-nine years," I say. "Why did my mother stay with him?"

"Why do most women stay in abusive situations? Fear of the unknown. Even with all her reading—and she was an avid reader—she had a fear of the unknown."

"She was happier when he was away," I say. "So was I."

"Well, your mother, she knew what kind of job he had, and what kind of man he was. He had to deal with all these women buyers, and she knew that some of these situations and relationships got more involved than others. And that's the sad part of it. It's not like he had one-night stands here and there. So she really had it rough. She really did. And sometimes, when they would fight, he would compare her to them. And that's what hurt her the most. Can you imagine?"

I don't have to imagine. I saw it. I heard it. But Aunt Ceil, the best egg, is telling me what my parents' marriage looked like from the outside and her judgment of what she saw makes me blink. If I believe in anything, I believe in my father's premise of his own distinction and in the one-of-a-kind rigors of my mother's suffering. And yet Aunt Ceil just used a word to describe their marriage that is commonplace in the extreme, and all the more hideous for that. My mother, like so many women, was trapped in an "abusive situation" and my father, like so many men, was . . . can I bring myself to call him "an abuser" even now? And how did I miss it, when all the time it's been so obvious?

"I was very close to my mom," I tell Aunt Ceil. "But I loved him too, and that bothered her."

"What bothered her was that you might be like him," Aunt Ceil says from across the table. "That was her one fear. She didn't want any of you to turn out like him. Your brother, your sister—she didn't want that for any of you. But she worried the most about you."

I don't see him coming. I don't have to. I feel the bristling vehemence of his approach as he brushes past me. I watch him order a shot of Jameson and down it. He doesn't turn around, though he knows very well I'm there. I walk up to the bar and stand next to him. I order two shots of Jameson, one for him and one for me. We clink the glasses before we speak, and then drink the whiskey straight down.

We are at another Irish bar in Queens but everything has changed. Three weeks after our first meeting at Saints & Sinners I wrote him an email asking for Vern Winick's phone number. He wrote back to tell me of the sleepless nights he'd endured "since what started off as a fun and interesting encounter took a terrible turn." He was terrified about the prospect of me approaching his sister, Lizanne, with "[my] and Dolores Klein's hypothesis." He feared that my quest to find out the truth about my father's life might "tear apart [Lizanne's] fabric of understanding" about her own. "Your truth is one thing," he wrote, "but the damage to the hearts and souls of those involved by revealing unnecessary truths is another."

We met the first time to discover what we might have in common.

We are meeting now to hash out our differences—and to distinguish between necessary and unnecessary truths. I have the advantage of being professionally conciliatory; he has the advantage of being genuinely aggrieved. There is an NFL playoff game on television and when my eyes drift toward the screen, Tom Monahan says, "Keep your eyes on me, please. Thank you." There is a discussion of something I wrote in the past, and when I describe what I do for a living—"You ask questions, you tell people's stories, and all of a sudden you're in a much deeper place than you ever thought you'd be"—his face hardens in judgment and something like scorn.

"Don't fucking do that!" Tommy snaps. "Don't ever fucking do that again!"

"Do what?"

"Compare *this* to all the other things you've done. Because it's not the fucking same. It's different."

There is nothing I can do but nod. He is right, and from then on we have an understanding. He is not my brother, he is not my friend, and he is not only my source or my subject. My father and his mother may have been lovers, but the sense of kinship I took away from the first meeting was in error. My father may have been brutally selfish and my mother endlessly betrayed but his father was brutally violent and his mother endlessly dead. We are not the same, and when he asks why I have decided to explore my family's secrets and I answer that my "life was built on a foundation of lies," he responds like a cardplayer who sees an opportunity to show his hand. "Well," he says, "my life was built on a foundation of trauma, and that makes all the difference." He doesn't let me forget that he has suffered more than I have. He also reminds me that his suffering gives him power.

"Here's what I've decided," he says. "I'm not going to help but I'm not going to sabotage you, either. And I could. I could, very easily. You know that, don't you?"

"I do."

"Well, that's all I have to say. I have to go home now and cook dinner."

But that's not what happens. He orders two more beers and I order two more shots. The bar gets crowded and close, and Tommy takes off his black puffer jacket and ties it around his waist by the sleeves. All around us people staring upward at the football game cheer and groan. It's become a boozy afternoon, and Tommy asks why I wanted to meet with him again, given that he's made clear how he feels about me contacting Lizanne.

"I guess I'm trying to figure out if my father was a villain when he had an affair with your mother, and if I, forty years later, am just repeating his history. I mean, I'm invading your family, just as he did. Is my father the villain in this story? Or am I?"

Tommy's eyes narrow in scrutiny. "Oh, I think you know the answer to that question," he says.

I head to the bathroom. I don't have to use it; I just need a break. I'm not even that wobbly, because I can't be—because I've found myself in a contest rather than a conversation, and I'm not about to quit. When I head back to the bar, Tommy keeps an eye on me. "I checked out your ass when you went to the bathroom," he says, when I pick up my beer. "You have an ass just like my sister. You're built just like her. Except that she has huge tits, and if she were here there'd be twenty people standing around her at the bar, and you'd be proud that she's your sister."

I ignore the provocation and go back to trying to cut a deal. "And I'm a villain for wanting to get to know her—to be part of that?"

Tommy shakes his head. He closes his eyes in forbearance, and when they open he does something he hasn't done since he walked into the bar and downed a shot—with the barest movement of his lips, he smiles. "No," he says. "You're not a villain."

It's like getting a reprieve from the governor. We find a table away from the bar and begin watching the game. A lot of gay men like football, he says, but he's not one of them. He's never watched a football game in his life, but on this day the game does its job and enables us to talk about our families. I talk about my Michael, and his history of bipolar illness, and he talks about his Michael, and his history of crime. "Michael's been to prison," he says.

"I know," I say, and despite all that I've learned about Michael—despite his connection to some fledgling mobsters and the main witness in his trial turning up in a canal outside Tampa—I tell Tommy I want to meet him.

And Tommy laughs, exactly as he did when I asked him a few

weeks earlier about the possibility that his father gave his mother a push. His head tilts back, a public gesture for what seems a private joke.

"Oh, you should definitely meet him," he says, roaring. But his abrupt change in manner puts me on alert.

"So do you want me to meet him so that he can beat the shit out of me?"

Tommy shakes his head and smiles ruefully. "No," he says. "I would never do that. But you will never meet another person like Michael. He is very unusual. He is like no one else."

He orders two more shots, and we both down them. "Now I really do have to go and cook dinner," he says. "Do you have any more questions?"

"I do," I say. "We've talked about your mother and your father, we've talked about Lizanne and Michael. But we haven't talked about your brother Johnny."

"What do you want to know?"

"Well," I say, "who is he?"

Tommy looks at me, and holds his gaze for an extra beat as he makes his last play.

"He's your brother," he says, and heads for the door.

I can still hear her voice. I believe I heard it long ago, in the summer of 1964, when my father told me to sing "Fly Me to the Moon" to a woman in Florida, and I can still remember her response: "I hope I can meet you one day." Her voice: it would be old now, uneven in pitch and timbre, but had she and my father carried out their plans . . . had they run away together . . . had she become my stepmother . . . had she not fallen down the stairs and lived now in a retirement community in Florida . . . I would still want to hear it, because of its music.

There is no music in the voice on the phone. It is an old voice, a tired voice, a Midwestern voice, a colorless voice, a level alto voice stripped of everything but urgency—and yet that urgency makes it come alive like an aria. "Hello, this is Vern Winick. You wrote me a letter about my friend Peggy. She was very dear to me. You are writing a book about her?"

"No, about my father," I answer.

"I don't know very much about your father, except that he and Peggy were very close. He was in the leather business, wasn't he? He used to send her handbags. I never met him. But I can talk to you about Peggy. I've never really gotten over the way she died."

"I'd like to come down and see you," I say.

"Come down and see me? I'm an old woman now, and I haven't been well."

Her voice is so emphatically no-nonsense that it doesn't discourage me. Instead, it recalls the last conversation I had with my father, when he left me with a final admonition: "Well, you better hurry up then." I didn't listen to what he was saying and I missed him. I'm not about to miss Vern Winick.

"How about tomorrow?" I ask, and buy a plane ticket for Fort Lauderdale as soon as I hang up.

They were a generation of molls. They were great beauties freed by the dislocations of war and postwar plenty, smart and funny and fierce and outspoken but none of them college girls, and therefore bound to the men they outshone. There was Peggy and Valerie and Dolores and, yes, Fran—and there was Vern Winick, carrying herself now as the last of the breed. Tall and blond and game, she came to Florida from Chicago in the early 1950s and married Arnold Winick, one of America's most prominent trainers and traders of horseflesh. She was class all the way, and became the kind of woman my mom envied, the kind who attended the Kentucky Derby in extravagant hats, a woman with horses.

She is eighty-eight now, and when her nurse allows me into her townhome in a guarded and gated development in Hollywood, I hear her before I see her, the forthright voice from the phone shouting orders from her bedroom. I see her *house* before I see her, and recognize it—the gilt and glass and French provincial flourishes made for the bright lights of the past rather than the stifling afternoon shadows of the present, the home itself a memorial to the home where once upon a time life really happened. "I'm in here, I'm in here!" she calls out when she registers my arrival, as if crying for help. I follow the sound, carrying a couple of coffees and a bag of glazed donuts. She's sitting up, next to her bed, with a walker set in front of her and a folding table to the side. She's wearing a nylon tracksuit, blue and white with yellow trim, and her long straight gray hair bunched on top of her head, like sheaves. She wears no makeup. She has big hands and an unvanquished posture and she's been waiting—waiting for me to get there, waiting these last forty-one years to talk about her friend Peggy.

They met, she says, at the airport, when she was flying back home with Arnold from a trip to Chicago and Peggy was a stewardess for National Airlines. She was tall and dark and exotic with a growl of a laugh and a discordantly dry sense of humor and Vern recognized her immediately as an equal. When Peggy married John Monahan, it turns out she married a friend of Arnold Winick, and when the Monahans built one of the first houses on Diplomat Parkway, the Winicks built another, on the same side of the street. From then on, the two women lived in each other's homes, and called each other "Mom." They baked in the sun together, they went to the Palm Bay Club and the Jockey Club together, they drank champagne cocktails in the afternoons. "Peggy drank—sure she did. We all did. I did. But she didn't get drunk. She wasn't like that."

What she did get was down—"depressed and forlorn," especially as time revealed the distance between the show the Monahans were putting on and reality of their home life. "Peggy was a beautiful woman who knew she was beautiful, and she could really flirt," Vern says. She walked around her house in a leopard-skin bikini, and the celebrities who stayed at the Diplomat would knock on her door just to spend time with her. Gordon McRae, Lloyd Bridges, Buddy Hackett—they all fell in love with her. "All these men wanted Peggy, and the sad thing was that John Monahan had her and didn't know what to do with her. He didn't know how to treat her. He was an egotist—it was all about him. He was the one who wanted to shine, and I don't think he liked women." He wore a bikini around the house too, and drove a motorcycle with Peggy in the sidecar, husband and wife in matching fringe outfits. But he was withholding not only of his love but of his money, and he was violent with the children.

"They had swinging doors to the kitchen," Vern says, "Peggy would call me, and say, 'Oh, Mom, the doors are off the hinges again.' That meant that John knocked one of the kids through the swinging doors, hit them so hard the doors came loose." The opulent pretense of her life began to wear Peggy down, and her friend Vern began to counsel her that maybe it was time to put away the leopard-skin bikini—"Mom, it's getting a little late for the bikini." Then one morning she saw Peggy wandering Diplomat Parkway as if in a trance, "wearing a *schmatte*. You know what a *schmatte* is? It's a housedress. And that wasn't Peggy either. Peggy Monahan did *not* wear *schmattes*. I said, 'Where are you going, Mom?' She said, 'I'm going to your house.' But she was so dejected and forlorn, I went home and told Arnold, 'You have to talk to your friend John. You can't let him keep doing this to her. He's killing her.' And Arnold did go down and ask, 'John, what are you doing?' He tried to talk some sense into him. But the next thing I know, she had the accident. And it was always on my mind: was it an accident, or wasn't it?"

She does not know when the man she calls Peggy's "friend" entered her life. She does not know how they met, nor where they carried out their assignations. She didn't know his last name until my letter wound up in her mailbox. "I just knew there was a man named Lou, and he was in her life a long time and it was an ongoing thing. She knew he cared for her—that she had someone who cared for her. It pained me when she was unhappy, so whatever your father provided for her, if it was happiness, I'm happy with that. I'm truly happy that she got some pleasure, some happiness. I remember that she would get phone calls from Lou. He would call her when she was particularly down, and she would hear from him and it would give her a lift. She would come down to my house and show me a beautiful purse he had given her and say, 'John doesn't even notice. He didn't pay for it and he doesn't even care where I got it.' "

She does not know if Peggy was planning to leave her husband for my father when she died, nor if John had found out about "her friend." She doesn't believe that John Monahan pushed her down the stairs—"that's just nasty gossip." But she still wonders about Peggy's death. "The question was always did she slip, did she fall, or did she just . . . let go? I never knew. I don't know to this day." And she blamed him—she blamed John Monahan for grinding his wife down, for destroying her will to live. After Peggy died, Vern

Winick didn't talk to him for seven years, until one day, when her husband, Arnold, was out of town, John invited her to dinner. "He had Peggy's place at the table set for me. He pulled out her chair for me, and asked me to sit down. I did. We started talking again after that. It was his apology, and I returned to the fold."

She's never stopped thinking of her friend Peggy. But she hasn't thought of Peggy's friend Lou since Peggy died, has never wondered what became of him. She doesn't remember the details of Peggy's funeral, much less my father's faltering presence there; she never heard of Dolores Klein, much less her suspicion that at least one of Peggy's children was Lou's offspring. She accepts what Peggy told her about him—"he cared for her and was a wonderful man"—and when I mention that he might have been wonderful to Peggy but not to my mother, Vern Winick says, "Peggy was unhappy with John and your mother was unhappy with your father. It's funny how things work out." I think now of what their lives might have been like if Peggy had only lived. It seems for the first time a realistic prospect instead of just a fanciful one.

Imagine: my father, a wonderful man.

I don't simply dress like my father when I head west to pay her a visit. I dress in my father's clothes. I wear his shirt, a short-sleeved Ban-Lon as green as his eyes. I have seen photos of him wearing it in Wantagh, back around the time when I was just born and he was beginning his affair with her. Now I am wearing it as I stand at the door of her house in the desert, in heat that makes me want to get out of the sun the way I would want to get out of the rain.

"My God," she says, when she opens the door. "You look just like your *fatha*."

"Thank you," I say, guessing she intends a compliment. "A lot of people say that as I get older."

"I never saw it before," she says. "But now it's all over you."

Valerie McBryde—formerly Schocket—is eighty-one years old, so thin she looks lanky, with a Parkinsonian tremor that seems to center her face around her prominent teeth. She has gray hair, cut even shorter than it was when our neighbors in Wantagh were taken aback by her "pixie" hairstyle, and wears hippieish clothes that remind me of how young she was in comparison to my parents:

a striped black-and-white jersey, gauzy muslin pants tied with a drawstring, Teva sandals. She was only twenty-three when she bore my friend Michael, nearly twenty years younger than my mother. And yet she has only to speak for me to remember how formidable she was back then, how intimidating, not only calling my father "Louis," with a tender and lingering sibilance, but doing so right in front of his wife.

It is April 12, 2017, six days after Vern Winick, and here I am, with another woman from another time. The house is dark inside, shuttered against the heat. Valerie doesn't turn on any lights, but she shows me her office, its walls bedecked with the photos of her pluckily glamorous past, when she was a water-skier at Cypress Gardens and then a model in Los Angeles and New York. She lingers over a framed two-page spread from a Los Angeles newspaper, an advertisement from the May Company department store that features her in a collage of black-and-white photographs, each of which makes the point that whether she is wearing a hat or a bathing suit or an evening dress she is young and fresh-faced and slightly exotic, a new kind of girl. "Wasn't I *something*?" she asks.

I always knew she was, in some way, like my father; now I see she, like my father, was self-created. She did not know how to water-ski when she went to Cypress Gardens, but she met a man who said he could teach her and after two weeks of skiing eight hours a day she could ski in a pyramid, flashing a smile. She knew nothing about modeling but when she went to LA and stood in front of a photographer she understood that "it was nothing but acting, acting, acting" and when she got bored by LA she went to New York on a train and "Eileen Ford signed me as soon as she met me and I lived with all the other models in the Barbizon Hotel. Oh, it was so easy back then, Tommy. I thought everything was going to be a lark."

"And then you met Chip," I say, my first little nudge.

"And then I met Chip."

"And then you met my dad," I say, the first nudge she can feel. She looks at me with a renewal of interest.

"And then I met your dad," she says.

We are eating in the restaurant in the community center, filled with tanned men and women fresh from the golf course. "The food is good here," she says, ordering a club sandwich. She asks me if I'm in LA interviewing a film star.

"No, I'm interviewing you," I say.

"Me! Why would you want to interview me?"

"For a book I'm writing."

"What's the book about?"

"About my father."

Her face changes, not with surprise, but with an inward smile that suggests I haven't fooled her and never will. "I'm writing a book too," she says. "Do you want to know the title?"

"Sure."

"It's called *Just Me*."

"That's a great title. Is it a memoir?"

"It's the story of my life," Valerie says, by way of correction. "I wasn't supposed to have a life, you know. But the life I've had I've built myself, and I've done everything I wanted to do, with no regrets. I've gone around the world. I've even gone skydiving."

"Have you ever been in love?" I ask.

She leans back, and even dabbing with a napkin at the bits of food spotting her teeth she is cagey and brightened by memories unshared. "I think I have," she says. "I think you could say that I've been in love."

"Were you in love with my father?"

She puts the napkin down on her plate. She tilts back toward me, with narrowed eyes and the suggestion of a smile. "Now why," she asks iambically, "would you ask . . . a question . . . like . . . that?"

"Because I was there," I say. "Because I saw it."

"You must be a hell of a writer if you could see that back then. You were just a baby."

"I was my mother's companion. I had no choice. Seeing it was my job."

"Well," she says. "*That* I'm not going to tell you, because *that* belongs to me."

I eat, and watch her struggle to do the same. We are quiet. "What kind of man was my father?"

I expect her to duck it—"Oh, Tommy, why do you want to go back to the past?" Instead, she pauses, and looks right at me. "Your father was the kind of man who sang . . . in clubs."

I nod. I don't know exactly what she means, but the judgment seems final.

"You heard him sing?"

"I heard him sing."

"Was he a good singer?"

"He was a good singer. In a club."

"What kind of man was Chip?"

She exhales with a force that causes her to slump a little. "He was the strangest man I've ever known. I remember sitting in his car when he took me out to Montauk to get married. I kept telling myself, 'Stay in the car. Don't get out.' I didn't listen. I was like a child misbehaving."

"Was Chip in love with my father?"

It is not a prepared question. It is a hunch, a thing I grab from the air as it floats by. "*Now* you're onto something," she says. "Do you know that after I got pregnant he wouldn't touch me? He wouldn't touch me. Oh, it was strange, it was bizarre, it was not normal."

Her face rearranges itself around her mouth's expression of distaste and dismay. "Put that in your book!" she says.

She manages to finish half her sandwich, then asks the waiter to box the rest so she can bring it home. I walk her to the car, and the heat brings on a sense of exhaustion, and the exhaustion tells me something. Time is running out. Do this.

"You say that you were in love. Are you going to write about your love affair in your memoir?"

She stares straight ahead. "I know what you're doing," she says. "You're needling me, and I'm not going to fall for it."

It was what she had called Chip, her ex-husband. It's what her son Michael had called him too. "I'm not a needler," I say.

She sighs. "Oh, I know you're not. I just don't know why you need to ask all these questions."

She doesn't invite me in when we reach her house but I follow her through the door, like a presumptuous date. She goes to an easy chair in the corner of the living room, and slumps down into its enveloping arms. The silence gathers. I let it gather, until it becomes something I can't bear. I inhale, and I hear myself say:

"Valerie, did you have an affair with my father?"

Her tremor has worsened as she has grown tired, but now she is still and composed. She stares at me as if from a distance and says, with sudden incredulous gusto, "You just can't *stand* it, can you?"

"No."

"Why? Why do you need to know?"

"Because I was born to know," I say. "My parents used to argue whenever you visited. You almost ended their marriage when I was three years old."

"Then I'm not going to lie to you," she says. "Yes. I had an affair with your father. It lasted a long time, probably five years."

"Thank you," I whisper, in a voice that seems to emerge from a place somewhere close to me but distinct from me, from another mouth next to my head.

"But there's something you need to know. I had nothing with Chip. That doesn't make it right. I would never have done it today. But I was very young, and I had nothing. Nothing. Oh, Tommy. I don't even know how it started."

"I imagine at Chip's instigation."

"Yes," Valerie says. "Yes, it was. Chip was impotent, and your father used to come to the house. Chip was a latent homosexual who couldn't stand himself. So he was a sadist. That's what happens to a lot of people who can't stand themselves. The only time he ever touched me was after Lou made love to me. Then he would try to take me into the bedroom and have sex with me."

I don't know what to say, so I don't say anything. I am surprised, however, by what I feel—an almost physical manifestation of gratitude. Something passes between Valerie and me, a sense of ease and intimacy. She looked older than her eighty-one years when she first opened the door and now she looks younger, as if she's just woken up from a long and recuperative sleep.

"When you talked about being in love—was that my father?"

"Yes," Valerie says, softly and thoughtfully. "Yes, I think so. I think he was."

I don't say anything else, just watch the shine come to her eyes, liquid in the dark. I think of kissing her goodbye then, as I might a child, and leaving her where she sits, easy in her easy chair. Instead, she says sharply, "Well, you did it. You pulled me back to where I didn't want to go. You pulled me back to the past."

She stands up, and walks with me to the door, her age reasserting itself, her hardiness as well. "The last thing you ever expect is to be sitting there telling a man's son that you had an affair with his father," she says as she opens the door and steps out into the heat and the light. The burning brightness halts her, but as I turn back to hug her where she stands, she says that there is something I need to know. "He always loved your mother. He used to tell me that—that after your mother he loved me the most. But your mother was number one."

I don't have the heart to tell her about Peggy Monahan.

22

There's a scenic view—a restaurant built on the top of a butte, and a parking lot where diners come to see the panorama of Phoenix at night. The heat of the day has finally expended itself, and a fragile breeze, a desert breeze, has arisen in its place. A woman sits on the low concrete wall that marks the end of the restaurant's property, crossing her legs with the city's silver sprawl behind her and the breeze stirring her silver hair. I take her photograph, although I barely know her.

Her name is Vicki Oglesbee. She is about ten years older than I am, with bangs cut into her shoulder-length hair. She wears black pants just past her knees, a sky-blue cotton blouse and sandals. She has a narrow face, with soft brown eyes and a sharp nose. Her wide smile shows off both her white teeth and her easygoing amiability. Though not shy, she is very soft-spoken, almost deferential, in conversation. She is averse to making a show of herself, and yet . . . I can't keep my eyes off her. It must be her mouth, I think—how wide it is, and how straight, with the kind of rectitude one sees in old photographs. Or maybe it's her chin, which . . . yes . . . is my grandma's chin, my father's chin, my chin.

More than a century ago, my grandmother, born Elizabeth Schmeckenbecher but married at age sixteen to Arthur Reisman, left her two-year-old daughter Annette in order to have an affair with a man named Louis Junod. They, mother and daughter, never saw each other again. But I swung out to the western desert not only to squeeze secrets out of Valerie McBryde; I came to find Annette Reisman's daughter. My grandma Bess's granddaughter. My father's niece. My own cousin. My father never accepted the existence of his lost sister Annette, even when I told him I had documentation—"never happened," was his line. And now here sits Vicki Oglesbee, in the parking lot of a cowboy-themed restaurant, one part of her face in agreement with mine, living proof of an ancient infamy turned into the basis for reconciliation.

Yes, it *happened,* and I am surprised at how happy she makes me. I am surprised at how easily we get along. It is not simply that I have gained another cousin, in whom I see a deeply coded resemblance. It's that I have another cousin who's somehow innocent of being a Junod; who's never been to Levittown; who never had to deal with Bess and who's never met Lou; who doesn't have our history. People have been asking why I am so interested in revealing my family's secrets, as though I have a taste for both inflicting and enduring punishment. But it's only by my determination to talk to someone like Valerie that I've put myself in position to meet someone like Vicki, and in her company I don't feel bound to some unspeakable past; I feel like I've been given a fresh start. She lives outside Phoenix with her partner John in an RV, and in late spring they hit the road and wander. "A vagabond," her brother Steve calls her, and yet now she has returned to the fold almost as certainly as I have left it. I take her picture; John takes our picture together; and when I leave, she says, "We're heading east this summer. I hope I can see you, cuz."

Aunt Ellie still has something for me. She always does, and it's always the same thing. "Tommy," she says, as soon as I step inside her home in Levittown, "do you want a Yoo-hoo? I have a Yoo-hoo for you." She has stocked her refrigerator with the stuff since I was a little boy. She doesn't drink it herself; she never has, and now that she's ninety-one years old in the summer of 2017 and my own hair is going gray, I can't imagine refusing her. She's wearing the same outfit of housedress and slippers she always wears. She's smoking the same Kent cigarettes she always smokes, with the same stub of a finger, and drinking the same Pabst Blue Ribbon or Budweiser. She goes to the old spare refrigerator in the sunporch and comes back with a bottle of Yoo-hoo, already opened, unaware that on this visit I have brought something for her—something that threatens to turn her life upside down when her life is almost over.

I have always loved her. I have always loved her spunk, her defiance, her anger, her courage, her loyalty, her compassion, her epic grudges, this tiny woman's outsized heart. When I was young, I loved her refusal to kowtow to my dad, and drew strength from her success at making him back down. He was afraid of her, so I wasn't. She might have repeated the story a hundred times, but I never grew tired of her telling me about the time she was fifteen years old and he tried to stop her from leaving the house in a red dress and she lifted her knee into his groin and left him writhing on the floor. "How could you do this?" he moaned, and she said, "Louie, you taught me how."

I admired her all my life but only began to understand her when Janet and I were not able to conceive a child. She was the one member of my family who knew the extent of our pain firsthand, and so I came to know what lay behind her devotion to her husband, Frank; her sister Millie; and her mother, whom she called "my heartbeat." I made sure to call or visit her every Mother's Day, and when my own mother was initially unenthusiastic about the prospect of Janet and me adopting a child from China, Ellie took me aside and whispered with harsh and tender urgency: "If you can adopt that baby, do it. Do it now. No one wanted babies as much as me. But Frank was too sick to adopt. I was born to take care of him and my mother. But it's a tiny little goddamned void that drives you crazy. Adopt a baby, it will fill your life."

She was right. Now I try bringing Nia to 112 Old Farm Road as often as I can, and laugh when Ellie does with my daughter what she used to do with me, standing back-to-back with her and cracking wise about her own stature. But today I have come alone. Yes, I brought sweets. But I have never forgotten what Aunt Marie told me twenty years ago when I visited her in upstate New York and she started gossiping about her sisters—about their origins. Aunt Ellie, she said, was not a Junod, but rather the daughter of "the little Italian man" from the neighborhood in Brooklyn. And so in addition to pignoli cakes from the local Italian bakery, I have brought a DNA test to Aunt Ellie's house.

I don't hide it. I display it on the Formica table in the kitchen, where the yellow box matches the Yoo-hoo bottle. But I don't tell her what I'm trying to find out, which makes me feel squirmily dishonest in the home of the family truth-teller. And yet I should never underestimate Ellie Peragine. I might think that she's taken out some old family photo albums simply as a warm-up to the voluntary relinquishment of her genetic material, but she has some truths yet to tell, particularly about my mother and father. I turn the pages and she talks about them and from the way she talks about them I feel compelled to ask a question:

"Did you like my mother?"

"No, we never took to each other. It eased a little when we got older. But I always thought she was a conceited snob. That's why I so rarely went out to Westhampton. I went once or twice, and I ended up so tense, I was shaking, coming home. I couldn't care less for Frances. I just disliked her intensely. I couldn't shake it. Of course, she had her own troubles with my brother. He lived his own life, always. Once I said to him, 'You sure go down to Florida a lot. You must really like it there.'

"He said, 'I do.'

"I said, 'You got a broad down there?'

"He didn't answer.

"I said, 'You got a *family* down there?'

"He shook his head. He said, 'I adore Frances. But man, is she a cold fish.' "

The testing doesn't start until my cousin Betty Ann arrives. She's in a rush; she spits in the plastic vial first to show Aunt Ellie how, and it takes about two minutes for her to complete her own test. I hand Aunt Ellie her vial and she takes it as if she's about to down it, *salute*. But instead she stares at it and begins to swallow and lick her lips, which have turned to jerky. She says, "I could use a beer," but I pour her a glass of water and after she drinks she starts over, a woman trying to spit in the desert. After a half hour, she hands the vial to me, filled just short of the line. I take it and cap it, a saliva sample that she may as well have produced by the *molecule*—gene by gene. She puts her hands on her hips, and says, "So now you're gonna know who's who and what's what, huh?" I hug her in gratitude but she keeps nodding through my embrace. My parents didn't fool her. Neither do I.

Peggy was a model. Peggy was dark haired and statuesque. Peggy was born in the North and moved to the South. Peggy married a smart, ambitious man and for a while she helped him become the toast of the town. Peggy lived in an elaborate home she loved and was known for the parties she threw. People looked up to Peggy and Peggy never looked down on anyone. Peggy liked to drink and flirt but Peggy kept her family together not by force of will but rather by the power of her presence—the life in her. Peggy liked to go downtown with her husband and frequent the bars and clubs where everyone knew her name. When the family business slumped the husband stopped going out, so Peggy went alone. Peggy drank too much. The bartenders would call home and tell her husband or her son Ken to come get her. There was talk; her husband was afraid of losing his money and Peggy was afraid of losing her looks—

I almost want her to stop. I am sitting in a stand-alone beauty parlor in Columbus, Georgia, and Shelly Tubbs is telling me the story of the life and death of Peggy Friedlander, the woman who kissed me good night in front of the Plaza Hotel in the summer of 1978. Shelly is one of the last people alive who knew Peggy well enough to bear witness to her beauty and her sorrow. It's a sad story and I know how it ends. But what's most unsettling about it is that it doesn't exist in isolation. I've known for a long time that there were two Peggys in my father's life and they both left his life in the most sudden and tragic manner possible. But until now I couldn't see the parallels between their lives and their deaths. I can't hear one story without hearing the other; I can't hear both without hearing my father crying alone in his bedroom.

Peggy Friedlander was a disappointed woman, Shelly says. She and her husband had to sell the Tudor mansion in the heart of town and move to a smaller house on the outskirts. In the summer of 1978 Friedy promised to take Peggy to Monte Carlo but he didn't have the money for the trip and she wound up going to New York City with her sister-in-law Ann instead. Peggy grew despondent when she came home and later in the summer she asked her daughter Jill to come stay with her for the weekend so she wouldn't be alone. But Jill had plans to go to the lake house and on the evening of Friday, August 18, Peggy called Friedy at the store they owned. He was working late as usual but he was just about to head home. She asked him to stop on the way and buy her some peanuts. She was reading a bestseller, Judith Krantz's *Scruples,* about the scandalous adventures of a woman who owned a store in Hollywood. She left the book open on a counter and went to her daughter Cindy's room. Cindy had lived in Atlanta for a while and there she had bought a little derringer for her own protection. She brought the derringer home with her and now Peggy found it in a drawer. She sat on Cindy's bed and shot herself in the head. Cindy returned home to a quiet house and was the first to find her. She has never been able to speak about it, and when I called she asked if I could speak to Shelly instead. She is still alive when Shelly and I meet. She will die a year later, in 2018, the last of Peggy's children to be buried in Moultrie.

"Peggy was the rock," Shelly says, "and once she was gone, there was nothing left." Jill Friedlander never forgave herself for refusing her mother's request for company and in 1980 she put a gun in her own mouth and pulled the trigger. She paralyzed herself instead of killing herself and endured the next ten years as a quadriplegic before she died in 1990. Shelly divorced Ken after Jill's attempt on her own life—leaving not only her husband but the Friedlander family, "because I knew where it was all headed." Judy began a life of drinking and drugging and changed her name at the behest of the spiritual leader she followed and Ken developed early-onset Alzheimer's and they are all in Moultrie now, back with their mother, where Shelly believes they wanted to be all along. "Peggy held everything and everyone together and there's no doubt in my mind that if she hadn't died we'd all still be together."

The story she tells is not about the death of one unhappy woman but rather about the destruction of an entire American family and so I tell her my own story. I was twenty years old when I met Peggy Friedlander and felt an instantaneous conviction that she and my father were intimate. I have wondered ever since if he broke her heart and contributed to the sweeping scale of the heartbreak that ensued. "I think that Peggy died of a chemical imbalance," Shelly says. "I doubt your father had anything to do with it, unless . . . unless your father just had that effect on women."

Did he? Even my mother acknowledged that he had a type—women who were dark, bold, daring, sensual. But I think now not just of the two Peggys but of Valerie and Mikie and wonder if instead of having a type he had . . . a *profile*. They, my father's women, had so much in common, including the unhappy ending of each of their stories. Did he seek them out because they were all so strikingly beautiful or because they were all so vulnerable . . . and, not incidentally, all so married? Did he try to save them from what awaited them or did he ensure that what awaited them devoured them? Did he fail in his attempts to rescue them or did he succeed all too well in bringing about their ruin?

I have a fantasy when I send my own spit off to Ancestry. Like a lot of people, I tell myself I am looking for the facts of my family's history—the hard facts that will answer all my questions, solve all my mysteries, confirm all my suspicions. But like most of the people who pony up the plastic vial, I am not immune to the fantasy that the DNA testing companies are selling. I hope that by finding out the facts I will discover that my family is somewhat different than the one I grew up with, more heroic, more tragic, more eccentric, with greater historic resonance and perhaps even a *past*, rich, royal, refined, ruined. From the past, I will find something—or someone—new.

I already have heard from my aunts and cousins that there is Eastern European aristocracy on my grandfather Louis Junod's side, that he was a direct descendant of a Romanian—or was it Hungarian?—count. But my fantasy is more specific than that, more purposeful, a product of my research and my labors. My family is *already* scandalous, thanks to the murderous jealousy of Arthur Reisman's second wife. But he remained married to his first wife, my grandma, for ten years before a judge finally signed the divorce decree, and as soon as I saw photos of him in his Depression-era prime—the tan skin, the big nose, the bald head, the dapper mustache, the cabin cruiser, the knickers, the argyle vests—I figured him for my father's father. I even imagined a narrative that complemented the whopper Grandma told the *Daily News: Before Arthur Reisman went off for World War I, she and the father of her child Annette had gotten back together. She got pregnant, and then heard that he had died and never saw him again. She had his baby, your father, bursting with Arthur Reisman's joie de vivre. And you, Reisman's grandson, are not only genetically invested in a scandal that occupied the front page of New York's tabloid newspapers in the heart of the Great Depression. You're also part Jewish.*

I take this narrative seriously. When I send my own saliva sample to Ancestry, I also send a kit to one of Arthur Reisman's grandchildren from his second marriage. I am Vicki Oglesbee's cousin because Elizabeth Schmeckenbecher is her grandmother. But I don't turn out to be cousins with any of Arthur Reisman's grandchildren by Etta Schmier, the kids who grew up in disbelief that the "Bubbe" who babysat them had also killed a young woman in cold blood on her driveway. I have no genetic connection with them at all, which means that their names don't show up at all on my Ancestry page. The names that do appear belong, in a few cases, to people I've known all my life or, mostly, to an endless assemblage of strangers. The great surprise is that there are no surprises—I am, embarrassingly, 99.9 percent gentile—except for one puzzling absence:

There are no Junods.

On a Sunday afternoon in late October, I receive a message on 23andMe, which I have just joined. It's from a guy named Ralph Pasqualina. It says, "hi this is Ralph, trying to figure out this connection." I write him back and give him my phone number. He calls and says, "Hi, I'm Ralph, who the hell are *you*?"

I have never heard his tough-guy voice. I have, for that matter, never heard his name. He is a complete stranger. And yet according to 23andMe he is my first cousin, and I share more genes with him than I do with any of the people I've known as my first cousins since I've known what first cousins *are*. Betty Ann and Vivian; Mitchell Brandshagen, one of Harry and Ceil's sons; and now Vicki Oglesbee: Ralph Pasqualina shows up above them on the list of genetic matches, just under my brother, Michael, and my niece Stacey. He is right there, near the top of the mix. He is family.

It's happened, then: the Ancestry *thing*, the 23andMe *thing*, what everyone secretly wants to happen when they spit in the tube and nobody is really prepared for. The fantasy of the inexplicable has come true. And yet, it feels at first like a glitch, like an oversight of the algorithm or an invitation gone astray. Ralph Pasqualina? Tom Junod? It's like we're each simultaneously crashing each other's party, and he's as suspicious of me as I am of him: "*What are you doing here?*" "*No, what are* you *doing here?*" But then we start talking, and we both become suspicious of something else, not the circumstances that have brought us together but rather the circumstances that have kept us apart.

We are the same age. We were born a month apart, in the same year. We both grew up on Long Island, he on the North Shore, me on the South, separated only by the Seaford–Oyster Bay Expressway. We like the same music, remember some of the same places. He might be a truck driver. He might be a "hood," self-proclaimed, who wore steel taps on his boots in school. But he has a stop in his voice on certain consonants that makes him also sound vulnerable when he's at his most voluble—when he's expressing his excitement at the prospect of the two of us being related. He's an only child, he says. He's the son of a mother who was an only child. His father, Ralph Pasqualina Sr., died when he was two years old. His stepfather committed suicide when he was five. He's lost track of most of his cousins. He's married and I can hear his wife in the background. But he's been alone in the world for a long time, and when he advances a theory that ties us together, I can hear the warmth, the hope, the ingenuity, the unmistakable sound of human need.

"So listen," he says. "When I was first trying to figure out who you were, I did a little research and saw a picture of your father, right? And he looks Italian. He's got an Italian nose. And then I started tossing some things around in my head. If you're my first cousin, that means your father is probably one of my father's brother's sons. Well, my mom used to always talk about my father's oldest brother. His name was Uncle Louie, right? And he never married. But there was always talk, that he had a child—an illegitimate child. Well, that's your dad. My father's brother is your father's father."

The conclusion has come so quickly I don't even feel it. "I'll do some research," I say. "I'll take a look and see what I can find out. What about your mother? What was your mother's maiden name?"

"Her name was Scharnberger, Marguerite Scharnberger. S-C-H-A-R-N . . . but you don't have to worry about that. That's not how we're related. We're related through the paternal side. Pasqualina. That's your father's name. And that would be your name too."

A month later, I call Ralph with the news. He's still the inexplicable presence on my 23andMe page, and I am still the inexplicable presence on his. Our genetic correspondence is a fact, and nothing changes it. But the narrative has to change. I tested the Pasqualina connection on 23andMe in the same way I tested the Reisman connection on Ancestry. I sent a test to one of Ralph's cousins, Bob Pasqualina, and the results showed no shared genes. "I'm not related to the Pasqualinas," I tell Ralph, "and you're not related to the Schmeckenbechers. But you're related to my brother and my niece and my nephew—to anyone who came down through my father. So that has to mean—"

"That has to mean we're connected through my mother," he says.

"That's right. So tell me about her."

She was born in 1921, he says. She was the daughter of Augustus Scharnberger and Elizabeth Martin. There were no other children. She was smart, she graduated high school at sixteen, the same year her father died. Augustus Scharnberger worked as foreman in the construction of the Midtown Tunnel and died in an accident in 1937, when he was forty-one years old. Marguerite went to work in New York City, and met Ralph Pasqualina during the war. He was twelve years older than Marguerite, and they were married in 1943. "I should have been born in 1945 or 1946," Ralph says. "But my parents couldn't have children. They were both sterile—both of them. My mother went to church every day and said a novena. I was born in 1958, fifteen years after they were married. I was the miracle baby."

"Where did your mother work?" I ask.

"She worked at Macy's for sixteen years."

"Where?"

"The one on Thirty-Fourth Street."

"Herald Square?"

"Yeah, the big one."

And then, suddenly, I have a theory of my own. My father worked around the block from Herald Square. He was in the wholesale business and Marguerite Pasqualina was in the retail business. I hope I can be forgiven for wondering if the strength of the genetic relationship between me and Ralph doesn't come from us being cousins but rather half brothers . . . if my father wasn't the miracle worker . . . if the story of Ralph Pasqualina Jr. doesn't start, like so many of the stories involving Lou Junod, with a vulnerable woman.

"Do you want a Yoo-hoo, Tommy?" Aunt Ellie asks as soon as I step inside her house.

"I'd love one," I say. "You stay here—I'll get it myself."

It's the first thing that's out of order. I never get the Yoo-hoo myself. She narrows her eyes and gives me the glare, trying to figure out the game I'm playing. "Don't be *ridiculous,*" she says, and trudges away to the refrigerator in her striped slacks, her flowered housecoat, her slippers. She returns and plants the cold bottle in the palm of my hand, as if it's a beer. I am standing next to her in the middle of her kitchen, a foot taller than she is, but she looks me up and down through the eyeglasses balanced at the end of her nose and sucks at her teeth, as if sizing me up for a brawl. "So . . . what's up?"

In the six decades I've been visiting her house, she's never asked why I've come. But three days earlier I came with Nia, and when I gave Ellie a squeeze I felt the bones under her skin, the jagged frailty held together with nothing but the memory of her fierce tensile strength. Now, four days after Christmas, I'm back. I'm back in the same place, walking through the same steps of a lifetime routine. But today I know something she doesn't, and I can't figure out how to tell her—or even if I *should* tell her. It makes Aunt Ellie's kitchen, for the first time, a foreign place.

"I just wanted to stop by and talk to you," I say, like a doctor with bad news.

"Oh, you were just in the neighborhood and decided to stop by. How *nice* of you." She gives me a wink, her tongue planted literally in her cheek, and I know—she lets me know—she's onto me.

"Remember that test you took a few months ago, that test about your ancestry?" I hear myself saying before I even sit down. "It came back."

And then she stops. She's been taking cold cuts out of the refrigerator even as she's been giving me the once-over, but now all her wound-up motion comes to a halt, the platter in her hands, the hooklike hairs barnacling her chin, all in almost defiant abeyance. Then her eyebrows go up, the only things on her face that move. "*That* bad, huh?"

"No!" I almost shout, ridiculously. "Not that bad!"

She places the platter in the middle of the kitchen table and moves into me, as if she's exchanging a confidence in her own home.

"Was my mother . . . a *busy* woman?" she asks.

"She was!" I answer, with a guffaw. "She was!"

I sit down at the table and pull my laptop from the briefcase I smuggled through the door. Aunt Ellie doesn't drive and she's never owned a cell phone, so my computer might as well be a UNIVAC. But I've come prepared, and I open to screenshots of her Ancestry page. She's sitting next to me now, chair against chair, the cold cuts in front of us untouched. I press my fingertip to the screen, the patient proctor, but even though it's four days after Christmas and I've had her results since August, I still can't quite believe what I see.

"See, Aunt El, here's your name, and here's your lineage. It says here that you're forty-nine point three percent Italian."

"Uh-*huh*."

"And here is a list of your relatives. You see I'm there, and so is Betty Ann, and Kim and Britt and Stacey. But you also see a lot of Italian names. Most of them are Ponessas."

"And they can do this? This is right—this is true?"

"I'm sure they make some mistakes. But these tests are usually pretty accurate, or else these companies would go out of business."

"I see," Aunt El says, and tilts her head to face mine. "So you're telling me that my father isn't my father?"

I try to take a breath. "That's right."

"I'm not a Junod?"

I put my hand on hers. I want to say I'm sorry, but I offer instead a pat and a squeeze.

"You know, the day before I married my Frank, my lovely father came over to pay me a visit. He looked at me, and he said, 'Just like you, to marry a dirty guinea.' I told him, 'You get out of my sight, you son of a bitch. You don't come to my wedding. You don't come to my house. You don't ever try to see me again.' And he never did. That was the last time I ever spoke to him, and that was how I wanted it. And you're telling me now that that piece of shit wasn't my father?"

I nod. There's nothing else to do.

"Tommy—you just gave me a late Christmas present," my aunt says. "You just gave me one of the best gifts I've ever gotten in my *life*."

I reach for a piece of Swiss cheese, hard at the corner. Aunt Marie, she was right—Aunt Millie was a Schmidt, and Aunt Ellie was a Ponessa, her father the little Italian man around the corner. There is a devastation around the old family tree, an ice storm, a wind storm, gypsy moths. But Ellie Peragine stands fast, this ninety-one-year-old woman relieved of the grudge she's carried since her wedding day, and when I ask her if the news changes her opinion about her mother, she tells me something I need to hear. This is the first time I've delivered genetic news to someone, and what my Aunt Ellie says allows it not to be the last.

"I loved my mother," she says. "What she did, she did—a lot of individuals do things the world can never understand. But I loved her. And when I love, I love. I don't dissect."

It turns out my closest cousin on my father's side doesn't look anything like me. He doesn't look anything like my dad or any of my other cousins. He doesn't really look like anyone I know. Ralph Pasqualina is a big man with an enormous bald head and a nose the size of a fist and when I see him waiting for me at the end of his driveway in his house in the woods he motions for me to get out of the car and envelops me like a fairy-tale giant.

We go inside; his wife, Gerry, is coaxing sweet smells from the spaghetti sauce, and we sit down at the dinner table and once again try to figure out how we're related. I had an idea I didn't even want to tell him when I first conceived it—the idea that my father spotted his mother at the Macy's in Herald Square on a lunch break and cured her of the sterility that had been her diagnosis since she was married fourteen years earlier. I thought, that is, that Ralph and I might be half brothers, until I visited a genetic counselor at Mount Sinai and she told me that the two of us don't share enough genes to be brothers. We're cousins and we just have to figure out the ancestor we have in common.

I remember how I felt when I first met my cousin Vicki Oglesbee a year and a half before at the cowboy steakhouse and I sat outside with her and she became part of the nightscape of Phoenix and I felt her addition to my life so keenly—I was one person less alone in the world. But I already knew exactly how Vicki and I were related and so there was a feeling of reunion, over time and distance and even ancient tragedy. Ralph and I are still trying to understand how and why we're suddenly intertwined, and so we're like mad scientists who every few minutes cook up a new theory about our own origins.

He's motivated, Cousin Ralph. He's lived and worked alone for long stretches of his life, from childhood on. First Ralph Pasqualina Sr. died, then his stepfather by his own hand. His mother, he says, started drinking "very, very heavily for the next five or six years and then she met this younger guy who's an ex-convict. Everybody on Long Island feared him, and that was what I had for a male role model. I grew up on Long Island with no father and a crazy stepfather and I hung around with all these older guys and I drank and I got into trouble. It's not murder and it's not sex crimes but I got into trouble."

He did time—"I'm an ex-convict"—and fell out of touch with both sides of his family, Pasqualina and Scharnberger. He quit drinking and gave his life to God and married a Christian woman and when she died he became a Gideon, distributing Bibles to hotel rooms. He started a trucking company and now he lives with Gerry at the end of a very long driveway in a house that can't be seen from the road. It's a godly house, and so a very quiet house until Ralph starts talking, with his rumbling stumbling voice and his happiness that after a life of so many subtractions he has, in me, what I knew I had in Vicki—that unlikely thing, a late-in-life addition.

Then he tells me about another subtraction in his life, his grandfather, Augustus Scharnberger. He was born in 1894, married in 1920, and became the father to Ralph's mother, Marguerite, a year later. He and his brother Henry made a lot of money in the 1920s, Henry as a real estate developer in the New York City boroughs and Augustus—Gus—as a builder of roads. They lived in fancy houses, and Ralph's mother spoke often of her coddled chauffeur-driven childhood in Queens. They even had a house in Bayville, Long Island, where they threw a clambake every year for the local Democratic Party. But Gus lost his savings in the Depression, and in 1937 he was working as a foreman of a construction crew in the Midtown Tunnel and a crane swung into his head and fractured his skull and killed him. He was forty-one years old. He had one child, Marguerite, and Marguerite's one child wouldn't be born for another nineteen years.

"So that's got to be him, right?" Ralph says. "That's got to be your grandfather—our grandfather."

"Let's not get ahead of ourselves," I say.

"No, no, no—look. We're half first cousins. You're not a Pasqualina. I'm not a Junod. So what else can it be?"

"Do you have any sort of artifact that might have your mother's DNA in it? A hairbrush, maybe?"

"No, nothing like that. All that stuff is gone."

"Where is your mother buried?"

"In Pinelawn, with my father. What do you want to do—dig her up?"

I think about this. "Well, it might be the only way we can prove the connection."

"You don't need to do that! Take a look at this."

He shows me a photograph of a woman on her wedding day—a dark-haired woman in a white gown standing next to a man in his dress uniform. "That's my father, right before he went off to war. And that's my mother. Take a look at her nose."

Marguerite Scharnberger has a pale round face under her dark permanent wave, with dark eyes and a nose extravagantly nostriled. In most people, nostrils are hidden, mere holes. Hers are prepossessing, two dots that find their way into the portrait—a feature.

"Okay," I say, hesitantly.

"You have the same nose! You both have wide nostrils. That's why I brought out the photo."

It is not something I ever talk about. My brother has my mother's nose, my sister a miniature of my father's. But I have spent hours staring at myself in the mirror, wondering where my capacious nostrils come from, susceptible as they are to harboring flecks of foreign matter. I decided years ago that my nose came from Ireland—that it's the nose of a scrapper, a pug. But there it is, in a wedding photo from 1943.

"And look at this," Ralph says, and shows me another photo, this one from his cousin Carol, a group photo of the Scharnberger family, circa two turns of the century ago, about 1900. Everyone is identified, even the dog, Trixie. Augustus Scharnberger, in a sailor's suit, is about seven years old and stands to the far right. In the middle, there is his uncle, by marriage, John Schmeckenbecher—who is also Grandma Bess's half brother from her father's first marriage. Grandma is not in the photo. But she and Gus Scharnberger were born two months apart in 1894, and the presence of her half brother John in Gus Scharnberger's life explains how they might have met. He is, by virtue of John Schmeckenbecher's marriage to his aunt Sarah Scharnberger, a cousin, and when he was in his early twenties he even lived with the Schmeckenbechers in the Bronx, not long before my father was born. Aunt Marie had told me that when she was in the back seat of cars with strange men, Grandma was up in front with her "half cousin" who wound up living in Queens. That is a description of Augustus Scharnberger.

I have grown up thinking that nobody in my family—that nobody in the world—looked like my father except Grandma herself, and that the two of them constituted their own singular tribe. But now Ralph shows me photos of a man who, as an adult in the 1930s, is swarthy and self-assured and formidable. He has jet-black hair and thick, dark brows and an imposing glare that gives me a chill. My grandmother's cousin by marriage turns out to be a prototype of my old man. Could he be my grandfather? Could he be anyone else?

I think of my Ancestry page. There are Brandshagen cousins. There are Schmeckenbecher cousins. There are no Junod cousins, even in the crowded ranks of distant relations. There are instead Scharnberger cousins, a third, a second and of course a first, Ralph himself, this repentant colossus who cracked the code of our common lineage.

"I'm getting kind of choked up, thinking about all this," he says. "My mother had a brother she never knew. Your father had a sister he never knew. But at least *we* know each other."

"We do," I say to my first cousin, the giant.

"God is good," he says, and then Gerry joins us and we all sit down to pray and finally to eat, that slow perfect sauce.

I stay overnight, and in the morning I drive back down the long driveway and head for Connecticut, where I plan to approach Lizanne Monahan Searing at her food truck in order to start the process of finding out if she is a Junod—this, on the first morning I have woken up as a Scharnberger.

23

It's there. It's there at 11 a.m. It's *right* there, on a little side street, in front of the sedate red brick of the psychology building. A line has formed on the sidewalk and the sun in the autumn sky has caught the food truck's silvery panels. It shines, beckoningly. I get the hell out of there before she sees me, even though she probably has no idea at all what I look like and is fifty yards away even if she does.

I go for a walk. I circle the campus on one of the perimeter roads. It's a long walk and I complete it once, twice, three times. I have been doing this for years, showing up where I am unwelcome, poking my nose in other people's business. I have knocked on doors that have been shut in my face and once, in South Carolina, a bail bondsman greeted me with an unholstered revolver. But I have never been as afraid of approaching someone as I am right now, because in all the other cases I was out for information. Now I need acceptance.

I have been warned. Her brother, a year and a half ago, warned that I had the power to destroy her with what he called my "unnecessary truths." But I have never shaken the memory of her face and back in the spring I drove to Storrs and parked near the truck and dispatched a friend to come back with a couple of sandwiches and a report. When he returned, he dropped a bag of cheeseburgers through the open passenger seat window and said, "She's your sister, man." Since then, I've been moving toward her, toward this, by proxy—by my discovery of my cousins Vicki and Steve and Ralph and by the news I broke to Aunt Ellie about her origins. That they survived my outreach enabled *me* to survive my outreach and has brought me to the University of Connecticut for the purpose of introducing myself to Lizanne Searing at her food truck, whether she wants to meet me or not.

I check the time. It's 1:20. I have been walking for a couple of hours and she closes at 2:00. I feel a little sick. Instead of walking around the campus one more time I find the narrow path that winds along the lake, to the sidewalk, to the corner where I have stood scared and stymied, to the side street where Lizanne Searing has sold food to students for nearly thirty years. I don't slow down, because my only chance is to give myself no choice. Five people are on line, and I join them. I also see her. There are two women working inside the truck but she is unmistakable. She is tan. She is tall. She is lanky. She is beaming, her hair slick from the shift but falling to her shoulders in tendrils. She has big hands and cords of muscle running the length of her bare forearms. She is wearing glasses, moving between the grill and the counter. I am standing on the sidewalk so I have to look up to look at her. She is wearing a T-shirt that says, in script, "Be Nice." She wipes her hands on the front of her apron and says, "Can I help you?"

I look at her and say, "Lizanne, I'm Tom Junod."

She continues wiping her hands but then the hands stop moving. Her wide mouth straightens out of its smile. She studies me. The other woman studies me and sneaks a glance at Lizanne. Everything stops. Then Lizanne's lips disappear and are replaced by a broad band of teeth so white they twinkle. The smile that returns to her face is like a pennant, and she says, "What the hell are you doing here?"

She knew I was coming. Maybe not today, but someday. I had written her several times, once by email and twice by post; I had written her eighty-something *uncle*, for God's sake, and told him about the secret of his sister and my father. Her family talked about me and what to do about me, Tommy especially, who had taken it upon himself to be Lizanne's protection ever since we met in Queens. So she knew it was only a matter of time before I showed up. What she didn't know was how she was going to respond when I did.

She definitely entertained the option of kicking my ass. She talked to Courtney, her sous-chef in the truck, and put her on notice: "You might have to back me up." But she had no real idea how she was going to respond—she put off her decision about how she was going to respond—until I got on line and instead of ordering a sandwich introduced myself.

"It could have gone one of two ways," she says when we meet a couple of hours later. "It could have gone the way it did or I could have told you to get out of my face. It was a toss-up."

"I figured you for a total badass and I *one hundred percent* expected you to say, 'Get out of my face.'"

"Well, I *am* a total badass," she says. "But as soon as I saw you I said to myself, 'Well, he's got balls, brass ones.' What can I say? Balls impress me. You have questions. I'll try my best to answer them, though I don't think that I have that much information for you."

Lizanne is sitting behind her desk in the little office that flanks the big commercial kitchen she keeps just a couple of miles from UConn. She's drinking a beer she pulled from one of the humming steel refrigerators and so am I, with a digital recorder positioned on the desk between us. She is still wearing glasses but her hair is tied back and though she's still smiling she's also extending me a personal and professional courtesy so she's no longer beaming. I'm in a chair, sharing space with promotional stuff from Lizzie's Curbside catering events—a giant replica of a whisk that shadows me like an eavesdropper and a sign imprinted with a line drawing of a woman batting her eyelashes under a toque. I can't help thinking that the portrait doesn't look like Lizanne. I look like Lizanne. She looks like me.

We talk then. We talk for the first time, Lou Junod's son, Peggy Monahan's daughter. We talk about *them,* all of them, Peggy and Lou, Fran and John, the common cause of all children, our unhappy parents. "I know my mother was miserable at the end of her life," she says. "We'd be at home and then my parents would be arguing and then she'd be taking us kids to a houseboat somewhere." She doesn't know where. She has trouble remembering anything before the day her mother fell down the stairs. She was twelve years old and she was the first to get to her. "I'm sorry," she says, wishing she could remember more.

I ask about her father, if he was devastated when Peggy died four days after the fall. "I remember being pulled out of school, being told she had passed away. I was in the sixth grade or something. And I remember my father sitting outside in the backyard with my brothers and I, saying that this had happened, that we'll get through this and everything will be okay. But as far as him being devastated, I don't remember. The funeral was a circus. There were more flowers, more people, at her funeral than I've ever seen to this day in my life in one place. I've never seen anything like it. And I remember being across the street on the golf course. We were just sitting there, watching this procession of people going in and out of the house, and there were hundreds and hundreds of flowers outside the house and inside the house and I was across the street because I had to get out of there. I remember my grandmother in the den, saying, 'Why didn't you take me, God—why don't you take me?' You know—instead of her daughter. But other than that, I don't remember people's emotions, because it was all so overwhelming. Because it was like a show. Well, not a show—it was a *job*. Do you know what I mean?"

I want to tell her about my father—I want to say that he went to the funeral, but that Frankie and Dolores Klein had to prop him up. I want to say that he loved her mother, but I've been selling my father all my life and I don't have to now. I *can't* now. I have to sell myself, working against the clock. We talk about the motorcycle Lizanne received on the Christmas after her mother died, about food and the food business, and about how strange it is that her husband, Joie—pronounced "Joey"—and I both grew up in Wantagh, New York. And then we both stop. There are, for the first time since I've sat down, a few ticks of silence. Lizanne lifts her chin and looks at me from across the desk, all business.

"What else?" she says.

She knew I was coming, but not much more. She didn't know what Tommy and I talked about; she didn't know why he won't return my calls or answer my messages; she didn't know about my hunch, my inkling, and where this conversation between us is about to turn. She's still as innocent of my intention as she was before I stood on line for a sandwich I never ordered, and I still have the chance to keep my mouth shut. But that would mean thanking her for the beer and walking away and never seeing her again. And I can't do that. The thing her brother enjoined me never to say is the thing I have to.

She, like Tommy, has no memory of a woman named Dolores Klein, much less of Dolores's stepdaughter Nancy. But I have no other evidence to produce, no more privileged information to share. All I have is my story, beginning with my father displaying a single emphatic digit at the Dune Deck twenty-two years ago and ending with this: "Nancy told me that before Dolores died she said that one of the Monahan children was Lou's."

Lizanne doesn't let go of her smile, not yet. She just adds a little puff of air, a soft incredulous snort. "Okay . . . Dolores said *what* . . . to *whom*?"

"Her stepdaughter."

"So . . . she didn't say which one?"

"She actually said she thought one of the boys was."

"So how does that make you feel?" she asks. It's a question I don't expect, a question that I expected to ask her. My answer takes me by surprise.

"I have been willing to forgive my dad a lot," I say. "But if it turns out that he has a son or a daughter out there that he didn't tell me about before he died, I think I'd be angry."

"Do you think he would know, and not tell you? Or just not know? Are you thinking he has offspring all over the place and you don't know?"

"It happens. And so when I met Tommy I was looking for some kind of resemblance."

"*No,*" Lizanne says flatly. "No way." Then, in the ensuing quiet, her face changes just a little bit, squinting and smiling at the same time. "You don't see a resemblance between *us,* do you?"

My voice shrinks. "When I look at you, I see . . . you know." I stare at her, and then retreat. "But that's just something I think. It's not proven. People say people resemble each other all the time. And now that I've met you, I'm not sure if we resemble each other as much as I first thought."

Her badass smile returns. "You're *lucky* if you resemble me."

"I wish I had your smile," I say. "Your teeth . . ."

"I go to the dentist tomorrow," she says. And then it's gone: though her white teeth remain on display, her smile disappears, replaced by a smarting grimace that strikes her face one, two, three, four times in rapid succession. "I don't know where to go with this, Tom."

"Does it flip you out?"

"Nothing much flips me out," she says. One, two, three, four seconds pass. "How much of this conversation we're speaking now stays right here?"

"How much do you want?"

She indicates the little digital recorder on the desk. "Is that on?"

"Yes."

"Turn it *off*!"

Twenty-five years have passed, and his body has never been found. It has never floated to the surface of the bay; no dog has ever dug it up in the backyard of a home in some new Southern California development. So complete is his disappearance that even the few rumors that arose in his sudden absence—that he went into witness protection, that he's living high on the hog in Jamaica, laughing at those he left behind—are just things that people once said. Because he is considered missing, his case is not closed. But the police aren't still looking for Raymond Carl Vincent. They never really started.

Eleven years ago, I celebrated my fiftieth birthday by finding out Peggy Monahan's name. Today, on the day of my sixty-first, I'm driving south from Newport Beach to a sprawling apartment complex off the interstate between Newport Beach and San Diego to find out about the nature of my father's friendship with Vinnie. It's old, though the architectural style was once called California Contemporary. The units are low, identical, sided with age-darkened cedar and outfitted with private patios protected by high wooden walls. The complex seems never-ending, but on top of one of those brown boxed patios, lining the entirety of the ledge, is a series of potted flowers, the pink petals picking up the spring breeze. I know exactly who lives there and find a place to park.

I knock. I hear her, a natural commotion audible behind two doors, one steel, one screen. The steel door opens. It's dark inside, but there she is, on the other side of the screen, a shadow in the shadow with curly gray hair. "Can I help you?" she asks, her lips rolling back from her teeth in an instantly identifiable smile.

"Mikie, I'm Tom Junod," I say, and the smile goes away. We are standing so close, the thinnest of membranes between us, but she slides back behind the steel door, her face peering around the edge.

"Mikie, I've been trying to get in touch with you. I just have a couple of questions about my dad. You two were so close . . ."

"I was in a really terrible situation with my husband back then," she says, "and I really don't want to talk about it." She swings the door shut and I wonder if there's anything else I can do until I realize I've already done it. Four decades after he gave me a glimpse of it, I still believed in my dad's dream of Shangri-la. I still believed that Mikie was part of Shangri-la. I still believed that she would be nostalgic for it because *I* was nostalgic for it—my father with his linguini and clam sauce. But there was no Shangri-la for Mikie, only a terrible situation with her husband. I did not just make a mistake. I was mistaken.

The next morning, the phone rings a few minutes shy of seven o'clock, when I'm still in my hotel bed. It's my brother's friend Skipper, who's been up all night. He roomed with Michael in college and he roomed with Vinnie on Balboa Island and after Mikie slammed the door in my face I gave him a call. He's been thinking about it ever since. He apologizes for a crude joke he made and wonders what else he should apologize for. "That house on Balboa Island, it was a frat house when I was living with Vinnie. Guys being guys, your dad included. But maybe it was more than some guys drinking beer on the deck. Maybe it was nefarious. And I keep wondering if I'm that guy—if I was complicit."

He is not proud of it. He's never thought of Mikie as a victim—he never allowed himself to see Mikie as a victim, despite the "visible marks" that Vinnie left on her and despite Vinnie using her ruthlessly for his own ends. "He was a genius con man," Skipper says, "and he used Mikie to close the deals. He had power over her and she gave him power over people. Your father was part of that. He loaned Vinnie money, if I recall correctly. Ten-thousand-, twenty-thousand-dollar loans—that was Vinnie's thing. I remember your dad saying that your mom flipped out."

"It's weird my dad got caught up in that," I say, because out of habit I still insist on believing my father was better than Vinnie.

And yet I also remember what Mike Adams told me—the story of Vinnie's student and Vinnie's switchblade. That story didn't involve just Ray Vincent, but also Lou Junod.

"I don't think it's weird at all," Skipper says. "Your dad and Vinnie, it was one con man meeting another. It was your dad's life, and I don't think he regretted it. I think he enjoyed it."

At six in the morning, July 19, 2019, I wake up and start putting my clothes on. I don't know why, I just do. "Where are you going?" Janet asks as she watches from our bed.

"I think I need to go to the hospital and see Aunt El."

"You were there all day yesterday. I thought you were going to go later today. You look so tired."

I give her a kiss and drive from Shelter Island back to Nassau County. It's not yet 8 a.m. on a Sunday morning when I reach Ellie's room. Nothing has changed. Two days ago, my cousin Betty Ann found her on the floor of 112 Old Farm Road in Levittown. She lost consciousness not long after she was admitted to the hospital and has not regained it. She is shrinking, contracting in her hospital bed. I sit next to her for a few minutes and then walk to the family waiting room. I'm about to call Janet when Betty Ann's daughter Linette walks in, wiping her eyes with a Kleenex. "Tommy!" she says, and embraces me. We are all alone. We sit with each other, talking about the decisions we'll have to make in the course of the day. We are practically whispering but a nurse appears at the door, asking if we need help.

"Not really," I say. "Our aunt is in a coma and we're her next of kin and we're just talking about what to do next."

"Is your aunt the little lady in the room around the corner?"

"That's her."

"She just told me to go fuck myself."

Linette and I look at each other. "Aunt El!" we shout, and run to her room. She is sitting up, with her head propped on a pillow and her hair tied with a scrunchy into a pale gathered girlish sheaf. Her false teeth are nowhere in sight and she's speaking through her toothless mouth, a black hole that freezes her face in an expression of strangely youthful surprise. I extend my hand and she gives it a tug. She doesn't have much time, but she has a lot left to say. "I love you," she whispers, and looks across the room at Linette. "Oh, I love you too. I love all of you. I love this family."

"They're coming," Linette says. "They're on their way, my mother and my brother." She knows this is a respite and respites are fleeting at the end of a life. She is telling Aunt Ellie to hang on.

"You have a brother," Ellie says to Linette. "Do you get along?"

"Yes," Linette says. "I love my brother very much."

I squeeze Ellie's hand. "You had a brother," I say. I hesitate. "Did you get along?"

She sits for a few moments, contemplating the question as if she's waiting for breakfast. Parts of her have changed color. Her hands are purple and her eyes are fading into a shade of something like stucco. "Lou and I never got along," she finally says. "Everybody knows that."

I find the phone in my pocket and call Michael in Atlanta. I hand her the phone and she talks to him and tells him she loves him. When Betty Ann and her son Chuck arrive, she tells them the same. We are ringed around her bed, in thrall to her toothless mouth, her colorless eyes. "I love all of you," she says, "and when I love, I love. My family."

She is a Ponessa and I am a Scharnberger but none of that matters now. We all nod, as if to be counted in. "Your family," we say.

Her nurses return to the room. "Mama, Mama, are you tired?" She is tired, and the ghost of a smile shapes the circle of her lips. She has said what she wanted to say. She falls back asleep and she never wakes up.

Your father would be so proud of you, people say. There's a movie about to hit the big screen and it's about his son's life—what could have made him happier? It was his dream, but now you're living it.

I am not so sure. Yes, a movie based on a magazine article I wrote—based on my friendship with Fred Rogers—is about to make its premiere at the 2019 Toronto Film Festival with Tom Hanks cast in the lead role and Matthew Rhys playing none other than a character based on me. And yes, *A Beautiful Day in the Neighborhood* is about the reconciliation of a long-estranged father and son courtesy of a great man's lessons in forgiveness and kindness.

But if my father were alive the first thing he'd say is that he was never estranged from either of his sons—in fact, he was not just a father but a friend. The second thing he'd say is that he was much better looking than the actor who played the father, and would have never worn a dark shirt with a dark blazer to . . . a wedding, like the character in the movie.

And yet I can't help but wonder if he could have seen the truth in the movie, which is that Matthew Rhys seeks out the spiritual counsel of Mister Rogers because he's seeking an alternative father *figure* of patience and grace. In *A Beautiful Day in the Neighborhood,* Fred Rogers ends up comforting Chris Cooper on his deathbed. In real life, Fred talked a lot about my dad, assuring me of his love. But my dad never understood my friendship with Fred, whom he thought "effeminate" and never met.

It is a lovely movie, and for a short time it makes me something of a public person. People want to know not only what Fred was like, but what I'm like after all the time I spent with him. They want to know if he made me a better person, and if the conversion experience portrayed on-screen actually, well, *took*. I wish it did. Some days, I even tell myself it did. But in truth, when I talk about Fred I often wind up talking about my dad, by way of contrast—and then receive compliments about how *different* I am from my father, and how, with Fred's help, I've gone in a different direction from Lou Junod, an opposite one. But that's not simply an untruth. It's a lie, and I've been living it for twenty-three years.

One night, a few days before I am scheduled to leave for Toronto, I do not sleep. I wake up early and make the coffee. I neglect to turn on the lights. I sit on the couch as the sun comes up with our philosophical pit bull Dexter. I hope he will not be ashamed of me. When Janet wakes up and walks through the house, she has to swim through the cool shadows. She pours some coffee for herself and I ask her to sit down. She does not sit next to me. She sits alone. "I have something to tell you," I say.

When I tell people what it was like growing up with my father, they often feel at liberty to ask whether I have followed or rejected his example as a driven philanderer. Janet never does. She has never asked me a question about my fidelity, because from the very start of our romance she has known about my dad and she has known how much I don't want to be like him. She has given me her trust, and that gift, in turn, has given me my life. Now I look her in the eyes and say, "In 1996, I had an affair. We went to bed just once. But it was no small thing. It was a big deal for me and for her. I'm so sorry."

"When you asked me to sit down, I thought, 'Divorce or cancer,'" she says. "Not this." She is not entirely surprised, because she remembers how I was back then—how angry I was. She remembers a charge from Tiffany that I had a hard time explaining, and a note she saw on my desk, among my papers, that was so personal she slipped it back into its envelope without reading further. She refused to believe what it suggested because she refused to believe any less of me. Now I've made her question not only me but herself; I've made her feel foolish, hoodwinked, naïve, a patsy. She does not have to tell me that I've made her feel the way I saw my mother feel under the tyranny of Lou. I look at her face and tell that to myself.

No tears have fallen. But a seepage of salt shines in the narrowed corners of her eyes, and stays there. Her irises are gray and given over to a windy, winter-beach desolation—I have chased the color away. She is still tall, still built like a tennis player, still almost arrogantly pretty, her face entirely innocent of lipstick or makeup but her cheeks pink with hurt. I wish I could kiss her, as if that would undo what I've done, first the affair, now the confession. But my charm has no place here. Dexter stands up, resettles against her, as always going where needed.

"What did she have that I didn't?" she asks.

"She didn't have history," I say. "She was new. She didn't know me when you knew me—when I thought I was weak, when I thought my father had broken me. She only knew me when I thought I was a big deal. She made me feel smart. She made me feel like a superstar."

"I never knew that about you—that you're the kind of guy who just wants to be the big swinging dick."

I want to make sure she understands something about the circumstance. I want to make sure she knows that the affair started on the very day my father told me about Peggy Monahan, after I dropped him at Aunt Elizabeth's after our weekend at the Dune Deck. She is not impressed. She's not going to let me get away with using my dad as an excuse. I refer to the affair as a "relationship," and she says,

"For her it was a relationship. For you it was an affair." I remind her that it all happened twenty-three years ago, and she says, "For you, that's a long time. For me, this is brand-new." I say, in truth, that the affair counted as the unhappiest time in my life, meaning the unhappiest time since I met her and my life really began.

"My marriage to you is the best thing I've ever done, and I thought you felt the same way," she says. "I never thought I'd have to worry about it. I thought you were as committed to it as I was."

She looks at me with those beach-glass eyes, squeezed wet where her cheeks rise up and her eyelids angle down. "Do you still want to stick it out?" she asks.

We have been together since 1977. We have been married since 1984. But she is giving me a choice and a chance, right *now,* and the soft and stark surprise of her invitation makes me feel everything I have left to lose and all I have yet to gain. "Yes," I say, grabbing again at the grace she offers, in a universe without end.

24

They started on celluloid, and I watched them in the basement with my parents, on a portable movie screen that operated like a window shade. They migrated to VHS, and I watched them with Janet and the rest of my family in the TV room of the first house we bought. Now I can take them to a little shop and pay for them to be transferred to a thumb drive. These I watch on a laptop, alone, stopping the action with just a click and watching certain scenes over and over again. They were shot when I was a child; I am miraculously able to watch them again, as an adult, and yet watching home movies is, for me, like *being* a child, even though I am sixty years old instead of six.

I see things. I see things I am still not supposed to see, not supposed to talk about. I am supposed to be basking in the beauty and warmth of my family and friends, my mom and my dad and my brother and my sister, the people I loved and the people who loved me. I am supposed to be giving myself over to the tantalizing glow of nostalgia. But the things I see I am never quite able to unsee. I see them as if from the corner of my eye, and they suggest that things aren't—that things are *never*—as they seem.

The first time I watched a VHS version of my parents' home movies I saw my father scoop up Valerie Schocket at the New Year's Eve party in Wantagh and carry her up the stairs in her green dress. She looked like she was surrendering to him. He looked like he was taking her. They didn't bother to hide it.

Now I am visiting Michael Schocket at his home south of San Francisco. We are in his living room and he's showing me around, some of the old furniture he salvaged from Chip's pad in New York City. He is not nostalgic, exactly; he's haunted by the past, like me, and so the old flocked chair that has somehow made the journey from Sutton Place to Redwood City has symbolic value. It is what his father *believed* in, and when Michael invites me to sit in it, I do, and that's when I see something else. The TV is on. At first I think it's just something he keeps running, the way that some people keep CNN or ESPN on in the background. But then I take a closer look, and I'm transfixed. They're home movies—Uncle Chip's home movies.

It is the summer of 1961. There's Michael and there's me—two little boys on the beach in Westhampton, both of us three years old. We're chasing each other around in the sand, so small and so spindly we look like sandpipers. In the next clip, Dad and one of his buddies have picked me and Michael up and they are *jousting* with us—jousting with our bodies—on the edge of the surf, the contestants jabbing me at Michael and Michael at me. And then . . .

"There they are," Michael says.

He doesn't mean the general crowd of people scattered around the sand. He means my father, his mother, Lou and Valerie. They are sitting next to each other on a blanket, my dad in swim trunks, Valerie in a sweater and white slacks and sunglasses. They sit very close, but when the camera comes around—and there is no doubt Chip is behind the lens—my father puts his arm around her and draws her in. They both smile and they both look beautiful.

"There they are," I repeat.

"That's them, all right," Michael says, in that way of his, of not letting anyone know exactly what he's thinking. He's in the mental-health field, the head of a service that finds jobs for the mentally ill, and he's still soft-spoken and observant, the same guy my mother once described as "all Valerie."

"Couldn't be anyone else," I say, and then I ask if I can take the two VHS tapes back home to Atlanta and have them transferred to a digital format, so that I can watch them on my laptop. I can't watch most home movies without wondering how many others have been lost forever. But now that I have the chance to watch and scrutinize home movies *Chip Schocket* shot, I have all the evidence I could ever need.

There they are, on a boat, a wooden cabin cruiser, with Chip at the helm and behind the camera. Lou and Valerie are at the stern, the wake spreading out before them, since their backs are to the camera. Valerie is wearing orange shorts, my father a pair of squared-off trunks. She is standing against him, sideways, her knees pressed into his. She looks back over her shoulder, at her husband, her tan face full of daring and defiance. My father also takes a backward glance, but he doesn't appear nearly as carefree. She whispers in his ear, then kisses it; she runs her fingers from the nape of his neck to the opening of his bathing suit. The circumspect camera shifts to her feet, which are delicately crossed, one on top of the other. They untwist themselves and begin playing footsie with my father, until at last, one extended toe finds my father's calf and begins to climb his leg. The camera shuts off and the scene ends with a kind of wink, like a romantic interlude in an old movie.

The answer comes as no surprise. I ask my brother-in-law Ronnie if I can talk to him about my family and he says, "I've been waiting for you to ask me that question for forty years." It's a vehement response, sure—but that's Ronnie. He's a vehement guy, loud and quick-tempered. He started dating my sister when I was four years old, so I've known him almost as long as I've known Cathy and Michael, my blood siblings. I've known him as a high school distance runner of national renown, as an ironworker, as one of the hard hats who took it upon himself to excavate the ruins of the World Trade Center after 9/11 and now, mostly, as the caretaker of my sister as she sinks into the thrashing melancholy of Alzheimer's disease. I have had my differences with him; I have had harsh and sometimes bitter words with him, because nobody argues with Ron Gustafson without feeling pushed to their limits. But I've also admired him, not just for his refusal to give up on Cathy but also for being a person upon whom little is lost. He sees, he listens, he feels, he remembers and when he says he's *aching* to talk, I think that's just Ronnie—it's only natural for him to have something to say about a family he's seen close-up since 1962.

I meet him in a bar in Hilton Head Island, South Carolina, where he moved with Cathy shortly after her diagnosis. I drove from Atlanta with Michael, who is staying back at the house with Cathy so I can talk to Ronnie alone. The bar is dim and cool, the kind of place that's open on a Monday afternoon in the coastal South, full of raspy-voiced men in Hawaiian shirts buying liquor for raspy-voiced women with indoor tans. I drink beer; Ronnie, Captain Morgan straight up.

I am well-versed in the story of Ronnie and my mother. Just about everyone in my family knows that she not only wanted her daughter to "marry an officer," she came right out and said it. Instead, Cathy, in Ronnie's phrase, "got knocked up" by an enlisted man home on leave from his clerical duties on a base in Germany. Fran Junod never stopped finding ways to remind Ronnie Gustafson that he might have been good enough to do odd jobs around her house but never to marry her daughter.

I know much less about the story of Ronnie and my father. Ronnie likes to talk about the first time he called Cathy and heard in the background a deep-voiced man bewailing the loss of his hair, but that was the most common sort of anecdote about Lou Junod. I want to hear something else, though I can't quite say what. Ronnie, by this time, has turned seventy, and has been married to Cathy for fifty years. He is defined, in my eyes and perhaps his own, as the son-in-law, and so maybe amusing vignettes about my father are all he's *supposed* to have. He got off easy, after all—he could enjoy my father's shine without having to step into his pervasive shadow. But it turns out he has plenty to say about my father because he has plenty to say about his own.

They weren't that different, Lou Junod and George Gustafson. They were both womanizers of an unrepentant stripe. But George

Gustafson conducted his trysts in the shed behind the gas station he ran, and then had the nerve to flaunt them to his wife. Lou was hardly discreet; when Ronnie was dating Cathy Junod, his crowd of high school pals had somehow heard all about her father's conquests, some of them with famous women—"Michael is the only one who didn't know," he tells me. But my father had the talent of making betrayal look classy, instead of cheap. "I was very impressed with your dad," Ronnie says. "I thought many times that I wish my dad had that kind of polish—my dad had no polish at all, and as I got to know your father, I lost a lot of respect for my own father. Your father became the father I wished I had."

He left my family's—and my father's—orbit for a while. He received a full scholarship to run track at the University of Houston, then had trouble with his grades, got drafted, and barely saw my sister for almost two years. In the summer of 1968, he came home from the army on leave, and stopped by 1463 Britton Street. He wasn't just visiting her; he was visiting *us,* and when he pulled up to our house the first person he met was my dad, just back from the beach, standing in the driveway in his bathing suit and hosing down his car. He told Ronnie that Cathy was upstairs in her bedroom; then he said, "Go on up." Ronnie went on up, and just like that he was back in the place where he might not have belonged but very much wanted to be, a flawed but beguiling version of home. "I took Cathy out for a couple of dates, and when I went back to Germany she sent me a letter saying she was pregnant."

I know what happened next, of course—I remained in the dark about the circumstances of Cathy's pregnancy until I was forty years old. Ronnie laughs at that, laughs at me and laughs at his daughter Stacey, who just found out that she was "a love child" and that her parents got married because her grandfather made them. But Ronnie hasn't picked a bar and ordered hard liquor to tell me what I already know. I have been talking to him in the belief that we've *just* been talking, brother-in-law to brother-in-law. Then suddenly Ronnie is telling me about returning to the States with his new wife and daughter in the summer of 1969. "Are you going to punch me if I say something?" he asks.

I've seen Ronnie change with the years. He was, when I met him, lean as a Slant-Six, with a flattop. All those hollows filled in as he aged, especially when the falls he suffered as an ironworker ended his ability to run. Now I watch him change again. His mouth goes dry, and he orders another drink. He raises his fist to his mouth to clench down on a sudden cough, and when he turns to me on the bar stool, he leans forward as if he's heard a loud noise and can't help but duck.

"I'm not going to punch you," I say. "Why would I punch you?"

"Your father had a friend, Chip Schocket. Do you remember him?"

"Of course I do. *Uncle Chip.*"

"I was suspicious of Chip being a switch-hitter."

"He was."

"Thank you," Ronnie says, with a nod. "Then I'm not wrong. I was also suspicious of your father. Being a switch-hitter."

"I'm not going to punch you. Keep going."

"Do you remember the outdoor shower in Westhampton? Whenever I was in the shower your father would come over and look down. And he wasn't looking me in the eyes. I used to feel very uneasy about that. You would think I wouldn't be, after coming out of the military and taking gang showers. But this was my *father-in-law.* But that was secondary. When Stacey was an infant—I don't know where you were, you weren't in the house in Westhampton that night . . ."

He stops. He breathes. A few seconds pass.

"Frannie and Cathy went out to the movies and left me and Louie watching TV. Remember there was that one double bed in the bedroom and the little TV? Well, we were watching TV. Stacey's in her bassinet. We were babysitting. So we're watching TV . . ."

Two seconds.

"I'm laying on the pillow like this. Your father's laying like this, facing me. He keeps inching over. Very slowly."

Ronnie shows me his hand, almost but not quite motionless.

"Over a period of time, lasting a half hour or so. I finally got to the point where I felt very uncomfortable with it. Had no idea where it might be going."

He coughs and looks to the bartender. "Can I have a glass of water?" He takes a sip.

"I get up to go out to the deck through the screen door in the kitchen. It's locked, from the inside. That door is *never* locked. I'm just out of the army, in great shape, and your father is a tough guy. Who the fuck is going to bother *us*? Why do we need to lock the door? Unless Frannie and Cathy came home. Tommy, I really felt . . ."

His voice changes. It shrinks a little bit, pushes up against the next register.

"I really felt he was looking to make a move on me. I swear to God. Like I said, I hope you don't want to punch me. I can't make that up. How could someone make something like that up?"

"I don't think you're making it up," I say, and Ronnie orders another Captain Morgan. He has just told me something he has never told another human being. I can't say I know exactly what happened, but something did, something involving the trust he had in a man who was more than a father-in-law to him. "This," he says, "has been haunting me my entire life, a thorn in my heart."

I drive home the next day without telling Michael, and Ronnie tells not another living soul. Six years pass, and the thorn—the secret—becomes something we share.

I stop and see Cathy and Ronnie as I drive from Long Island to Atlanta. My sister no longer remembers my name, but she hugs me and tells me how much she's missed me. I dance with her to the soul music she still loves and sing with her to the songs she still knows. She might not know who I am, but she knows I am someone to *her,* and in some ways I feel closer to her than I have since I was a little boy and she taught me how to tie my shoelaces.

I stay a night, and when I leave in the morning Ronnie asks if I want to take a box of home movies. "There are a couple of you playing football, a couple of Westhampton." They are on the original celluloid, wound up around blue plastic spools, Super 8. I head to Atlanta with them in a cardboard box, and deliver them for digital transfer before I even reach home. I hope I will find that blessed moment when we were all together on the deck in Westhampton, Michael and Cathy and Lou and Fran and Ronnie and Stacey and me, and "In the Year 2525" and "My Cherie Amour" were playing on the radio and men were about to walk on the moon.

I pick up the digital thumb drive when I come home from the

movie premiere in Toronto. I make dinner and Janet tells me that she wants to be alone. I begin watching the short films on my laptop, eight in all. I am disappointed at first because half of them were shot at various construction sites where Ronnie worked. The ones of me playing football in seventh grade were shot from the stands, and they appear sped up, like silent films. But the last two reels allow me a glimpse into a past that is at first familiar and then utterly foreign. In one, my parents are going to a wedding. My mother is wearing a chiffon dress, and my father, dressed in a seersucker jacket over tuxedo pants and shirt, is escorting her to the Cadillac, a comic turn in which he bows like a butler. He does not kiss her, but then Cathy rides by on a bicycle, with her very young daughter Stacey in the child seat. My father kisses Stacey softly and then Cathy tenderly, with Cathy's face between his palms. I remember him talking about this day, because he believed that the choice of a casual sport coat and formal pants represented a sartorial innovation. On this day, he told me, he was at the height of his powers, and I have always wanted to see it. Now I have.

The second—the last—film is in Westhampton, around 1970. Ronnie is operating the camera; he pans across the ocean from the top of the dunes and then the house. The sky is low and tinged with encroaching twilight. There are surfboards, leaning against the deck; there is the Cadillac in the driveway, along with the red Camaro Super Sport my father bought for Michael and Cathy. My father is in front of the house grilling steaks, and the camera captures him hamming it up in a bone-colored Ban-Lon shirt that I now wear every summer. Then a woman appears out of the background, sauntering toward my father in a long white man-tailored dress shirt. She is young and she is tan and she is blond and when she reaches my father he immediately bends her backward over his knee, like a celebratory swain on V-E Day in Manhattan. He kisses her on the mouth, and then pats her behind. She walks toward the camera, toward her husband, and pokes her tongue at him.

I call for Janet. She is washing the dishes, and is reluctant to come over. But I ask again, and after a while she sits next to me. We watch again the young woman in the white dress shirt step out of the shadows, waving, and we watch again my father taking her into his embrace and bending her over his knee. And then we watch one more time. I keep thinking, She should be my mother but she's not. She shouldn't be my sister but she is. The woman in the white shirt is Cathy. "This is wrong on so many levels," Janet says.

I watch over and over again when Janet goes back to the kitchen and I'm alone. I watch it with a vain hope, with a desperate wish that I will see something different, that it will change with repeated viewings. I wish that Cathy will express surprise when my clowning father embraces her. I wish that she will scold him, or make a face at him, or push him away, or even just laugh.

She never does.

The next morning, I am back on the couch, talking to Janet. I am explaining myself again, and though Janet doesn't want to hear any excuses, I'm beginning to tell her things she's never known, and she's beginning to understand my father is not just the charismatic man who became her father-in-law. She's beginning to learn that he did *damage*. "I always thought you just *had* this," she says. "I always thought that you might have had a complicated upbringing but you just had it all under control, no problem. But I'm starting to see how much it affected you."

"It affected all of us," I say. "It affected me, it affected Michael, and it affected Cathy. The only difference is that I . . ." And suddenly there's that word again, the word I spoke when I left Michael at the hospital fifteen years earlier. I made it my vow then—"I'll survive this, no matter what." Now I think of Cathy and the terrible accumulating absence of her Alzheimer's disease, and I wonder if a vow to survive counts if you can't quite say what you're surviving. "Oh, my poor sister," I say, and as I look to my wife, my face seems to crack and give way as words and tears begin pouring from me. "She didn't do nothing wrong. She never hurt nobody. She didn't deserve what she got . . ." And I can hear myself, speaking in the syntax of a boy, and crying like a baby.

They pull into the parking space near the restaurant. They get out of the car. They stop at the meter and pay. They walk to the restaurant. He is a man with a formidable neck and a rolling woodchuck's walk. She is tall and rangy, wearing a long belted sweater and cowboy boots—she's a cowgirl. I stay in my car and watch them. I wait for them to go inside, then I follow. I have watched many people get out of cars in my life. I've never watched someone get out of a car who looks like me—and I must say it's a spectacle. It's brand-new. The whole world is brand-new and rife with possibility.

It's a Thai restaurant and they are already talking to the owners. They know food, they know restaurants, they know Connecticut. I sit down and they tell me what they usually order—the lettuce rolls, the curry as hot as the chef can make it, along with some cocktails. I gladly defer to them and when the cocktails arrive I drink mine down. I've gone to the food truck a couple of times since I first met Lizanne but this is the first time I've sat down with her for a meal and the first time I've met her husband, Joie, with his shrewd pink-cheeked face and his time-resistant head of brown hair. I suspect that she's brought him to dinner to run interference, to deflect my questions. But when he gets up and heads for the bathroom and I use his absence as an opportunity to probe, she stops me cold with that voice of hers—that frank voice not much higher than mine and entirely free from my habits of hesitation and hairsplitting. "Joie saved me," she says. "I was a mess when I came up here and he pulled me out of a horrible situation. There's nothing we don't know about each other and so there's no question you can't ask in front of him. We hold nothing back. If I don't know the answer, he will."

Joie returns. He calls her Lizzie, with a soft plea in his voice, with an occasionally intrusive patience, as if he's most comfortable helping her out of a jam. "I have two questions," I say, "and the first one is about the morning your mother died." They look at each other, and come to a sort of silent agreement. She repeats what she told me a year and a half ago, that she doesn't remember much of the past and prefers not to spend much time there. But then to the past she goes, to the morning of October 17, 1976. Her mother was going to an event. She was wearing a long robe. The robe was—like most of the clothes she wore, like most of the clothes she tried to get her tomboy daughter to wear—"glamfab." She tripped and fell—"she was probably drunk"—and Lizanne, in the kitchen with the maid, ran to her. Her head was bleeding on the monogram, the family M, at the foot of the stairs. "I held her. I held her head while someone called 911."

She doesn't remember where her father was, or, for that matter, anyone else. "The moment was *her,*" she says, the part of the past she doesn't like to revisit. When she tries to remember her mother, "even the good memories are bad." When she looks at pictures of her, "even the great pictures are bad pictures, because every picture is of a great mother who is gone." She can only reclaim the past by living in the present, by being what she always was and always will be, her mother's daughter. "My mother is like me and I am like my mother. I *am* Peggy Madeline Sheehan Monahan. I'm not glam. But I'm her in a country way, and she was fucking awesome. She was taken away and she's gone, and all I have of her is what I see in the mirror."

I was afraid, when I first sought her out, of hurting her. Now I tell myself that I can help her, that indeed I *am* helping her by giving her a better idea of who her mother was and what she went through. But when I tell Lizanne I hope our conversations can help her heal, she says, "They're healing for you because that's how you're wired. I'm wired in a different way. I don't go back there. My mother was unhappy and she had an affair. Okay—I'm sad she was unhappy. But I'm not proud she had an affair. Men were lining up to kiss her next. Your father was just one of them."

We look at each other across the table. Then Joie asks, "What's your other question?"

We both turn toward him, slightly mystified.

"You said you have two questions," says Joie from Wantagh.

"Maybe I answered it already," Lizanne says.

"You didn't," I say.

"Okay."

"The second question is harder," I say.

"Okay."

"It's the question I asked you a year and a half ago. Do you think that me and you, or me and one of your brothers, could be related?"

"Could you repeat that?" Lizanne says.

"Do you think that my father is your father instead of your father?"

"What do *you* think?" she asks. "Why are you hemming and hawing?"

"Because I want it to be true and I think it might be. But my conjecture isn't worth anything."

She turns to her husband. "What do you think? You have an artist's eye. Tell me." She met Joie when she first came to Connecticut. He was an audio engineer at an event she was catering. He asked for a beer. They've been together ever since. He can do anything; he does a little of everything, including art. He stares at me like a photographer framing a portrait and a politician seeking more time.

"His face is too familiar," he says.

"*What?*"

He speaks into her ear, as if she's hard of hearing. "From an artist's eye, it's too familiar."

Something goes out of Lizanne then, or maybe something returns to her. We are both wearing black turtlenecks. We both have wide shoulders, and hers, taut as a clothes hanger, finally relax when she exhales. "You're in," she says. "I didn't want anything to do with you and now we're having dinner and you're in."

I told them I had two questions. Now I have a third. "Will you take a genetic test?" I ask.

"I would," she says. But she's sitting with her hands folded in front of her like a schoolgirl, and when she glances up from them she says, with her wide mouth in a straight line in her face, "I have to warn you. This might take a long time."

"I don't care how long it takes."

"You're going to have to leave it to me. And you might have to wait."

"I'll wait," I say. "If it means knowing if we're connected, I'll wait and wait."

And I do. Two weeks later, the pandemic shuts down the world.

After I finish singing "Take Me Home, Country Roads" with Cathy in her living room, I take her for a walk. She lives in a new town now, High Point, North Carolina. She lives in a friendly new neighborhood designed for retirees. I walk with her in the sun, holding her hand. A man says, "Hi, Cathy!" She smiles and says hi but as we continue walking I see her lips moving, the words barely audible. I listen. I wonder if she is singing another verse of the John Denver song or maybe praying. She is not. She is saying, under her breath, "Fuck you, motherfucker, you think you can fuck with me? Huh? You think you can fuck with me?"

This is my new sister, the sister Alzheimer's disease is making. Cathy has never been emotionally accessible—I've seen her cry only once, when Mom died, and even her closest friends mention that they've never seen her cry at all. But she's always been easy to get along with, easy to hang out with, mostly because it's easy to make her laugh—and her laugh is a deep scornful guffaw that expresses her utter lack of pretension. Her dementia has never stopped her from laughing and for a while the erosion of inhibition made her the life of the party, a woman who would lift her shirt and show off her cleavage after she beat me in a backyard game of cornhole.

But that wasn't really Cathy. She had always been a private person, especially in regard to, well, her *person*—in addition to never seeing her cry, her college roommate had never seen her naked. Her newfound exhibitionism and her bawdy humor signaled that the frontal lobe of her brain was under attack and one morning in Hilton Head Ronnie had to call the police when she became violent while he attempted to give her a shower. They moved to High Point because their daughter Stacey lived there and because Ronnie was determined to care for Cathy at home and at the same time could no longer manage alone. But the move didn't slow the progression of the disease, nor the emergence of the muttering, profane and occasionally violent edition of Cathy whom Ronnie calls "the Sailor."

The Sailor is everything Cathy never was. Cathy never had a mean word to say about anyone; the Sailor never has a kind one. The Sailor is not only profane, but also brutally, pointedly, personally honest, with an instinct for individual weakness that gives her a kind of dangerous swagger. The Sailor comes out at night. The Sailor comes out after dinner. The Sailor especially shows up after Cathy uses the toilet or is led into the shower. Any touch of her privates, even by her husband or her daughter in the course of hygiene, transforms Cathy's body into a fortress, and summons the Sailor as its enforcer. Cathy has always been known for her athleticism, but she is even stronger than she is athletic. She packs a wallop. Nobody wants to mess with the Sailor.

Once I hear the Sailor speak during our walk, I can't stop hearing *her*, the growling undercurrent that turns out to be perpetual. What is she saying and why is she saying it? Stacey and Scott endure her insults by dismissing them—"That's not my mother." And of course they are to some degree right. They know their mother better than I do, and I am only just now beginning to understand that Alzheimer's disease is a descent not only into oblivion but into insanity. But I spend a lot of time with Cathy when I visit. Sometimes I just watch TV with her, holding her hand. And when she gives my hand a squeeze and says, "I miss you," I don't think she's lost her mind. I think she's still there. I think that something has been peeled away, not just her modesty but her reticence, and that the gentle wounded woman who dances and sings with me is in some way more my sister than ever.

I receive a video from Stacey in September 2021, seven years after Cathy's diagnosis. There's something beautiful about it, the morning light sweet and clement, Cathy at the kitchen table, Stacey trying to convince her to eat breakfast. Cathy hasn't worn makeup in years, but that's to her advantage, her strong face, her softly shaded green eyes, her hair swirled salt and pepper, all caught now in pondering profile. She's barely picking at her food. She's talking to herself again, whispering to herself, telling herself secrets: "Someone hurt me real bad. Someone hurt me real, real bad." I don't know what she's saying exactly, or about whom. But I don't think I'm hearing a madwoman and I know I'm not hearing the Sailor. I'm hearing Cathy Junod Gustafson, trying to tell the truth.

It was funny. She was funny, the sounds she used to make. She used to do an imitation of Stan Laurel, the skinny one from Laurel & Hardy, with her fingers scratching the crown of her hair and her voice tuned perfectly to the hapless apology "I'm sorry, Ollie." Even better was the gulping sound she'd make at the dinner table. She'd swallow so hard that I could hear it, so hard that it would make a cartoony noise, and I realized how the word "gulp" came to be—that was the sound Cathy made. It was an onomatopoeia. My brother rocked in bed to calm himself, my sister gulped. I didn't understand until much later that Cathy only gulped when she was really nervous.

I am surprised, then, when she starts gulping at the hospital. It is January 2005, and Michael is about to be discharged after his two-week stay. My sister and I have been called for a session with his lead therapist—me and my sister as his next of kin, although my parents are still living upstairs in his town home. The therapist asks all three of us to tell our family story, and we do, enthusiastically, all that made us so different—so colorful—and all that, in Cathy's recollection, made us an average family, same as everyone else. Then he asks, "What about your father?" and the conversation stops. We look at one another. Who's going to tell this story and what's going to be said? But the therapist has already heard the hiccup, already registered the silence. "Is something wrong?" he asks. Our three sets of eyes skitter. He takes a breath. "Did something happen you're not telling me? What's going on that I need to know?" I don't know why but my eyes fall on Cathy. Her hands are folded in front of her. She shakes her head in a shiver. None of us speak, not even the therapist. That's when I hear the gulping.

Seventeen years later, she is not gulping. She is cursing. It is December 2021, and Michael and I have driven up from Atlanta to spend time with her before Christmas. Last night was a difficult one, because she tried to leave, she tried to get out of the house, and the effort to bring her back brought out the Sailor in full force. Today, Michael is napping, Ronnie has stepped out, and I am alone with her. All day, I've been watching music documentaries with her, and I've managed to talk to her and forget what she called me in the throes of struggle. I sit close to her. But then I show her to the bathroom, and she stays behind the closed door a long time, and when she comes back she's speaking under her breath again. I try to change the subject but I can't, because the subject is not some stranger in the street, it's not even me. It's *someone,* an offstage antagonist who has occupied more and more of her attention since she moved to High Point, an invisible but apparently identifiable presence she can excoriate and upbraid for *hours.* "You think you're so fucking smart," she says. "But you're fucking stupid. You think you're not going to get caught? Ha. Ha ha ha ha ha. That's funny. You stupid fuck. You sick fucking bastard . . ."

She is sitting at the table, at the edge of a chair. I stand behind her and try giving her the same kind of neck rub I used to give our mom. Her unyielding shoulders feel like rocks. I sit down next to her and stroke her hand. She looks at me, takes me in, cagily. "Cathy, who are you talking to? Who are you talking about?"

She pulls her hand away. "Ho ho ho ho ho ho ho. That's for me to know and you to find out!"

"You sound so angry, Cath. You can talk about what's making you angry, you know. You can talk about it, and it'll make you feel much better."

She studies me in apparent consideration. Her face relaxes and her eyes relent. I think, for a moment, that she's returned to me, that the next time she opens her mouth the Sailor will be silenced and Cathy Junod from 1463 Britton Street will speak. She narrows her eyes, and then, with perfect diction, and in what seems like perfect lucidity, she answers me.

"No," my sister says.

The doctor meets with us at seven to talk about Cathy, about the unchecked internal bleeding caused by her heretofore undiagnosed bladder cancer. We crowd the small dim family room at the end of the hall the way college students might—we're all over the place, and Stacey, herself a nurse out on call, talks through my phone, her voice pouring loud through the little machine on the floor. Fourteen years earlier, I made this decision by myself when my mother was dying—the decision to let her die. I have no vote here, among my sister's family, only advice and the occasional interpretation of what the doctor has to say. There is, of course, no real debate, not in the face of Cathy's shocking suffering. Ronnie and Stacey and Scott elect to change the advance directive; Cathy will receive only palliative care. She will die, perhaps even tonight.

We thank the doctor and head back to the room. We are walking down the hallway, all of us, the whole family, and then we begin to hustle, we begin to run. We open the door to Cathy's hospital room and she is nestled in fresh white linens and recently transfused. We begin, all of us, to reach for her and touch her, her hands, her feet, her cheeks, the whole family transformed into a phalanx of extended arms. Stacey kisses her, in tears; Scott too, while Ronnie dips to a knee as if he's courting her. She is not exactly awake through this . . . this offering. But she is not unconscious either, and she knows what she wants. "Michael, Michael," she cries.

Michael is partially deaf. He is sitting in a chair with his face in his hands and doesn't move.

We alert him. Stacey shakes his shoulder. "Michael—she's calling for you!"

He lifts his face from his palms. He walks to the bed and takes Cathy's hand and looks in her eyes. "Michael," she says, and then I begin to cry. She has known him longer than she has known Scott and Stacey, longer than she has known Ronnie, longer than she has known me, longer than she knew my dad or knew what my mother looked like. Michael is her twin; they grew together in the womb, and in calling for him she is true to the soul she tried so hard to preserve. She is at the end, and she is going back to the beginning.

They were so alike. Their tans, their emphasis on their own looks, their sartorial overkill, their self-appointed expertise in the precepts of masculinity, their infidelities, the gorgeous wives they flashed around like expensive accessories, their head-turning charisma, their self-made wealth, their self-inflicted penury: John Monahan and Lou Junod were each a product of their time and place, and since they each occupied the *same* time and place, midcentury Miami Beach, I cannot help but look at them as rivals. Did they know each other? My father had indicated that he'd encountered John at least once or twice—he knew him well enough to tell me he didn't like him. But why would the big man at the Diplomat bother with Lou Junod when he had everything Lou Junod wanted? He had the plane, he had the publicity, he had the famous friends, he had mobsters packing his wife's funeral, he kept an eye on Meyer Lansky's daughter when she visited the Diplomat and he could have called Lansky himself for a favor any time he needed one. The man had real power. All Lou Junod had was the love of the man's wife.

It was inevitable that two of his sons would hate me. I haven't heard from Tom Monahan since I first visited Lizanne in her office and her phone rang and she handed it to me and I heard a voice shivery with contempt: "I *knew* you were going to do this!" "Do what?" I asked. "Stalk my sister," he said. I've never exchanged a word with Michael—the one time I called he slammed the phone down as soon as I said my name—but I've been warned about him. He thinks I'm out not only to disgrace his family name but to make his beloved mother out to be some kind of tramp. He's an ex-con; he did five years in the federal penitentiary for his role in a mob-adjacent extortion plot that cost a man his life, and he's said he's ready to go back to prison if I show up at his door. I have not shown up at his door. But I have kept in touch with their sister, always wondering what compels me to—wondering if it's something in my genes or something in my father's legacy, wondering if I'm simply doing what he did, and taking her away from them.

And yet when I go to see Lizanne a few months after Cathy's death on May 31, 2022, I no longer feel like an interloper dispatched by my old man. We meet at a Mexican restaurant near her home in Connecticut—her call, of course; another place where the servers don't bother asking for her order. She's at the bar, with Joie, talking to the bartender. I walk in and he moves over. He keeps talking to the bartender. I talk to Lizanne, her hair tied back, her big eyeglasses propped up between her heraldic eyebrows and her starburst cheekbones, her mouth and her eyes in a smiling contest. She is wearing a burgundy sweater with a V-neck trimmed in white. She brought me a couple of bottles of esoteric hot sauce, and I use it on my chips instead of the house salsa.

I tell this woman I suspect of being my sibling what it's like to lose a sibling—the ghostly narrowing of my world. She answers by telling me she's in the process of losing a sibling herself. It's bad enough that she hasn't talked to Tommy for a long time, "because Tommy loves drama." But Michael hasn't just started drinking again. He's started drinking again with determination and a final purpose; he's drinking to die. She loves Michael—all the Monahans do, along with their friends, despite his criminal history. But she can't do it anymore. It's too stressful watching him kill himself day by day; it's so stressful her hair began falling out. She had to cut him off, she says, once and for all. "I told him, 'I'll come down and bury you but I'm not going to watch you die.'"

I wonder if I had anything to do with it, all the stress and the estrangement. "You know that I have no intention of ever making your mom look bad, right?"

"Michael is Michael," she says. "He's made a decision, and once he does that you just can't stop him. I don't think you have anything to do with it, though you still better keep away from him. It's a little different with Tommy. He was on your side at first, but then he changed his mind. You freaked him out. You freaked everybody out. You were going back to a past most of us didn't want to think about. And you were pushy."

"I was pushy?"

She rolls her eyes. "You sent a letter to my *aunt and uncle*."

"I didn't push you."

"That's because I can't be pushed."

She sips from her margarita and I sip from mine, the most relaxed we've ever been together. But at the same time, I sense the room beginning to speed up in advance of another irrevocable moment. I met her four years ago. I am happy I am friendly with her, and I decide, right there at the bar, that even if we end up connected by friendship rather than by genes I'll try to keep the relationship alive—I enjoy her company that much. But at the same time I think of my sister Cathy and her brother Michael and her mother, Peggy, and her father, John, and my father, Lou, and all the terrible things those two men did and I can see a future in which Lizanne and I are just about all that's left, the last lonely survivors gabbing on the phone about hot sauces. "I hope this doesn't sound stupid," I say. "But I really want you to be my sister. Because I've already decided—if you turn out to be my sister, I'm all in. I'm all in as your brother."

She smiles and nods, a curt gesture of faith I can recognize. "I'm all in too," she says.

The three of us find a table and have dinner, the hot sauce going around and around. When we are done she walks me to my car. There is no evidence as yet linking her genes to mine. What if I made it all up, on a guess, on a feeling? What if I dreamed it all up, as if to make myself whole? She slings her arm around my shoulder as if to console me, as if we've known each other a long time. "We'll figure this out," she says.

Three weeks later, I send her an Ancestry test.

It's bucolic. That's what my father said, anyway. The place mystified him. He didn't get it. He especially didn't get why we bought a house there when we could have bought one in Westhampton or some other place that boasted "a little action"—a hot spot down the road like the Dune Deck. One day he asked Michael what he thought of Shelter Island. "What's there to say?" my brother responded. "It's . . . bucolic."

"Exactly," my father said. A year or two later, after he died, we found a little notepad in the guest bedroom where he and my mother slept when they visited. In his handwriting, there were two underlined words: "too bucolic." He thought it was a synonym for "lonely" and "desolate." Lou Junod didn't do bucolic.

But he's right, sort of. Shelter Island, where we've had a house since 2000, is bucolic both in the intended sense and in the haphazard sense my father heard in the word's exotic music. It's quiet and peaceful and still somewhat unspoiled but it can also be very lonely on winter nights and a few years after the deaths of our parents Janet and I began having a Christmas Eve party that is an annual attempt to find, in "bucolic," a synonym for "home." We invite friends who don't have any family nearby, who have lost their parents or don't have any kids. We celebrate the peace of the place and answer the loneliness. I cook all day, a non-Italian English major's attempt to fulfill the exacting math of the Feast of the Seven Fishes. There have been years I missed by one; there have been years I've cooked smelts or eels and the seventh and eighth fish go emphatically uneaten. In 2022, though, I'm determined to serve seven fishes, because it's the year my dog died and I broke my first bone and I lost my first sibling and yes, I need the luck. I invite a local oysterman—one fish. I rub the spare ribs with anchovies—two fish. I cook like a possessed person all day long—three, four, five, six, seven fishes, for the ten people who will come to our table. We start eating around seven fifteen and a little more than an hour later we stop filling our plates. We continue pouring wine and when the Nat King Cole Christmas CD comes to an end I stand up to change the music.

There's a request: Johnny Cash. I start flipping through the old CDs, the plastic cases making their tinkling, obsolete music, as the postprandial conversation from the table in the next room roars. I come upon Frank Sinatra instead, and hear the whisper in my head: Play it now or you'll never get another chance. I put the CD in the tray to acknowledge my father's insistent presence on this of all nights—as Michael never tires of saying, "Dad *loved* Christmas Eve." When the music begins to play, the cornball version of "Jingle

Bells" that opens the record, I pull my phone out of my pocket to check my messages. Maybe someone who couldn't make it to our table has texted a greeting from afar. Maybe my brother has sent a photo of his new grandchildren from Atlanta. It's 8:23 p.m., and there's a text under the name Lizanne Searing from 7:03: "So the email just came in that the results are in? What am I supposed to do and how do we figure it out."

I don't have to ask what results she means. I read the message three, four, five times standing up; then I read it three, four, five times sitting down on the old couch in the living room. I no longer recognize the music. I no longer follow the conversation of my family and my friends through the kitchen. I no longer feel the wine. At 8:26, I text back: "Does the email give you a link to follow?" Then: "You probably have to register. The account will be free unless you want it to be 'premium.' But you'll have to have a log-in, etc. Then you go to 'DNA matches.' It's a little confusing, and if you want to go over it tomorrow with me, I'll call you. But if they offer you a link, try to follow it."

There is no response, and I sit alone counting the minutes. The world came to a stop; now it goes wheeling away, and the talk at the table rises and falls like breathing. I have no idea how much time passes and Lizanne's silence makes my heart sink. Then I realize something. She is not the only one who will receive the results. The results are shared if DNA is shared. I open my Ancestry page on my phone. It looks the same as it always does, with the name Michael Junod at the top. They are all there, my cousins and even my late aunt Ellie, the familiarity an obfuscating force. I let out a sigh. Then, as if I've been nudged, I look again. There is a name in lowercase right under Michael and two levels above Ralph Pasqualina. The name is brand-new.

And just like that, it is as if the past has been remade. It is as if my parents have finally divorced. It is as if all pretense has been thrown off and just as I feared when I was a boy I have to decide whether to live with my father or my mother. And it is as if Peggy Monahan never died. I stand up and walk back to the dining room table and discover that dinner has gone on without me—the world has gone on without me. There are at least three discussions in progress, each of them very loud and emphatic. There is laughter. I stop in my tracks without sitting back down in my chair. I stand and look at my wife and my daughter and all our guests. The first discussion ends; then the second; then the third. There is silence, and as I stand staring I feel an overwhelming love for everything and everybody, not just Janet and Nia and the friends who have gathered in our home but Lou and Fran and Peggy and John and on and on and on. I spread my arms so far and so wide that my fingertips tingle with the encompassing strain and I say, I *announce,* "Lizanne Searing is my sister."

My friends look at me, these fellow refugees from a bucolic island. They have no idea who Lizanne Searing is. I am looking at Janet, who is facing me from the middle of the table. Her eyes are fixed on me, and our friends follow my eyes back to her. The whole table watches her. Her face reddens and then crumples, and with a little cough she begins to shed glistening tears.

25

I am up early, Christmas morning, and this time it's not out of habit, it's not because I'm still clinging to the days when we had to beat Nia to the tree with the last few gifts we'd kept hidden. It's because the world feels brand-new, refurbished not just in the present but in the past. I make coffee and the sun comes through the window and when it stings my eyes I say to myself, Yes, that's how it's supposed to feel. Janet comes downstairs and we talk in the quiet house until, at 7:38, I receive a text from Lizanne Searing.

It's like most of her texts, short and direct and surprising. It says, "Merry 🎄 Bro."

I answer as if learning a new language: "Morning Sis! Feliz Navidad! How are you doing?"

"Not sure . . . you?"

These are good questions that neither of us will answer for a while. I know how I *want* to answer—it's one of the greatest days of my life. I've just received the greatest Christmas gift of my life.

I started with nothing, and here I am, with a sister. I wanted this to happen, and it did. I rescued a primary human relationship—a sibling relationship—from the famished maw of the past, from secrets kept and then swallowed whole. I honored my father. I honored Peggy. I honored their love affair, not as something that might have been but something that *was*, and so on a Christmas morning decades after their deaths they're somehow still alive. What I want to do is celebrate with laughter and tears and then start my life anew, minus one secret.

I can't celebrate, though—I can't even say I want to celebrate—because of . . . because of my *sister*, my kid sister. She needs room and she needs time. She didn't want what I wanted. She went along with what I wanted. She was not, she said from the beginning, "a looker-backer," and now that she's looked back all the way to her biological beginnings she has found her past upended. We both might have gained something: a brother, a sister. But she and she alone also lost something. She lost a lot. She might not have gotten along with John Monahan, but at least she knew him, or thought she did. He *raised* her. He built his life on the conviction that she was his daughter as much as she built hers on the certainty that he was her father. And her mother, Margaret Madeline Sheehan Monahan—her mother was wrenched from her, right in front of her. Did Lizanne have to lose her all over again? Did she have to lose her mother as her father did, to this leathery Lothario named Lou? Did she have to find out that in addition to being Peggy's daughter she was also Peggy's secret?

We talk as soon as we can find time alone on Christmas morning, calling each other "Sis" and "Bro" with a moonshot of awkwardness and a splashdown of joy. She tells me not to worry about her. She's in Florida, her happy place, the condo in Hallandale where her father lived after moving out of the house with the stairs on Diplomat Parkway. She's baking eggs in spicy tomato sauce. She has a lot of friends in Florida and she's cooking for them. But later on Christmas Day she starts feeling sick and tests positive for COVID the day after. Three days after Christmas she texts with an apology for not answering my phone calls: "LOL I am fine but I am positive it's hard for me to process our situation but I will deal with it fine, I'm one tough lady."

She is a tough lady, promiscuous with the word "fine." But I know damned well how hard it is for her to be another man's child, and I know this because I know myself. I know it's hard on her because it would be hard on me, and I'm her brother.

I want her to meet Michael. She won't know me until she meets Michael. She won't know my father until she meets Michael. And Michael, when I call him Christmas morning, wants to meet her. There's my celebration: my conversation with my brother. The first thing he says is "Oh my God." The second thing is "Wow, that's amazing," repeated any number of times. I have to tell him the whole story, beginning to end—how I first saw Lizanne's face on Facebook in 2015 and then, last night, how I saw her text message on my phone while making the decision to play Frank Sinatra instead of Johnny Cash—and I realize how solitary I've been in pursuit of a connection with Peggy Monahan's daughter, how deeply alone I've been in my quest to ease my loneliness. But he's with me now, my brother. He brings up Cathy's death, and how it adds to the emotional resonance of connecting with Lizanne. He talks about flying up to Shelter Island in the summer to meet *his* new sister. And, of course, he says that there has to be some meaning to the coincidence that we found out about Lizanne on "Dad's favorite night of the year. He loved Christmas Eve," Michael says, "and just the other day I was looking at a picture of him in his red sweater, with a drink in his hand . . ."

He calls again the next day. His voice is different, more ruminative. He's had some time to think about it, he says, and he tells me something that doesn't surprise me but rings with Michael's enduring capacity to *be* surprised: "I'm disappointed in Dad." What bothers him is the duration of our father's affair with Peggy. "If Lizanne was born in 1964, that means you were five years old when she was conceived—*five*. That means I was fifteen. I used to think that Dad and Peggy started their relationship in the seventies, and it was just an accessory to his life with us. It turns out that we were the accessory to their lives. I just wonder how big it was. I wonder if it was bigger than us."

—

Do you think he knew? Janet asks on Christmas Day. So does Michael. So do Stacey and Scott, Kim and Britt. The only person who doesn't ask is Lizanne. *Did Lou Junod know that he had a daughter with Peggy Monahan?*

"Oh, he knew," I say.

How are you so sure?

"I'm pretty sure I sang 'Fly Me to the Moon' to Peggy in the summer of 1964, right after Lizanne was born. He had to be helped to her funeral in 1976. Frankie said they were planning to go off together. How could he not have known?"

Maybe she didn't tell him.

"You have to see pictures of Lizzie when she was young. She was dark—very dark. She was all eyes and eyebrows. She was Little Louie."

He went to her home to say goodbye. He was eighty-five years old. He was leaving—leaving Levittown, where he had lived on the largesse of his favorite sister, and thereby leaving Long Island forever. He knew he was never coming back, and so one last time he went to see the woman who for eleven years had been his lover. Did he love her? Did she love him? Maybe. But they weren't in it for love. They were in it for something else, and so the visit shocked her.

"He came to my house," Muntu Law told me in one of my last meetings with her. "He was . . . emaciated. You know, you always want to remember someone as they were. But he was so frail. There was no one home but me. He wanted a hug so I gave him one. He wanted a kiss so I kissed him on the cheek. Then he had the nerve to say, 'That's all I get?' Can you believe it? But that's just the way he was."

On a cold day in January, I take a bus from Shelter Island to LaGuardia. It's a long trip, and I buy a cup of coffee for the woman sitting next to me. She asks if I had a happy holiday, and I tell her about Lizanne. Then I can't help myself—I tell her everything. For the next two hours, I hold forth, until the bus nears its destination and I begin reaching for my bags. "Can I ask you one question about your father?" she asks.

"Of course."

"Why aren't you angry at him?"

It's not a trick question—I've heard versions of it before—but on this morning it registers as one. "I'm writing about him," I answer. "Isn't that angry enough?"

"You might be angry when you write about him. But you're definitely not when you talk about him. You still hold him in high regard. I can tell. Why?"

She waits for an answer, so I try to think of one. Why did I do the gentlemanly thing and buy her a coffee when I bought mine? Because of my dad. Why has the discovery of Lizanne Searing come to mean so much to me? Because of my dad. Why was it so important that the discovery came on Christmas Eve? Because of my dad. Why, when I was asked to play Johnny Cash, did I look for Sinatra instead? Because of my dad. Why do I love music so much? Because of my dad. Why do I love language so much? Because of my dad. Why am I a writer in the first place? Because of my dad. I took so much from him, I owe so much to him, and when I respond to the world I am often responding through him, for better and for worse. He taught me how to *live,* man—and he gave me permission to enjoy life. He might not have been a good man but he was an elemental one, and I feel his presence when I eat, when I drink, when I make love, when I breathe. Anger never had . . . a chance.

"When I was a little boy," I say with something like bravado, "my father took me out into the ocean and when we got past the breakers he would say, 'It's so clean, you can drink it.' Then he'd scoop handfuls of the water into his mouth. I thought the ocean belonged to him."

"So? That's what narcissists *do*."

"So how can I be angry at him?" I ask. "He gave me the ocean."

The two slides are still at the bottom of the big plastic bin. They probably weren't supposed to be there, but they've gone decades without being discovered and nobody has been looking for them, not even me. I've just chanced upon them, and now that I've found them I still can't make them out. They are slides, after all, and the Junods were never the kind of family to own a slide machine. I've been sifting through the endless envelopes and plastic bags of photos that Mom kept in dresser drawers and that we—Janet and I—rescued and haphazardly preserved after she moved to assisted living. The slides intrigue me because the bin contains so few of them and because of the date stamped on the cardboard margins: "JUL 76."

I remember July 1976.

I cannot forget July 1976 and so I put the two slides into a Ziploc and in the spring of 2023, when I hear about an iPhone app engineered to read old slides and negatives, I download it. I've held the slides to a lightbulb and already know that they are photographs of my dad. But their details remain mysterious until they're subjected to the scrutiny of Photomyne; then I see, and figure out why the images have been so perplexing and elusive.

They are photographs of my dad in the shower. They are photographs of him taking a shower taken by someone who is in the shower with him. They aren't particularly revealing, but they are intimate, shot very close. He is grinning. He is very brown and his hair is white with lather. In one photo, he's facing the camera straight on; in the other, his head is angled to the side—it's an action shot, as if he's just surrendered to laughter after stubbornly resisting it. In both, he looks different somehow, different from the man I knew, because in both he looks free.

Some part of me thinks—hopes—that Mom took them in the outdoor shower in Westhampton. But of course she didn't. The outdoor shower in the photographs is not the whitewashed cinder block shower of Dune Road and Mom never *took* showers, much less took them with my dad. No, he is somewhere else, away from home, and he is at ease with the person behind the camera. He is not performing for the person behind the camera because he is transformed by the person behind the camera. He doesn't look younger so much as he looks like a fifty-seven-year-old boy, cocksure and yet, at the same time, a word I never apply to him: innocent. The camera loves him. The person behind the camera loves him. It's the shock of these slides: he looks loved.

I have always believed what Frankie told me back in 2008. I have always believed that my dad was ready to leave Mom and go off with Peggy because I always remembered how it was between me and him in the summer of 1976. He had never mistreated me, but that summer he hit me, he called me a zero, he dared me to fight him, he called me a coward. Later, when Frankie told me his plans, I figured that he was sabotaging our relationship so that he'd have less to lose when he left us. But when I see the slides I see *why* he might have been leaving in the first place because I see him in the presence of someone who brought out the best in him—because I see him, I think, in the presence of Peggy Monahan.

He is not alone in the shower in JUL 76, and neither is the person taking the pictures. They are together. It is impossible to view the slides without feeling both of them, without recognizing that the image is the record of an interaction, and without understanding that he doesn't just look happy—he is standing with the person with whom he is about to make a bid for happiness.

They don't make it. And so there is a presentiment of tragedy in Dad's exuberant face, a kind of oblivious nobility. He came so close to getting what he wanted. But he was not meant for happiness; perhaps, as hard as this is to say, he didn't deserve happiness. He tried and tried. He just never got there.

And so this is how it ends instead: Thirty years later, he is raving, and my mother is scared. He's not . . . doing well, even after visiting the VA hospital the day before. Fluid is accumulating in his extremities, and he's not thinking clearly. He's been confused all day, but as darkness comes he makes accusations, and she feels threatened. She calls Michael and asks him to come to their apartment. She needs her son.

It is September 16, 2006. I am far away, on the beach in Shelter Island with Janet and Nia and my friends, milking joy from the last days of summer. Cathy is in upstate New York, at a cabin with Ronnie. It's all up to Michael, but if anyone can calm Dad down, he can; even two years after his hospitalization, he is what Dad would call "a rock," especially in times of crisis. He lives close by and although he gets there quickly he is shocked by how far things have gone when Mom opens the door. Dad is agitated, wild, and as he paces the floor he blames his wife of fifty-nine years for all his unhappiness: "You don't love me! You never loved me! You just loved me for my money! You know what a woman who loves a man for money is called? *That's* what you are . . ."

Michael tries to convince him to go to bed. It is not easy, but Michael can talk to Dad with love and unstinting admiration in almost any situation, and he finally succeeds. He settles Dad in bed and kisses him good night. "Forgive me," our father says. Michael goes out to the living room to speak to Mom and reassure her. One day has ended; a new one has begun, Sunday, September 17, and they are relieved for the quiet. Dad mutters a few things they don't understand, but after a while he settles into the darkness of his bedroom and they assume he's finally fallen asleep. He cries out, and they listen. He releases one terrible shriek, and he is gone.

Michael calls me at home right after he calls the ambulance, and, a half hour into the new day, I topple to the floor.

She is afraid of the dark. She lives out in the country, in a wooded area with no streetlights, so she should be used to it. But on this particular night our neighborhood in Shelter Island is stygian in its gloom; she can't see her hand in front of her face, and she thinks I'm as crazy for walking in it as I would be for walking in a storm. But we've been drinking, all of us, and I insist on going for a stroll as a way of clearing our heads. It's a cool night, with a shivery breeze, and about halfway into the walk she begins shaking. I think at first that she must be cold. But she isn't. She's scared.

She is visiting our house for the first time. I invited her back in the early spring, hoping that she and my brother, Michael, might be able to meet as guests in Shelter Island and become more than what Ancestry calls "DNA Relatives." But it was too soon; she backed out of the invitation with a text that suggested she was backing out of the bond we'd been trying to build: "I am sorry, but I got blindsided today with this whole situation and it's reality. I'm really not ready to meet your family and your brother let alone come out to Shelter Island and change my life indefinitely. I'm a simple girl living in the country just living a simple life and don't want to be a part of any book on the trauma. Any lifelong old school issues. That's just not my world. I'm sorry."

I didn't push her. I told her I'd be ready when she was and it turns out she was ready in less than a week. She didn't want to be the curiosity at the center of a family reunion of complete strangers. But she and Joie wanted to come see Janet and me and so I began trying to figure out a date. They arrived four days short of the six-month anniversary of Ancestry's holiday confirmation of our genetic connection. They stayed at a hotel, but they visited our home and I dared cook spaghetti and clam sauce and in the shadow of a sign salvaged from my father's bar in Wantagh—"Lou's Bistro"—she asked for the first time, "What was he like?" and a few minutes later she wrapped her arm around my shoulders and offered the both of us up to Janet's inspection and said: "Well, what do you think?" And yet the effort of the evening has exhausted her, and now, walking around the block, she seems unable to go any further. She seems about to cry.

The next day, on our way to a restaurant, Janet sees something in us. Lizanne and I are walking side by side; Janet and Joie are following about ten feet behind us. They can't see our faces. But they can see that we are walking in step, and that we mirror each other. Our gaits; the angles of our feet and knees; our broad shoulders; our bony legs; our absent asses. It's uncanny. Janet raises her camera and takes the picture. "Well, what do you think?" Lizanne asked the night before. Now she has her answer.

A year later, when I'm visiting in Connecticut, Lizzie takes me to meet one of her friends for lunch. She's an artist, and she notes the resemblance in our faces. "You should see us from behind," I say, and tell her all about Janet's photo. "Does it look anything like this?" she asks, and produces a framed oil painting from a bag she's stashed under the table. It's based on the photograph, but it also interprets it, for we appear to be not only walking together but also toward something far off—the future, perhaps. My sister Lizzie commissioned it, and now she gives it to me as a gift, and perhaps as an acknowledgment of how far we've already come.

The painting is a vision based on a vision. As we finish our lunch, the painter asks about our father, and I tell her a little about him—about how he, at his best, could make food taste better, music sound sweeter, the sun burn hotter, the ocean sparkle in a deeper shade of blue.

Lizzie turns to me. She asks, "Do you think he knew about me?"

She rarely asks questions about him. This one I feel in my gut, her natural optimism deepening the ache.

"Yes," I say. "Absolutely. There's no way he didn't."

She nods and doesn't ask the question I see on her face—*Then why didn't he ever try to meet me?* And perhaps she sees what I'm thinking but also not saying:

He would have loved you. He would have loved everything about you, both what you took from your mom and what you took from him. He would have loved your spunk, your defiance, your inability to bullshit or to take bullshit, your magnetism. And that he didn't know you—and that I don't want him anywhere *near* you—might be the punishment he deserves.

On July 16, 2023, Michael Monahan makes good on his mission, dying alone in his apartment of the complications of his alcoholism. His sister, Lizanne, makes good on her promise and flies down to Fort Lauderdale to arrange for his cremation. It is a tough trip. For one thing, she's not feeling well. For another, Michael was trying to die for a long time, and his apartment is not so different from a crime scene. She leaves on a Monday, flies back on a Saturday, and on Sunday she works twelve hours in her food truck at a farmer's market. I am in New England for work and try to contact her so I can see her on the way home. In just over a year I have lost a sister and she has a lost a brother and we have somehow found each other. I want her to know that although I can't take Michael's place I can still be there for her as a big brother.

On Thursday, July 25, I wake up early in a hotel room in Massachusetts. I check my phone and find a message from late the night before: "Tom This is Joie Searing. Bad news Lizzie was Life Starred to Hartford hospital in critical condition. Found her on her kitchen floor convulsing she had been there for a while. At hospital will let you know any news. Pray."

I pray. I *beg,* and I drive to Hartford. I find the waiting room for the intensive care unit in the big public hospital and use the intercom to call the nurses' station and find out that Elizabeth Anne Searing is still critical. She's limited to two visitors at a time, and Joie is always one. So I find a seat until one of Lizanne's friends opens the door. "Are you waiting to see Lizzie?"

"Yes," I say, and resolve to call her that name from now on.

"Are you her brother?"

I don't know what to say. I don't know what my sister has told people. I don't know if I am her secret, as she was my father's. But I am proud, and I tell the truth.

"Yes."

"What's your name?"

"Tom."

"Oh! You came all the way from New York!"

"No, I was in Massachusetts for work," I say, knowing she has confused me with Tom Monahan.

I go to her room and I see Joie slumped over in a chair with his hands folded. He's rocking a little and talking to her in a singsong voice. I put my hand on his shoulder and see my sister. She's on life support. She has a tube in her mouth, connected by a ridged hose to the machine that's breathing for her. There are hoses, tubes, screens, the tangle of care. Her brain waves and her heartbeat are displayed on separate screens, running in parallel. The room is dim and she is wearing a blue gown and a white cap that makes her look slightly Amish. The swelling of her face has made it smooth, almost plain, but I can still see her mother in it—the skeptical black eyebrows—and our father. She has been wrested from death and so the machines seem dedicated not only to her survival but to her creation, as if she were a premature baby instead of a fifty-nine-year-old woman. They move and make noise. She is still and silent.

Joie puts his face in his hands, wondering if he found her too late. He had been calling her commercial kitchen. She hadn't been answering. Finally he went to see her. She was on the floor, her eyes rolled back. She had been there for hours and she was convulsing and gurgling. The EMTs took her to a local hospital and then a Life Star helicopter flew her to Hartford. She had a temperature of 104.6 when she was admitted. She is on antibiotics now and the doctors are trying to cool her down. They have no idea what's wrong. They have no idea how much damage has been done, especially to her brain. When Joie folds himself into a courtship pose next to her and takes her hand, he resumes the singsong declaration that is also a plea for her to hear him: "I love you, Lizzie, I love you, I love you, Lizzie, I love you . . ."

He gets up after a while and heads out to the waiting room—"I'll give you some alone time with her," he says. I wait for him to go.

I wait for everyone to go, and take one of her hands. She has large hands hardened by decades of labor on the grill. They are brown, very tan, also swollen. My squeezes leave dents. I think of my sister Cathy. I think of Annette Reisman and Marguerite Scharnberger, the two sisters my father either never knew he had or refused to believe he had. I look around, because I feel as if I am about to tell Lizzie my secret, and I speak as Joie did, hoping against all evidence that she can hear me: "Lizzie, I'm so so glad you are my sister. I'm so so glad you are my sister . . ."

I stay the next two days. The second day is the same as the first but on the third day I am there when she opens her eyes. Her best friends from Florida have flown up to be with her and when she sees me standing with them and the hospital chaplain by her bedside, smiles on our faces, she stares at us one by one and then all together, her eyes skittering about in mounting terror. The chaplain assures her that our presence does not mean she's dying but she never entirely loses that panicky glare and she never stops straining against the discomfort and silence imposed by the breathing tube stuffed in her mouth.

I go out to the waiting room and see Johnny Monahan. I've met him before but I can see all over again why Lizzie and Tommy Monahan and even Janet think he's my brother. He has my father's and my grandmother's eyes to an extent no one in my own family ever did, except maybe Cathy. But he and I took a paternity test together a few months back and the results were deemed "inconclusive" and since then we've both just let the matter lie. Now, though, he's shaking his head with shock in his eyes. He visited Lizzie earlier. "She looks just like my mother when she was in the hospital," he says. "I mean, exactly. That's how my mother looked the last time I saw her alive."

I think about Peggy and how she died and I am back to where I began. I am back worrying if my father's entrance into her life was her doom and I am back wondering whether history is repeating itself with my presence in the hospital. I started something. Is this where it ends?

The next morning, I stop by the hospital to say goodbye and the nurses come in and announce that the ventilator tube is coming out. Lizzie's going to be able to talk. I stand there smiling at her, just me and one of the Florida friends—Joie isn't there, he's down in the cafeteria. Lizzie has responded well to the antibiotics and the prevailing theory behind the crisis is that the convulsions were caused by unchecked Lyme disease. The medical team kicks us out and then invites us back in, carrying the tube away. Her friend grasps Lizzie's hands. But she's smiling, that broad banner of teeth, and looking straight at me. She appears ready to start laughing but I suspect her voice is going to be faint so I draw closer to her. I remember the first time I approached her at the food truck and had no idea what she was going to say and thought she might say anything. It feels like that again, except that now she takes my hand before she speaks. "What . . . the hell . . . are . . . you . . . doing . . . here?" she asks all over again, but this time both of us know the answer.

We're family.

EPILOGUE

Dear Dad:

When I was a boy, sitting up in bed and listening to you and Mom arguing in the bedroom down the hall, I used to wonder who I'd live with if you divorced. You argued often, so this was not a one-time exercise: I had many opportunities to revise my conclusions. Some nights, I weighed the benefits of staying with my saintly mother in Wantagh; others, I contemplated the temptations of living with my exciting father in Manhattan. I loved both of you, so you'd be surprised at how often the contest ended in a virtual stalemate. But that doesn't mean you won, Dad; it just means the competition was close. In fact, you never won, because no matter how many advantages I allowed you, I came to the same jarring conclusion.

"Okay, I'll go with Dad."

You can't go with Dad.

"Why not?"

Because Dad is going to hell.

I told myself to take it back. I told myself that you weren't really going to hell; that Mom had told you to go to hell so many times that she put the idea in my head. But all these years later I can tell you the truth, Dad: the idea was mine. It would come to me spontaneously, like a pang of my own conscience. It had nothing to do with Mom at all; I thought you were going to hell because of what I already knew.

You came so close, Dad—so close to getting away with it. You've been dead now for nearly twenty years and you are resting in peace at a national cemetery, your body already consumed by fire. You and Mom are together, your ashes under a plaque stamped with the words "MOM AND DAD." You bother nobody and nobody bothers you. Fewer and fewer people remember you. Fewer and fewer people are *alive* to remember you, but those who do remember do so fondly. To the sons and daughters of your sisters and best friends, you remain "Uncle Lou"; to your grandchildren, you are "Pop-Pop"; to Michael and me, you are and will always be "Dad," a one-note word that we sing with a wistful extra beat, in the minor key. To everyone else, you are a colorful character who did nothing worse than live beyond your time and your bank account. You were old-school. You didn't do anybody any harm, except perhaps your long-suffering wife.

Even the story of your life was settled. A long time ago, I asked why you didn't want to be buried with your mother in the Schmeckenbecher plot in Queens. You said, "That's you and your . . . history. Why go digging in the dirt unless you can find a rose? I made my own life, kid—remember that." And you were right. You didn't have a history; you barely had a past. You weren't just a self-made man, in the economic sense; you were self-created, in the mythological one. You were thirteen pounds at birth, just like Sinatra. Your father and namesake was a mortician and a drunk. Your mother kept your family ahead of the bill collectors and outraged landlords by playing piano for silent movies. You had four sisters, and were the man of the house. Your sister Marie was the great beauty but she "ruined herself." You had no role models except Gable, Cagney, Astaire, Cary Grant—you learned how to dress as well as how to be a man at the movie theater. You got a job driving rivets at the shipyard in Brooklyn; that's how you got your "physique." You had an exemption from the draft but you enlisted because you didn't like the way people looked at you in the streets—"Who's this big *brute* and why isn't he in uniform? He must be yellow." You fought in the hedgerows of Normandy and after being wounded by a German grenade you received a Purple Heart. You were headed back to the front but you saved yourself by singing. You sang all over Europe and sang in Paris with Django Reinhardt, who wanted to make you a star. You came back home because you missed your mother and you missed Mom. You didn't make it as a singer because of your teeth. You married Mom and moved to Levittown. You had the twins, Michael and Cathy. You drove all over the American South in a red Oldsmobile. You used a reflector on Fifth Avenue. You moved to Wantagh when I was born. Cathy was the athlete—"she should have been the boy." Michael was good-looking and good-hearted. I was the love baby. You made your own life and you made us. We were the Junods, and because of you we were a breed apart.

I know this story so well because I wrote it, twice, for men's magazines. I was aware of many of your secrets but kept them to myself and wrote the stories with the intention of giving you the celebrity you'd always craved. I printed the legend, as the saying goes—and I found out that people not only loved the legend but were devoted to protecting it. They were devoted to protecting you, because you gave them something they needed and didn't otherwise have. You were a man of style in a drab and slovenly world. In a time of confusion you had conviction . . . no, *certainty.* You had not only standards but rules that boiled the tricky questions of being a man down to their quotable essence—"The turtleneck is the most flattering thing a man can wear." You were a war hero *and* a crooner. You were a he-man *and* a ladies' man *and* a family man and even women you tried to seduce would later tell me that all you talked about was your kids. When I wrote your eulogy and titled it "If You're Going to Be a Bear, Be a Grizzly," I had no reason to believe I was referencing anything but one of your maxims—no reason to suspect that the maxim was itself an echo from your secret life. And when you were turned to ash and laid to rest with a twenty-one-gun salute there was not a person in the world who needed to know anything else about you, maybe not even Mom. You were often mistaken for a celebrity: *that* was your celebrity. Now you began the long slide toward the mercy of eternal anonymity, the luxury of no one knowing you or what you were capable of. My work was done. So was yours.

It was Michael, the most faithful of your sons, who shook the crypt. He didn't know what Muntu was getting at when she spoke at your funeral, and so when he met her for lunch and she told him she'd had an eleven-year affair with you, he called me. The affair was *obvious,* Muntu had said; neither she nor you had tried to hide it. He called to ask if *I* knew, and in my doubled answer—my practically simultaneous "Of course I knew" and "No way I knew"—I felt the trembling of a divided self. I felt, in the heart of me, the crack that ran through our household, the irreconcilable split between your deep family feeling and your insistence on sexual license. You were a family man who flaunted himself on every possible occasion and in every conceivable manner; you were a family man who counted on his family's silence to ensure his freedom. We complied without being asked and without being told. But when I followed up with Muntu and she said, "Tommy, you're just going to have to accept that your father was a Casanova," the irreconcilable became unbearable. And when I saw Lizanne's face on Facebook . . . well, here I am, nine years later, with a story of my own, a story about your story.

You were not the man of your family. There were many men, passing through. In 1910, your mother, Elizabeth Schmeckenbecher, married Aaron (later Arthur) Reisman. She was sixteen. Two years later, she had a daughter, your first sister, Annette. Two years after that, she had an affair with Louis Augustus Henry Junod, and got caught. Her own mother testified against her in court and the disgusted judge gave Arthur Reisman custody of Annette in an emergency order. Elizabeth Reisman never saw her again and when a child was born from the affair with Louis Junod—your brother, known to New York City birth records as "Wm. M. Junod"—she surrendered him for adoption. In 1916, she married Louis Junod while still married to Arthur Reisman. It would take five more years for her divorce to become final.

When I was growing up, it was not just an article of faith but a matter of fact that Grandma had five children with your father Louis, "the only man who ever turned me on." But nothing in that assertion is true. She was never legally married to Louis Junod. She had seven children by five different men, and your father was Augustus Scharnberger, her cousin by marriage.

Did you know this? Did you know that you were "illegitimate"? Did you know that the man you called your father was not really your father? Did you know Louis Junod Jr.—your name in the 1925 census—was not really Louis Junod at all? I assume you did, because then the statement you repeated over and over when I was a boy—"I never had a father"—would make sense. You were trying to say something, Dad, but either you couldn't bring yourself to come out and say it plain or I couldn't understand it. I'm glad I understand now because it helps me understand you. You hated answering questions about the past because the past was pain. In 1935, your mother gave birth at age forty-one to the baby, Millie; she was the daughter of the lodger who lived with you on Coney Island Avenue, John Schmidt. A few months later, the murder of Virginia Seigh by Arthur Reisman's second wife put the adulteries of his first wife, Elizabeth Schmeckenbecher, on the front page. The *Daily News* even sent a photographer to Coney Island Avenue and printed a picture of Grandma and her children in the centerfold. But the photo included only Marie and Elizabeth, her children with Louis Junod; Aunt Ellie, a Ponessa, remembered being home that day, and being shooed to a back room.

You were sixteen when your mother became a scandal and eighteen when your father Augustus Scharnberger was killed in an accident during the construction of the Midtown Tunnel. Your boyhood was not only a matter of moving from place to place and singing to your dates on the way home from the movies. You were humiliated by your mother's romance with the lodger and then her public infamy. I know, because John Schmidt lived with "Elizabeth Becker"—your mother's name as it appears on Mildred Schmidt's birth certificate—for at least sixteen years, until Grandma moved in with Ellie in Levittown. You never mentioned his name, not even once, to Michael and me. And there is an extensive newspaper record attesting to the existence of Annette Reisman and also your mother's prominence in the "love triangle" scandal of 1935. I mentioned it to you once, wondering if you wanted me to find your lost and forgotten sister. You glared and snapped at me with such vehemence that I was afraid of you one last time.

You were not just a self-made man. You were a self-made dad. You wanted to be a good dad, you were driven to be a good dad, and you were, at least to your sons. So many people I talk to—so many men—wish their dads had said they loved them. You never shortchanged me on that score. You spent time with me, you took an interest in me, you ran the beach with me, you boxed with me, you threw the football with me, you went to my football games even when I sat the bench, you trusted me as your tout, you saved up for our trip to Paris, you bought me an MG, you watched movies with me, you taught me to dress, you taught me how to drive, you defended me to a coach who cut me from an all-star team, you spent the whole night at an Express Passport operation when my passport was lost before a school trip to Mexico, you made me laugh, you were able to laugh at yourself and taught me to laugh at myself, you spoke in an idiom all your own and made me try to write in the same way, and when I finally had some success you let me know you were proud of me—"I'm bursting my buttons," you said. You loved me. You told me you loved me. You were my dad, you were never anything but, and God knows how I loved you back.

So why was I so fucking terrified of you for so many years?

I wasn't afraid that you would hit me. I wasn't afraid that you would yell at me. As you often remarked, all you had to do was look my way and I would start falling apart. Maybe I was a born coward. Maybe I was overwhelmed by your sheer physicality. Maybe I couldn't help but take after Mom. Or maybe the only power I had terrified me even more than you did. I had nothing in my quiver except what I knew—except what I saw and heard and thought. I knew that you did wrong, Dad. But how could I tell on you? How could I tell about Valerie and about the lady you visited when you took me out for a sundae? How could I say anything to anybody about the lady who listened to me sing "Fly Me to the Moon" and said she'd like to meet me one day? I couldn't. I knew not to, because what I risked by opening my mouth was not your anger, or even a slap in the face. It was the obliteration of everything I knew and loved.

I kept quiet to protect our family. And I protected Mom by protecting you. The subjugation porn and mallet-sized dildos in your briefcase? The date with Peggy Friedlander? Zsa Zsa and Eva and Vinnie and Mikie? And finally, at the end, "the One" you told me about at Dune Deck? I told nobody for years, because I understood the terrible consequences for me and for you—for all of us. I was too young for that kind of power, too fragile, too weak—I didn't want it. But of course I kept on looking for it, because it was the only power I had. A crack opened right down the middle of my soul, between my fear and worship of you, between my love for you and my love for Mom, and between wanting to know and feeling the need to shut up. I am so grateful to be your son—so grateful for the *opportunity* to be your son. But I loved you in order to survive you.

You wouldn't talk about the pain, ever, because you couldn't talk about your illegitimacy and your beloved mother's promiscuity. But there's something else, something I find hard to talk about as well. Aunt Marie didn't "ruin herself," Dad. She was ruined, by Grandma. She was turned out to make rent in the back seats of cars when she was barely a teenager. She was sexually abused and then spent the rest of her life trying to make her mother love her. Her daughter Vivian was sexually abused in turn by Joe Laura, and spent the rest of her life angry at her mother for not protecting her. Aunt Ellie was groped and grabbed by John Schmidt, and to the day she died she spoke of him with a spitting hatred that rose well above her routine antipathies. And you, Dad: what happened when you were in your teens and Grandma directed you to the home of her bewigged friend? You probably wouldn't have called it abuse; you probably would have called it initiation. But you were so young, and sixty-two years later you recoiled when you told me about it. And I'll *bet* you Grandma got paid.

It took Ronnie nearly fifty years to tell someone about what happened between you and him in the bedroom of the Westhampton house the summer after he and Cathy came home from Germany—the "encroachment" that became his lifelong secret . . . what he never fails to call his "deepest, darkest secret." He happened to tell me first, and in the six years it took him to tell his daughter, Stacey, and his son, Scott, that secret became my own—because that's how secrets *work*. I couldn't tell anyone else about it, and Ronnie and I sometimes argued about it. He believed it wasn't homosexual behavior on your part, but rather a sin: the sin of lust. I believed that it was an abuse of power and trust—you were his father-in-law, for God's sake—and that it should be talked about. That he did eventually talk about it with his children and other loved ones was nothing less than an act of courage, because I know how powerful you still are, Dad, even twenty years in the grave.

Was Cathy also courageous? I sure thought so—she was the only one of your children brave enough to disobey and defy you. You seemed to think so too, speaking as you often did of all that she would have attained had she just been a boy. But she wasn't a boy, Dad, and I never knew how vulnerable she was until Ronnie provided me with a box of home movies in 2019 and I saw you bending Cathy over your knee forty years earlier and kissing her on the mouth. I am not here to prosecute you; I don't have the evidence. But I am Cathy's brother and I am Nia's father, and I can tell you that I've never reconciled myself to those few frames of film, no matter how fast they fly by; I felt that film in my body, and I still do. And so I suspect a few things about Cathy, and her courage. I suspect that when she returned home from her two-year bid at a Baptist college in Virginia she wanted *out,* and got pregnant. I suspect that when in the last years of her life she carried on a bitter and never-ending colloquy with a tormentor invisible to all eyes but her own, she was engaging with you, the offstage antagonist. And I don't just suspect—I *know,* from Ronnie—that when you died she never shed a tear. You have four children I can count, Dad. The two boys, grown now to men, have never stopped mourning you. The two girls never started. Cathy shocked me by melting in tears when she had to leave Mom in her urn at the cemetery, but she didn't so much as blink an eye for you. Lizanne you never met, or at least never knew. That duty, that privilege, that pleasure, that future, you somehow left to me.

A few years ago, Michael called me because he was missing you. We've never stopped doing that, calling each other to talk about you, to quote you, to shake our heads and laugh about you. We call not just out of nostalgia or respect but because it was intoxicating, living in your world, and when we talk about you we go back there—it's a high. "I hope that there's a heaven," Michael said, "because I would really like to talk to Dad again."

I didn't know what to say. I don't think you're in hell, Dad; I reject Christianity in part because I refuse any belief that puts me under the obligation to think of you subject to eternal fire. I think of what you said at the end: *forgive me.* I think of what your sister Ellie said: "When I love, I love. I don't dissect." Well, all I do is dissect, and I *still* love you. Now it's done. And if there's anything I know in this life, it's that you're not in heaven. For one thing, you were . . . what? A seducer? A philanderer? An adulterer? A libertine? A bedroom gangster? A shameless and inveterate sinner? For another, you had your heaven, here with us.

It was never enough.

Your son,
Tommy

ACKNOWLEDGMENTS

People often ask how long I've been working on this book. The glib answer is also the correct one: I've been working on it all my life. I became a writer in order to write this book. It might have taken me a while to get to it. But everything else I've written is prelude to this.

This is a memoir. I remembered as I wrote and I wrote as I remembered. But the story it tells is the story I have not been able to forget. Some of the incidental conversation is based on what my father and other participants might have said, and is true to their voices. But the scenes and incidents and statements recounted here are the scenes and incidents and statements that have stayed with me, verbatim—"swear on my life."

I have used pseudonyms in a few instances: Timmy Titimski; the Rose family; Brendan Clancy; the Wantagh hoods, Billy Knott, Jackie Costello, Richie Loudermilk, and Paul McCracken; Skipper; my friend Jack. The names are the only liberties taken.

I have understood the truth about my father since I was a child. But I began trying to *uncover* the truth about my father in 2015. There was something I wanted to find out, and I spent eight years doing it. To that end, I called upon my memory but also upon family members, friends, and people from my father's past. I did hundreds of interviews, made use of documents dating back to the 1800s, found old court cases, and read the accounts of newspapers long dead. I also surrendered my DNA to Ancestry and 23andMe. In the end, I found not just stories, but people who are now part of my life. History has a heartbeat, and I can prove it.

I am grateful to so many. But this book wouldn't have been possible without the people who did the most difficult thing:

They told the truth.

So many of them are gone now. I have tried to honor them in these pages, but my debt to them goes on and on. I can never adequately thank the beautiful and formidable women who told me what it was like to be in love with my father:

The late Valerie McBryde and the late Muntu Law.

I also wish to thank the late Vern Winick, who was so steadfast in her love for Peggy Monahan that she agreed to talk to the son of the man who loved her.

My thanks to the late Cindy Friedlander, who couldn't bear to speak of the tragedy of her mother, Peggy, and directed me to talk to Shelly Tubbs instead.

And thank you to Ceil Brandshagen, Aunt Ceil, the good egg who shared what only she could know: how much my mom suffered and endured being married to my dad.

My deepest thanks to the late Frankie Klein and his family, Kelly Lewis Rabin, the late Rick Lewis, and, especially, Nancy Klein McCann, who has been for me what her father, Frankie, was to my father: a confidant and a boon companion. This book started with them.

I am grateful to the late Helen Klein, the late Mike Adams, the late Jerry Gelbwacks, the late Lou Taylor, Kenny Orr, Ron Lozoff, Judi Di Domenico, Nancy Lewis, Sue Coleman, Carla Klepper, Susan Schindehette, Peter Hough, David Loiselle, Dan Christensen, the late Dick Cami, Sandra Lansky, the late Dolores Savarese, Judy Sayfie, Scott Stockholm, Teri Brown, Stacey Winick, Sandy Fritzmaier, and Gail Thomas Burkley, "the most beautiful woman on this beach."

I am grateful to Art and David Reisman for the magic of their mother, Lee.

I am grateful to Vivian Yee of *The New York Times* for the burning warehouse.

I am grateful to Heidi and Jamie Vincent, and am sorry that I could never find out what happened to their father.

I am grateful to Kathryn Harrison for answering my questions.

I am grateful to Lama Elkhoury for her help in untangling the family tree. I am grateful to Dr. Daniel David, who week in and week out gave me permission to keep going. I know, I know—the bad boy is the good boy and the good boy is the bad. One day, I'll figure it out.

I am grateful to Amy Wallace for the Heimlich. I'm grateful to two artists, Margaret Garrett and Stephanie Molnar, for their visions. I am grateful to Marion Ettlinger for the photo that shows Lou Junod as "Big Lou" for the last time.

And I am grateful and indebted to Steven Grossman, who, long ago, at gunpoint in a hotel room in Los Angeles, saved my life.

My father lived the last third of his life convinced that he lived under a cloud—that he was endlessly and fundamentally unlucky. It was a source of contention between us, as I tried to tell him that he was the luckiest man alive because so many loved him. I am not only determined not to repeat his mistake; I have written a book that has made repeating his mistake impossible. I could not have written it without the support of people who remind me of just how lucky I am.

First, my editors, who have from the beginning been able to change not just my stories but also my life with a note or a phone call: the late Gene Cudworth, Sylvia Wrobel, Neil Shister, Lee Walburn, Chris Wohlwend, the late Art Cooper, the late Jay Lovinger, John Huey, Denise Wills, Ryan D'Agostino, Peter Griffin, John Kenney, and the great Mark Warren. I am especially grateful to David Granger, who made me believe that every single freaking story could and should be life-changing, and to my dear friend and collaborator Eric Neel, who taught me to listen for what I can't always hear. The Wolf is *not* overrated.

Second, my friends, too many to thank properly. From the earliest days, Michael Schocket, who was part of this book long before I began working on it. From Wantagh: Robert and Joann McGarty, always family; Ray Labella, ditto; Steven Ciccarello; Eddie Wengler; and the late Chris Leahy, troublemaker and inspiration. From high school: Terry Erb and Jim Lowe and Cynthia Van Nostrand; Jim Blair and Cathy Piche and Nancy Hughes. From college: Gerry and Belinda Privin, Kevin Gray, Will and Beth Bashan, Steve Boyka, and the late great Howell Neal Powder; Ira Gleser, Mary T. Johnson, and Paul Grondahl. From Texas: John Kovas and Bob Gold, the Legend. From Atlanta: Sue Spann, the late Neil T. Harkins, and their children, Ian and Sophie; Graham Anthony; Margaret Anthony; Vince Coppola; Kevin Sack; Esther Muench; Frank Reiss; Loring Kemp; Holli Hutson; David Boatright; Steve Shlansky; Jay Underwood; Beth Burns; Maryann Doring; Mark Baker and Charles McNair, the Cousins; Mel Konner and Chantal James, the Verbalists; Justin Heckert, Amanda Brown, and Tom Lake; Bob Townsend; Candice Michelle Dyer; Ann Hardie and my pal Drew Jubera. From the neighborhood: the Fosters, the Gibsons, the Lawsons, the Heeges, the Gaults, Geoff Frost, Cal and Sandy Tax, "Sal and Candy." From the Biz: Scott Raab; Lisa Hintelmann; Robyn Crawford; T Cooper and Allison Glock; Anna Peele; Alex Belth; Jeff Gordinier; Lee Crum; Michael Hainey; Mim Udovitch; Laura Lee Huttenbach; Jeff Hooten; Amy Burgess; Noah Harpster; Micah Fitzerman-Blue; John Lee Hancock; Matthew Rhys; Lucy Stille; and my Long Island exemplars, JR Moehringer and Taffy Brodesser-Akner. From my work at ESPN: Paula Lavigne; John Skipper; Chris Buckle; Scott Burton; Mike Drago; Don Van Natta; Susie Arth; Nicole Noren; Rayna Banks; Dante Stewart; Jeremy Williams; Martin Khodabakhshian; Mike Sciallis; Neely Lohmann; Dwayne Bray; Steve Fainaru; Bonnie Ford; Dotun Okinoye; Tommy Tomlinson. From the Thread: Seth Wickersham, Wright Thompson, and Kevin Van Valkenburg—Hemingway and Fitzgerald might have had Paris, but we have our daily dose of each other. From Shelter Island: David Browne and Maggie Murphy and, of course, Maeve; Bob Lipsyte and Lois Morris; Gary Kagawa and the late John Miller; Dan Ouellette and Yvonne Schibsted; Jackson and Jen Rohrer; Shannon Coyne, Chris Coyne, and Julia Romanchuk; Susan Morrison and Loudon Wainwright; Kathy Heintzelman; Dawn and Michael at the Black Cat; Finley Shaw; Holly Carter; The Cahills; Glenn Petry and Alissa Friedman; Stephen and Tricia Fearing. Bill Grimbol and Bronwen Dickey, thanks for listening. "Jack" and Maura, I miss you, and guess I always will. My dear Fred and Joanne Rogers: you are my friends, forever.

Third: my family, which is the heartbeat of everything I've written here, as participants, as sources, as witnesses, as my audience, as the people I really want to impress. You lived it, and I have tried to love you as lavishly on the page as I do in life. I'll start with Levittown: Marie Peters; Frank and Ellie Peragine; Elizabeth and Harry Nolan; Jack and Millie Thimons. They are all gone now. But, Aunt Ellie, you are the spirit of this book, and Aunt Marie, you are its aching heart.

The Junod cousins, as I once called them though none of them bear that name: the late Vivian DeMase; the late Billy Nolan; Wendy Nolan; Betty Ann Feldman; Judy Eisgruber; Linette Sica; Chuck Ragona. "I hear you're writing . . . a *book,*" Viv said. "About the *family.*" Yes—and you guys never blinked. I so wish Cousin Billy could listen to this story from beginning to end.

Thanks to my Brandshagen cousins Mitchell and Michael for telling me about the secret language my father spoke when you were going out on dates—I thought I knew everything. I didn't.

Thanks to the Folks for taking me in: the late George and Helen; Lee Ann Folk and Den Devers; Jon Folk and Amy Kasuga; and Artemis and Daniel.

There is plenty of pain to go around in this book and a lot of loss. But there's also something of a miracle: family members whom I would otherwise never have known and whose presence in my life justifies my quest to find them. Thank you, my cousins Vicki Oglesbee and Steve Goodman, for staying on the phone when I first called, and for staying open to everything else since. And thank you, my first cousin Ralph Pasqualina, for making a Scharnberger out of me. I feel that through all of you my father finally met his sisters Annette Reisman and Marguerite Scharnberger.

Nine years ago, I sent an email to Tom Monahan telling him that his mother, Peggy, had a long affair with a man named Lou Junod. I am indebted to Tommy for meeting with me and hope the day will come when he doesn't regret his decision. I am grateful to John Monahan for his unflagging kindness and consideration and I pray that Michael Monahan rests in peace. I thank Joie Searing from Wantagh for remaining gracious and unflappable in the face of what must have seemed an impossible situation.

As for Elizabeth Anne Monahan Searing: I'm all in, Sis. It is one of the impossible gifts of my life that you are too. I love you.

I lost my sister Cathy while working on this book. I love you, Cathy, and miss you more and more as time goes on and on. I can't listen to soul music without thinking of you. And I listen to a *lot* of soul music.

I am grateful to Ron Gustafson for doing so many hard things—for staying with Cathy through the end and for staying with me when he wanted nothing to do with my book. You are a brave man and a truth-teller and you have been my brother-in-law for most of my life but you have also become a brother to me.

I have been grateful for my brother, Michael, from the day I was born. You are simply the best big brother a guy could have. You might think Dad was my role model. But that has always been you, Bro.

I am grateful to my nieces and my nephew, Stacey and Scott and Kim and Britt, as well as their spouses, Mike, Dion, Jon, and Brian. You listened to the story of Pop-Pop without flinching and you pretended that you weren't concerned when the years rolled by with the book still unfinished. Thanks, you guys. I love you all.

There are a few people who have been part of the book from the beginning—who knew it was a book before I did and had to wait for me to come around. David Black has been my agent and my friend for decades. I also did not write a book for decades—that's how I know he's my friend. He has represented me fiercely without any financial benefit, and he has never pushed me to write a book for the money. We have been through so much together, and now we finally have the chance to go through this—a book. I thank you, David, for everything, but mostly for being yourself, a whisperer on the phone and a shouter at Jets games and a wise man for all seasons. Love to Melissa and Mitchell.

Bill Thomas of Doubleday saw the potential of this book as soon as the words "my father's women" left my mouth. He then read every single one of the fusillade of words that followed and never lost hope when I concluded the case was hopeless. A born coach, he never let me get too far up or too far down, literally handing me a title and then pulling off one of the great edits of a raw first draft. Bill, you are a Major Dude with a heart and a half, and I look forward to the next book, though perhaps not the next draft.

I will be frank: My mother, Frances Brandshagen Junod, would be mortified by this book. But it wouldn't exist without her and her dogged belief that I pooped gold. Mom, you were in Dad's shadow for so long, and I wanted the world to know you. And no, I *never* forget who raised me, kid.

I've been working on this book about half of my daughter Nia's life. She did not go to Disney World because of it, and now she has to find out how truly "messy" her Pop-Pop was. But, Nia, I can still hear you singing to him, and I can still hear him calling you "tiger." Through you, the good in him lives on.

My dear Janet. I did it. We did it, all of it. This story is also your story, and I wouldn't have been able to write it if you hadn't offered the strength of your steadfast heart. You're gorgeous and I love you.

God Only Knows.